HISTORY OF EDUCATION IN AMERICA

HISTORY OF EDUCATION IN AMERICA

Sixth Edition

John D. Pulliam
Professor Emeritus
University of Montana

James Van Patten
University of Arkansas-Fayetteville

Merrill,
an imprint of Prentice Hall

Englewood Cliffs, New Jersey   Columbus, Ohio

Library of Congress Cataloging-in-Publication Data

Pulliam, John D.

    History of education in America / John Pulliam and James Van Patten.—6th ed.

        p.   cm.

    Includes bibliographical references and index.

    ISBN 0-02-396818-4

      1. Education—United States—History. I. Van Patten, James J. II. Title.

LA205.P84   1994

370'.973—dc20

                                           94-6031

                                           CIP

Cover photos: Nebraska State Historical Society (top, left); Arthur Rothstein (top, right); State Historical Society of Iowa—Iowa City (bottom, left); Bettmann Archives (bottom, right)
Editor: Debra A. Stollenwerk
Production Editor: Rex Davidson
Text Designer: Julia Zonnenveld Van Hook
Cover Designer: Brian Deep
Production Buyer: Deidra M. Schwartz
Electronic Text Management: Marilyn Wilson Phelps, Matthew Williams, Jane Lopez, Karen L. Bretz

This book was set in Cheltenham BT by Prentice Hall and was printed and bound by Book Press, Inc., a Quebecor America Book Group Company. The cover was printed by Phoenix Color Corp.

Prentice-Hall International (UK) Limited, *London*
Prentice-Hall of Australia Pty. Limited, *Sydney*
Prentice-Hall of Canada, Inc., *Toronto*
Prentice-Hall Hispanoamericana, S. A., *Mexico*
Prentice-Hall of India Private Limited, *New Delhi*
Prentice-Hall of Japan, Inc., *Tokyo*
Simon & Schuster Asia Pte. Ltd., *Singapore*
Editora Prentice-Hall do Brasil, Ltda., *Rio de Janeiro*

PREFACE

There is a saying circulating in the universities these days which goes:

Georgie Porgie, Puddin' and pie,
Kissed the girls; they didn't cry.
When the boys came back to play,
A sexual harassment subpeona barred their way.
Georgina, Porgiana claim rights to the pies.
Times, they've changed right before our eyes.

Indeed, the times are changing so rapidly that keeping up with any field is extremely difficult. The knowledge explosion affects all scholars as they seek to keep abreast of their fields by understanding the latest research. Many students of education find that they must reduce the scope of their reading in order to concentrate on their own special areas. At the same time knowledge of the entire field is necessary. It provides the foundation for understanding the profession and enables the scholar to gain perspective on his or her own role. As we place current events in historical perspective, cycles of proactive and reactive thinking and action are revealed. Thus we revisit concepts previously discarded and, by putting new wine in an old bottle, proclaim innovations and frontiers for education without being aware that they are educational history. As historian Christopher Lasch pointed out in the *Culture of Narcissism*, people with no understanding of their history are lost in the present and unable to plan for the future.

Alvin Toffler in *War and Anti-War* notes that we are living at a fantastic moment of human history. He finds the world system taking on Prigoginian characteristics—looking more like the physical, chemical, and social systems described by Ilya Prigogine, the Nobel prize-winning scientist who identified what he called "dissipative-structures." In these structures, all parts of the system are in constant fluctuation. Parts of each system become extremely vulnerable to external influences. Educators and their institutions are facing flux and instability as attempts are made to respond to all sorts of new external and internal pressures and influences. Educational historians have an opportunity to place these changes in proper perspective.

The purpose of this book is to provide an overview of the history of American education and to serve as a quick reference to the most important persons, dates, events, and movements that shaped the nation's system of education. A capsule presentation is made of the basic concepts and theories that underlie educational practice. In order to pack as much information as possible into a succinct volume, interpretation is left largely to the reader or to professors who use the book as a text. Certainly the raging controversy between the traditionalists and revisionists is important. The differences between Michael Katz and H. Giroux (radical revisionists) and David Tyack (interpreter of social forces) are pronounced. Before judgments of interpretation can be made, there must be a wealth of faculty knowledge, and that is provided in this book.

Features of the Sixth Edition

- ❏ The chapter on Contemporary Philosophy of Education includes a section on *postmodernism* together with a chart delineating the various philosophies and their educational implications. Early contributors to educational philosophy are included in Chapter 2.
- ❏ *Comprehensive coverage* is presented in the same compact, readable format of earlier editions. Quotes from leading authors of the period introduce each chapter.
- ❏ *Unique time-line charts* and "Then and Now" sections provide ease in understanding the various periods.
- ❏ Current legislation, court decisions, and governmental policies are examined, including programs initiated by the current administration such as the *National Service Legislation* and efforts to enhance the learning environment of children at risk.
- ❏ *Thorough updating* reflects the impact on education of recent development and controversial issues. Inclusion for exceptional children, outcomes-based education, and multiculturalism are explored.
- ❏ The Civil Rights Act of 1991, the *Americans with Disabilities Act of 1990* and efforts to achieve women's equity are included in this volume.
- ❏ *A chapter on the future of education* projects current trends into the 21st Century and reflects the work of such popular authors as Arthur Wirth, John Naisbitt, Alvin Toffler, Joseph Coats, and C. Owen Paepke. Changing demographics and delivery systems are included in this edition.
- ❏ Selective chapter and general *bibliographies* are provided as guides for more detailed study. The reader is also urged to pursue original documents as well as interpretative histories.

We are indebted to Linda Sullivan for the encouragement to produce a sixth edition, to Rex Davidson for his production guidance, and to copyeditor Regina Shelley. In addition, Dr. Timothy J. Bergen Jr., Dr. Fred Kierstead, Dr. Paul D. Travers, and Dr. James Swartz made valuable suggestions about material to be included in this edition. Their suggestions were invaluable as was the work of Roberta Clark with her computer expertise, cheerful disposition, and readiness to assist in manuscript completion. Special thanks go to Walter Kreeger, who with his expertise in proofreading with our university press, identified many needed modifications. I also thank Wendy Thornton for her proofreading help, and Deans Roderick McDavis and David C. Smith, both at the University of Florida, for their inspiration for the project. Finally, we want to thank the reviewers for this edition: Malcolm Campbell, Bowling Green State University; Fred Kierstead, University of Houston; Joseph McCarthy, Suffolk University; Albert Miller, University of Houston; Harvey Neufeldt, Tennessee Tech University; and Franklin Parker, Western Carolina University.

BRIEF CONTENTS

CONTENTS

INTRODUCTION

Lycurgus would never reduce his laws into writing . . . for he thought that the most material points . . . such as . . . the public welfare, being imprinted on the hearts of their youth by a good discipline . . . would find a stronger security, than any compulsion would be, in the principles of action formed in them by their best lawgiver, education.

Plutarch

As Alvin Toffler has demonstrated in *Future Shock*, the pace of change and the birth of new information are the most significant characteristics of modern society. As a major social institution, the schools are constantly bombarded with new demands and challenged with alternative ideas about how goals might be achieved and problems solved. In a broader sense, education is called upon to provide all members of modern society with the skills, values, information, and attitudes needed to survive in an uncertain world. The very nature of an unknown and dangerous future creates controversy in educational matters. Never before in American history have so many issues involving the social, economic, and political aspects of the culture been so hotly debated. The progressive and dynamic nature of American society has long allowed opposing viewpoints to be passionately expressed; but controversy is more intense today because basic values and the public philosophy are at stake.

In a world marked by war, inflation, recession, population explosion, careening technology, pollution, racial strife, unemployment, energy crises, starvation, ecological suicide, and anxiety about the future, education and schooling cannot be taken for granted. The teacher today is likely to be overwhelmed by the number and variety of demands made and conflicting theories about how demands should be met. In a time of information overload, it is especially important for educators to have some sort of theoretical base to serve as a map through the labyrinth of facts and opinions. Misconceptions and misunderstandings may often be avoided if teachers and the general public have a sound understanding of the historical forces which served as the foundation for our present culture.

While the history of education does not provide the teacher with a blueprint for classroom practices, it may serve to recall previous techniques and concepts with which others have had success or failure. Much of what is regarded as new or innovative in education has a long historical record. For example, individual instruction, team teaching, open classrooms, schools without walls, alternative schools for secondary students, work-study programs, nongraded schools, and competency based programs were all tried in one form or another by the progressive educators of the 1930s. It is incredible that some modern educators have overlooked the progressive experiments which can supply valuable information on proposed educational changes. Without a knowledge of history, teachers find themselves "re-inventing the wheel."

1

Greek City States	Roman Republic	BC	AD	Roman Empire	Dark Ages
c 900	Cato		First Century		
Homer			Hebrew Elementary Schools		
	Cicero		Quintilian		
Athens			Tacitus		
Sparta					
Fifth and Fourth		University of		360	
Centuries		Alexandria		Julian Revived	
Socrates				Classical	
Plato				Learning	
Aristotle					
Isocrates				529	
				Justinian Closed	
				the Pagan Universities	

More importantly, knowing educational history provides a basis for reassessing educational and cultural traditions and a guide for making judgments about the future. Accepted practice and tradition are simply not good enough at a time when the very survival of the race depends upon educating children who are able to cope with the mammoth problems surrounding us now and future ones that can barely be imagined. Today a critic like Ivan Illich, who advocates deschooling society because he believes that the values carried by formal educational institutions are unwholesome and dangerous, must be taken seriously. In the 1950s Illich would have been the object of ridicule. The concept of "culture lag," central to William F. Ogburn's *Social Change*, is now so much a part of reality that it is taken for granted; but school planners must still find ways of keeping education from falling hopelessly behind. The age of electronic communication, computers, cybernation, and mushrooming scientific discovery is upon us.

Teachers must have an appreciation of the culture in which schools operate if they are to influence programs and choices of curriculum. To understand problems in a world of exponential change, educators need to know how problems have developed, what dangers and opportunities are linked with them, and what future developments may reasonably be predicted. A teacher who has excellent techniques for communicating with and stimulating students may achieve great success in teaching. However, *what* is taught may be vital or useless to the student, depending on the state of the culture and the rapidity of change. Many American high school students now receive training in job skills that will not be needed in the future.

Education locked into a rigid pattern with few alternatives is a blueprint for disaster. To deal with an issue of this kind, educators must understand the culture—the social, political, and economic forces at work. To this end, the history of education should be treated as social and intellectual history. It is the significant forces, movements, ideas,

Middle Ages		Renaissance	Reformation
569-632 Mohammed	776-586 Alcuin	1158 University of Paris	1466-1536 Erasmus and Humanism
800 Learning Revived by Charlemagne	Chivalry	1225-1274 Thomas Aquinas	1517 Luther's 95 Theses
Monasticism		Scholasticism	1509-1565 Calvin
		Growth of the Universities	1550 Knox and English Puritans

and conflicts which shaped the American school system that are vital to a comprehension of the present.

Further, professional educators need to understand the close functional relationship between theory and practice. This requires more than accuracy in reporting events, authenticity of records, and credibility of sources (although all these are vital). While the historian must attempt to determine the meaning of the record, that record must always be interpreted and there is always the possibility of bias. The authors of this book take responsibility for the validity of the material presented and for efforts to show relationships, evaluate trends, and understand context. Interpretation, however, assumes the active participation of the reader, who must draw upon his or her experience in addition to the historical facts.

A complete history of American education in a book of this length is impossible. Many excellent treatments with more detail and depth are available, most of which are included in the chapter bibliographies of this text. An adequate historical reassessment of our cultural and educational foundations requires examination of the documents upon which history is based. The object of this work is to give an outline of the most significant educational events and movements which shaped the American schools. It is designed to provide a sound historical base from which to evaluate and judge modern educational theory and practice. The level of information provided is about what most American universities expect graduate students in education (not majoring in educational foundations) to know about the field. The book may therefore prove useful to those studying for preliminary or general examinations.

The broad chronological organization of this book is justified by the ease with which the novice may find topics and grasp the material. Time lines, section headings, a glossary, and an index are included for the same reason. Nevertheless, it should be remembered that events, dates, laws, and administrative structures are less important than evaluating, understanding, and criticizing the historical material.

HISTORY AND PURPOSES OF EDUCATIONAL HISTORY

As subjects of study or "disciplines" go, the history of education is relatively new. In a general way it has been included as part of the field of history, but intellectual and cultural history (of which the history of education is a segment) is much more recent than military and political history. Systematic study of the history of education has developed in America largely within the past century, although there were many earlier accounts of the training of particular individuals or unique groups. Thus, literature contains some history of education, as in the case of the life of Lycurgus in Plutarch's *The Lives of the Noble Grecians and Romans*, which provides considerable information about the training of boys in the ancient Greek city-state of Sparta. Biography is obviously a rich source of information about educational practices in times past, since authors nearly always attempt to account for character development by describing childhood experiences, schooling included. Historians have also been attracted by customs or practices which they considered rare or bizarre, so that atypical educational systems often have been described in some detail.

Modern history of education received its greatest stimulation from the theory that teachers should have a knowledge of the development of at least their own national school system as part of their professional equipment. Obviously, this belief was dependent upon some sort of formal training for teachers—something which did not occur in the United States until after 1825, and then only to a limited degree. The common assumption that educational historiography started in the nineteenth century is largely true, even though one may point to numerous efforts to trace school development in earlier times. Quintilian, the Roman educator of the first century, included some history of education in his *Institutio Oratoria*, while Robert Goulet's book, *Compendium on the Magnificence, Dignity, and Excellence of the University of Paris in the Year of Grace 1517*, helps us understand the origins of our modern university as well as linkages with our present secondary education system. Similarly, Goulet's *On the Origins of the University of Paris*, published in 1517, could be considered educational history. Professor Harry Good identifies Claude Fleury's *Treatise on the Selection and Methods of Studies* (France, circa 1700) as the oldest systematic history of education. There were numerous histories of institutions of higher learning and some efforts to describe higher education generally, such as that of the Puritan minister Cotton Mather who wrote about New England college programs around the year 1700.

Nevertheless, the history of American education was hardly a field for systematic study until Ellwood P. Cubberley of Stanford University published his *Public Education in the United States*, followed by books of readings in the history of education and critically annotated bibliographies on the subject. Cubberley, who produced his books just after 1900, was a widely respected educator and scholar who had considerable influence upon the inclusion of the history of American education among standard subjects in teacher-training programs. Since normal-school education had become common by the beginning of the twentieth century and education departments were by then established in many of the nation's leading universities, courses dealing with history of education in the United States sprang up all over the country. Historians who were not also educators continued to avoid the field; but scholars such as Paul Monroe with his *Founding of the American Public School Systems, 1940* and I. L. Kandel's *International Yearbook of the International Institute of Teachers College, (1st–21st editions), 1942–1944,* that explored adult education in other countries, contributed vastly to our knowledge.

History of education was identified by its broad area of coverage compared to other kinds of history. The emphasis of historians who were also interested in teacher preparation and school improvement was not simply on the development of the public system of education but also upon the social factors which gave rise to the system. In this sense, the history of education may be called the earliest systematic treatment of cultural and intellectual factors affecting the American people. No full understanding of the current educational situation in a nation is possible without a knowledge of the evolution of the school system, together with the practices and theories which contributed to its growth. Thus, the educational historians do not limit themselves to a single field of knowledge but draw upon information from such disciplines as economics, sociology, anthropology, and psychology in an effort to get a true conception of educational development. For this reason, their approach should be considered interdisciplinary.

Differing Points of View.   Leading historians of education have been more interested in the application of their studies to professional improvement of teaching than to the study of "pure" history for its own sake. This fact and the educators' point of view have led to disagreements between modern historians of education and professors of history who are interested in studying education. Both groups add to the existing body of knowledge about education. The historian contributes special skill in the detailed study of limited periods, geographical areas, and special topics. Educational historians are usually interested in interpreting broad cultural trends in order to clarify the goals and aims of education, as well as intensive work on specific topics related to schooling.

Historians of education have differed on the interpretation of the facts, especially since the field was entered by scholars with a strong interest in sociology. Bernard Bailyn is an example of an author who feels the schools have generally supported educational equality, while Michael Katz argues that they have served the special interests of the dominant middle-class whites. Much of the current historical literature in education aligns itself with one of these interpretations of the role of education in American culture.

Influence of Recent Changes.   A number of changes have taken place in education during the past few years which have had a marked influence upon the study of the history of education. Among the more important developments are the following: (a) rapid increase in scientific activity and the accumulation of knowledge, together with an extension of average time spent in school and a major increase in adult education and training by private industries; (b) substantial involvement of the federal government in educational matters, especially after the success of the Soviet space effort in 1957; (c) growth of graduate work in education due to a much larger demand for teachers with advanced degrees, bringing many more scholars to the field of history of education; (d) an increased interest in foreign school systems, the role of education in emerging nations, and the problems of social class, racial integration, and poverty in America; (e) the work of critics of the school system in the United States who have taken issue with the organization, methods, and especially the curriculum of our public schools.

The history of education is therefore a developing rather than a finished area of study. It is concerned with building a full understanding of the current educational situation through the study of the evolution of educational practices, ideas, and institutions in social context. In a 1964 lecture to the Department of Education of Johns Hopkins University, William W. Brickman described educational history as that branch of history which deals with the development of thought, practice, materials, personnel, administration, organization, and problems of schools. Educational history also includes institutions and organizations which instruct both the young and the mature, the mass media, and other learning experiences.

INTELLECTUAL BACKGROUND

American education is western education and therefore the intellectual roots for it extend back to ancient Greece and Rome. Plato and Aristotle formed the basis of the school curriculum and also laid the foundation for educational theory. Classical studies especially stressed Latin and the culture of the Greeks and Romans. Humanism in the age of Erasmus looked back to Cicero and Quintilian for models of literary style. Leaders of the American Revolution were familiar with writings of classical antiquity and often quoted the ancient writers. (See Chapter 2 for a philosophic discussion of early writers.)

Force of Medieval Tradition.   With the decline and fall of the Roman Empire, an intellectual and social stagnation began in Europe that continued until the several revivals of learning known collectively as the Renaissance. Feudal patterns of social structure and economics developed in this era, while philosophy and learning were handmaidens of the Church. Education was at a low ebb, the monasteries and a few cathedral schools being the chief instruments of instruction. Charlemagne made an effort to revive learning at the end of the eighth century, but theological questions continued to occupy the minds of the learned elite while the great bulk of the people remained ignorant in an "otherworldly" society.

A reintroduction of ancient classical learning, especially the Arabic translations of Aristotle in the thirteenth century, gave rise to the higher level scholarship of Albert the Great and Thomas Aquinas. Medieval universities and the scholasticism of Thomas

Aquinas eventually provided a basis for moving beyond the traditions of the Middle Ages. Nevertheless, medieval influences were still very strong at the time of American colonization. They are to be found in the social structure, the dominance of religion, superstitions, and other beliefs widely held by settlers from all parts of Europe.

Impact of the Renaissance. The Renaissance, or rebirth of learning, began in the 1200s and lasted through the Reformation of the 1500s. There are many aspects of this movement which had some influence on American development. The Renaissance replaced a religious point of view with a secular one, making man rather than God the focal point with reference to art, literature, and the government. Humanism, as it is sometimes called, was based partly upon the transfer of wealth and political power from the Church to laymen and nation states. The Renaissance also included a revival of interest in the ancient classical culture of Greece and Rome. Humanists studied and imitated the manuscripts of the great writers of the past. They also examined the ancient social order (especially of Rome) and made critical comparisons with their own time. Classicism protested against the narrow religious nature of education in the Middle Ages. Erasmus made editions of the New Testament in Latin and Greek and also criticized the ignorance of the clergy and the injustice of society. Renaissance emphasis on the development of the individual helped to purge ignorance and encourage education.

Significant and new inventions made rapid progress in learning possible. As the Renaissance swept through Europe, a great desire for books developed that hand copying or block printing could not satisfy. Johannes Gutenberg developed his technique for using separate pieces of raised metal type in a press about 1440. The resulting revolution in the production and availability of printed information had a profound impact on education in the Western world. The availability of books at a low cost allowed many more members of society to read and think for themselves, instead of accepting everything on the authority of scholars. Growth of cities, revival of trade, exploration, and increased mobility of scholars helped to spread information and expedited the exchange of ideas.

Impact of Scientific Thinking. From 1500 to 1700 significant changes were taking place in Europe such as geographic exploration, religious revolution, the growth of nationalism, and the discovery of science. While the classical humanism of the Renaissance period continued to be the dominant educational force, commercial interests and cultural diversity gave rise to the growth of scientific facts and methods.

Around 1500, Leonardo da Vinci called attention to the importance of observation and experimentation in learning. Francis Bacon (1561–1626) popularized the scientific technique in Novum Organum. The astronomical discoveries of Copernicus, Kepler, Galileo, and Bruno challenged traditional conceptions of the universe. William Gilbert made studies of electricity, Robert Boyle examined the chemical properties of gases, and Isaac Newton published basic laws of physics and mechanics. Mathematical support for science was found in the contributions made to calculus and analytical geometry by Leibniz, Descartes, and Newton.

Science was still suspect when the American colonies were founded. Very few learned people accepted the materialism and the concept of a machine universe expounded by Thomas Hobbes or Pierre Gassendi. Nevertheless, the scientific method of thinking did provide a challenge to established beliefs and laid a foundation for the enlightenment of the eighteenth century. William Harvey's theory of the circulation of the blood was discussed at Harvard while that institution remained a theological college strongly opposed to science.

Significance of Religious Revolutions.   Probably no single movement so greatly affected colonial America as the Protestant Reformation and the Catholic Counter-Reformation. The tremendous impact of the Reformation on social, economic, and political life was of paramount importance in the formation of the United States, and some of the influences are still felt today.

In 1517, when Martin Luther posted his Ninety-five Theses on the church door in Wittenberg, Germany, the Catholic Church was the most important educational agency in the world. At the close of the Thirty Years War, all institutions and every aspect of the culture had been affected. Most of the Europeans who came to America were Protestants, but there were many denominations. Lutherans from Germany and Scandinavia settled in the middle colonies, especially Pennsylvania. Followers of John Calvin were represented by Puritans, Presbyterians, Huguenots and several smaller sects. Anabaptists (followers of Huldreich Zwingli [1484–1531]) were persecuted by both Catholic and Protestant authorities and therefore sought freedom in the New World. Much of the struggle known as the Reformation centered upon efforts to capture the minds of men, and therefore great emphasis was placed upon the written word. Obviously, schools were needed by both sides to foster the growth of each denomination or sect.

Luther's doctrine of the "priesthood of all believers" made it necessary for boys and girls to learn to read the Scriptures. Educational programs which were intended to give the masses the ability to read the Bible in the vernacular were started by Protestant groups in Germany and wherever Luther's concepts spread. While the schools were often rudimentary, they offered universal education for all children regardless of wealth and were supported by both church and state. Protestants also provided secondary education of higher quality for the elite destined to enter positions in the government or the Church. While Catholics played a substantially smaller role in colonial America, they were very much part of the Counter-Reformation. Catholics in Maryland were influenced by leaders such as Jean Baptiste de la Salle and St. Ignatius of Loyola.

In England, the break with the Catholic Church came when Clement VII refused to annul Henry VIII's marriage to Catherine of Aragon. By the Act of Supremacy in 1534, Henry became head of the Church in England and proceeded to break up the monasteries. The English Church remained very much the same during Henry's time, with the Reformation really starting under Edward VI. Catholicism was briefly restored by Mary I, but during the long reign of Elizabeth, Anglicanism was firmly established. Anglicanism is a moderate form of Protestantism which preserves most of the organizational structure of the Catholic Church. English Calvinists who wanted to change or purify the Anglican Church became known as Puritans and were very important in the settlement of New England. Other dissenters from the Anglican faith included some called Separatists, who denied the establishment of religion and held that each man must be free to worship as he thought fit. Followers of John Knox (1505–1572) in Scotland (Presbyterians), Quakers, and Catholics tended to move to America when the political tide was against them in England. For example, the great Puritan migrations took place in the 1630s because of the persecution directed by Anglican Archbishop Laud.

Conservative Traditions.   Students sometimes get the idea that the Renaissance and the Reformation were entirely progressive movements. In fact, they were often reactionary. Humanism looked to the past rather than the future for its model. The Reformation had a tendency to make religion once again the dominant intellectual interest of mankind. There were, however, other forces which tended to counteract the importance of the Reformation and the Renaissance. The American colonies were an integral part of a great English colonial empire. They were not isolated outposts or temporary communities but a portion of a larger capitalistic scheme brought about by a strong middle class for the purpose of material gain. The rise of capitalism was one of the strongest factors in the development of this nation. American civilization, from the first, was profoundly affected by economic motives and interests. Even the New England Puritan, who came to a "stern and rockbound coast" in order to escape religious oppression, was not without economic concern. The soil in New England was shallow and unproductive. Pilgrims and Puritans soon turned to timber cutting, ship building, fishing for cod, manufacturing, and trade in order to make a living.

In addition to capitalism, the parliamentary form of government was brought by the colonists to America. The New Englanders especially supported Parliament against the King. They wished to substitute their own body politic for the authority which had been vested in the crown. Thus, the effort of the Pilgrim fathers in making the Mayflower Compact, which served as a constitution and defined the responsibilities of the people as well as centering authority in the people, could hardly have occurred without the struggle for parliamentary supremacy which had taken place in the mother country.

Many other potent forces played a part in the intellectual climate out of which American educational institutions developed. The rise of science, British empiricism, the forces of rationalism, and the movement toward greater intellectual discovery all had their effect on the birth of American schools. The point to be made is that American educational and intellectual foundations have roots which run very deep into the European past. While many of the most conservative ideas, such as the evil nature of man, were preserved in America, there were also factors tending to develop an attitude of change.

THEN TO NOW

The casual student of history may not immediately see the relationship of the remote past to the age in which we live. Nevertheless, connections do exist between the world of today and those past traditions which were once dominant. A better understanding of modern attitudes and ideas can be gleaned from an analysis of historical forces. Consider, for example, the curriculum of present schools and colleges. Medieval universities offered studies which had been derived from ancient educational interests reaching back to Aristotle. These were the seven liberal arts which scholars believed to be essential to the life of the mind and the education of men. The basic or tool subjects were grammar, logic, and rhetoric. Advanced studies consisted of arithmetic, geometry, astronomy, and harmony. Although the names have sometimes changed (music for harmony and language arts for grammar), it is obvious that these medieval curriculum offerings are still found in the schools. It is also true that modern groupings into natural sciences, social sciences, and the humanities are based on these early subjects and that we still speak of a liberal arts curriculum in reference to such studies. There have been many modifications and additions but the curriculum of the universities of the Middle Ages has not disappeared. The whole idea of a university stems from the medieval organization of a guild of teachers and a guild of students. The modern master's degree is named after the guild practice of awarding master craftsman status for those who had demonstrated excellence in their work. Our most modern research universities still have deans, lecture halls, student organizations and rectors (presidents) all of which were part of the early universities.

The rebirth of learning known as the Renaissance has never really ceased. Ideas from the classical past together with the humanism of scholars like Erasmus produced a new desire to understand the forces that shape human society. When modern sociologists attempt to analyze the actions of groups of people, they are involved in the spirit of inquiry that was the heart of the Renaissance. Educators today still debate the role of humanistic studies in an age of scientific research and specialization. Likewise the invention of the printing press led to improved production and distribution of information which is still accelerating. Modern telecommunications, information superhighways, electronic media, and computer-based research are current aspects of the revolution started by Gutenberg. It should be obvious also that the secular scientific thinking started by Bacon, Galileo, Gilbert, and others has continued to grow and expand at a rapid rate. The study of the history of science in many universities and popular television programs like *Connections* illustrate the need for understanding the past in order to cope with the present. Current issues over tax support for religious schools may be linked to the struggles of the Protestant Reformation and the Catholic Counter-Reformation.

While we are able to get a better picture of the forces that shaped values and attitudes in historical times than we are today, currents of opinion and climates of thought are difficult to isolate in any age. It is easy enough to mark the founding of the English settlement on the American seaboard with Jamestown in 1607 and the first major school law with the "Old Deluder Satan Act," but it is another matter to trace the cultural forces that shaped the minds and deeds of the colonists. Nevertheless, whatever light can be cast on the intellectual, social, ethical, and philosophic forces which created colonial culture will be useful in helping to gain a better understanding of our own times. Just as the Puritan ethic of early America still casts its shadow over modern educational theory and practice (as in the case of Bible reading and prayer in public schools), so the Puritans themselves were influenced by mainstreams of thought going back at least to medieval times. As difficult as the task may be, cultural and intellectual history must try to identify main currents of thought and influential values that set the parameters of basic cultural beliefs. In this way, history can be a most useful tool in helping us to understand ourselves and the times in which we live.

Because we tend to think in a contemporary time frame, it is important to recall that many of the movements considered in this book required several years. The Protestant Reformation and the Catholic Counter-Reformation were not single events like those reported every day on the CBS News. They were revolutions of many facets of society which took centuries to develop, decades to complete, and their aftermath continues to be felt in contemporary society. Due to the brief treatment given to colonial history in the common school history courses, it is easy to make the error of thinking of the colonial period as brief. Actually the years between Jamestown and the American Revolution cover almost half of the time that has elapsed since 1607. In the passing of nearly two centuries, changes occurred in colonial America that were dramatic and vast, even though they took place at a slower rate than modern transformations. The revolt against England and the birth of a new nation could hardly have taken place in the conservative climate of opinion that existed in the beginning of the seventeenth century.

Educational development in colonial America and its influence on the schools of later times can only be appreciated against the backdrop of an earlier Old World culture. What is happening in education today must also be evaluated in terms of changing world conditions. For the first time in history, all of the school age children in mainland China actually attend school. Mass starvation in East Africa makes it impossible for children there to reach their full potential or to achieve educational goals. Currently, what used to be the Soviet Union is in the throes of trying to reconcile Western Capitalism with the demands of citizens for jobs and sustenance protection offered by the old communist regime. The Bosnian conflict also reflects a return to the balance of power system among nations so prevalent in history. Russia has emerged as a power broker, influencing competing interests in Bosnia. Our economic system will be influenced by the continuing pressures of an interdependent global community. All people living on earth are affected by the ways in which natural resources are used, and all are demanding more human services, education included. An airport or a computer is much the same whether it is found in New York, Manila, or Buenos Aires. Our educational history began with influences from many areas and traditions; the future of education also depends on events and developments that are global in nature.

Many causes were at work in the settlement of the American colonies. Adventure, money, love of God, and a desire to convert the Indians gave rise to the colonies. Many wished to escape oppressive governments and the hard times in Europe such as the English depression of 1595. The first settlers were Europeans, dominated by English traditions. Modern society in the United States has been greatly modified by the influx of other people and ideas, but the Protestant religions and the English language remain dominant today. This dominance, like that of middle-class values in schools, creates a major educational problem in equal treatment of students whose first language is other than English or who represent religious backgrounds other than Protestant Christian.

Most of the time and effort of teachers and administrators in schools is spent dealing with contemporary needs and problems. It is all too easy for us to think of events in the remote past as having no relevance for modern educators, if we think of such events at all. This is a fundamental mistake which may prevent us from making the best decisions for the well-being of our students and their communities. Religious conflicts starting with the protests of Martin Luther are still evident in current arguments over prayer in public schools. Attacks by the "ultra right wing" on "secular humanism," as well as various other special interest groups including advocates of home schooling, can be clarified by an understanding of conservative theology, Renaissance humanism, and *laissez faire* politics. Several states have passed or are considering a law requiring schools to give equal time to the Biblical theory of creation and to the theory of evolution. It is not enough to link this with the work of Darwin or with the Scopes trial in 1925. The educator needs also to consider it in the light of the opposition to scientific knowledge in the time of Copernicus and Bruno. Historical knowledge is vital for placing current issues into perspective and making decisions that will stand critical analysis.

Sources of educational history include deeds, contracts, oral history, archival records, newspaper morgues, personal correspondence, archaeological discoveries, museums, art, tools, garments, flyers, government documents, artifacts, charters, archives, journals, texts and diaries of the period, all of which provide avenues to understanding our past.

BIBLIOGRAPHY

Bailyn, Bernard. *Education in the Forming of American Society: Needs and Opportunities for Study.* New York: W. W. Norton, 1962.

Barrow, Robin. *Plato and Education.* Boston: Routledge & Kegan Paul, 1976.

Brann, Eva. *Paradoxes of Education in a Republic.* Chicago: The University of Chicago Press, 1979.

Church, Robert L. *Education in the United States.* New York: The Free Press, 1976.

Clough, A. H. *Plutarch's Lives.* New York: Bigelow, Smith and Co., 1911.

Cremin, Lawrence A. *American Education, The Colonial Experience.* New York: Harper & Row, 1970.

Curtis, Stanley, and M. E. A. Boultwood. *A Short History of Educational Ideas.* 3d ed. London: University Tutorial Press, 1964.

Grant, Gerald, ed. *Review of Research in Education: Section 11 History and Philosophy.* Washington, D.C.: American Educational Research Association, 1992.

Gross, Richard, ed. *Heritage of American Education.* Boston: Allyn & Bacon, 1962.

Gwynn, Aubrey. *Roman Education from Cicero to Quintilian.* rev. ed. New York: Teachers College Press, 1966.

Holley, Raymond. *Religious Education and Religious Understanding.* Boston: Routledge & Kegan Paul, 1978.

McMillan, James H., and Sally Schumacher. *Research in Education: A Conceptual Introduction.* New York: Harper Collins, College Publishers, 1993.

Meyer, Adolphe. *Grandmasters of Educational Thought.* New York: McGraw-Hill, 1975.

Mulhern, James. *A History of Education.* 2d ed. New York: Ronald, 1959.

Perkinson, Harry. *Two Hundred Years of American Educational Thought*. New York: David McKay Company, Inc., 1976.

Pounds, Ralph. *The Development of Education in Western Culture*. New York: Appleton-Century-Crofts, 1968.

Ravitch, Diane. *The Revisionists Revisited: A Critique of the Radical Attack on the Schools*. New York: Basic Books, 1978.

Rusk, Robert. *The Doctrines of the Great Educators*. rev. ed. New York: Macmillan, 1969.

Sherman, Robert, ed. *Understanding History of Education*. rev. ed. Cambridge, MA: Schenkaman Publishing Company, Inc., 1984.

Spring, Joel. *The American School: 1642-1990*. New York: Longman, 1990.

Wood, Norman. *The Reformation and English Education*. London: University Tutorial Press, 1931.

EUROPEAN HERITAGE AND COLONIAL INFLUENCE ON AMERICAN EDUCATION

It being one chief object of that old deluder, Satan, to keep men from the knowledge of the scriptures, . . . it is therefore ordered, that every township . . . after the Lord hath increased them to the number of fifty householders, . . . shall . . . appoint one within their town to teach all children as shall resort to him to read and write. It is further ordered, that where any town shall increase to the number of one hundred families . . . they shall set up a grammar school, the master thereof being able to instruct youth so far as they may be fitted for the university.

Old Deluder Satan Act of 1647—Massachusetts Laws of 1647.

The first American educational theory and practice tended to reflect European patterns, but the instances of transplantation without modification were few. Early but relatively slight in influence on later developments were the settlements of the Spanish in Florida and the French in the Mississippi Valley—settlements in which European institutions, including schools, were copied as closely as the new environment would allow. This was true in St. Augustine, which was founded by Pedro Menendez in 1565, and in the French settlements at Montreal, Quebec, Kaskaskia, and New Orleans. Spanish monasteries were educational as well as religious institutions and the duty of teaching Indians the Spanish language was required by royal order in 1643. Convents and schools founded by French and Spanish Catholics reached much of North America, including California where Father Junipero Serra was active.

British colonials, on the other hand, began to incorporate distinctive new features in the models they took from their homeland. The apprenticeship system, elementary reading schools, the Latin grammar school, and even Harvard College were not exact duplicates of their English counterparts. The Reformation had suggested the principle of universal education, but in England it had also allowed church property to be used for secular purposes, nearly destroying elementary schools. Philanthropists, therefore, began endowing British charity schools, while the middle-class children attended schools taught by private masters

15

BC	AD	Protestant Reformation			Glorious Revolution	
427-347 Plato		1601 English Poor Law	1620 Plymouth Colony		1664 New Amsterdam became New York	
384-322 Aristotle		1607 Jamestown	1636 Harvard College		1688 William and Mary	
		1619 Black Slaves in Virginia	1642 Massachusetts Compulsory School Law	1647 Old Deluder Satan Act	1689 English Act of Toleration	

for fees. In America, charity education provided by such agencies as the Society for the Propagation of the Gospel in Foreign Parts (SPG) became popular. The SPG, an agency of the Anglican church, provided money, books, teachers, and physical facilities for American children who otherwise would have had no opportunity to attend school. Of course, philanthropic education usually had special interests attached, such as furthering the cause of a particular religion or fostering a set of values esteemed by those who contributed funds. The English pattern of high quality private schools catering to the children of the well to do and supported by tuition was not followed to a great extent in the colonies. Secondary educational institutions modeled on Westminister, Eton, or other English "public" schools were uncommon in America. Private venture schools tended to offer practical courses such as surveying, navigation, or bookkeeping. In those areas where religion was the driving force of a community, education became an instrument for social control through transmitting and preserving the beliefs of the sect. Such efforts had often been discouraged by the authorities in England. All schools underwent changes as a result of cultural forces in the colonies and the experience of coping with the American wilderness. Apprenticeship and the tutorial system remained dominant educational practices in the colonies, as was the case in England.

Generally the educational aims of colonial schools and teachers represented stability, tradition, authority, discipline and preordained value systems that were marks of idealism and classical realism. Many of the European educators discussed in Chapter Three reflected the ideology of Idealism and Classical Realism. Friedrich Froebel's educational writings reflect Idealism while the others reflected various forms of Realism.

IDEOLOGICAL AND PHILOSOPHICAL FOUNDATIONS OF AMERICA'S EUROPEAN EDUCATIONAL HERITAGE

Idealism.   Idealism is a very old traditional philosophy, and Plato (427–347 BC) is credited with providing the philosophic principles upon which it rests. The term refers to the

French and Indian War	Boston Massacre	
1690 New England Primer	1751 Franklin's Academy in Philadelphia	
		1763 Treaty of Paris Ended the French and Indian War
1693 William and Mary College in Virginia	1762 Rousseau's *Emile* Published in France	1765 Stamp Act

reality of ideas, or mind, spirit, and reason. Idealism is in opposition to materialism and realism. Plato held that only mental or spiritual aspects of experience are ultimately real. He used the myth of the cave and the allegory of the divided line to convince his followers that ordinary common-sense objects exist only as copies of absolute ideas or "forms." In the cave, a person held captive from birth experiences only the dim light and shadows on the wall made by his captors and objects they manipulate. Eventually he breaks loose and emerges from the cave where he experiences the "real" world of sunshine, other people, farms, and the sea. Having once "seen the light" he can never again believe in the reality of the cave.

In the divided line, Plato shows that our senses are often fooled by dreams, shadows, mirages, and the like. These dreams, shadows, and mirages are related to sense objects, which have a higher order of reality. By the same argument, Plato claims that sense objects are related to constructs and concepts which are more real than the objects and that the concepts and constructs refer to pure ideas or forms. The order for water on this theory would be first, a mirage of water on a dry road; second, water in a glass; third, H_2O; and finally, the form water.

If only ideas are real, then pure ideas should be the objects of education. For example, once the pure idea "justice" is understood, the learner has a basis for judging all human acts just or unjust. Plato also placed all human beings into a hierarchy of categories according to aspects of their souls. The largest and lowest group are those dominated by appetite, and they should be the workers in society. The middle group is dominated by spirit, and they make good soldiers. At the top are those dominated by reason, and they should be the philosopher kings who rule the state. Education is intended to sort out those who have rational souls and to enable them to "remember" the forms that represent ultimate truth. A mathematical concept such as a point or a line cannot be found in the sense world but must be described in theory. Constructs of plane geometry are, therefore, excellent studies for philosopher-kings. Plato's Republic is the first full statement of a philosophy of education. It describes the organization and the curriculum of ideal education in detail, and its scope is from early childhood through adult life.

Since the universal mind is real for idealists and the individual's spiritual essence, or soul, is permanent, the philosophy is compatible with organized religion. St. Augustine (354–430) had been a teacher of rhetoric as a young man. He employed many of the ideas of Plato in the church and made idealism a Christian theology. The seven liberal arts consisting of the trivium (logic, grammar, and rhetoric) and the quadrivium (music, arithmetic, geometry, and astronomy) were Platonic subjects, modified by the fathers of the church. They persisted into the medieval universities and are still found in the modern curriculum.

Other famous idealists include Rene Descartes (1596–1650), George Berkeley (1685–1753), Immanuel Kant (1724–1804), and George W. F. Hegel (1770–1831). Berkeley took an extreme position which held that physical objects cannot exist on their own but depend on some mind for their reality. Kant's transcendental idealism stated that an object consisted of ideas in our mind but that a thing observed might exist "in itself" independent of the knowing mind. For Hegel's "absolute idealism," both the object itself and the object known to us are ideas of the universal mind. If the universal mind is defined as God, it is easy to see why this philosophy dominated religious institutions and influenced American transcendentalists such as Emerson and Thoreau. We have seen that American education in the nineteenth century was greatly influenced by Friedrich Froebel and William Torey Harris, both idealists. Josiah Royce (1855–1916) and Herman Horne (1874–1946), contemporaries of John Dewey, were idealists in America. J. Donald Butler was an ardent spokesman for American educational idealism.

Idealists think only the spiritual is ultimately real and that the universe is the expression of a universal mind or a generalized intelligence. This mind is permanent, regular, orderly, and eternal, and the truth it represents is absolute and universal. Through education, the individual mind or soul may come to understand and appreciate these unalterable truths. Plato argued that ideas do not come into the mind from an outside source but are always present as a manifestation of the universal mind and may be recalled through the intellectual process of working with ideas. Teaching, for idealists, is bringing forth the latent knowledge so that a general awareness of universal truths will emerge.

Intellectual disciplines or conceptional systems, such as mathematics, language, ethical studies, history, and the sciences, represent a synthesis of the universal mind. The liberal arts and all other formal intellectual disciplines lead to the highest order of knowledge about reality. Integration of all subjects is important to idealistic pedagogy. Logic and mathematics are powerful tools which cultivate the ability of the student to deal with abstractions and the most sophisticated aspects of the cultural heritage. Vocational subjects, or those which have a practical outcome, are not valued highly. Natural and physical sciences are useful because they deal with cause and effect. History and literature hold a higher place in the curriculum because they provide cultural models. At the top of the hierarchy are the general disciplines of philosophy and theology, which are the most abstract and which transcend time and space. Clearly an idealist school or college would lean heavily toward the arts and sciences and would stress general or what is termed "liberal" education of the arts. Idealists will not tolerate an elective system by which students may choose to boycott general education and concentrate on job preparation.

Although idealism as a philosophy of education is still found among educators in the United States, it is no longer a dominant theory as was the case in the nineteenth century. The vast expansion of science and technology has also contributed to the decline of idealism, so it is now more of a protest philosophy than a mainstream one. Idealism still finds its advocates however, as in Mortimer Adler's call for universal knowlege that all individuals ought to have as members of the human race.

Friedrich Froebel, founder of the kindergarten, followed the tenets of idealism in both theory and practice in his work with childhood education. William Van Til in *Education: A Beginning* noted that Froebel's own childhood experiences of loneliness led to his deep religious faith and emphasis on a home united by love which was reflected in his educational philosophy.

Educational aims of 17th and 18th century American colleges included moral and ethical conduct, universal truths and knowledge, and expounding the best ideals of humankind. Although often honored more in the breach than the observance, these idealistic values were taught in colonial colleges as well as in their European models. Religion and idealism were often interrelated in schools and colleges of the period.

Realism.   Realism is a school of philosophy which stresses objective knowledge and information that comes from the senses. These philosophers hold that there is a real world not constructed by human minds which can be known by the mind. Knowledge of reality is the only reliable means of guiding individual and social conduct. Reality is found in the realm of objects and perceptions about objects, and these objects are matter. There is no division of object and form as the idealists say. Human beings can know reality through examination of objects and through reason.

Plato's student, Aristotle (384–322 BC), is considered to be the father of philosophic realism. While not rejecting the existence of ideas or forms, Aristotle found it impossible to separate the study of sense objects from their blueprints or forms. Plato would consider the idea of a rectangular solid in the abstract. Aristotle insisted on examining the object itself. For example, a brick takes the form of a rectangular solid, and that is its basic plan or idea. The brick is made of straw, sand, and clay, and that is its materialistic nature. Aristotle was also interested in the force that made the object (the brickmaker) and the purpose for which it was intended, such as a brick wall (final cause). He invented many of the standard ways of looking at things, such as classification into categories and the examination of individuals within a class. We can know objects directly through sensation and indirectly through contemplation or abstraction. When a number of individual objects have the same characteristics, we can generalize about them. This is a spectator epistemology in that the learner is an onlooker who sorts and classifies objects in his/her environment. Spectators may verify conceptions by correspondence with objects in the sense world. This is the empirical principle of John Locke, which is covered in Chapter Three.

Just as Plato's ideas were adapted to the church by St. Augustine, those of Aristotle were brought into harmony with Christian doctrine by St. Thomas Aquinas (1225–1274). He held that God is pure reason, and by use of reason, we could come to know the truth of reality. Proofs of the existence of God rely heavily upon observation so that scientific activity, while subordinate to reason, is justified. Aquinas saw philosophy as the handmaiden of theology and, therefore, a tool for reaching God. Knowledge can be gained from sense experience, and reason may be applied to sense data, revealing the divine plan. A proper education recognizes both the material and the spiritual nature of man. Thomism is still the philosophy of education for Roman Catholic institutions and has greatly influenced other branches of Christianity as well.

The term "sense realism" refers to the process of sorting objects in the environment and gaining an understanding of reality through observation and classification. In this sense, Bacon, Locke, Comenius, Rousseau, and Pestalozzi were realists. Sense realism, as in the case of Comenius, may be combined with religious or rational realism. For the sense realist, the learning environment must be rich in objects against which conceptions can be tested. A field trip to a farm for kindergarten children or a chemistry laboratory for secondary students meets this requirement. Objects have characteristics that may be used to classify or categorize them, and realism stresses placing everything into an objective order according to shared characteristics or similarities. Thus, realists feel zoological criteria for listing animals in groups should be learned and practiced early in the educational process. The curriculum should be organized into separate subjects in order to create an efficient and effective means of learning about the real world. The school then becomes a reflection of the systematic way in which the intellectual disciplines are organized in the university, and those, in turn, reflect the universal order of the world. For the realist, knowledge comes through pursuit of the ordered and disciplined inquiry of bodies of knowledge and subject matters. Realists also value prescriptions to govern intelligent behavior. Such behavior is rational when it conforms to the way objects behave in reality as they follow natural laws or physical laws. The educated person must live according to the rules of civilized social organization and must exhibit rational characteristics.

Essentialism is a recurring theme in education. Back to basics, essential knowledge that is the same for all people at all places everywhere, and intellectual discipline have been themes of realism from John Locke to William Bagley to the America 2000 National Education Goals.

COLONIAL MELTING POT

Theories of educational idealism and realism were modified in theory and practice in Colonial America. Modifications may be attributed to environmental difficulties, such as the struggle to produce food, the communication problem, disease, isolation, and hostile natives. Economic stresses and strains have always played a part in education. Other changes were caused by the new intellectual climate illustrated by the many nonconformist or religiously dissenting settlers and the shift of the center of civil authority represented by the signing of the Mayflower Compact. Of course, the colonists remained Englishmen and the crown retained sovereignty until the American Revolution, but local control and some degree of political independence began to emerge quite early. Dissatisfaction with conditions in the homeland caused the migration of thousands of individuals who were not anxious to restore the agencies of their grief and oppression. The availability of free land and the desire of the English to encourage settlement made it possible for almost every group of people to find a place where they could practice their own religion and follow their own lifestyle. Quakers sought freedom from restrictions on their religious activities, while indentured servants wanted freedom from bondage and the opportunity for social advancement.

However, European schools themselves were not the objects of attack by dissatisfied groups. The fact that educational facilities in the homelands were often decadent and offered very limited opportunity for the children of many who stayed behind did little to harm their reputation in America or undermine the attempt to imitate them. In an effort to preserve the European civilization of which they were a part, the colonists tried to copy the educational institutions they knew best. English textbooks and school methods were widely accepted in all the American colonies. Nevertheless, schools in the colonies were not merely transplanted but also revolutionized in spirit and sometimes in form. While the colonies were never a melting pot in the sense of mixing all the people together into one homogeneous mass, cultural diversity and the presence of many different religious denominations had a considerable influence on colonial schools.

Colonial legislatures, royal governors, proprietors, and stock companies were delegated educational authority along with political powers by the British crown. However, the degree to which civil governments took an interest in education differed greatly from one colony to another. Established churches and European governments exchanged mutual support in seventeenth-century culture. This alliance was also found throughout the colonies, although the nature of established churches differed considerably from Puritan New England to Anglican Virginia. Some degree of religious toleration developed in Rhode Island, Pennsylvania, New York, and Maryland.

RELIGIOUS SECTARIANISM

Religion played a very important part in colonial schools and colleges, both in the conduct of the institutions and in the curriculum. Although Bible reading and prayer continued to be a major part of common school practice well into the national period, control of education gradually shifted away from sectarian authorities. Just as the several states in modern America delegate authority to local school boards, so the colonial governments allowed private individuals and religious groups to establish schools of their own. In part, this was caused by the failure of governments to support schools with tax revenues, and, in part, it was due to the rise of numerous religious sects which demanded the freedom to educate children in their own way. As a general rule, the central civil government did not engage in close supervision of schools which were built and financed by local or church agencies. This was true throughout the colonies in the eighteenth century and was especially obvious in frontier settlements.

In a very real sense the desire for greater religious freedom contributed to the doctrine of separation of church and state. Roger Williams was driven from Massachusetts partly for supporting such separation, and he made it a policy in his Rhode Island settlement. The various sects eventually obtained freedom of worship and since there was no consensus concerning religious principles to be taught in schools founded by civil authorities, the various denominations conducted and controlled their own schools. In New England, the selectmen of a town, the General Court, or the ministers constituted ultimate educational authority. Royal governors and towns gave charters for schools in the Middle colonies. In the Anglican South, the Bishop of London was responsible for licensing teachers.

SOCIAL CLASS IN THE COLONIAL ENVIRONMENT

English feudal structure was not equally superimposed on all parts of the American colonial culture, but social class stratification was marked. Southern plantations usually contained every social class from slaves to owners of estates. Virginia reflected British class divisions almost exactly, and even feudal practices such as primogeniture (passing an estate to the eldest son) and entail (making sale or exchange of real property unlawful) were found in that colony. Indentured servants and at least a few slaves lived in all of the colonies. New England had no gentlemen-planter class, but ministers and magistrates had great prestige, and Puritan emphasis on work and frugality soon produced wealthy merchants. Middle colonies like Maryland had a well-developed middle class consisting of artisans and skilled workers, but the middle classes grew everywhere as trade developed and the population increased. Scarcity of labor, and especially of skilled labor, made it easy for the ambitious man to improve his social status through hard work. It was difficult to prevent a servant from becoming an independent frontier farmer.

While social class mobility was a feature of colonial society, the schools remained class-centered. Latin preparatory schools and theological colleges favored the upper classes. For many years, Harvard College class roles were arranged by social rank. Public demand for new skills resulted in a special school—the academy—which catered to the practical requirements of the commercial class. Nevertheless, many students obtained only rudimentary education and many of the earlier settlers of the lower classes could not read or write. Even in New England, where schools were in operation by 1636, the level of instruction was low and not all children could attend. Before American independence, there were trends toward a more flexible and democratic school pattern, but the rigid class system and the strong religious atmosphere continued to influence education until comparatively recent times.

Few experiences in England fitted colonists for the difficulties of sustaining life in a wilderness. Nor were the colonies similar in climate, landforms, or population so that quite different lifestyles emerged. Thus the South concentrated on agriculture and created great plantations with a social system resembling that of England, while economic complexity in New England led to towns and villages sufficiently dense in population for the maintenance of schools. Each colony also had different community patterns. Land was too cheap to sustain the feudal privileges of southern planters, and soon a new breed of small farmers and hunters emerged. These rough and ready pioneers were not at all like the gentlemen who owned large estates planted in indigo, rice, or tobacco. They were not cultured or highly educated and they had little leisure time to pursue the intellectual graces commonly acquired by wealthy slaveholders, but they soon became a political and economic force. This new class of independent people had little use for the classics or the Latin grammar schools, but they wanted their children to have the basic skills of reading and writing. In England the sons of working men and farmers seldom had an opportunity for formal schooling. In America the possibility for a better life in the future for children of all classes created a demand for some sort of schooling in every community. The most common practice among working and middle-class parents was to apprentice their sons to skilled tradesmen or shopkeepers to learn skills.

THE SOUTHERN COLONIES

Of the English colonies on the eastern seaboard, Maryland, Virginia, the Carolinas, and Georgia most closely resembled the British homeland in cultural and social patterns. Economic factors were responsible for most of the migration of English gentlemen to the South. They were not dissatisfied with conditions in the homeland, and therefore expected to replicate English institutions in America without substantial change. Southern planters devoted their energy to business and the development of their estates. They remained loyal to the Anglican church and the values of the British landed gentry. Plantation owners emphasized the enjoyment of the cultured life which included gambling, dancing, literature, music, art, books, and the breeding of fine horses. Religion was reverently practiced by prayer and church attendance, but it did not become the dominating force of life as in New England. There was no Puritan zeal for having every person taught to read the Bible for himself. The clergy was responsible for interpreting scripture and clerical authority was vested in the Anglican hierarchy. Educational matters also rested with the decisions of the Archbishop of Canterbury or the Bishop of London. Since both church and state favored the landed gentry and large estates were the rule, social equality did not develop in the South. Those not favored by conditions of birth and wealth were expected to be satisfied with their station in life and the decisions made for them by their "betters." In 1671, Governor Sir William Berkeley of Virginia held that every man should instruct his own children according to his means. He said:

> . . . I thank God, *that there are no free schools nor printing*, and I hope we shall not have
> them these hundred years, for *learning* has brought disobedience, and heresy, and sects
> into the world, and *printing* has divulged them, and libels against the best government.

Berkeley no doubt spoke for many Virginians, but some free schools did develop in spite of the opposition. Occasionally a parish built and maintained a school which was open to children who could not pay tuition. There were numerous endowments for schools such as those provided in the wills of Benjamin Syms (1634) and Thomas Eaton (1659), both of whom gave land and goods for the maintenance of an "able schoolmaster" to teach poor children. Nevertheless, free schools remained rare in Virginia, and large areas of the South had no formal education of any kind.

The planters did devote a good deal of time to intellectual pursuits beyond the instruction of their children. The art of writing letters was highly developed and many newspapers were circulated. Even the remote plantations usually had a good collection of books from England and other European nations. Some private libraries were excellent: that of William Byrd contained some four thousand volumes. An excellent account of the intellectual and social life of the colonial South is found in the diary of Philip Fithian. Fithian was a graduate of Princeton and served as tutor to the Carter family of northern Virginia. Tutorial education was common practice in the South.

Leading elements of the social order attempted to copy the customs and mores of wealthy Englishmen in everything, including schools. Southern educational institutions reflected more English ideals than schools in other parts of the colonies, and every planter who could afford it wished to send his son to Oxford or Cambridge Universities, or the Inns of Court (London law schools) for training.

Rigid southern social class distinctions allowed few opportunities for the indentured servants, the slaves, and the poverty-stricken freemen to engage in cultural pursuits or to improve their minds. The persons lowest in social rank were entirely dependent upon the wealthy and powerful for what little education they received. Skills needed to operate farms and plantations were not taught in schools, nor was education very clearly related to success patterns of nonprivileged southerners.

Gentlemen thought of themselves as natural political leaders, as well as guardians of refined manners, learning, justice, hospitality, and religion. No effort was spared to initiate sons of the planter class into the intellectual pursuits of their fathers. They were given generalized readings in the Greek and Roman classics. French was widely taught along with English literature and the Bible, and studies such as painting and architecture were commonly included.

No single educational pattern developed in the Southern Colonies, making it difficult to generalize. While diversity of educational practice was at a maximum in the South, public interest in education was at a minimum. Virginia had money earmarked for education as early as 1618, but the revocation of the charter for the Virginia Company seven years later stopped these funds. From that time until 1660, Virginia passed laws which required children to be taught religion, although public financial support was lacking. Since southern leaders came from the upper classes of England, the Anglican church was dominant and exercised considerable influence over the existing educational programs. Schools, however, were only indirectly controlled by law or the church because education was considered a private matter left in the hands of individual citizens. Exceptions were apprenticeship education, which was carefully regulated by law, and efforts of philanthropic or religious societies in behalf of the poor, the Indians, and the slaves. Attempts to save souls of native Americans met with slight success, but continuous appeals were made for giving slaves the rudiments of a religious education, especially by suggesting that Christianity would make them more content and harder working.

Tutorial Schools.   Tutorial schools existed throughout the South, although they varied widely in form. Very wealthy planters hired learned tutors to train their sons and frequently their daughters as well. When there was time and interest, a similar tutorial system was also used by others attached to the plantation, such as the sons of foremen or managers. Teachers were often Anglican ministers who served churches in the proximity of the estate, but private schoolmasters were also employed to teach. Sometimes it proved cheaper or more expedient to buy the services of an indentured servant for teaching. Many well-trained Scots who knew Latin and Greek were included in the shiploads of indentured persons entering southern ports, and their time could be purchased at a lower rate than that of skilled labor. Private tutorial schools were sometimes sufficient to prepare boys for college in England. The curriculum was usually classical, but practical subjects such as surveying and mathematics were by no means excluded. Girls were instructed in French, music, dancing, and polite manners by their tutors, and for them the instruction was terminal. Boys who had mastered Lilly's *Latin Grammar* were often sent to one of the private preparatory schools (great public schools) in England.

Travel was considered to be a major part of education even for boys who did not attend Latin grammar schools or colleges in England. High standards of scholarship were maintained by such educational leaders as James Blair and the Reverend Thomas Bray of Virginia. The universal employment of tutors indicated a greater interest in education by American planters than by their English counterparts.

Other Southern Colonial Schools.   Schools for those not favored by birth were limited in the Southern Colonies. Early efforts to provide endowed schools for all children, including Indians, failed. Some laws required education for pauper children, but little was actually done. Like England, the southern governments made an effort to keep the poor from starving and to see that children of paupers learned a trade, but the Virginia law requiring training of "bound" boys was not passed until 1705. Virginians saw nothing odd in imposing requirements upon parents and ministers for religious instruction without giving financial aid to education. Teachers in private schools were seldom examined on their qualifications beyond the ability to read and write but were expected to prove their orthodoxy in religion.

Meager efforts were made to establish chartered or publicly aided schools in the Carolinas. Maryland fared a little better with a provision in 1671 for a "School or College" and a system of secondary county schools founded in 1728. Duties on tobacco and fines for crimes were used to support such schools, but only a small proportion of the population had access to them. Maryland had a quasi-public corporation made up of church and government officials to make policy and secure funds for schools in each county. Georgia was the last Southern Colony to be settled and little progress toward an educational program was made there before the Revolution.

Old Field School.   One southern innovation was the old field school. This was a local elementary school built by members of a community on one of the fallow "old" fields which had lost its productivity through over-use. Sometimes Anglican ministers taught in these schools as they did on the plantations, but the masters were often persons with very little education. Old field schools were usually maintained by private subscriptions with some sort of scholarship or other provision for impoverished scholars. Control of the schools, including the securing of teacher and materials, was in the hands of the local community. These schools were similar to later ones established in frontier towns during the national period. They commonly were in operation for only a few months each year.

Dame School.   In most colonies including the South dame schools were found. These were not really schools at all, but consisted of rudimentary instruction given by a woman in her own home, usually while she carried on household duties. The lessons were limited to the alphabet, counting, prayers, the catechism, and perhaps reading a few sentences from the Bible. A standard instrument in the dame school was the horn book, which consisted of a single printed page attached to a wooden paddle, covered with a transparent film made by boiling down the horns of cows. Hornbooks often were inscribed with the alphabet, numerals from one to nine, and the Lord's Prayer. They were a means of keeping "letters faire from fingers damp" and were used throughout the colonies. Dames who offered instruction were often barely literate themselves. One is recorded as saying, "T'is little they pays me and little I learns em."

Secondary and Higher Education.   Plans for a Latin grammar school were made in Virginia before 1630. Property bequested by Syms and Eaton apparently was used for such classical schools. Thomas Jefferson graduated from a Latin school before entering William and Mary College. Nevertheless, due to preference for sending sons to preparatory schools in England and the sparse early population, few secondary schools developed. Some towns were able to maintain academies. Those in Charleston were supported by a combination of fees and grants. Some academies were classical schools for college preparation and some taught only practical or commercial subjects. William and Mary was the only institution of higher learning in the southern region during the colonial period. It began granting degrees in 1700.

Charity Education.   Other educational measures were taken by philanthropic societies, most of which were organized by religious institutions. The Anglican church encouraged slaveholders to teach their charges Christianity. Charity schools were operated in England, and this idea soon spread to America for the training of orphans and paupers. By far the most active group was the SPG of the Anglican church, which raised funds in England and used the money to send out teachers and to buy textbooks for the colonies. Many able instructors (often young ministers) brought their knowledge and missionary zeal to the colonial schools for the poor. The best charity schools, and also the most numerous ones in the Southern and Middle Colonies were provided by this Anglican society. It printed and distributed books on history, agriculture, and mathematics, as well as religious tracts.

Perhaps the most conspicuous thing about education in the South before the American Revolution was the lack of public interest in schools. Several factors contributed to this attitude, some of which continued to affect public schools in the national period. It was strongly believed by the dominant planter class that each man was responsible for the education of his own children. Further, it was against the prevailing custom to tax one person for the education of the sons of others. Southern colonies had widely scattered populations not concentrated in cities and towns. Even if the people had wanted one, physical remoteness made an educational system almost impossible. Secondary schools of either the Latin grammar or practical academy type did not develop. The classes most interested in education could afford to hire tutors or to send their sons to England, while many of the smaller landowners and pioneer hunters were more concerned with the practical skills necessary for survival than with formal schooling. Also, the southern attitude toward religion failed to bring about the New England emphasis on education as a means of salvation, hence one of the most important duties of every Christian man. Southern colonial education remained very much like education in England. Nevertheless, many of the most learned and able leaders in the revolutionary period were from the South.

THE MIDDLE COLONIES

Diversity and parochialism are perhaps the best words to describe the colonial settlements of Delaware, New Jersey, New York, and Pennsylvania. Settlers from Holland, Germany, Sweden, England, Wales, and Scotland came to the Middle colonies in large numbers. Disparity in religion was even more pronounced than differences in nationality so that the colonies became a potpourri of faiths, languages, and ethnic cultures. It is said that thirteen languages were spoken in Dutch New Amsterdam before it became New York in 1664. So many different religious denominations were represented in the region that toleration soon became a necessity. The Quakers of Pennsylvania were theoretically opposed to persecution. Commerce and trade worked better in an open society, and no single religious sect had the numerical power to force its will on the others. Although the Catholics in Maryland had been protected in Lord Baltimore's time, religious freedom was limited there after 1654. Other Middle colonies and Rhode Island then became the haven for all persons escaping from any form of religious persecution. It was this freedom that attracted the Pietist scholar Francis Daniel Pastorius (1651–1720), who was the best educated man in America at the time. Pastorius wrote a primer called *The True Reading, Spelling, and Writing of English*, published in New York in 1697. New York, like Philadelphia (the largest British city in America during the eighteenth century) was a center for intellectual activity.

Mennonites, Quakers, Lutherans, Calvinists, Moravians, Huguenots, Separate Baptists, and Episcopalians established educational practices of their own. Small numbers of Dunkards, Jews, disciples of John Hus, and other minor sects emigrated to America and set up schools. In short, the Middle colonies were the ones with the largest number of national and religious groups; therefore, they tended to develop many kinds of schools. There was also a considerable urban growth in this area and constant communication with the most sophisticated centers of Europe. Intellectual freedom (and tolerance) was possible in the central coastal cities to a degree unheard of in New England or the South.

From its very beginning the Dutch West India Company accepted its obligation to provide schools, and it demanded careful records showing every expenditure down to and including paper and ink. All nine villages chartered in New Netherlands probably had schools. The schoolmaster was not only a teacher but also a minor church official. He was picked for his orthodoxy and had other duties such as reading Scriptures on Sunday, digging graves, and acting as church sexton. When the English became dominant, Dutch schools continued to exist very much as they had before, but they became parochial institutions supported by local church congregations or private schools supported by towns.

Except for insisting on the right to license teachers, practically no laws were made concerning schools. The SPG of the Anglican church was responsible for the majority of the common schools in New York, which were intended for the poor and thus were charitable institutions. These enjoyed the favor and support of the governor and his offices but were seldom entirely free, each student paying what his family could afford. This system of charging different amounts was known as the "rate bill" and was widely adopted. Private instruction was sometimes similar to the plantation schools of the South, but individual tutors were rare.

Private venture schools in towns sometimes taught such practical subjects as bookkeeping, geography, and navigation. Each denomination was permitted to set up its own school system, and therefore schools were nonpublic in nature and intolerant of individuals representing other views. Nevertheless, religious differences kept the schools out of the hands of the central civil government and made them the responsibillty of the churches. It was common, therefore, in the Middle colonies to have many sectarian schools together with a considerable number of charitable institutions for education.

Where the Quaker faith was strong, there was much support for primary education. Pennsylvania, with its Quaker commonwealth, had many laws regulating morality, including punishment for such offenses as drunkenness, dancing, gambling, and profanity. Nevertheless, jailing for debts was abolished and a great deal of freedom of speech and religion was allowed. Since the colony was open to all creeds, Pennsylvania attracted Mennonites, Moravians, Lutherans, and Anglicans in addition to the large numbers of Quakers.

Denominational Influence.   Dissenting factions in Pennsylvania caused many Quakers to fear for the unity of their church and to be suspicious of college education, but they remained active in their support for elementary schools. Quaker schools were excellent in quality. They taught reading, writing, arithmetic, and probably bookkeeping as well as religion, and they were not closed either to the poor or to girls. Quaker teachers received an apprenticeship training, the first teacher education in America. That some control was used is shown by the record that one Thomas Meking was rebuked by the Council of Philadelphia for teaching in a Friends public school without a license. The first American education for freed blacks was provided by Quaker schools. Smaller religious sects known as "dissenters" also established schools and colleges. The "log college" opened by Presbyterians in 1726 trained boys for the ministry. In Philadelphia, the William Penn Charter School taught both the classics and an English curriculum. The German scholar Francis Pastorius taught there. Baptists and Moravians set up denominational schools that were also open to the public. Governor Nicholson set aside land for a free Catholic school in Maryland.

Academy.   Vocational education was more significant in the Middle colonies than elsewhere in colonial America. English poor laws of 1562 and 1601 proposed the establishment of working schools as well as forced apprenticeship for the poor. William Penn was influential in bringing the idea of trade training for pauper children to Pennsylvania, and John Locke's concern for practical subjects was well known in the colonies. The academy, a terminal secondary school which prepared students for a vocation, did not become highly significant until the national period. Nevertheless, both elementary and secondary schools in the Middle colonies offered such practical subjects as merchandising, navigation, trade, and mechanics. Benjamin Franklin's academy in Philadelphia opened in 1751 and became a model for others. While it was organized in part as a Latin school, the academy was intended for the heterogeneous population of Pennsylvania. Franklin was particularly interested in training teachers for rural schools and officials for the government. The seeds of the American comprehensive high school were planted in the private and parochial schools of the Middle colonies which offered vocational subjects.

Latin Grammar Schools.   Secondary schools of the Latin grammar type were necessary for college preparation. New York, Pennsylvania, New Jersey, and Maryland had such schools. Higher English schools and Latin schools existed together in Quaker Pennsylvania, and denominational support for both was common.

The teachers were usually ministers who had no church to serve and the purpose was college preparation, leading eventually to political or church positions. Latin secondary schools and colleges were strictly for men. The curriculum often included Juvenal, Ovid, Virgil, Caesar, Cicero, and Horace, with perhaps some Greek grammar.

Religious sectarianism was a major force in Middle colony education even though freedom of choice was respected. Schools were used for propaganda and there was often bitter condemnation of other groups, especially Catholics.

Common Schools.   Private education in Pennsylvania was largely the prerogative of the upper classes. However, there were some accommodations for sons of workmen and artisans of the middle class. A night school teaching writing, arithmetic, and some mathematics was opened in Philadelphia in 1731. Navigation, surveying, and mathematics were taught in another night school in the same city. Later in the eighteenth century, private evening schools for accounting, mathematics, and modern languages were advertised in many cities. Public lectures on natural science, astronomy, and mechanics attracted large crowds. Private circulating libraries were available for a fee. Journals, books, and newspapers were numerous in larger cities. Philadelphia continued to be a major center for learning throughout the colonial era. Although New England led in universal education during the colonial period, there was a great deal of school activity on the elementary level in the Middle colonies.

Higher Education.   The Middle colonies also had their share of denominational colleges as well as the College of Philadelphia (1755) which was the only nonsectarian institution of higher learning. The College of New Jersey (Princeton) was established by Presbyterians in 1746. King's College (Columbia) was an Anglican effort of 1754, and Queen's College (Rutgers) was founded in 1766 by the Dutch Reformed Church. The College of Rhode Island (Brown) was created by the Baptists in 1764. Of the nine colonial colleges in America, five were in the Middle colonies. Early graduates of American colleges often found work as tutors to well-off children in the Middle colonies and the South.

The cultural variety which characterized the Middle colonies made education quite different from both the North and the South. Particularly significant were the early influences of settlers from Holland and the later emigration of large numbers of Germans. There was no one single powerful ruling church, and therefore no establishment of religion. Tolerance was greater than in New England or in the South and many more sectarian schools developed. Class differences in the Middle colonies were less distinct than in the South, and the central colonies became a melting pot for many nationalities and many social positions. But by and large, less interest was shown in educational development in the Middle colonies than in New England.

THE NEW ENGLAND COLONIES

In many ways, education in New England was most significant for the growth of later American schools. The influence of parliamentary rule and the Christian duty of educating each child caused the theocratic governments in New England to take great interest in schools. The Puritans wanted a state church ruled by congregations rather than by bishops, and a government which substituted the authority of the people for the divine right of a king. New England colonies made laws requiring education of the children, but left details to local communities—thereby creating the traditions of local autonomy and the district system. These colonies provided both for universal elementary education and for the training of ministers, which tended to perpetuate the English dual system of education. But it is wrong to assume that Puritan efforts fostered religious freedom or democracy.

Puritan Philosophy.   Part of their educational interest stemmed from a concept of the nature of man which is found in the Calvinistic creed. The Puritans assumed that man is by nature evil, having fallen in the sin of Adam. Not only is man bad, but he also has an active nature which must be controlled to prevent the Devil from becoming his master. This notion of man's being bad and active gave rise to the establishment of schools, which should prevent idleness and show mankind the way to overcome the evil in his nature. Assuming that man is depraved, there must be an effort to bring him to salvation. This, together with the Protestant notion of the priesthood of all believers, made it mandatory that the New England Puritans establish elementary schools.

In Massachusetts, New Hampshire, and Connecticut, Puritans were determined to build their own religious orthodoxy in the way Calvin had suggested. They established theocracies in which the church and state ruled by means of public disapproval, whipping, banishment, and fines. It was common for them to use the General Court and the authority of the minister to enforce conformity both in behavior and in belief. Such positive support of religion required not only that schools be created, but also that every child be able to read and understand both the Scriptures and the capital laws.

There were numerous Puritan ministers who wrote works in theology and philosophy which reinforced this educational theory. In his book, *A Family Well-Ordered*, Cotton Mather dwelt upon the duties of parents and the obligations of children. John Cotton reflected the same view, and even the learned Jonathan Edwards (1703-58) made his idealism the servant of a narrow Calvinistic theology. The views of these Puritan theorists are clearly seen in the religious nature of textbooks like the New *England Primer* of 1690 which included:

> In Adam's Fall
> We Sinned all
> . . .Thy Life to Mend
> This Book Attend
> . . .The Idle Fool
> Is Whipt at School.

As previously stated, in New England the farm land was not especially fertile, and people turned early to such occupations as shipbuilding, manufacturing, and trade. A merchant class developed which had need of people who could take care of business accounts and work with all sorts of business documents. It was therefore an economic necessity to have large numbers of people able not only to read and write but also to cast accounts. Even so, the New England schools were primarily established for the propagation of the Gospel and the control of new generations. It was usual for children to spend only a few years in the common school. There were, however, Latin grammar schools established for the use of the elite.

The Pilgrims insisted that education be taken care of by the parents. As early as 1642, however, the General Court of Massachusetts came to the conclusion that many parents were neglecting the training of their children. The court therefore ordered that the selectmen of every town should require that all parents and masters undertake the education of their children. After a short time, it was found that this provision was not working well. In 1647, therefore, the General Court passed its famous Old Deluder of Satan Act. This law required that every town set up a school, or that it pay a sum of money to the next larger town for the support of education. A precedent was thus made for requiring the towns (or townships) to take the responsibility for establishing and maintaining schools. The theocracy not only required education, it also set both the curriculum and the standard procedures for operation. These early efforts of Massachusetts were soon picked up by other parts of New England.

The first tax on property for local schools was in Dedham, Massachusetts, in 1648. New Hampshire required towns to support elementary schools as early as 1693. Taxes were used to pay the wages of teachers and to build school buildings, but tuition fees were universally charged in the New England colonies. The curriculum of the early New England schools was almost entirely religious, for these institutions were viewed officially as being indispensable to the stability of Puritan society. Such books as the Bible, the *New England Primer*, and the catechism were widely used in schools. Education was for salvation as well as for getting along in life. It was a primary duty of parents to bring their children up according to the orthodox religious beliefs of Puritan society.

The Puritans feared leaving an illiterate ministry to the people. For this reason they established Harvard College (1636) almost as early as the town schools. The college was primarily for the education of ministers of the Gospel, though after a few years students preparing for professions such as law attended as well. Once the college had been established, it was necessary that Latin grammar schools be provided so that the boys wishing to enter Harvard could get the necessary preparatory studies. The first of these schools was established in Boston. A famous teacher, Ezekiel Cheever, taught for over fifty years in the Ipswich Grammar School and in the Boston Latin Grammar School with considerable influence on the prestige of the teaching profession in the New England area. Almost no curriculum choice was offered in any of the colonial schools and the methods were both fixed and harsh. It was ordained that school masters be examined and certified by the minister of the town or the adjoining towns where the school was to be held. Education was generally narrow, limited, elementary, and moral in character. In Massachusetts it was common for masters who failed to carry out their responsibilities adequately to be fined and sometimes even thrown out of their jobs.

Educational Conditions.   In the lower schools there was normally one master for a room full of children of various ages. Supervision of the school was provided by the local minister and the "selectmen" of the town. Buildings were of the log cabin or clap-board variety, furnished with benches, a fireplace, shelves around the walls for writing, and a few small windows. The master usually had a chair and lectern, but the meager equipment seldom included blackboards or maps. A whipping post was commonly erected by the school door. Severe floggings were administered for misbehavior or break-ing the rules, since Puritan philosophy called for literally beating the Devil out of the child. Massachusetts law allowed children to be confined in stocks for some offenses, and fathers had a legal right to execute their children if they could not be controlled, although this extreme was never practiced. There are records of pupils who were tortured by hav-ing a stick of flat wood (whispering stick) placed like a bit between their teeth, pupils made to kneel on hard pebbles, or made to wear heavy wooden yokes. The school in colonial New England was not a pleasant place, either physically or psychologically. Great emphasis was placed on the shortness of life, the torments of hell and the fear that one's behavior might not be acceptable for salvation. Children in dull and grim schools memorized passages such as:

I in the Burying Place may see Graves shorter there than I;
From Death's Arrest no Age is free,
Young Children too must die.
Oh God may such an Awful Sight Awakening to Me be,
That by Early Grace I shall, For Death Prepared be.

The elementary curriculum consisted of the four R's: religion, reading, writing, and arithmetic. Boys and girls entered the school at the age of six or seven. They began with the hornbook or a similar instrument printed on stiff paper called a battledore. Next they were given the New England Primer, a crudely illustrated reading text that included the *Westminister Shorter Catechism*, a picture of the martyr John Rogers being burned at the stake in England, a dialogue between Christ, a youth, and the devil, and John Cotton's *Spiritual Milk for American Babes drawn from Both Brests of the Testements for their Souls' Nourshment*. Many children remained in school only three or four years and did not progress beyond the primer. For those who remained longer, there was the *Psalter* (Book of Psalms) and the Bible. Paper was scarce and of very poor quality. It came in large unlined sheets and had to be folded, sewn together, and marked with pieces of lead in order to make a tablet for the children. Hornbooks, crude slates, and quill pens were provided by the students themselves. Often the masters would canvass the community to determine the availability of books, and whatever they found would be used as reading material for older pupils.

The school normally operated six days each week, except in the summer. There were long periods of prayer and Bible reading both morning and evening. Most of the subject matter was memorized by the student and tested in a cue and recitation session before the master. There were no group activities or mass assignments. Students were not encouraged to express opinions or to ask questions. The word of the master and the text were regarded as absolute authorities. Teachers had no pedagogical training as such, but in New England the school masters were often among the best educated members of the community. The pay was extremely low and many communities required masters to "board around" in order to save money.

Latin School and College Programs.   Boston had a free Latin grammar school and many other New England towns developed secondary schools supported by tuition. These "higher track" schools for the social and intellectual elite were intended to prepare boys for college and were always taught by college graduates—often ministers. Boys usually entered the Latin school at the age of eight after having learned to read English at home or in a lower school. The curriculum consisted of three years of Latin grammar "accidence" and practice in parsing Latin sentences. Thereafter, the scholars began to "make Latin" and to translate Latin literature into English. The program continued from six to eight years and included some Greek and Hebrew in the last two years. All the students in the Latin grammar school hoped to be admitted to a college for that was the entire purpose of such schools. Entrance requirements for Harvard College indicated the curriculum of that institution:

> When any Schollar is able to understand Tully, or such like classical Latine Author extempore, and make and speake true Latine Verse and Prose, . . . and decline perfectly the Paradigm's of Nounes and Verbes in the Greek toungue: Let him then and not before be capable of admission into the College.

Since the first Puritan ministers were graduates of Oxford and Cambridge, colleges in New England closely copied those English institutions. Until 1653, Harvard was a three-year college with a fixed course offering one subject at a time, so that all classes could be taught by the president. Classical and theological studies were the mainstay of the program. Aristotelian logic and physics, arithmetic, geometry, astronomy, grammar, rhetoric, dialectic, etymology, syntax, and prosodia were taught for the purpose of disciplining the mind. Upperclassmen studied Greek and Hebrew grammar and there were occasional lectures in history and natural science. Students were expected to declaim once a month, and great stress was placed on study of the Bible. For a degree, the student had to present evidence of his ability to read the Scriptures in Latin and to resolve them logically, "withall being of godly life and conversation."

Yale College was founded in 1701, and Dartmouth in 1769. All three New England colleges were Congregationalist and similar in curriculum. They were theological seminaries, not schools for professional men in other fields such as law, medicine, or science.

Religious Cycles.   Education in New England during the colonial period was highly influenced by religion, but the degree of religious activity varied greatly. Harvard and the early town schools of Massachusetts were established during the time of religious enthusiasm of the great Puritan migration. Economic interests and secular views soon created apathy which caused a decline of educational zeal. Between 1661 and 1681, enrollment at Harvard dropped steadily and the district schools had difficulty obtaining support. But in the first half of the eighteenth century, there occurred a fervent religious revival known as the Great Awakening. While the movement was largely evangelistic, it also sparked renewed interest in schools at all levels. Yale College opened at the beginning of that period of new religious enthusiasm and produced the most famous preacher of the time, Jonathan Edwards. Edwards was an eloquent speaker, well known for his fiery "Hell and Damnation" sermons. He was also a learned scholar and the author of many pamphlets widely used in schools and colleges. The Great Awakening and the efforts of Edwards caused numerous conflicts, such as the issue over predestination that split the "Old Lights" from the "New Lights," but it also caused a major revival of educational activity. The new demand for ministers led Eleazar Wheelock to found a school in Connecticut in 1754, which was later moved to New Hampshire and renamed Dartmouth College. The College of Rhode Island, founded by the Baptists, was also a product of the Great Awakening.

New England schools were crude in form, narrow in curriculum, and poorly supported, but the significant fact remains that they existed in quantity. Long before the United States became a nation, traditions of education, including the ideas of universal schooling and public support, had been formed. Americans had already started to demand what was to become standard—better education for children than their parents had enjoyed.

THEN TO NOW

Life in pre-Revolutionary colonial American culture seems to bear very little direct relationship to present conditions, at least at first glance. Educational institutions such as dame schools, academies, old field schools, and Latin grammar schools have long since disappeared. Of course, the New England pattern of district schools, compulsory education, taxation, and distinct educational levels continues to exist in highly modified form. More important than the schools themselves, however, is the vast heritage of beliefs, values, and attitudes inherited from the Puritans. Modern citizens are more highly influenced by the colonial past than they might imagine because systems of value tend to persist over generations. As the theory of culture lag suggests, materialistic and technological inventions occur rapidly while concepts of proper conduct and ideas about the good life change so slowly that they appear to remain constant. Alteration of values is likely to be slow and evolutionary while changes in material aspects of the culture are quick and revolutionary. This is obviously important, because schools have a major role in transmitting the core values from one generation to the next. Teaching values or value clarification is always difficult, but it is even more complicated in a multicultural society where some children come from families more influenced by the Puritan ethic than others. Choosing and reinforcing values for survival and maximum realization of the human potential in the present and the future is central to the socialization function of education. Socialization can hardly be accomplished without a basic understanding of the Puritan ethic of old Massachusetts Bay colony. Puritan beliefs about the evil nature of the children and their support for corporal punishment are no longer popular, but the basic values are found in the "pioneer spirit," the work ethic, and middle-class values.

Since the Puritans held that God allowed his elect to prosper and that idle hands did the work of the devil, they stressed productive work and striving for economic improvement. Today, justification of one's existence through hard work and social service is supported by schools. Puritans were not supposed to display their wealth and therefore they invested in land and various commercial enterprises. Frugal life style, saving money, preparing for the future, and investing were New England values that proved useful to business and commercial interests. These values are not limited to the Puritan tradition (they are practiced also in Japan) but they are central to the American cultural core.

Socialization requires that the most important aspects of the dominant culture be taught. Using models of accepted behavior and sanctions, schools attempt to get students to accept and internalize values cherished by the institutions and the leaders of the dominant culture. Some of these values which can be traced to the Puritan heritage are:

- respect for authority
- postponing immediate gratification
- neatness
- punctuality
- responsibility for one's own work
- honesty
- patriotism and loyalty
- striving for personal achievement
- competition
- repression of aggression and overt sexual expression
- respect for the rights and property of others
- obeying rules and regulations.

Without making a judgment about these values, it may be pointed out that teaching them creates certain problems. Ours is a multicultural society in which minority and ethnic groups differ in the emphasis they place on traditional values of the majority culture. Contemporary American society is also stratified and the various social classes do not exhibit the same esteem for all behaviors prized by schools. For example, American Indian and Hispanic cultures have had a more casual attitude toward time than the middle-class Caucasian society. As a result, they cherish punctuality less, and their children may not understand the school's demand that homework be turned in on time. Lower-class youngsters seldom have the future orientation which is the ordinary timeframe of the middle class. Living for the immediate moment and letting tomorrow take care of itself is an attitude sure to be in conflict with schools that require planning and a postponement of rewards. Competition may be discouraged by some ethnic groups even when it is encouraged by schools. Urban African-American youngsters are not apt to appear neat to white teachers, even when their appearance is quite acceptable to their parents and peers. The "macho" image many lower-class boys need to create for peer acceptance makes them seem rude and loud in school. Expression of sexual interest may be tolerated and encouraged in a lower-class environment in ways likely to be unacceptable and punished in middle-class schools. Extreme concern about respect for property and the need to be still while others speak may be more difficult for students with no experience in valuing such behavior. Puritans were not tolerant of any violation of their social norms. They were quick to condemn and punish any who dared to challenge the authority of their institutions or to break the rules. Modern versions of the Puritan ethic may be insisted upon by middle-class teachers but many of the students find that ethic incompatible with their own cultural backgrounds. The critical literature on contemporary education indicates that children of ethnic groups and minorities are more likely to fail in school if the school attempts to teach values foreign to them.

Of course, Puritans did not believe in democracy; however, modern education must attempt to promote democratic values in order to deal constructively and creatively with the confusions and conflicts of the modern world. Puritans also had the church, the family, and the local community in absolute support of their educational efforts, while contemporary schools exist in an environment of special interests and conflicting beliefs.

Not all middle-class people from the dominant culture support the traditional values of the schools. Sociologists say that there are emerging values in American culture that are in conflict with the traditional ones. The family is no longer the major socializing agent, but if that duty is passed to schools, the schools need support. While many families now stress hedonism, materialism, living the good life, social interaction, and the value of leisure, others with single parent households struggle to make ends meet, relying on schools to pick up some of the child care duties. These are examples of emergent values in conflict with traditional ones. The peer subculture of American adolescents is unconcerned with older traditional belief systems. Rock and roll music, experimentation with drugs, and permissive attitudes toward sex dominate the interests of teenagers.

Another potent force in value formation is the mass media. Television especially fosters values in conflict with those of traditional schools and the Puritan ethic. Television urges people to gratify their every desire, to "buy now and pay later," and to enjoy life without concern for future consequences. No one viewing television gets the impression that hard work, striving, and deferring to authority are necessary for success or the good life. Many members of the modern society have no faith that honesty really is the best policy or that patriotism is a higher value than individual gratification.

Dissolution of the traditional family unit with its support network, single parent families, the challenges of AIDS (HIV), teenage suicide, teenage pregnancy, increase in crime (on and off school campuses), random violence with children killing or maiming children, children whose health has been affected by parental use of drugs entering public schools in ever greater numbers, together with inner city riots that wipe out savings of a lifetime in a matter of minutes, are part of the American culture as we approach the twenty-first century.

Reports of child abuse have grown exponentially in the 1990s with few solutions in sight. Whatever the causes of these challenges to the social fabric, whether increased unemployment, lack of skills to cope with an increasingly complex society, emotional instability, or uncontrollable drug use, there are ever growing numbers of families and children at risk. These challenges lead to social fragmentation which conflict with goals of consensus and social unity in democracy. Currently there are increasingly strident calls for character, value and moral education in our schools to deal with these issues.

Minority, single-parent, and nontraditional families are less likely to agree with the Puritan ethic than are middle-class, majority culture parents. If they do agree with the ethic, they are less able to reinforce the values of schools at home. Some Americans reflect the fierce independence shown by the early colonists. An example is the litigation known as *Wisconsin v. Yoder* (1972), in which Amish families won exemption for children from the compulsory education laws of the state. Like early colonists, the Amish were willing to challenge secular authority on religious grounds and to define their own values. Another example is the home school movement. Some parents wish to teach their children at home in order to "protect" them from values taught at school.

Some educators also believe the school should work for diversity, tolerance, open-mindedness, and the development of self-concept. They do not agree with the function of transmitting an authoritative body of knowledge, and they do not want the school to impose values on children. Nevertheless, modern American schools still reflect many Puritan values.

It remains to be seen just how effective the schools will be in supporting traditional values or in teaching emerging ones. It may be that some of the Puritan values are not at all appropriate for a future learning society where leisure and cooperation are more important than work. Schools tend to be quite conservative, but there are many other institutions that carry cultural values. In Puritan America, the family and the church supported values taught in schools. Contemporary society finds the schools often in conflict with such agents as the mass media and advertising. At present, the Moral Majority as well as other fundamentalist conservative religious groups are trying to win support for the values of the Puritan ethic while others push for diversity, free choice, and multiculturalism. Laurel Walters in his article *Religious Right Win Seats on School Boards Across the US*, noted that religious right candidates won school board election in 12 states in 1992–93. People for the American Way also are working to elect school board candidates to represent their point of view. These groups represent increased public interest in education decision making. Regardless of the position, educators need to understand the historical link with the colonial past and the Puritan heritage if they are to understand the present culture and prepare for a viable future. Beliefs of the early settlers of colonial New England still cast a shadow over values in the modern American society. Those who do not appreciate this historical fact are ill-prepared to understand the value conflicts that are central to so many modern educational issues.

BIBLIOGRAPHY

Butts, R. Freeman, and Lawrence A. Cremin. *A History of Education in American Culture.* New York: Rinehart and Winston, 1953.

Church, Robert. *Education in the United States: An Interpretive History,* New York: The Free Press, 1977.

Cohen, Sheldon. *A History of Colonial Education, 1607–1776.* New York: Wiley, 1974.

Curti, Merle. *The Social Ideas of American Educators.* Patterson, NJ: Littlefield, Adams, 1959.

Edwards, Newton, and Herman G. Richey. *The School in the American Social Order.* Boston: Houghton Mifflin, 1963.

Good, Harry, and James Teller. *A History of American Education.* 2d ed. New York: Macmillan, 1973.

Havinghurst, Robert, and Daniel Levine. *Society and Education.* 5th ed. Boston: Allyn and Bacon, 1975.

Jernegan, Marcus. *Laboring and Dependent Classes in Colonial America, 1607–1783.* New York: Frederick Ungar, 1960.

Knight, Edgar W. *Education in the United States.* Boston: Ginn and Co., 1951.

Miller, Perry, ed. *The American Puritans: Their Prose and Poetry.* Garden City, NY: Doubleday, 1956.

Morrison, Samuel Eliot. *The Intellectual Life of Colonial New England.* New York: New York University Press, 1956.

Potter, Robert. *The Stream of American Education.* New York: American Book Company, 1967.

Rippa, S. Alexander. *Education in a Free Society: An American History.* 7th ed. New York: Longman, 1992.

Rippa, S. Alexander, ed. *Educational Ideas in America: A Documentary History.* New York: David McKay, 1969.

Van Til, William. *Education: A Beginning.* Boston: Houghton Mifflin, 1974.

Walters, Laurel. "Religious Right Win Seats on School Boards Across the US." *Christian Science Monitor* (August 9, 1993): 1,20.

Warren, Donald, ed. *History, Education, and Public Policy.* Berkeley, CA: McCutchan, 1978.

3 THE PERIOD OF THE AMERICAN REVOLUTION

Although I do not, with some enthusiasts, believe that the human condition will ever advance to such a state of perfection as that there shall no longer be pain or vice in the world, yet I believe it susceptible of much improvement, and most of all, in matters of government and religion, and that the diffusion of knowledge among the people is to be the instrument by which it is to be effected.

Thomas Jefferson

Before the time of the Revolutionary War, the population of the American colonies had grown to more than two and one-half million people. An expanding frontier fostered perseverance, ingenuity, self-confidence, and a defiant individualism among the western settlers. This frontier character was unique to America, as was the mixture of nationalities and religions found in the Middle Colonies. The district system with its decentralization and local control continued to dominate New England schools before and after the Revolution, and the idea of free, compulsory, universal education was central to the ideal of self-government there. While schools varied widely in number and quality in the New England colonies and later in the New England states, America looked to Massachusetts, Rhode Island, and Connecticut for educational leadership. Religious denominational or parochial schools remained common in the Middle Colonies until the country became independent, but such sectarian schools were weakened by the withdrawal of English financial support and by the separation of church and state.

DEMOCRATIC IDEALS

The rising tide of democracy threatened a dual system of education in which the elite enjoyed good schools and the masses were largely ignored. This factor accounts for the shrinking influence of Latin grammar schools and the vast growth of the academy. The

American Revolution		
1776 Declaration of Independence	1780 English Sunday School Founded by Robert Raikes	1785 Northwest Ordinance Land Grant
Thomas Paine's *Common Sense*	1781 Battle of Yorktown	1787 Constitutional Convention
Adam Smith's *Wealth* *of Nations*	1783 Treaty of Paris Ended War with England	1789 Constitution Accepted without Mentioning Education

revolutionary period saw academies, with their emphasis on practical subjects such as bookkeeping, navigation, and surveying increase in popularity. Town schools in the most populated areas and even crude schools of the remote frontier settlements became more numerous as the eighteenth century closed, and such educational institutions did not cater to an aristocracy. Southern educational patterns altered little during the revolutionary era except that students did not study in England and many of the charity schools were closed.

CHANGES IN COLONIAL CULTURE

American capitalism was providing general growth and prosperity in the economic order and in intercolonial trade before the Revolution. New York, Boston, Philadelphia, and Charleston had become large cities with sophisticated populations interested in all sorts of European ideas. There was a diffusion of culture between the various parts of the colonies, as well as much travel and correspondence. Colonial intellectual life was stimulated by newspapers like the Boston News Letter and other periodicals such as *Poor Richard's Almanac* published by Benjamin Franklin. At the outbreak of hostilities in 1775, there were thirty-seven newspapers in regular publication.

College, private, and city libraries were found throughout the colonies, although many did not permit the free circulation of books. Subscription libraries were available at a small fee. Only a few Americans published books before the Revolution, but British volumes were for sale in most large towns. Bookstalls had the works of Bacon, Locke, Boyle, Newton, Swift, Milton, Hume, Voltaire, and Addison, among others. Learned professions like law and medicine made progress in the late eighteenth century and

French Revolution		War of 1812
1791 Bill of Rights Ratified	1798 Joseph Lancaster and Andrew Bell Start Monitorial Schools	1805 New York Free School Society
Philadelphia Sunday School Society	1802 West Point	1806 New York Monitorial Schools
	1803 Louisiana Purchase	1812 State Superintendent Appointed in New York

gained in respect. Experiments in science and medicine were as popular as speculation in philosophy. The American Philosophical Society, which developed from a proposal by Franklin, brought Americans into contact with the learned world of Europe. Not many colonial minds were on a par with the cosmopolitan Benjamin Franklin or the theologian-philosopher Jonathan Edwards, but there were well educated, widely read, cultured Americans before the Revolution. Leaders in public life like Patrick Henry, John Adams, and Thomas Jefferson were much influenced by intellectual changes in Europe.

THE SHIFT IN THE COLONIAL MIND

Dissatisfaction with conditions in Europe was one reason for the first American settlements, but this feeling shifted to dissatisfaction with English colonial policies such as mercantile capitalism. The American Revolution was a combination of native efforts and contributions from foreign thinkers and movements. The rationale for the American experiment in self-government was provided by political philosophers like John Locke and Jean Jacques Rousseau, philosophers whose effect on education was both direct and indirect.

Locke's Influence. The English philosopher John Locke (1632–1704) not only provided a theoretical basis for the Declaration of Independence, but also contributed to American educational thought. Locke's political ideas concerning the inalienable rights of man and the contract relationship between a people and its government were accepted almost without qualification by Thomas Jefferson and other leaders in the movement for independence. The high reputation Locke enjoyed among Americans caused his philosophical writings to be widely circulated in the colonies and later in the United States. Locke had severely altered the direction of educational thought through his denial of the existence of innate ideas and his insistence that the mind at birth is passive and like a blank tablet (tabula rasa) upon which experience writes. He believed that all our ideas come from experience and that the measure of the truth of an idea is its correspondence with concrete, objective, common-sense reality (empirical principle). Emphasis on experience, good study habits, a utilitarian curriculum, and sense-realism aided the scientific and practical elements in American education. Franklin's belief in self-education for practical utility, his broad interest in empirical science, and his desire to provide educational opportunity for anyone who wanted to learn were all in keeping with Locke's theories. The emergence of a strong middle class with large numbers of lawyers and merchants was an event of the late colonial period which helped to support the ideas of Locke. Franklin and Locke emphasized the secular aspects of education as opposed to the ecclesiasticism of the schools supported by religious organizations. While sectionalism, a lack of money, disunity, and religious sectarianism prevented any common educational program in colonial America, the theoretical foundation for free, universal, and public schools was laid.

Comenius.   An outstanding spokesman for the power of education in improving the human condition was John Amos Comenius (1592-1671). Born in the village of Nivnitz in Moravia, Comenius became bishop of the Moravian Brethren, a Hussite religious sect persecuted by both Lutherans and Catholics. In spite of exile, the murder of his family, and the destruction of his library, Comenius managed to develop a philosophy of education and to write some of the most influential school books produced in Europe. His *Great Didactic* and *Door of the Languages Unlocked* (an introduction to Latin grammar) were produced while he was rector of the Gymnasium at Lissa, Poland. Influential Englishmen invited Comenius to present his plan for universal knowledge and a world university to Parliament, but the English Civil War of 1642 prevented his appearance. For six years he wrote textbooks for Latin schools in Sweden and later established a school at Sanosptak, Hungary. There, Comenius developed his idea of schools in graded order from "the school at the mother's knee" to the university. In 1658, while living in Amsterdam, he published his *Orbis Sensualism Pictus*, the first popular illustrated textbook for children. Cotton Mather claimed that Comenius was invited to become president of Harvard in 1654. He was a highly respected educator whose ideas fell on fertile soil in America.

While the religious background of Comenius caused him to accept the doctrine of original sin, he agreed with Locke that ideas come from experience and that our sense organs are our teachers. This sense realism lent support to empirical investigation, practical education, and the potential of science. Comenius believed that war could be prevented if scholars were brought together to work out solutions to international problems. To this end he proposed a pansophic university with functions faintly similar to those of the United Nations. He felt that universal education could improve civilization through the discovery and dissemination of practical information on subjects such as economics, medicine, agriculture, and sanitation. Although a linguist himself, Comenius believed that primary instruction should be given in the vernacular. He encouraged the publication of dictionaries, textbooks, and encyclopedias in order to simplify instruction. He thought a science of education was possible and that teachers could be trained to practice that science. Comenius influenced American education through his textbooks, his support for science, and his belief that education must be practical. The growth of the academy and the concept of self-education made popular by Franklin were also part of the educational theory of Comenius.

Impact of European Movements. The sense realism of Comenius, the empiricism of Locke, and the scientific movement in Europe paved the way for new conceptions of man and society. The verbal or humanistic realism of John Milton advocated encyclopedic studies and general education. In place of the narrow religious view and conservatism of the New England Puritans, Englishmen were substituting a secular, realistic, liberal world view.

The life of the mind in the American colonies varied from theological arguments in the early Puritan settlements to broad scientific and secular issues addressed by men like Franklin in the urban centers of the Middle Colonies. The scientific revolution of seventeenth century Europe reached America by degrees and had a major impact after 1750. Findings of the Royal Society of London for Improving Natural Knowledge excited American interests and stimulated discussion, especially of the physical sciences. Empiricism, sense-realism, and scientific discovery foreshadowed the movement of the late seventeenth and early eighteenth centuries known as the Enlightenment.

The Enlightenment was a rational, liberal, humanistic, and scientific trend in thought which vastly altered the climate of opinion in Europe. It was grounded in the natural and social theories of Comenius and Locke, but found new expression in the works of Diderot, Voltaire, Rousseau, Hume, Paine, and Kant. Kant described the Enlightenment as the liberation of man from his self-caused state of minority. The Enlightenment was a protest against authority which insisted upon man's ability to understand the universe without divine revelation. It held that men as individuals have worth and dignity and that they are able to judge truth for themselves. It fostered belief in a universe governed by natural law which reason could penetrate. The Enlightenment was a protest against both the authority of Christian dogma and absolute monarchs. Its leaders sought a balanced social order free from the control of a single powerful class. Enlightenment thought favored autonomous economic enterprise and parliamentary forms of government. It created an attitude of distrust for despotic monarchs and all other forms of strong centralized government. British mercantile capitalism, which exploited colonies as sources of raw materials and dumping grounds for surplus manufactured goods, was attacked by the theorists of the Enlightenment. Scottish economist Adam Smith, with his ideas of value placed on labor, laissez-faire, and a free market, appealed to leaders of the Enlightenment.

Humanism looked to the past through a study of classics for solutions to problems of the world. Great interest was shown in the social and governmental arrangements of ancient Greece and Rome. Men like Jefferson used classical models for the new republic and for institutions such as the University of Virginia. Sense realism placed man (not God) at the focal point and sought knowledge through ordinary experience or scientific observation. American revolutionary leaders were much influenced by books written by liberals like the humanitarian, Montesquieu. Cultural changes of the Enlightenment helped to plant the ideas which grew in the fertile soil of a comparatively free society and became the timber of revolution. It should also be remembered that more than one hundred and fifty years of colonial growth and development before the Revolution provided ample time for a major alteration of values and beliefs. The intellectual climate of 1776 was far different from that of 1650.

COLONIAL LIBERALISM

By no means were all of the colonial settlers conservative and narrow in their beliefs, in spite of restrictions imposed by Puritan and Anglican authorities. James Oglethorpe proposed colonization of Georgia as an experiment in humanitarianism after he had visited English prisons. The Quakers of Pennsylvania were not only tolerant of other religious beliefs, but also were concerned about the dignity and worth of all persons without regard to color, creed, or social position. Catholics in Maryland brought a different tradition to America, and they were hardly in a position to resist religious freedom.

The Puritans were outspoken in their opposition to secular authority that overran the "just bounds" which they defined as God's word and the common interest, although they were not willing to grant religious freedom. Even so, Roger Williams, Thomas Hooker, Jonathan Mayhew, and John Wise were Puritans who dissented from church authority with considerable success. Puritan schools were dominated by orthodox teachers like Ezekiel Cheever, who was praised by Cotton Mather as much for his preaching as for his pedagogy; but tolerance and liberalism became widespread ideals before the Revolution.

Other systems of thought had considerable influence on the cultural climate before the United States emerged as a nation. The Puritan theologian Jonathan Edwards was hard pressed to defend his religion against science. Samuel Johnson was attracted to the idealism of Bishop Berkeley, while deism (the belief that God created the world and then withdrew to let it operate according to natural law) was popular with many intellectuals. The naturalism of Rousseau and his concept of government were known in America, although his influence on education was severely curtailed by the conservative reaction that followed the war for independence. Adam Smith's *Wealth of Nations* appeared in 1776 and became the basic economic theory of the new nation. Thomas Paine was one of the great champions of the American Revolution because of such writings as *Common Sense* which had an enormous circulation and which proclaimed independence. But later Paine's *Age of Reason* was considered radical in the conservative period that followed the Revolution, and its author lost his influence in the United States.

EDUCATIONAL CHANGES IN THE LATE COLONIAL PERIOD

Several of the colonial colleges were founded in what may be called the revolutionary era. Harvard College, William and Mary College, Yale College, and the College of New Jersey were founded between 1636 and 1746. King's College, the College of Philadelphia, the College of Rhode Island, Queen's College, and Dartmouth College were all founded between 1750 and 1776. Some of the political leaders in the movement for freedom from England were products of the colonial colleges, which were basically conservative institutions. The total enrollment of the nine colonial colleges operating on the eve of the Revolution was about 750 students.

On the secondary level, Latin grammar schools declined in importance with respect to the academy. Academies were more democratic in organization and far more geared to the needs of an expanding economy. Franklin's first effort at Philadelphia in 1751 was secular, practical, and widely copied. Courses in Latin and Greek were included in some academies but modern languages, including French and German, were more popular. Gauging, drawing in perspective, merchant's accounts, logic, chronology, astronomy, and rhetoric were added to the older subjects of history, geography, bookkeeping, writing, surveying, and navigation.

Academies and some private venture secondary schools flourished in the larger towns in the decades before the war. As colonial interest shifted from religion to shipping, commerce, and agriculture, civil town governments became more important in education. Many efforts were made to obtain town schools in which children without means could receive rudimentary training, and town schools often had secondary departments for those who could pay.

Elementary schools continued to operate with crude instruction and equipment. Several factors led to the decline of certain kinds of schools, but the educational tradition continued. The early New England writing school, which had never been in great demand, expired before the Revolution. In Pennsylvania, the SPG gave up in disgust after 1763, while the decline of New England theocracies made schools more difficult to support. Massachusetts, Connecticut, and Rhode Island did not abandon efforts to educate all the children, but some towns were without schools and many provided them for only a few winter months. Denominational efforts such as the Reverend Wiliiam Tennant's Log College (a classical secondary school for training Presbyterian preachers) declined after 1742. Nevertheless, elementary education was provided for most colonial children who could pay a small fee. A larger and more prosperous population gave rise to more schools in the Middle Colonies than had been the case earlier.

THE WAR AND AFTER

The Revolutionary War directed men's energies away from education and science, as De Witt Clinton observed years later. Illiteracy increased because rural schools had to close their doors and even the larger town Latin grammar schools were crippled. British occupation of New York caused schools to be abandoned there. New England schools continued to operate but they suffered from a lack of funds and teachers.

Higher education was restricted in part because many talented teachers were Loyalists. Books were scarce since they came from England and colonial printers could not maintain their presses without outside supplies. Yale College was broken up into groups centered in different towns, while Harvard's buildings and those of the College of Rhode Island housed provincial troops. Dartmouth had neither money nor books, and classes had to be discontinued at the College of Philadelphia. The College of New Jersey and William and Mary also suffered but were not closed.

British support, as in the case of the Anglican SPG, was cut off and never revived. Lack of money and the interruption of the normal economic process made the operation of educational institutions almost impossible. Teachers and scholars joined the fighting forces while school buildings were converted into barracks. Tory or Loyalist teachers were turned out of their schools. Sometimes the schools were burned and libraries scattered or destroyed. Nevertheless, the conflict was restricted to certain parts of the colonial territory, and areas that escaped destruction continued with education. Peace allowed for a restoration of many schools even though the money was scarce and authority uncertain.

Sway of Independence.   The Revolution dealt harsh blows to intellectual life in America, but it also provided the seeds for intellectual activity independent of Europe. As long as the colonists were tied to the value system of the mother country, it was almost impossible for the native culture to rival the established and sophisticated English life of the mind. But the Revolution broke those ties and stimulated considerable literary activity, expressed in antimonarchical and predemocratic pamphlets and books. Further, the heroes of the Revolution were elevated to a dignified and popular social and political status in the new nation. Their ideas gained immediate support. Many revolutionary leaders attempted to put ideas central to the struggle for liberty, such as natural rights, freedom, equality, patriotism, and resistance to tyranny, into the laws. A free press and freedom of speech called attention to the need for schools if the new government of the people was to be successful.

EDUCATIONAL EFFORTS OF THE FOUNDING FATHERS

Many of the men who contributed to the birth of the new nation had plans for schools or other educational institutions. Few of these were actually realized for a variety of reasons including the national debt of seventy-five million dollars (which seemed a staggering sum at the time) and Federalist conservatism.

Freedom of Religion.   Patrick Henry first became involved in the struggle for religious freedom in 1763 when he defended a group of Virginia farmers against Anglican ministers who were suing for their back pay. He lost the suit but the jury fixed the pay of the ministers at one penny which was a victory for the opponents of established religion. James Madison and Thomas Jefferson carried the banner of freedom of religion during the war. They offered a bill in 1776 to exempt dissenters from paying the church tax. In 1779 Jefferson sponsored a bill establishing religious freedom but it was unsuccessful. Patrick Henry proposed a law in the Virginia legislature which would have provided tax support for Teachers of the Christian Religion, without regard to denomination. Madison feared the creation of a "multiple establishment of religion" and in 1785 he managed to push through Jefferson's earlier proposal. Virginia became the first state to have a law guaranteeing freedom of religion. Jefferson returned from his mission in France in 1787. Finding no constitutional guarantees for individual rights, he refused to support ratification of the Constitution without the series of amendments known as the Bill of Rights.

The First Amendment specifically prevented Congress from making any law respecting the establishment of religion or prohibiting religious practice. Connecticut, Maryland, Massachusetts, and New Hampshire did have constitutional provisions for tax-supported religion but these were abolished by 1833. While the long range effects of disestablishment and religious freedom were beneficial to public schools, the immediate result was to take away public funds which had been used to support church-related schools. Separation of church and state also gave rise to educational problems which persist today, such as the issue over prayer and Bible reading in public schools. Nevertheless, sectarian control over public education was broken by the provision for religious freedom.

National University. James Madison and Charles Pinckney attempted to include a provision for a national university in the Constitution. Although it failed, interest in the idea was expressed by several national leaders including Washington. His farewell speech to the army emphasized the need for the promotion and diffusion of knowledge. Several times Washington attempted to get Congress to establish a national university and he left part of his estate to the proposed institution. John Jay, James Monroe, and John Quincy Adams shared the desire for a national university with Washington, Jefferson, and Madison. The university was never built, partly because Congress failed to act and partly because of legal and financial arguments.

Plans for a National System. Despite the omission of education from the Constitution, a number of proposals for a national school system were made by revolutionary statesmen. In 1795, the American Philosophical Society offered a prize for the best essay on the subject of a national system of education. Many plans were submitted including those of Benjamin Rush, Noah Webster, Samuel Smith, Samuel Knox, and P. S. Du Pont de Nemours. Knox and Rush shared the prize. All these plans were founded on the theory that a public system of education is necessary for a free and self-governing republic. Consideration was given in the plans for public control, public support, a practical curriculum, compulsory attendance, and all levels of schools including a national university. The plans differed: one in particular designed by Rush, offered a very extensive system with supervision of schools and academies for teacher training. Support for an American school system also came from essayists such as Robert Coram of Delaware and Revolutionary War officer Nathaniel Chipman. In spite of the interest, all plans for a national system were rejected by Congress.

REVOLUTIONARY PERIOD EDUCATIONAL LEADERSHIP

Many men aided the cause of schools during the period of the American Revolution. Benjamin Franklin lent his great prestige to all intellectual and cultural causes, although he supported practical self-education more than public schools. Benjamin Rush, a signer of the Declaration of Independence, wrote numerous essays on education in addition to his plan for a national system. Perhaps the most important influence of the era came from Noah Webster and Thomas Jefferson.

Noah Webster.   Known as the "Schoolmaster to America" because of the popularity of his textbooks, Noah Webster (1758–1843) was a major educational force for many years. His *Compendious Dictionary* (1806) was the first of a series of dictionaries and lexicons which made his name a household word in the United States. While keeping a classical school in New York, Webster began his Grammatical Institute of the English Language, of which the first section, often revised, became the famous "blue-backed speller." It is estimated that this book had sold nineteen million copies by the time of Webster's death, and by all measures it was the most successful textbook ever produced in America. He also wrote books on grammar, reading, and history, all with a strong patriotic and nationalistic flavor. As a young man, Webster was caught up in the liberal ideas of the Enlightenment and the Revolution. He supported free schools, a national language as a band of union, and separation of church and state.

The French Revolution shocked Webster, and he repudiated his earlier republican principles in favor of conservative federalism. His later works stressed religious morality, respect for government and a patriotism that sometimes bordered upon the fanatic. He believed that all books, schools, masters, and programs for the schools of the republic should be strictly American and even suggested that the first word taught to an infant should be "Washington." Webster called for strict teaching and supported traditional methods of instruction, but he was against corporal punishment. He wanted education for girls because they would be the mothers of future citizens and the teachers of youth. Webster felt that no legislature should ignore the need for free schools in which all American children could learn the virtues of liberty, just laws, morality, hard work, and patriotism.

Thomas Jefferson.   Jefferson's contribution to education would constitute ample material for an entire book. He provided the ideology for extending educational opportunity to all citizens and argued that no democratic society is safe without an educated population. For more than fifty years, Jefferson was personally active in efforts to put his educational theory into actual practice. As a young man he worked to reform the schools of Virginia, while much of his old age was devoted to building the University of Virginia. The basic theme of Jefferson's educational policy was academic excellence with equality of opportunity for all. He was not, like Hamilton, a supporter of strong federal government and therefore his efforts to improve schools were on a local and state level. Jefferson did not agree with the schemes for a national system of education, although he did not oppose a national university.

Jefferson's Bill for a More General Diffusion of Knowledge in Virginia was widely circulated and used as a model. The plan called for a state system of free elementary schools with local control. Secondary schools were to be tuition institutions, with a provision for scholarships to meet the needs of poor but gifted boys. A state university was to crown the educational system. Jefferson submitted three bills to the Virginia Assembly but he was not successful in passing any of his proposals except that for the University of Virginia. His effort to overcome the danger of an ignorant populace was very modest; the Bill called for only three years of public schooling. His organizational pattern with decentralized control and localization of financial responsibility became popular even though Virginia failed to adopt the plan. For example, Edward Coles became governor of Illinois in 1818 and promptly submitted a plan for a school system in that state which borrowed many of Jefferson's ideas.

After attempting to reform the College of William and Mary, Jefferson became convinced that an entirely new university was required. Few institutions have reflected one person's views as closely as the University of Virginia reflected those of Thomas Jefferson. Not only was he the driving force for the creation of the university, he organized the curriculum, hired the faculty, planned many of the buildings, purchased and catalogued the books for the library, and generally supervised the entire operation. In 1825, Jefferson saw his creation open with forty students. The University of Virginia became the first state university and one with a "modern" curriculum.

EARLY GOVERNMENT PROPOSALS

It was the prevailing view of the founding fathers that while knowledge was the best guardian of liberty, education did not belong in federal hands. James Madison wanted a general tax for schools, and Samuel Knox argued that private schools were subversive in a republic, but such reasoning did not convince the Constitutional Convention. The Constitution, therefore, contains no reference to education, although state control and nonsectarian public schools are assured by the First and Tenth Amendments. Other measures significant in the development of education came out of the early national period.

Early National Legislation.   In 1785, Congress outlined regulations for the national territory west of the Alleghenies, north of the Ohio River, and east of the Mississippi River. This Northwest Territory was to be laid out in townships consisting of thirty-six sections. By the Ordinance of 1785 (also called the Northwest Ordinance) the sixteenth section (one mile square) in each township in the territory was reserved for the support of schools within the township. A second Ordinance two years later authorized not more than two full townships in each new state to be reserved for a university. The act contained a statement that schools and education should forever be encouraged for the benefit of human happiness and good government. These acts became a precedent for land grants to the states for public schools and colleges. By later acts, most new states entering the Union received federal land for educational purposes.

In 1802, Congress established the national military academy at West Point. This was the first of many federal acts which created special educational institutions with specialized functions. West Point had the first American training center for engineers.

State Efforts.   Seven of the state constitutions adopted before 1800 mentioned education. Those of Pennsylvania, North Carolina, and Vermont called for the establishment of schools in each county with some public financial support. The Pennsylvania Constitution, accepted in 1776, became a model for several others. It required that the state pay salaries of teachers in public schools. New Hampshire and Massachusetts stressed the need for wisdom and knowledge as a means of preserving liberty, but their constitutions did not require schools. Massachusetts legalized its traditional local district school system and in 1789 admitted girls to district schools. New York made public lands and certain other funds available to free schools.

Before 1812, the Union had grown considerably with the purchase of the Louisiana Territory in 1803 and the admission of the new states of Vermont, Kentucky, Tennessee, Ohio, and Louisiana. The constitutions for these states all indicated some concern about education, and several set up a system of schools in law. As the nation grew, each new state adopted a constitution modeled after those which were admitted earlier. The tradition of having educational provisions in the state constitutions became common.

OTHER EDUCATIONAL MOVEMENTS

Lacking public school systems and the ability to obtain laws for education, a number of leaders tried to support schools by other means. Many church-related institutions continued to offer charity education as they had in the colonial period.

Monitorial Schools.   Monitorial schools originated in England through the work of Joseph Lancaster and Andrew Bell. This type of school provided for inexpensive education that could be given to the masses by a minimum teaching staff. Students of ability were selected as monitors or student teachers, and these monitors were instructed by the master. The monitors, in turn, taught the lessons they had learned to small groups of pupils. Simple lessons were memorized and slates or chalk boards were used. The Lancasterian monitorial system allowed one teacher to instruct hundreds of children. One of these schools appeared in New York City in 1806 and the idea spread. Lancaster himself came to America in 1818, where he promoted his mass education program until 1830.

Sunday Schools. Another English educational plan introduced in America was the Sunday school. Not a church school in the modern sense, the purpose of the Sunday school was to provide basic education to the poor. Its champion was Robert Raikes of Gloucester. Raikes wanted to rescue children of factory workers from their filth, ignorance, and sin. Since the children worked in the mills all week, schools could be provided only on Sundays. Several religious groups, especially Methodists, supported the Sunday school with money and teachers. Children were supervised and given instruction in rudimentary principles during their free time on the Sabbath.

In 1791, A Sunday School Society was organized in Philadelphia. American Sunday schools developed in most of the major cities. They were primarily for the poor, but were not confined to factory or mill workers. Generally, the schools operated from six to ten o'clock on Sunday morning and again from two to six in the afternoon, leaving time for worship. Many children learned to read in these institutions, although they could hardly have provided more than the bare fundamentals of education.

Free School Societies. School societies were organized to develop monitorial schools, Sunday schools, and free public schools in certain areas. The Connecticut school societies were authorized to be district school authorities, while the New York Free School Society promoted several types of education. Schools for girls and for the poor were founded by the New York group which later became the Public School Society of New York. It was assumed in this period that students who could afford private schools would attend them, and indeed they did. Public schools and free schools carried the stigma of poverty because they were charity institutions.

SCHOOL IDEAS AND THE CURRICULUM

Independence brought about the development of a native American culture and a set of national institutions. Education was a reflection of this new spirit, as were self-reliance, optimism, individualism, and democracy. Farmers wanted more schooling for their children in order that they might gain the full benefit of the democratic society, for schooling was a mark of achievement and a step up the social ladder. The population of the new nation grew rapidly, increasing more than tenfold in a single century after the Revolution, and much of this growth came through immigration from European nations other than England. For these new citizens, education was the means of becoming "real Americans."

Improvements in transportation brought about social consciousness that was lacking in isolated colonies. It fostered an exchange of ideas and a national feeling which aided schooling. The start of the American industrial revolution shifted many people from rural to city areas, especially in the Northeast. Factory workers created special needs for free elementary education on a much larger scale. Doctrines of freedom and equality gave rise to free speech and a free press, which in turn fostered democracy.

But there was also a conservative reaction to the War for Independence. Liberals who fought for a free public system on the national level were opposed by those who feared the education of the masses and federal control. Lack of money and opposition to direct taxation prevented the building even of a national university. Yet there was keen interest in the building of state universities which soon became a unique American cornerstone of higher education. Educational interest was also expressed in state constitutions, land grants, school societies, and philanthropy. The start of free public schools for all the people can be found in the period before the War of 1812.

Separation of church and state did not take religion out of the schools. Both sectarian and public schools of the revolutionary era continued to use textbooks that were religiously centered. The Bible and the New England Primer were by no means expelled. Cheever's *Accidence*, the *Westminster Catechism*, and the Psalter continued to be used in New England schools after independence.

New Materials.   Changes did occur, however, in fields like mathematics, commerce, history, geography, and English grammar. Lindley Murray's *English Grammar* and the *Universal Geography* of Jedidiah Morse appeared before 1800. Samuel Goodrich wrote texts in reading under the pen name of Peter Parley, while Nicholas Pike's *A New and Complete System of Arithmetic* appeared in 1788. Noah Webster entered the field with his *Grammatical Institute of the English Language* in 1783.

In 1812, New York provided for a superintendent of common schools, but later abolished the office. Supervision was almost nil in the revolutionary period, except in Monitorial schools and in those operated by school societies. There was little effort to train teachers. Methods remained as crude as they had been earlier, with memorization the central concern. Liberal ideas from Europe and the frontier brought about changes in textbooks but not in the conduct of the schools, for it was still believed necessary to keep strict discipline by means of corporal punishment. Difficult subjects were learned for their value as a "discipline" to exercise the faculties of the mind. A more enlightened theory of learning was not to develop for more than fifty years.

THEN TO NOW

Anyone interested in describing an educational system must look for answers to several fundamental questions. Among the most important are: Who will be educated? What institution will control education? Who will provide the financial support? The colonial era was a period of transition from European educational patterns to ones more appropriate for life in the American environment. As we have seen, southern planters retained the English family-supported tutorial system while New England towns adopted a district system with some tax support. By the time of the rebellion against the British, no uniform educational policies had been established. Sectional differences in attitudes toward public schooling continued in the states as in the colonies. The great liberal leader Thomas Jefferson understood the need for citizens of a republic to be educated, but he did not believe in a federal system of schools. His *Bill for the More General Diffusion of Knowledge* proposed to the Virginia legislature in 1779 was a very modest plan which combined elements of an aristocratic attitude with a desire to broaden the educational opportunities of poor but able students. Even so, Jefferson's ideas were too liberal to gain the support of his colleagues from the South. Far-reaching plans for a national system of education such as those designed by Robert Coram, Benjamin Rush, and Noah Webster met with even more opposition. Yet the question of whether education should be public or private, supported centrally or locally, and managed by parents or governmental agencies, is still debated.

Although the fifty state systems of public schools have been operational for many years, Americans are still divided on numerous educational issues. An example is the argument over tuition tax credits for parents who send their children to private schools. These credits and the debate over the various voucher plans constitute significant support and control disputes about which many modern Americans obviously disagree.

Another example is the rejection by a growing number of parents of educational *outcomes* movements in which children are assessed on standards of performance that include values of tolerance and cooperation. Pennsylvania and other states are modifying outcomes assessment programs due in part to parental complaints that their chldren had to learn about and accept diversity in American culture. In a November 1993 election, Californians voted on a school-voucher system to expand parental choice of schools. Under the proposal parents would receive half the amount spent on each public school student or about $2500. Parents could choose private, parochial, or public schools. Although the voucher system proposal was rejected by a large margin of Californians, other states are considering the system.

Many of the founding fathers of the United States feared that leaving education in the hands of private families, churches, local communities, or philanthropic societies would not guarantee the survival of a democracy. Nevertheless, they were unable to promote a national system of education at any level. Considerable effort was made to obtain a national university but even that modest proposal was finally defeated. No educational provision was made in the Constitution, so the power to create schools fell to the states by default. Today there is continued conflict over what powers rightfully belong to the federal government, to the states, and to local school boards.

One of the major current issues in American education centers on the influence of political and governmental forces on community educational practices. The states were very slow in passing educational laws even though the right was stated in the enabling acts incorporated in the several state constitutions. Responsibility for public education was assumed by the states in the 1830s, modified by federal aid to education in the

Kennedy-Johnson era, and restored to the states under the administrations of Reagan and Bush. The Clinton administration is moving toward national models for educational standards, curriculae, and assessment to meet the need for equity among schools.

Early national practices allowed religious organizations, free school societies, and Monitorial schools to fill the void before state systems were developed. Laws provided for a great deal of autonomy to be delegated to local school boards while funding came largely from local property taxes. Under these conditions, it was natural for the district school authorities to consider themselves all powerful and without much control by the state. Leaders in the early national period like Horace Mann and Henry Barnard built their respective state school systems without taking away the policy making power of boards of education. The tradition of local autonomy has resulted in considerable conflict with state legislatures since World War II. State governments and state departments of education now take a more active role in teacher certification, establishing lists of approved course materials, and even mandating the curriculum. Many states now have a provision for *academic bankruptcy* whereby the state department of education takes over school districts when school achievement standards are not met. Federal pressure on local schools comes through court-ordered plans of desegregation, laws for equal educational opportunity (including disabled, disadvantaged, and non-English speaking children), and regulation of programs supported by federal taxes. There exists a great deal of resentment over the involvement of the central government in matters many consider to be the business of local boards. School boards and parents often feel that the bureaucrats in Washington have no understanding of local conditions and needs. Public sentiment for getting the federal government out of the schools and restoring local control was clearly demonstrated in the Reagan victory in the election of 1980. Much of the criticism of modern education from sources like "A Nation at Risk" is federal or national in origin, but the reforms mandated are to be carried out at state or local levels. The Clinton Administration is exploring the use of federal funds to assure that every school has the capacity to have all of its students reach high performance levels.

Two points need to be made here. The history of the early national period clearly indicates that education is a state function even though the states have traditionally permitted a high degree of local control. Secondly, although the federal Constitution did not deal with education, there has been a long tradition of federal aid to the states and to local schools as well. People who are trying to understand the current issue over local, state, and federal control of education should remember that all three levels have had input into educational policy since the founding of the nation. Granting federal land to the states for educational purposes began with the Northwest Ordinance of 1785. This practice was continued with the Morrill Act of the Civil War era which used federal land grants to create universities. Congress also established a number of schools for specific purposes and encouraged vocational education through legislation such as the Smith-Hughes Act. Recent federal acts such as the National Defense Education Act, the Elementary and Secondary Education Acts of 1965, the Equal Opportunity Act, National Service Legislation of 1993 (National and Community Trust Act) and Education of

All Handicapped Children Act of 1975 better known as Public Law 94-142 are merely current extensions of federal involvement in education reaching back to American historical beginnings.

The mood of the nation has often been reflected in political activity which has a direct bearing on education. The history of the United States Department of Education is an example. As we have seen, many of the founding fathers wanted to establish a federal system of education. In 1829, Congressman Joseph Richardson proposed a federal Committee on Education to coordinate the state programs. This was squelched by Congress but the idea kept emerging. Charles Brooks of Massachusetts (a Unitarian minister and school reformer) devoted thirty years to efforts at getting a national system. Although he failed, he stimulated educators to form communications networks to gather data and influenced Congress to consider federal aid to the South after the Civil War. Following the War, the National Association of School Superintendents proposed a bureau of education. In somewhat reduced form, the Bill creating a Department of Education was passed and signed into law by President Andrew Johnson in 1867. Henry Barnard, who had also lobbied for such a department, became the first commissioner. Barnard was not popular in Washington and the Department was soon reduced to a Bureau. General John Eaton, Barnard's successor, toned down the office and made its function mainly one of collecting information. For almost a century after its creation, the United States Office of Education kept a low profile and concentrated on statistics. Then, in the 1950s, with the Black revolution and the Civil Rights Movement, latter-day reformers found the Office a useful instrument for implementing the reforms of the Great Society. In the Kennedy-Johnson years, the Office gained great power and status. It was authorized to distribute vast sums of money to compensate for the inequality of educational opportunity and to stimulate plans for school integration. The Office was placed in the Department of Health, Education, and Welfare and its staff grew to enormous size. Under President Carter, it became a separate cabinet-level Department of Education. The administration of President Reagan, however, took a very dim view of social engineering through federal spending and reduced both the budget and the influence of the department. The Clinton Administration is seeking to reverse the Reagan and Bush educational spending programs by utilizing every avenue of the federal government to focus on updating and upgrading the educational effort nationwide. The focus will be on attempting to improve the education of children, especially those at risk in American society. All through history, the progress of education has been linked to the whims of politics and public attitudes. It should be remembered that the reason we do not have a federal system of public schools in the United States is because of the political climate at the time of the writing of the Constitution.

Another example is furnished by attempts of politicians to control higher education. During the American Revolution, criticism and attacks were directed at conservative colleges because they were considered to be insufficiently patriotic. William Smith, president of the College of Philadelphia, was an Anglican minister accused of Tory sentiments. In 1776, the College was investigated by the legislature. The board of trustees was dissolved and the faculty dismissed. A new institution called the University of the State of Pennsylvania was created by the legislature with a new board. The old college continued to function without legal status and finally, in 1789, the two institutions were joined to form the University of Pennsylvania. The case of the College of Philadelphia is similar to that of Dartmouth College, which will be treated in the next chapter. The point to be made is that political influence over education is nothing new in American history.

Periods of political unrest foster attacks on institutions of education. Notable modern examples include the investigations by Senator Joseph McCarthy following World War II and the controversy over loyalty oaths for teachers (Wieman v. Updegraff) in the 1950s. While education is legally a state function, all levels of government are involved in educational matters. The arguments over control and support of education that began in the period of the Revolution are very much alive today and may be expected to continue into the future.

BIBLIOGRAPHY

Arrowood, Charles Flinn. *Thomas Jefferson and Education in a Republic*. New York: McGraw-Hill, 1930.

Best, John Hardin, ed. *Benjamin Franklin on Education*. Teachers College, Columbia University Bureau of Publications, no. 14. New York: Columbia University Press, 1962.

Butts, R. Freeman, and Lawrence A. Cremin. *A History of Education in American Culture*. New York: Holt, Rinehart and Winston, 1953.

Church, Robert, and Michael Sedlak. *Education in the United States: An Interpretive History*. New York: Free Press, 1976.

Clinton, Bill, and Al Gore. *Putting People First*. New York: Random House-Time Books, 1992.

Davis, David. *The Problem of Slavery in the Age of Revolution, 1770-1823*. Ithaca, NY: Cornell University Press, 1975.

French, William M. *American's Educational Tradition, an Interpretive History*. Boston: D. C. Heath, 1964.

Gay, Peter. *John Locke on Education*. New York: Teachers College Press, Columbia University, 1964.

Gutek, Gerald. *An Historical Introduction to American Education*. New York: Thomas Crowell, 1970.

Hansen, Allen O. *Liberalism and American Education in the Eighteenth Century*. New York: Macmillan, 1926.

Hofstadter, Richard, and Wilson Smith. *American Higher Education: A Documentary History*. Chicago: The University of Chicago Press, 1961.

Jefferson, Thomas. "Letter to P. S. DuPont de Nemours, April 24, 1816." In *Jefferson on Religion in Public Education*, by Robert M. Healey, 181. New Haven, CT: Yale University Press, 1962.

Ketcham, Ralph. *From Colony to Country: The Revolution in American Thought, 1750-1820*. New York: Macmillan, 1974.

Meyer, Adolphe. *Grandmasters of Educational Thought*. New York: McGraw-Hill, 1975.

Perkinson, Henry J. *Since Socrates: Studies in the History of Educational Thought*. New York: Longman, 1980.

Thayer, V. T. *Formative Ideas in American Education*. New York: Dodd, Mead, 1965.

Travers, Paul, and Ronald Rebore. *Foundations of Education: Becoming a Teacher*. Englewood Cliffs, NJ: Prentice-Hall, 1987.

Ulich, Robert, ed. *Three Thousand Years of Educational Wisdom*. 2d ed. Cambridge: Harvard University Press, 1963.

Woody, Thomas. *Educational Views of Benjamin Franklin*. New York: McGraw-Hill, 1931.

4 AMERICAN EDUCATION 1812–1865

I believe in the existence of a great, immutable principle of natural law, or natural ethics—which provides the absolute right of every human being that comes into the world to an education; and which, of course, proves the correlative duty of every government to see that the means of that education are provided for all.

Horace Mann

Before the War of 1812, education was virtually a religious enterprise with the exception of some academies and free school societies. The period from 1812 to the Civil War was a transitional one during which educational leaders such as Horace Mann, James C. Carter, and Henry Barnard forged the first links in what has evolved as a free, public school system, supported and controlled by the state. The rise of nationalism and Jacksonian Democracy, the Industrial Revolution, and the forces of westward expansion, immigration, and population growth provided impetus to the concept of universal education. There was a rebirth in the growth of the elementary or common schools. The academies supplanted the elite-oriented Latin grammar schools, which flourished until their peak in 1850.

More important in this era was the birth of the American high school, an institution that would, in time, become the vital force of secondary education. This period saw the passing of the Morrill Act and the subsequent establishment of land grant colleges. European ideas were transplanted by innovations such as those of Victor Cousin, Joseph Lancaster, and Mrs. Carl Schurz. The curriculum was expanded. The sectarian stronghold gave way to a more secular orientation, and the concept of teacher training was realized in the establishment of the first normal school in 1839.

Jacksonian Democracy		
1817 Thomas Gallaudet Established School for the Deaf in Boston	1821 First American High School, Boston	1827 Massachusetts Required High Schools
1818 Robert Owen's Infant School	Emma Willard's School for Girls	1832 New York School for the Blind
1819 Dartmouth College Case	1825 Friedrich Froebel Published *Education of Man*	1837 Calvin Stowe's Report on Prussian Schools
University of Virginia	Henry Barnard Visits Prussian Schools	Horace Mann Made Secretary of Massachusetts School Board

SOCIAL, POLITICAL, AND ECONOMIC TRENDS

The period of time from the War of 1812 through the Civil War is often referred to as the age of the common man. This is true in part because of the impact of Jacksonian Democracy and the social, political, and economic developments of the nation. Throughout the land, the advancement of the common man carried the banner of education as a basic right and opportunity that should not be denied any citizen.

Common School Ideal.   The doctrine of equality of all citizens demanded mass education and made a system of separate schools for the elite social classes unacceptable. Equality led to the belief that all should read in order to participate in government and to have the opportunity to improve. The idea that schools could provide a ladder by which one might climb socially and economically was widespread. There was a demand for general education and for vocational skills as well. The attitude supported local control with no federal regulations. It was felt that common schools should be public in curriculum and tax supported. Separation of church and state was upheld, but no restrictions were placed on nondenominational religious instruction in public schools.

Impact of the Industrial Revolution.   The Industrial Revolution began in Europe and spread to America a few decades later. Its beginning in the United States occurred in the eighteenth century, but its development continued through the nineteenth

	Missouri Compromise		Civil War	
1839 First American Normal School, Lexington, Massachusetts	1848 Attempt to Teach Idiots in Boston		1855 German Speaking Kindergarten	
1840 Rhode Island Compulsory Education	1849 New York General Tax for Schools		1860 English Kindergarten in Boston 1861 M.I.T. Founded	
1846 Laboratory Sciences in Colleges	1852 Massachusetts Attendance Law		1861 War Begins 1862 Morrill Land-Grant College Act	

and twentieth. One effect of the change from an agricultural to an industrial economy was the demand for a terminal secondary school to train boys for the work for which they were destined. From 1830 to the Civil War, considerable pressure was generated for the expansion and improvement of public schools. The industrial working class became a political factor. Workers in urban areas could not afford to send their children to school at private expense. They wanted a better opportunity for their sons and daughters than they themselves had enjoyed. Therefore, the demand for universal free education became more pressing. In the East, the vast growth of cities and factories tended both to increase the desire for schools and to decrease the opportunity many children had to attend them. The factory system employed whole families. Some youngsters began working at the age of eight. The severity of this problem is evident in the fact that in the 1830s two-fifths of New England's working force was composed of children under sixteen years of age. This was also a period of geographical mobility. The labor supply was made up largely of immigrants and transplanted farmers. Vast improvement in industrial processes increased the wealth of the nation, but it also created slums, urban blight, and new social problems. Many reformers hoped to use education as a means of overcoming the difficulties produced by the Industrial Revolution, such as child labor, crime, drunkenness, and extreme poverty.

Public School Support.   Throughout this period there was an increase in the political power of the ordinary man and aristocratic birth came to be a political handicap. Private philanthropy, even by such a popular organization as the Public School Society of New York, could not really provide the answer, and increased agitation for tax-supported schools became commonplace. Bands of factory workers in cities formed working men's societies which tended to give their support to public education. Because they were important politically, the working men's societies had considerable effect.

The theory behind the taxation of every person for the education of all children was eventually accepted in most parts of the country, and the belief that schools must be both free and tax supported developed into general public policy before the Civil War. This did not mean that all states had established their school systems before 1865, nor that all resentment of tax support for education had disappeared, but the American people had generally accepted the notion of public support for common school education.

There was some feeling, particularly expressed by the New York Working Men's Advocate, that the public schools ought to board children so that those from poor families would not feel inferior to the sons and daughters of the rich, and equal educational opportunity would be a reality. This argument of 1830 serves as a reminder of some of the present controversy over civil rights legislation. It was also held that the curriculum ought to be the same for all students and that the classics should not be the basis, but a practical education which included the rudiments of the English language should be required.

Today the population explosion has manifest implications for education, but even in the early national period demographic changes had their educational impact. From 1820 to 1850 the centers of commerce, especially cities like Boston and New York, jumped vastly in population. Rapid growth of the cities and the subsequent surge of poverty and slums made reform and public concern with educational matters much more important. By 1845, the flow of people from foreign countries was so pronounced that cities like Boston had as many as one-third foreign-born residents. The nation's population exceeded thirty million in 1860.

Nationalization.   Many immigrants had customs and languages different from those of the native born population; therefore, the schools became a major instrument in the transfer of the American culture to the foreigners. One aspect of this "Americanization" was not limited to the newcomers. The two wars with England and the rapid growth of America had nurtured a growing nationalism. This resulted in an educational principle that the schools should pursue the inculcation of patriotism—love and respect for America, its ideals, its history, and its potential. Frontier equality aided public education because of the belief that the people ought to have equal educational opportunity without the stigma of charity. Hence, the new states with large frontier communities tended to provide for education as they provided for universal suffrage.

Frontier Impact.   Frederick Jackson Turner (1861—1932) was an American historian who became famous for his theory of the significance of the frontier in the development of the United States. He thought that an abundance of free land strengthened the democratic ideals and that western expansion provided a safety valve that prevented social revolution caused by economic stress. His view of the impact of western expansion and the moving frontier dominated American historical thinking for decades.

Other historians challenged Turner's ideas; but it is certainly true that free land, westward expansion and the constant development of new outposts of civilization, were significant factors in the creation of the United States. While it is true that there was a certain amount of anti-intellectualism on the frontier, it is also the case that most pioneer farmers wanted their children to have the rudiments of an education. The frontier towns were raw and unsophisticated but never dominated by only one class of people. Doctors, lawyers, and well-educated ministers were present along with farmers, ranchers, prospectors, and scouts. Pioneer virtues of thrift, hard work, self-reliance, and independence were often reflected in attitudes toward social institutions such as schools. The theory of minimum public education for every child found wide acceptance on the frontier, but getting tax money for schools often met with a good deal of opposition. The egalitarian view that one man was just as good as any other without regard to wealth, family, or social status became commonplace on the frontier and in American schools. The frontier fostered individual freedom and lack of governmental restraint—values that often made it difficult to support and regulate schools. There was also a general distrust of classical or "foreign" education on the American frontier, reliance being placed on practical wisdom and basic skills like reading.

The first quarter of the nineteenth century was remarkable in many ways; it brought about, in the various states of the country, the beginning of the school systems which still exist in one form or another today. This was the time of common school revival in which the older colonial educational programs which had developed in Massachusetts and the other New England states were re-established. Of course, there was widespread opposition. Many newspapers were against taxes for the support of schools, and it was not possible to raise revenues with the speed necessary to develop a genuinely good school system. But well before the Civil War, all the states had given at least some attention to the question of developing a system of public schools for the children of all the people.

First State Programs.   It was not thought necessary by the founders of the American common schools to guarantee a democratic system of education for all the people. The earliest state provisions usually created an ex officio superintendent of schools who also had other duties, such as being secretary of state. It was also common to empower local groups interested in education to establish an educational corporation for the purpose of building school buildings, hiring teachers, and whatever else seemed necessary to the making of a school. But the states moved slowly in the passage of laws which set up their various educational systems. The state superintendent of free schools or common schools, or the state superintendent of public instruction, as the officer was sometimes called, often had very feeble powers. Even when the states passed laws necessary for a real school system they tended to be very slow in the enforcement of those laws. For a long time it was difficult to collect school taxes and nearly impossible to insure compulsory attendance, even when such attendance was a legal requirement. Hence, the development of the state school systems varied as the interest of the people tended to wax and wane. Educational progress was hindered by the old tradition that children should be educated first by their parents and second by the church. However, in the long run frontier democracy overcame the prejudices against public schools.

THE AGE OF THE COMMON SCHOOL REVIVAL

Educational historians often refer to this period as the age of common school revival. It was during this time that the old New England demand for universal common education became an ideal for the American people. The common elementary school was established in the North and West, and it had the task of building social, political, and moral character needed in a democracy. In addition, it was concerned with the teaching of basic skills. The battle for free public education, supported and controlled by the state, was centered around the common school.

As the curtain rose on the nineteenth century, the condition of elementary school education was most depressing. The SPG withdrew its efforts after the split with England, and there were few schools which were for the benefit of the masses. Most existing schools required tuition, although some scholarships were available. Education was traditional, discipline was harsh. In the few public schools, most of which were in New England, the teachers' work loads were heavy and only the fundamentals were taught. For the most part school buildings and equipment were very poor, even in the private schools and academies. Textbooks, blackboards, and all working materials were in extremely short supply. Buildings were not kept up, lighting was not adequate, and quite often one poorly trained teacher was in charge not only of one school but of an entire district.

Teachers who possessed only an elementary school education were frequently hired. Of course, teachers in the Latin grammar schools and academies were educated; but there was certainly no formal teacher training system. There were some teachers of ability, but frequently men who were dreamers or who could not succeed in other professions became school masters. Perhaps people of better quality and training would have been attracted to teaching if the pay and conditions could have been improved, but this was beyond the capability of the settlers in most of the newer areas of the country. It is true that even on the frontier some well-educated and excellent teachers were to be found, but in most cases the quality of teaching was extremely low and the children could expect to gain little learning in return for the brief time and small fees which were required of them.

State Funds and State Laws.   Permanent school funds had been set up by a number of states during the early national period. Connecticut used the money from the sale of its Western Reserve for this purpose in 1795. New York and Virginia also had provisions for standing school funds before creating their state systems in law. While much educational support came from these funds, the tendency to rely on them probably retarded efforts to get real tax support.

One of the first acts commonly passed by states for education was a provision that local districts might tax themselves to support schools if the people in the district agreed. Such a law was passed in Pennsylvania in 1834. While no district was required to provide schools, more than half of the Pennsylvania districts did so. There was a great deal of opposition to school taxes in Pennsylvania, especially among Catholics and German-speaking farmers. Accordingly, the state senate voted repeal of the 1834 law and it was expected that the house would agree. At this point, one of the most unusual developments in the history of American education took place. An appeal was made to Thaddeus Stevens to support the repeal. Instead, Stevens made one of the most eloquent appeals known for free public schools. He offered a substitute law which would strengthen the public schools rather than repeal their support. Stevens used the common man ideal, the need for equality and the argument that public schools cost less than jails or welfare programs. Stevens was able to carry the day, and Pennsylvania accepted his substitute bill. Three years later Massachusetts passed a school law which established the right to use tax money for public schools. Other states soon passed similar legislation.

Curriculum Improvement.

Changes in the curriculum came gradually. Development was slow partly because most states could not afford teacher education or schools that offered much beyond the basic "R's." English grammar and spelling gained a place in school programs in the early national period. In western frontier towns, spelling sometimes was stressed more than reading and writing. American history was offered in some form to boys and girls who remained in school beyond three years. Geography was introduced into many of the elementary schools before 1825. Arithmetic was much improved by the addition of new texts and materials, but many pupils were taught only addition and simple multiplication "to the rule of three." As in colonial schools, reading, grammar, spelling, and later history and geography were treated orally by the recitation method. In 1836, William Holmes McGuffey began to publish his readers which sold over 120-million copies by 1920. These readers stressed individual virtue, literacy, hard work, and moral development.

Graded Primary Schools.

It had been the custom for mothers to teach their children to read and write before sending them to school, and therefore primary education was not considered the responsibility of the state. In Boston in 1818, primary schools were set up to take over this function. They were taught by women and eventually were consolidated with grammar and writing schools; this succeeded in forming the eight-year elementary school, a structure that is still prevalent in many areas today. Grading was not uniform, but the start of a graded elementary school can be traced to 1818 when the Boston Primary School was organized into six classes with the grammar or secondary school forming the seventh. In 1823 the grammar school was also divided into reading and writing sections. Many of the town schools had two rooms. Children were placed in the primary or the advanced room according to age. The person in charge of the older students was called the "principal teacher," which eventually led to an administrative distinction. The introduction of McGuffey's Eclectic Readers contributed to the grading movement as did the work of John D. Philbrick as principal of the Quincy Grammar School in Boston after 1848. Of course, many schools remained with no grades or divisions, especially in rural areas. In 1850, forty-five percent of the nation's youngsters attended school, and half of the states had established their school systems before the Civil War. Quality remained poor in most schools. The typical common elementary school of 1860 was a crowded one-room institution with poor lighting, bad ventilation, inadequate furniture, and no special equipment. Poorly educated and untrained teachers had no program to follow and much of the time was spent in individual recitations. Severe discipline and corporal punishment stifled creativity and imagination. Nevertheless, schools were growing in number and the principle of direct tax support for elementary education had been generally accepted.

BIRTH OF THE AMERICAN HIGH SCHOOL

Secondary education in the early national period consisted of the Latin grammar school, the academy, and the high school. Latin grammar schools were strictly for the preparation of the college-bound elite and high fees were charged. Academies also charged tuition but some had scholarships for poor students. A booming economy and the religious revival known as the Second Great Awakening contributed to the development of academies. Many were boarding schools which provided a protected moral environment for students. By 1860, one-quarter million students were enrolled in six thousand academies. However, a growing demand for terminal secondary education with free tax support was made by the middle class and many workers. Increasing urban growth and industrial expansion also contributed to the birth of the public high school.

In 1821, Boston opened the English Classical School and renamed it the English High School in 1824. This first American high school was established to meet the needs of boys who did not plan to attend college. Boys as young as age twelve were admitted by examination and very few poor or working-class youngsters were involved. English, mathematics, history, science, geography, philosophy, bookkeeping, and surveying were taught. Massachusetts passed a law in 1827 which required towns of four thousand or more to create a high school, but not all towns complied.

At first high schools grew slowly. There was competition from well-established academies and opposition to taxation for secondary schools. Still, the idea of a free secondary school or a "college for all the people" appealed to the middle class and grew in popularity. In 1826, Boston opened a female high school under the direction of Ebenezer Bailey. So many girls applied for admission that the school was closed for lack of funds.

In 1855, Boston established another school for girls that included teacher training in a "normal" department.

There were no electives in these high schools. Students were expected to take all of the courses offered but there was a choice between an English, classical, or commercial curriculum. Entrance requirements and standardization of courses varied. There were arguments over whether or not high schools should be terminal institutions only. When the Civil War began, there were over three hundred high schools, one third of which were in Massachusetts.

HIGHER EDUCATION BEFORE THE CIVIL WAR

Except for the College of Philadelphia, all the colonial institutions of higher learning had been church related. In spite of efforts to make them democratic, most colleges remained sectarian and aristocratic. Classics, theology, and mathematics dominated their curricula. Control was vested with religious leaders and with the wealthy. It was possible to prepare for college in a low cost academy, and some students worked their way through college by teaching school during vacation periods. But only a small fraction of the population attended college. A majority of the students were preparing for the ministry or for a life of leisure which their families could provide.

Dartmouth College Case.   The struggle over the question of public or private control of colleges came to a head with the Dartmouth College issue. Dartmouth had been founded through the efforts of Eleazar Wheelock, who was succeeded by his son John. A dominant figure, John Wheelock came into conflict with the trustees of the college. In 1815, the board removed Wheelock from the presidency of Dartmouth, but in 1816, the successful Jeffersonian Democrats converted Dartmouth into a state university and restored Wheelock. As a result, the students and faculty rebelled and the trustees filed suit to recover the college. In 1818, the case reached the Supreme Court of the United States. John Marshall wrote the decision which held that a private educational institution could not be taken over by a state against its will. This decision clearly established the right of private as well as state colleges to exist and to solicit gifts or grants for support.

State Universities   State universities were chartered first where no institution of higher learning existed. They reflected the theory of the Enlightenment that education should promote social improvement and individual happiness. The University of Georgia was created in 1785 and opened in 1800. North Carolina chartered its university in 1789, Vermont in 1791, and South Carolina in 1801. There was also Blount College in 1794, which later became the University of Tennessee. None of these colleges grew rapidly. They were state universities in name, but all were under the control of a private board and the curriculum included a large measure of classical studies. The best known of the early state universities was that of Virginia, which was dominated by Thomas Jefferson. There was a degree of academic freedom there: professors could select their own textbooks, and they held tenure. The curriculum was also much more liberal than at other colleges. Jefferson called for professors of ancient languages, modern languages, mathematics, natural philosophy, natural history, medicine, moral philosophy, and law. This was the first attempt to include such professional studies as law and medicine in a university program, and the students could select (or elect) the Program they wished to follow. In September of 1825, there were over one hundred students attending the University of Virginia.

While the new program at Virginia was getting underway, an effort was made to reform Harvard. George Ticknor, a professor of modern languages, proposed a series of changes based upon European universities which he had visited. Among his reforms were departmentalization of the university, strict examinations, teaching by the lecture method, and student election of some subjects. These reforms would have created a university similar to those of Germany, which had very high standards of scholarship. The reforms were unpopular with faculty members and Ticknor was forced to resign in 1835.

Resistance to change was also demonstrated by the Yale Report of 1828. This report placed stress on the status quo, emphasizing classical languages and theology as a means of gaining discipline over the mind. It put little faith in science and held that the foundation of a superior education is grounded in traditional subjects. The Yale Report called for recitations rather than lectures and placed stress on the "superintendence" of the faculty over all student activities. It supported the idea that traditional studies are a good foundation for all vocations including the learned professions. The Yale Report was a clear statement of the conservatism which continued to dominate most colleges until after the Civil War.

In addition to Harvard and Virginia, Union College in New York and Brown University began using the elective system. The major growth in higher education before 1860 was in the private and denominational colleges. Private and church-related colleges accepted the principles of the Yale Report and rejected the elective system. In 1810, there were about thirty private colleges and more than fifty in 1830. Eastern missionaries were especially active, founding colleges in western states like Ohio, Indiana, and Illinois. After the act which united Presbyterian and Congregationalist efforts, even more western denominational colleges were established. Methodists were also active. Many graduates of Princeton and Yale believed that creating new colleges was a way of reforming society and expressing religious beliefs. There were 182 American colleges in operation before the Civil War, although some of these may have offered only secondary instruction. Many of them ceased to exist before 1900.

State universities were also set up in the areas of westward expansion before 1861. In 1837, the University of Michigan was authorized to begin offering literary, scientific, and practical courses. There was also a branch for the education of primary school teachers. Indiana, Kentucky, Missouri, Mississippi, Iowa, Wisconsin, Minnesota,

Louisiana, and California chartered their state universities prior to 1860. Many of these institutions did not reach university status until later.

Technical and scientific education began to increase with the foundation of Rensselaer Polytechnic Institute in 1824. The Lawrence Scientific School at Harvard opened in 1847, and Yale created the Sheffield Scientific School in 1852. There was a great demand for people trained in scientific and engineering skills long before most universities developed professional schools. West Point-educated engineers were too few to meet the need and there were no universities where one could study agriculture. By 1850 considerable pressure for the establishment of scientific, agricultural, and engineering colleges was felt.

An adult education movement developing during the early part of the nineteenth century gave considerable attention to public schools as well as the educational improvement of older citizens. In 1826 Josiah Holbrook of Massachusetts organized the first "lyceum" which was an association of men and women for cultural advancement. By 1832, a national lyceum movement had been organized for the improvement of useful knowledge and the advancement of public schools. Lyceums especially encouraged female teachers and invited them to participate in local educational movements for better support of and higher quality in common schools. Lyceum meetings were similar to county institutes. The nonsectarian character of the lyceum provided common ground for persons of divergent religious persuasion to discuss educational matters.

Other literary and cultural activities helped to give indirect leadership to the school cause. Ralph Waldo Emerson and Walt Whitman idealized the common man. Transcendentalism supported raising the educational level of the whole people as a means of social improvement. Newspaper editorials and publications of workingmen's societies, such as the Mechanics' Free Press, continued to urge free schools throughout the nation.

Morrill Act. In 1857 Justin Morrill, congressman from Vermont, offered a bill for the grant of public lands to the states for colleges which would offer agriculture and the mechanical arts. The precedent of federal land grants of large size for schools and colleges had been established by the Ordinance of 1785. Morrill had the support of the farm interests in the South and West, but there was fear that it might cause the federal control of education. The Senate passed the bill, but it was vetoed by President Buchanan. Congress passed it again when Lincoln became president, and it became law in 1862.

The Morrill Act granted thirty thousand acres of public land to each state for each one of its senators and representatives. The land was to be used for the endowment and maintenance of at least one college in each state for the teaching of agriculture and the mechanical arts. Military science and tactics was also required, but the states retained control of the administration of the colleges and the remainder of the curriculum. Some states used the money to develop existing colleges, while others created new agricultural and mechanical universities. The actual development of these state institutions did not occur until after the war years. Congress made a number of supplementary cash grants to these colleges in later years.

AMERICAN EDUCATIONAL LEADERSHIP

Political Leaders.   Political support for educational reform came from many parts of society. De Witt Clinton of New York was a political leader who showed great interest in educational matters. He often urged that the legislature establish tax-supported common schools and institutions for teacher training. In 1827, Clinton was largely responsible for creating a fund for aiding academies and promoting teacher education. He promoted the creation of the first office of superintendent of schools in New York, to which Gideon Hawley was appointed in 1812.

Governor Wolf of Pennsylvania charged in 1833 that his state had failed to meet the constitutional requirement which charged the legislature to provide poor children with free education. Thaddeus Stevens helped put Pennsylvania at the forefront of the fight for common schools. Archibald Murphy in North Carolina, Calvin Stowe in Ohio, and Edward Coles in Illinois called for complete educational programs in their states. Governors and influential political leaders in all parts of the nation attempted to persuade the various legislatures to pass school laws and provide tax support. Of course, there was opposition and not many political figures had the success of Horace Mann and Henry Barnard, but many were trying.

Literary Support.   The *Connecticut Common School Journal* published by Barnard, William Russell's *American Journal of Education*, and the *Academician*, which appeared in 1818 are examples of early educational journals which aided the common school cause. The mission of the Western Literary Institute was to create favorable public opinion for free schools according to John Prickett, who founded the organization in 1831.

Professional Educators.   Cyrus Peirce, Samuel Hall, Edward Sheldon and Henry Barnard pioneered the normal school movement. Sheldon, school superintendent in Oswego, New York, implemented Pestalozzi's educational concepts in the United States. Catherine Beecher, Emma Hart Willard, founder of the Troy Female Seminary, and Mary Lyon were among the promoters of education for women. Frederick Rudolph in *The American College and University* identified challenges to women's education. He wrote of fears of men like Reverend John Todd who dreaded coeducation:

> Must we crowd education on our daughters, and for the sake of having them 'intellectual' make them puny, nervous, and their whole earthly existence a struggle between life and death.

Early female colleges were often only two stories, since there were fears any more stair climbing would completely unsex women.

Caleb Mills in Indiana, John D. Pierce in Michigan, Calvin Wiley in North Carolina, and John Swett in California were important early educators. Probably the greatest influence was exerted by James Carter, Horace Mann, and Henry Barnard.

Carter.   James G. Carter (1795–1845) was a pioneer educational reformer who worked his way through Harvard University by teaching in the Massachusetts district schools. He is often called the "father" of the Massachusetts school system and of normal schools. Carter was largely responsible for the passage of the Massachusetts school law of 1827, which provided for public secondary schools in that state. He made an effort to get Massachusetts to establish public normal schools for the training of common school teachers and he helped to set up the state board of education in 1837. Carter wrote essays on popular education in which he attacked the anti-democratic character of the private schools which existed in the early national period. He feared that private education, and especially private academies, would give rise to a differentiation between the classes of citizens which would be detrimental to America. Hence, in addition to his direct work with the schools, which included not only his efforts to pass school laws but also some personal experiments with private schools, Carter contributed vastly to the belief in democratic education for all people without regard for social class or wealth.

Mann.   Horace Mann (1796–1859) was perhaps the best known of the important leaders in developing the American public school system. Mann worked with Carter to persuade the Commonwealth of Massachusetts to establish a board of education, and then Mann resigned from the legislature in order to become secretary of that board. During his twelve years as secretary, he was the most active leader of the movement for common school education in the country. *The Common School Journal,* of which Mann was editor, was circulated throughout the nation and in foreign lands as well. Mann often received letters from educational reformers and others interested in the schools beyond his own state, and he himself made many lectures and public appearances in the cause of education. Mann became the acknowledged leader in American school organization, and he created a revival in Massachusetts which spread throughout the land.

The twelve annual reports published during his period as secretary of the board contained much information about how the schools could be improved. Mann was an enemy of the old district schools of Massachusetts, and he believed that education should be little influenced by private or religious societies. He succeeded in obtaining the support of the state legislature for liberal taxation which increased educational opportunities through better salaries for teachers and new buildings. From 1839 to 1840, Mann organized three of the first normal schools in the country. He also created fifty new high schools and had a marked effect on increased attendance in public schools at all levels. He worked, too, for improvement of teaching methods and for a better curriculum for the common schools. He attempted to use the schools to improve social conditions as well as to provide an opportunity for those who were on the bottom of the economic order.

Mann's work was so respected that his influence was very great throughout the United States, and his system for Massachusetts was widely copied as the development of common schools and high schools progressed in the rest of the nation.

Barnard.   Henry Barnard (1811–1900) played a role in Connecticut and Rhode Island similar to the role played by Mann in Massachusetts. He was secretary of the board of education in Connecticut, principal of a normal school there, and became the state superintendent of Rhode Island in 1845. Barnard's major contribution came through his editorship of educational publications, particularly the American Journal of Education published between 1855 and 1881. Barnard initiated the teacher's institute movement in 1839 and became a popular disseminator of information about better schools. A member of the Connecticut legislature, in 1838 he sponsored successful legislation similar to the Massachusetts bill of 1837 which created a state school board. He became the first secretary of the board of education and stirred much interest in education, although the legislature soon abolished his own office.

Next, Barnard moved to Rhode Island where, after a two-year campaign to awaken the citizens to the problems of the schools, he managed to get a law passed creating public schools, which he administered as commissioner until 1849. Connecticut made some efforts to reverse its previous error in firing Barnard by setting up a normal school and inviting him to be its principal. He held both positions for a number of years, and during this time he also produced many letters, articles, and educational studies. Barnard was also chancellor at the University of Wisconsin, president of St. John's College at Annapolis, and the first U.S. commissioner of education from 1867 to 1870. His greatest success lay in democratic philosophy and his ability to rouse public interest through the dissemination of information about education. Barnard is sometimes called the "father of American school administration," as well as the founder of American educational journalism.

EUROPEAN INFLUENCES

While it is true that American education was formed and molded by many factors that were uniquely American, the importance of transplanted European movements should not be underestimated. In the period from 1810 to 1865, the influence of European ideas was quite evident in the evolution of American preschool institutions.

Infant Schools.   The infant school of England, originated by Robert Owen and modified by Samuel Wilderspin, ministered to toddlers from the age of three. Owen's version encompassed a sort of informal education centered around health, physical training, and spontaneous activity. Wilderspin defined the school's function in more traditional terms, and his schools have been described as "intellectual packing-houses." In 1818, Boston made provisions for the first American infant school with an allocation of five thousand dollars. Dubbed the "primary school," this institution catered to children who had attained their fourth birthday. Within a decade, similar schools had sprouted in New York, Philadelphia, and Providence. The American infant or primary school was influenced by both originators, but the Wilderspin format enjoyed the greatest development.

By mid-century, the primary school had been absorbed into the common elementary schools. Infant schools were started to help the children of poor factory workers, but they did not satisfy the demand for free public schools.

Kindergartens.   European educators instituted the kindergarten as the proper foundation for education. The "garden of children" nurtured growth with the concept of activity, accenting the importance of play, songs, and stories. Froebel's educational ideas formed a complex and sophisticated philosophical position, but the kindergarten movement in America only encompassed the outward manifestations of his theory. Strangely enough, the kindergarten met with stern resistance in Froebel's homeland of Germany, and its greatest development was in the United States.

In the midst of a wave of German immigration following the Prussian Revolution in 1848, Mrs. Carl Schurz, a former pupil of Froebel, established the first American kindergarten. Formed in Watertown, Wisconsin, in 1856, Mrs. Schurz's school was really a German kindergarten on American soil, with German language as the means of communication. The growth of American kindergartens was considerably fostered by Elizabeth Peabody, who in 1860 established in Boston the first English-speaking kindergarten. In 1873, the kindergarten was brought into the realm of the public schools, due to the efforts of Superintendent William T. Harris in St. Louis, with the assistance of Susan E. Blow, who published *Educational Issues in the Kindergarten* in 1908. The movement was expanded in the private arena with contributions of philanthropic societies. In the early years kindergarten meant ages 3–7. By the 1970s it encompassed ages 3–5.

The kindergarten has become a stable part of the modern educational system with more than ninety percent of America's five-year-olds enrolled. Many of the ideas made operational by the progressives in the twentieth century trace their roots to Froebel and the kindergarten.

European School Model.   If the American schools were not altogether adequate, there was at least an awareness that better programs for education were available in other parts of the world. The influence of reports on European education can hardly be overemphasized, and the most influential of the lot was by Victor Cousin. His detailed monograph on Prussian schools was first published in 1831 and translated into English in 1834. It was widely circulated in America, and its impact can be judged from the fact that shortly after it gained prominence, a number of important educators journeyed to

Europe with the intent of studying the European systems and Prussia's in particular. Calvin Stowe's visit resulted in his treatise, *Elementary Education in Europe* (1837). Mann made the trip in 1843 and gathered material for his famous *Seventh Annual Report to the Massachusetts Board of Education*. While he disapproved of Prussian purposes, Mann found great merit in their efficient methods, universality, high quality buildings, broad curriculum, and significantly effective teacher training. Almost all the American educators who had an opportunity to visit schools on the European mainland returned with favorable impressions. They used German or Prussian schools as a model for making the American educational program more uniform and efficient.

European Educational Theory.   While some of the advances made in European schools were the result of national or political forces, there was also a new philosophic basis for change. In addition to Comenius and Locke (discussed in chapter 3) major educational concepts were developed by Jean Jacques Rousseau (1712–78), Johann Basedow (1734–90), Johann H. Pestalozzi (1746–1827), Johann Herbart (1776–1841), and Friedrich Froebel (1782–1852).

Rousseau was a critic of conventional civilization, which he viewed as depraved and artificial. Rejecting the doctrine of original sin, he held that the basic nature of man is good and only social institutions, such as governments, churches, and schools, cause evil. Rousseau demanded a return to nature and an opportunity for the child to pass through natural stages of development without being molded by degenerate social forces. Although better known for his *Social Contract,* Rousseau's *Emile* became a major educational classic. In it, he advocated emotional, intellectual, and educational freedom for children. Distrusting books and standard pedagogical techniques of his day, Rousseau believed that children should learn directly from experience. Thus, physical activity, field trips, learning by doing (including manual or vocational experiences), freedom to pursue natural interests, and play were advocated as means for developing the latent potentialities of the child. Rousseau suggested that people be aware of "negative education," by which he meant protecting the student from the influences of superficial social institutions. Rousseau's attack on formalism and support for natural interests had little direct influence on American education until the period of John Dewey and the progressive educators. His effect on European educators and schools had an indirect bearing on American schools at an earlier date.

The German educator Johann Basedow attempted to put many of Rousseau's ideas into operation in his Philanthropinum. This school was open to all students, regardless of wealth or class. It stressed natural development, teaching through conversation and sense experience, play, physical activity, and object lessons. Basedow included health, sex education, vocational training, and "world citizenship" in his curriculum, and wrote a book on his theories, *Elementary Work*. He also advocated teacher training. One of the teachers at the Philanthropinum, Christian Salzmann, later created his own school. Salzmann required his students to learn gardening, pursue gymnastics, and develop vocational skills; but there was also time for play, nature study, and formal classes. Other disciples of Basedow, such as J. H. Campe and Johann Guts-Muths, developed German children's literature and the physical education program for the German states.

The Swiss educator Johann H. Pestalozzi experimented with some of the more practical ideas of Rousseau's *Emile* and applied many of his own theories as well. Pestalozzi's major books included *Leonard and Gertrude, How Gertrude Teaches Her Children, Book for Mothers,* and the *Evening Hours of the Hermit*. Pestalozzi conducted schools at Neuhof, Stanz, Burgdorf, Hofwyl, and Yverdon. Starting with his own son's education, about which he kept a careful diary of observations, Pestalozzi developed educational programs for impoverished children and methods that were useful for teaching the children of the common people. Pestalozzi looked upon the child's mind as a union of separate moral, physical, and intellectual faculties. He believed that education was the natural, progressive, and harmonious development of the natural faculties and powers. He trusted children's natural instincts and thought they should provide the motives for learning. Instead of threats and corporal punishment, Pestalozzi believed that cooperation and sympathy could produce discipline in a homelike atmosphere. He saw education as a mutual effort by the student and the teacher which produced mutual respect. Like Rousseau, Pestalozzi believed that the child unfolds or develops through various natural stages, according to the principle of growth. He thought that sense impressions were the foundation of all knowledge. Pestalozzi wanted to develop each child's potential to the maximum and therefore spoke of educating the "hand and the heart," as well as the "head." Moral education and vocational training were just as important to Pestalozzi as intellectual subjects.

For Pestalozzi education was based upon actual observations rather than on books and theories. He relied on object lessons to develop the child's senses of sight, touch, and sound. Plants, animals, music, tools, and the natural environment were important in his education. Unlike the earliest sense realists, he did not view the mind as a passive receptor of sense impressions. He insisted that the mind is active in perceiving, analyzing, and selecting. Pestalozzi believed that society could be improved through adequate educational opportunity for all. Teachers from all over Europe came to observe his methods, and Pestalozzi offered them training. He believed that the basis for teaching should be close observation of the attitudes and activities of children.

In England, the ideas of Pestalozzi were made popular by Charles Mayo. American followers included Joseph Neef, who wrote *Methods of Instruction*, and Edward Sheldon, who created the Oswego movement (see chapter 5).

Froebel.   Since the advent of the kindergarten, educational leaders have been much influenced by Friedrich Froebel's theories concerning education of the very young. Froebel became a follower of Pestalozzi while teaching at a small private school at Frankfurt, Germany. In 1816, he opened a school of his own and six years later published *The Education of Man*. At Blankenburg, Froebel finally was able to establish his educational institution offering programs for children between the ages of three and eight. (The German term for his school was Kleinkinderbeschaftingungsanstalt which was later reduced to kindergarten.)

Froebel was basically an idealist who looked upon the child as the agency for the realization of God's will in human nature. A mystic, Froebel believed that the spirit of the child could be linked with the absolute through the unity of experience and divine nature. From a practical standpoint, the significance of Froebel was in his conception of the educative process as something which must begin with a child of only three or four years of age. Early childhood educational activities centering on play, music, and physical activity made him famous. Froebel created new respect for children, especially for their individuality and for the dynamic and active qualities of their nature. Constructive use of objects, story-telling, and cooperative social activities were supported in Froebel's program. Children were also free to express themselves and to build good relationships with others in the kindergarten. While later educators often disagreed with Froebel's mystical concepts, his efforts to create early childhood education had a profound effect. Froebel greatly influenced both Maria Montessori and John Dewey.

Growth of Academies.   The age of the common school revival was also a time of expansion for academies. Those which developed in colonial times were terminal private venture schools with practical programs. Many of those in operation before the Civil War offered college preparatory courses. Some were denominational, while others were governed by a local board or city government. Most academies charged tuition, but several enjoyed some sort of private endowment as well. Various schemes for public support of academies were tried, and a large number did benefit from some degree of public finance. The curriculum of the academy was never fixed; many offered a wide range of courses. Reading, writing, grammar, arithmetic, and higher mathematics were usually offered. Chemistry, botany, mineralogy, logic, moral philosophy, and natural science were sometimes in the program. Many academies offered modern languages and music. Some claimed to prepare students for teaching and other professions. A large number of academies admitted girls and some were designated as "female seminaries" or schools for girls only. After 1860, academies declined in number, due largely to the vast increase in public high schools. The census of 1850 numbered 6,085 private schools and academies in the United States. New York had over 800 incorporated academies. Both Ohio and Virginia chartered more than 200 before 1860. The majority were located in eastern states, but there were frontier academies in newly settled regions as well. Many academies closed after a few months because of lack of support. Some were only elementary schools and others largely vocational, but most American communities had access to some sort of academy for those who could afford tuition.

Normal Schools and Institutes.   Private academies for the training of teachers did not satisfy educational leaders like Mann, Barnard, and the Reverend Charles Brooks. Brooks began a campaign for state normal schools in Massachusetts in 1835, using the Prussian model of teacher education as a guide. Brooks had some influence on the school board, and in 1838 when Edmund Dwight offered ten thousand dollars for educational improvement, three normal schools were founded. The state matched

Dwight's grant and used the funds for salaries and operating expenses of the teacher-training institutions. In 1846, the normal school at Bridgewater got its own building. The name "normal" school came from the model or practice school in which the standard or normal curriculum and methods were observed. Cyrus Peirce, the first principal of the normal school at Lexington, stressed the review of common subjects and practice teaching under his own observation.

New York created a state normal school at Albany in 1844 but state money was also used to subsidize private academies for teachers. David Page, principal at Albany, wrote *Theory and Practice of Teaching* which became a standard text for teacher education. Only twelve normal schools were created in the United States before the Civil War. Many districts were satisfied with the untrained young ladies they hired as elementary teachers.

Henry Barnard started the teacher's institute. This was a meeting of a group of teachers for instruction and usually lasted only a few weeks. County superintendents of schools often conducted institutes for teachers in summer months. A similar effort was made by the NEA Teacher Center, popular in the 1870s.

Educational Opportunity for Women. The growth of academies provided a much greater opportunity for secondary and higher education for women. A few girls' schools in colonial times offered courses in ornamental needlework, polite manners, music, French, and other subjects deemed proper for females. The curriculum was expanded by the many academies for young ladies in operation before 1860. There was some opposition to teaching girls Latin, logic, and the sciences, but all other courses were offered in at least some of the schools for girls. Coeducation was rare; most academies admitted one sex or the other, but not both. Employment of male teachers only, except in the Dame schools, ended during the early national period. Horace Mann and other educational leaders encouraged women to teach in elementary schools. It became common for many academies to offer courses in "schoolkeeping" for girls. Preparation of common school teachers was largely confined to a review of the common branches and a series of highly moralistic lectures on the "duties" of teachers; however, it was often the only teacher training available. Samuel Hall's *Lectures on Schoolkeeping* was the basic text for teacher training until normal schools such as Edward Sheldon's opened in 1853 in Oswego, New York.

Catherine Beecher, Mary Lyon, Almira Phelps, and Emma Willard were leaders in the movement for girls' secondary education. In 1821, Mrs. Willard opened the Troy Female Seminary, while Mary Lyon founded Mt. Holyoke Female Seminary in 1837. Catherine Beecher founded the American Women's Education Association, and Almira Phelps wrote a series of *Lectures to Young Ladies*. The efforts of these women educators helped to establish the first coeducational college program at Oberlin in 1838.

Minority Education. Very little progress was made in providing educational opportunity for minority children before 1861. Early Indian schools which had been established by missionaries were largely unsuccessful, because the teachers misunderstood native American culture and attitudes. An occasional Indian learned to read English, but formal schooling was almost nonexistent for the American Indian population.

In the colonial period, many slave owners permitted blacks to read. Some felt it was their duty to teach slaves something about the Bible and the tenets of religion. A few free blacks made their way into Quaker schools in the North, which were open to all. In 1833, a Quaker teacher named Prudence Crandall was criticized for admitting black girls to her school in Connecticut. In 1846, Benjamin Roberts of Boston filed suit, because his son was forced to attend a segregated school for black boys. The Massachusetts Supreme Court held that the school committees had a right to keep schools segregated. However, by 1857, Massachusetts passed a law preventing discrimination. The school laws in most states before the Civil War did not provide for black scholars. Those of Indiana and Illinois specifically required schools for white children.

Even in the South, blacks were occasionally educated. John Chavis was a teacher and a licensed Presbyterian minister until North Carolina passed a law against black preachers in 1832. Most southern states prohibited the teaching of blacks after Nat Turner's rebellion of 1831.

THEN TO NOW

The age of the common school revival was a period in which equality of educational opportunity was stressed. Horace Mann was a great champion of education for all. He and Henry Barnard believed that the schools had the power to unite the United States into an integrated national community. Economic, social, racial, ethnic, and religious diversity were to be subsumed under one democratic system of education which would unite all the people into a single indivisible nation. Education was to be used as the chief instrument for assimilating the foreign born into the mainstream of American life and culture. Schools did have a considerable measure of success in creating a single culture. Some thirty-five million immigrants came to America in the nineteenth century and they were Americanized largely by the public schools. Still, the aim of Mann and Barnard to achieve equality and social integration was not fully realized. Many persons living in the United States today are excluded from full participation in the social and economic life of the nation. Contemporary concerns about equality for ethnic groups and Blacks are clear indications that the melting pot ideal has not been fulfilled. Mann also wanted to move away from the extreme differences between rich and poor. He believed that a strong nation must provide opportunity for all and that differences between the haves and the have-nots must be reduced. Although many Americans have achieved affluence in the modern era, there are still many who are poor or the victims of discrimination.

Black education in the South was almost nonexistent before the Civil War and very limited in northern states. About four million slaves were liberated by President Lincoln, almost all of them illiterate. The Fourteenth Amendment (ratified 1868) specified that states should not deprive any person of life, liberty, or property without due process of law. Nevertheless, they remained second-class citizens. Jim Crow laws of the 1880s were passed to "keep the Colored in their place" and discrimination was universally practiced. The separate but equal doctrine of *Plessy v. Ferguson* in 1896 legalized racial segregation until 1954. Private black colleges and those created by the Second Morrill Act helped to improve the quality of teachers but black schools lacked funds and the extreme poverty of the people made progress very slow. States claimed to provide equal support for black and white schools but many actually put more dollars into education for the majority race.

This difficulty has not been resolved in the modern era. An end to legal segregation and plans for achieving racial balance in school systems have had an impact, but problems remain. Many American cities are still segregated de facto. This situation is not improving in many areas that are becoming almost totally populated by one race or ethnic group. Affluent blacks (and other minorities) who represent the professions or the middle class have little difficulty in assimilating with white society. Integration in schools works well when all the students come from a similar socio-economic background. However, there are major problems when black children from urban slums are placed in classrooms with students from more affluent families. The issue is especially clear when busing is used as a means of bringing together students from different races, ethnic groups, and socio-economic backgrounds. Demographic patterns in many large cities are shifting so rapidly that efforts to integrate schools are frustrated. Atlanta, Houston, Washington D.C., and Newark are cities that have experienced dramatic increases in the number of minority students just when they began to implement plans for desegregation.

Desegregation efforts are illustrated by the Little Rock, Arkansas school districts which are under a Federal Court Order to desegregate. Ann Brown, Federal Monitor to the Office of Desegregation Monitoring reported that in 1993, the three districts of the system, Little Rock, North Little Rock, and Pulaski County had a racial black-white balance of approximately 60–40; 50–50 and 30–70. Magnet schools were created which draw on an approximately 50–50% racial basis from throughout the districts. There were seven racially identifiable schools. These were schools with such a high black enrollment that they were designated double funded incentive schools. The double funding was designed to compensate for the racially isolated environment and to provide an incentive for white students to transfer to these schools.

With an increasing number of immigrants, some states such as California may be dominated by ethnic minorities by or before 2050. The dominant groups in the state may be Hispanics and Asian-Americans with Caucasians in a minority group. Penny Loeb, Dorian Friedman and Mary C. Lord in an article "To Make A Nation," noted that in the 1980s over 8.6 million newcomers mainly from Asia, Latin America, and the Caribbean—the greatest influx since the 1920s—came to the United States. Although all parts of the country were influenced by an increase of 63 percent between 1980 and 1990 over the previous decade, most foreign born arrivals settled in five states—California, New York, Texas, Florida, and New Jersey. Loeb et al. noted that on the whole the new immigrants are not much different from the rest of the United States in their attitudes toward government, crime, and welfare. Increased burdens are placed on the educational systems to meet new demands on their facilities and services.

In the years covered by this chapter, much effort was devoted to creating and expanding public schools, high schools included. Educational leaders like James Carter were doing their best to make schools available to all and to improve their quality. The goal of providing equal educational opportunity to everyone and also of having excellent programs is still a difficult one to reach.

Even before Thurgood Marshall argued that segregated schools are inherently unequal (as lawyer for the NAACP in 1954), there was general agreement that minority schools had lower standards. It could have hardly been otherwise, for those schools enrolled many children who were poor and culturally deprived. Black schools had less equipment, worse buildings, and teachers with very limited training. Beyond question, minority students have gained a great deal since desegregation. It stands to reason that placing children in better schools will be of some benefit to them. Still, many schools have not been integrated, and critics say that progress in those that have been is not satisfactory. Lower overall achievement sometimes occurs when children with a poor educational background are placed in the same classrooms with those who have done better. This is especially true if the school is not used as an agency of selection to weed out those who are slow. The current attacks on social promotion and soft pedagogy reflect public dissatisfaction with attempts to meet all children where they are and to allow them to learn at their own speed.

There are also many current issues over attempts to teach the same values in schools and to Americanize all the youth. Ethnic and minority groups often argue that this takes away from the unique characteristics of children who are not of the white, middle-class, dominant culture. The struggle for equality and for excellence is far from over in American education.

BIBLIOGRAPHY

Bailyn, Bernard. *Education in the Forming of American Society*. New York: Random House, 1960.

Binder, Frederick. *The Age of the Common School, 1830–1865*. New York: Wiley, 1974.

Brown, Ann. *Federal Monitor to the Office of Desegregation Monitoring*. Little Rock: U.S. Government Printing Office, 1993.

Brubacher, John. *Henry Barnard on Education*. New York: McGraw-Hill, 1931.

Burton, Warren. *The District School as It Was*. Boston: Lee & Shepard, 1897.

Butts, Freeman. *The American Tradition in Religion and Education*. Boston: Beacon Press, 1950.

Cremin, Lawrence, ed. *The Republic and the School: Horace Mann on the Education of Free Man*. New York: Teachers College Press, 1957.

Curti, Merle. *The Social Ideas of American Educators*. New York: Littlefield Adams, 1966.

Good, Harry G., and James D. Teller. *A History of American Education*. New York: Macmillan, 1973.

Loeb, Penny, Dorian Friedman, Mary C. Lord, Dan McGraw, and Kukula Glastris. "To Make A

Nation." *U.S. News and World Report*. (October 4, 1993):47-54.

MacMullen, Edith Nye. *In the Cause of True Education: Henry Barnard and Nineteenth Century Educational Reform*. New Haven, Connecticut: Yale University Press, 1991.

Mann, Horace. *Lectures and Annual Reports on Education*, Cambridge, MA: Cornhill Press of Boston, 1867.

Mann, Horace. "Tenth Annual Report (1846)." In *The Republic and the School: Horace Mann*, Lawrence A. Cremin, ed., 63. New York: Teachers College Press, Columbia University, 1957.

Pratte, Richard. *Ideology and Education*. New York: Wiley, 1977.

Rudolph, Frederick. *The American College and University, Athens*. Athens, Georgia: University of Georgia Press, 1990. Original printing 1962.

Rusk, Robert, and James Scotland. *Doctrines of the Great Educators*. New York: St. Martin's Press, 1979.

Silver, Harold, ed. *Robert Owen on Education*. Cambridge, MA: Harvard University Press, 1969.

Veblen, Thorstein. *The Higher Learning in America*. New York: B. W. Huebsch, 1918.

Woody, Thomas. *A History of Women's Education in the United States*. New York: Farrar Strauss, Octagon Books, 1966.

5 AMERICAN EDUCATION 1865–1918

> We want education for ourselves . . . adequate, expertly taught, and
> continuing through the elementary grades, through high school and as
> far beyond that as proven gift and desert show is clearly for human
> welfare, no matter what the race, sex or religion of the recipient. This
> education is a public duty and should be at public expense. It should
> continue beyond school years, and in the form of adult education for
> all.
>
> W. E. DuBois

Wars are by no means the most significant checkpoints in educational chronology, but the period between the Civil War and the First World War was the era for the development of the modern American school system. Westward expansion and the growth of industry, agriculture, and population put vastly increased demands upon existing schools and required the building not only of new schools, but of whole new educational systems. By 1890 the frontier had almost ceased to be and with the addition of New Mexico and Arizona to the union in 1912, the continental United States was formed. Industrial growth carried with it the new problem of educating children in the urban slums and the need for Americanizing immigrants on a grand scale. Natural increase and immigration swelled the population from just over thirty million in 1860 to more than one hundred million by 1920.

Before 1860, the northern states had largely developed the outlines of their educational systems, and some had made substantial progress in bringing state education to all the people. States were not uniform in their growth; those first to be settled usually developed their systems earlier. By 1873, laws for the organization of a state school system, including the school tax and some form of state control, were to be found all over the nation. Before World War I, public school education in America typically included an eight-year elementary school and a four-year high school. State universities capped the systems, although only a small percentage of the people could take advantage of them.

Reconstruction	Herbartian Movement	Progressive Era
1865 Slavery Abolished by Thirteenth Amendment	1870 School Superintendents in 28 American Cities	1890 Second Morrill Act Provided Black A. M. and N. Colleges
1868 Fourteenth Amendment Protects Life and Property	1874 Kalamazoo Case Made Tax Support Legal for High Schools	1893 Rhode Island Begins Special Education Programs
1869 Fifteenth Amendment Guarantees Civil Rights	1890 National Herbart Society	

Public kindergartens, junior high schools, and junior colleges were found in only a few areas before 1920 and were not yet a significant part of the public school organization.

Educational theory passed through a series of stages which included sectarian dominance, *laissez faire*, slavish copying of European models, and the scientific-progressive movement. Professional training for teachers and administrators became firmly established as an ideal with the growth of normal schools and colleges or departments of education in the universities. Compulsory attendance, expanded curriculum, fully graded common schools, public high schools, and large increases in spending for buildings and equipment marked the period. However, the late nineteenth century witnessed extreme sectional differences in educational structure and quality.

INHIBITED DEVELOPMENT OF EDUCATION IN THE SOUTH

The War Between the States interfered with education all over the nation, causing schools to be closed and governmental revenues to be directed to the immediate expenses of the conflict. But northern states were able to continue their school programs in spite of the reduction in available money and the loss of many teachers. Sometimes an entire student body and faculty went off to join the army, as in the case of Illinois College at Jacksonville, Illinois, but elementary schools in the Union states continued to operate through the wartime years. It was not so in the South where battle devastation and increased sacrifice to support the war severely crippled the embryonic school systems. Southern states spent many years recovering even the low educational level they had enjoyed before the national strife, and some of the scars are still visible in the slower school development of the rural South.

Urban and Industrial Growth		Social and Political Reform
1909 Junior High School in Berkeley, California	1913 Thorndike Published His *Educational Psychology*	1916 Dewey Published *Democracy and Education*
1910 Junior College in Fresno, California	1914 Smith-Lever Act Encouraged Agriculture	1917 Smith-Hughes Act Encouraged Vocational Schools
Vast Growth of High Schools		

Southern Collapse. The war left southern states in physical and economic ruin with crops destroyed, buildings burned, livestock slaughtered, and the labor force demoralized. Civil authority broke down, courts were nonexistent, and four million black citizens were without economic resources or leadership. Presidents Lincoln and Johnson hoped to enlist the cooperation of former Confederate leaders in rebuilding the South, but the radical Republicans in Congress wanted to punish the southern states. In the struggle, Andrew Johnson was nearly impeached, and a military reconstruction government dominated by northern interests was imposed. These governments, consisting of "carpetbaggers," former slaves, and fortune seekers, failed to obtain the support of the southern white majority.

By 1876, when the radical reconstruction government finally ended and the Union army of the occupation was removed, very little real progress had been made. Southerners, bitter about their treatment after the conflict and fearful of black power, set about to undo the acts of the reconstruction era. Measures providing for public education, especially where racially mixed schools were concerned, were either ignored or removed from the books. Sectional hatred and opposition to black schools might have paralyzed education even if money had been available, but the war and the waste of the first post-war governments left the South bankrupt.

New-found freedom did nothing to improve the living standards of the southern blacks. Most of them were as economically dependent and as subject to exploitation as they had been in slavery. Economic expansion was slow to develop and both races remained poor, especially small farmers and sharecroppers. Industry received a boost in the 1880s with the founding of textile mills. Tobacco products, lumber, and even steel mills in Alabama contributed to a stronger economy. But agriculture continued to be the mainstay of southern economy, and very little tax money was available for school purposes until the twentieth century. Many southern statesmen deplored the low level and retarded growth of public schools, but were powerless to provide adequate support.

African-American Education.   Some money for educating the newly freed citizens came from private and church associations which sent teachers to the South in considerable numbers. The Peabody and other philanthropic funds provided some assistance but control remained in the hands of whites. In 1869 there were about nine thousand such teachers, working mostly in schools for freedmen. Several societies for the aid of freed slaves were formed, the most important of which were the American Freedman's Union (secular) and the American Missionary Association (religious). Congress established the Freedmen's Bureau in 1865. Its head, O. O. Howard, considered education to be the most pressing need of blacks in the South.

There was considerable enthusiasm for schooling among former slaves in the period immediately following the war, but adults soon learned that education was something for which they had neither the time nor the preparation. The economic support was often sporadic, and it appears that many of the schools were very ill-equipped and of poor quality. Social liberals and political propagandists among the teachers from the North were unpopular. Like all things "Yankee," the freedmen's schools became objects of attack once the power of reconstruction government was broken after 1873. While the South was still organized as a series of military provinces, new constitutions were adopted which included provisions for education. But for all practical purposes the states of the South were bankrupt, so that little more than a paper system of education existed in 1870.

Hoar Bill.   In 1870, a bill was introduced in Congress by George F. Hoar of Massachusetts which would have established a federal school system in southern states. The measure was designed to compel the establishment of a system of instruction and the appointment of a federal superintendent in all states where a minimum standard was not met. Textbooks were to be prescribed by the United States Commissioner of Education, and the schools were to be supported by a centrally collected direct tax. The bill was defeated partly because of the opposition of the National Education Association and Superintendent Wickersham of Pennsylvania. They felt that national control over part of the nation's schools could not be tolerated, although gifts of federal money with local autonomy could be. Roots of the modern day issue over federal aid to education can be seen in the arguments over the Hoar Bill.

Blair Bill.   A second effort to get national aid for states unable to maintain schools came in the form of a proposed national school fund from the sale of public land in the tradition of the Ordinance of 1785. When it appeared that this plan would not be adopted, Senator Henry Blair of New Hampshire introduced a bill in 1882 to help states with the greatest educational need. The Blair Bill (in final form) provided for seventy-seven million dollars to be divided among the states in proportion to the number of illiterates in each. The money was to be used as the states saw fit, provided that it was used only for education. This measure passed the Senate three times, but was never successful in the House of Representatives. No further bills of this nature were proposed until recent times, although the federal government continued to aid colleges through the second Morrill Act of 1892.

Philanthropy.   Private agencies made an effort to fill the educational void in the South and to stimulate greater local effort. George Peabody gave two million dollars for this purpose. The Peabody fund was administered by a board of trustees headed in turn by Barnas Sears, Horace Mann, and J. L. M. Curry. Curry was a southerner, under whose direction the money was used to develop a limited number of high quality schools as models. Part of the Peabody Fund went to normal schools for women teachers of both races and also to what became George Peabody College for Teachers in Nashville. Agents who supervised private funds also visited schools and opened lines of communication between groups interested in school improvement.

Southern Associations.   Thirty years after the Civil War, a Conference for Education in the South was organized and numerous meetings were held for the purpose of improving education. Out of this grew the Southern Education Board and the General Education Board (1903). A Southern Association of Colleges and Schools was established as well as many private boards which were connected with philanthropic societies, such as the Carnegie Foundation and the Rosenwald Fund. While stimulation and information were given, the public systems tended to make only limited progress before 1920. Only meager tax support was available in agricultural areas, and even southern cities were poor by northern standards. The educational conservatism of the pre-war period and hostility toward schools introduced in the reconstruction era dampened interest in public schools. The most negative factor of all was insistence on separation of white and black schools. This segregation required the building and maintenance of a dual system with duplication of buildings and teachers in states that could least afford them. While schools for black children were seldom given equal support, their very existence divided funds and lowered the capability of communities to give quality instruction. This was a major factor in keeping the educational level of southern states lower than that of the rest of the nation for several decades.

In the early 1900s, the South was still marked by short school terms (seventy days in North Carolina), high illiteracy, ineffective administration, poorly trained teachers, and meager tax support. Salaries of southern teachers in 1900 averaged about half that of northern ones, and black teachers were paid lowest of all.

NATIONAL AFFAIRS AND PROGRESS

If progress was slow in the southern states between the Civil War and World War I, those years also marked the transition from an old agrarian to a modern, industrial

America. In less than half a century, wounds of the Civil War were largely healed and America entered the era of industrial world powers. Territorial expansion had given way to a greater and faster development of northern industrial capacities. The growth and development of industry was at least as important a factor as immigration in the population growth figure. This was the period in which it was possible for the Goulds, Carnegies, and the Rockefellers to build vast industrial empires and accumulate great fortunes due to a favorable attitude by the government, untapped industrial resources, and cheap labor. Many of the industrial barons were interested in education and helped to found colleges, universities, and better public schools.

Industrial Exploitation.   The other side of the Industrial Revolution had a negative effect on education. Exploitation of children and working men was widespread, and it was not uncommon for immigrants in the cities to labor sixteen hours a day. The growth of great industry swallowed up the small businessman, and there was much corruption in government at all levels. City slums also presented a different kind of educational problem. The need for reform was seen, but many of the people in power sought to make more severe laws and to develop additional penitentiaries, rather than to cure the problem through education.

The Republican Party dominated politics and held control of the presidency between the end of the Civil War and the election of Woodrow Wilson in 1913, with the single exception of the two terms of Grover Cleveland. Distinctly, the party of business, industrial, and commercial interests, it did not promote mass educational reform supported by federal and state governments. What was done for the education of the masses in the cities was done largely through private enterprise and with the interests of individuals who saw most clearly the need for reform. The dissatisfaction of the laboring masses began to show itself in the latter part of the nineteenth century. Numerous labor reform parties came into being in the 1870s, and the agrarian and labor groups organized the Independent or Greenback Party in 1874. Later, several independent groups organized the Populist Party, which became part of the Democratic Party in 1896 and came very close to electing William Jennings Bryan over William McKinley.

The tremendous increase in industrial growth in the United States, which was especially obvious in the northern and eastern sections, together with the growth of large corporations controlling vast amounts of wealth, changed the nature of American society considerably. There was a strong belief in a hands-off, or laissez faire, governmental policy. This was the period of change of the basic nature of American society from rural to urban. The great cities were beginning to take their present-day shape, and the idea of the independent farmer class as the dominant one in America was beginning to fade.

Agricultural, Population, and Vocational Changes.   There was also a revolution in farming due to such inventions as McCormick's reaper and the new scientific knowledge about agriculture which had been greatly advanced by the agricultural colleges set up under the Morrill Acts. The farmer, however, did not immediately benefit from the better technology because the increase in production caused prices to fall. Hence, the period from 1865 to 1900 saw the rise of many farm organizations designed to aid the plight of the farmer with his decreasing income. This, too, was the beginning of the period of organized labor in America. The Knights of Labor gave way to the American Federation of Labor and the union movement was well underway by 1900.

The character of the population changed at this time. Immigrants coming to the United States had previously been largely from northwestern Europe, especially England, Ireland, Germany, and Scandinavia. But the people who arrived after the Civil War came from other parts of Europe such as Spain, Russia, Austria, Hungary, and Italy. There were also a few from non-European nations such as Japan and Mexico. This meant that the immigrant population became radically different during this period of time, making the educational task considerably more difficult. Tremendous growth in communication and the transportation system, together with an increased centralization in American life, also had an effect on the educational needs of the people.

THE PUBLIC SCHOOL IDEAL

A major principle of education put into practice after the Civil War was that public education should be free to all. In contrast with the European dual system, where elementary education was for the lower classes and secondary reserved for the elite, the United States established a ladder system by which one might advance from the first grade through college in a series of yearly steps. In theory at least, each child was free to begin at the lowest level and progress as fast as his or her abilities would allow. It was an American belief that the schools could be used for advancement up the social ladder, and the person of ability could qualify for a high paying job by acquiring education. This was an age of social revolution in which the industrial and financial leaders accumulated great wealth as industrial and technological expansion increased. With the commercial production of petroleum starting in 1859, the opening of the West to farmers and ranchers, and the joining of the Union Pacific with the Central Pacific to make the first transcontinental railroad line in 1869, growth of wealth and commerce accelerated. While wealthy families seldom sent their children to public schools before 1900, class distinctions were foreign to the educational ideal. Laboring and middle-class families demanded high quality public schools for their sons and daughters. Training for making a good living was important, but so too was education for citizenship, morality, and self-improvement. Common elementary schools for all citizens were established in theory before the Civil War. They became a reality between 1865 and 1900 for the majority of Americans. The theory was extended upward to include secondary education before World War I. The standard American high school became a major part of the educational program and cultural experience of the nation. Dewey's *Democracy and Education* published in 1916 addressed the role of education in a pluralistic society.

THE AMERICAN PUBLIC HIGH SCHOOL

The academy reached its zenith of popularity by the middle of the nineteenth century and declined rapidly after that time. Growth of high schools was slow at first. In 1875, there were fewer than 25,000 students enrolled in public high schools. In the 1880s more students attended high schools than academies, and by 1890 some 2,500 high schools enrolled more than 200,000 students. By 1900, there were more than 6,000 high school operating in the United States with over 500,000 students.

Kalamazoo Case. While the age of the common school revival clearly established the principle of free, tax-supported elementary schools, considerable controversy continued over taxation for high schools. Public secondary schools in some states were financed from common school funds while others charged tuition. Since one major function of high schools was to prepare students for college, and they were not patronized by all children, some citizens felt the states had no right to tax the public for their support. Others, led by such spokesmen as California superintendent Ezra Carr, argued that high schools were an important part of the basic public educational system.

The best known case dealing with tax support for high schools came after the town of Kalamazoo, Michigan created a public secondary school in 1858. Three taxpayers brought suit to restrain the school board from collecting and using taxes to support the high school. The case reached the Supreme Court of Michigan, which decided in favor of the school authorities in 1874. The opinion, written by Justice Cooley, held that high schools are common schools and they constitute a vital link between elementary schools and the state university. He pointed out that the absence of public secondary schools would discriminate in favor of the rich and prevent others from entering college. While other cases were tried, the Kalamazoo decision became a precedent which established the right of the several states to levy taxes for public high schools. This precedent contributed to the vast growth of high schools in the period before World War I.

Curriculum. High schools offered both traditional and practical programs, but the emphasis was usually placed on the college preparatory curriculum. In spite of the fact that only about one tenth of the students in high schools in 1900 expected to enter college, the "classical" course was taken by a majority of youngsters. Latin and algebra were the subjects which had the highest enrollment. Sometimes the college course was divided so that a student could elect an English or a scientific major, but there was no free choice of subjects. Many schools had whole programs or courses such as "manual training or commercial," for the terminal student; many studied the "English" course even if they had no plans for higher education. A few high schools had specialized vocational courses and some offered preparation for teaching. Physical education, art, music, and religion were included in the subjects offered by many high schools at the end of the nineteenth century. There was very little standardization. Some high schools offered as a four-year course what others gave in one semester or one year.

Standardizing Associations and the NEA. The United States had developed a large number of secondary schools. Many difficulties arose concerning the subjects of the curriculum, the length of time spent on each subject, and the quality of the instruction. Associations of standardization were created to deal with these issues. They also considered the preparation of teachers, the length of the school year, libraries, physical facilities, and graduation requirements. The New England Association of Colleges and Secondary Schools was founded in 1789. It was followed by the Middle Atlantic States Association (1892), the North Central Association (1894), the Association of College and Preparatory Schools of the Southern States (1895), and the Northwest Association of Secondary and Higher Schools in 1918. All of these organizations had the purpose of improving and making standard the offerings of various secondary schools and some colleges.

In 1857, forty-three leaders from ten state teachers' associations organized the National Teachers' Association in Philadelphia. This organization merged with the National Association of School Superintendents and the American Normal School Association to form the NEA in 1870. The National Education Association held an annual convention and published reports dealing with all aspects of education. Later, it became involved in defining the functions and standards for schools at all levels. Congress granted a charter to the NEA in 1905.

Committee of Ten. Confusion over standards in secondary schools, curriculum issues, and the argument between "modernists" and "traditionalists" caused the National Education Association to take action in 1892. In that year the NEA appointed a Committee of Ten to examine the high school curriculum and to make recommendations about methods, standards, and programs. Commissioner W. T. Harris and Harvard president Charles W. Eliot were well-known members of the Committee. There were four other college presidents, two headmasters, one professor, and one high school administrator, but no high school teachers. College interests dominated in the Committee of Ten, and the report was a bastion of educational conservatism.

One of the major weaknesses of the report of the Committee was that it based its findings on the psychology of mental discipline. The assumption was made that all subjects for general education had equal value for training the powers of the mind, such as expression, memory, reasoning, and observation. At a time when faculty psychology and mental discipline were already under attack, the Committee of Ten held that all its recommended subjects were of equal value for building sound mental habits in children. There were subcommittees on Latin, Greek, English, modern languages, mathematics, physical sciences, biological sciences, history, and geography. These subjects represented vested interests and were given support by the Committee, but vocational and commercial courses were largely ignored. In every case, the purpose of studying a subject was held to be mental discipline and exercise of the powers of the mind. It was also held that any recommended subject which was studied for one period each day, five days each week for a year was equal to any other recommended subject studied for the same length of time.

The Committee of Ten influenced the Committee on College Entrance Requirements (1895) and the subsequent work of the Carnegie Foundation for the Advancement of Teaching. The result was the establishment of the standard unit of credit for high school subjects (Carnegie unit), the support of traditional subjects and faculty psychology, and the limitation of any new or innovative high school programs. The Committee of Ten recommended intensive study of a few subjects for long periods of time in the high schools. It supported an eight-year elementary school followed by a four-year high school. No special subjects or methods were recommended for students who expected to terminate their formal education with high school graduation.

Accreditation.   The NEA Committee on College Entrance Requirements not only defined units of study in secondary schools but also recommended a set of constant or core subjects to be taken by all students. In 1902, the North Central Association set up a Committee on Unit Courses which required fifteen units for high school graduation. For college entrance, the Committee recommended at least three units of English and two of mathematics. Those recommendations became standard requirements in accreditation for all high schools. A College Entrance Examination Board was also established.

Cardinal Principles.   In 1918, a Commission on the Reorganization of Secondary Education was appointed by the NEA. This Commission recognized the high schools as instruments for social integration and building values. It warned against specialized schools which would divide the population of students and supported the idea of a comprehensive secondary school offering a variety of subjects and courses.

While providing some theoretical basis for the later development of a truly comprehensive secondary school, the Commission is best known for issuing its seven Cardinal Principles of Secondary Education. These became standard objectives for teachers, school boards, and administrators. They were:

1. health
2. command of fundamental processes
3. worthy home membership
4. vocation
5. citizenship
6. worthy use of leisure time
7. ethical character

Obviously, these principles could serve as a guide for curriculum and methodology, but they did not fill the need for a carefully articulated educational philosophy. The meaning of each principle may be interpreted in a variety of ways.

Rapid growth of high schools continued even though most of those before 1920 were noncomprehensive and strictly college preparatory in curriculum. By 1900, the public high schools were almost all coeducational and more than half of the students were girls.

In the early decades of the twentieth century, high schools doubled in enrollment every ten years, until they became common schools in fact as well as name.

Reorganization.   Public high schools retained the same general characteristics and organizational structure well into the twentieth century. In addition to a principal and his staff, the schools usually had departmental divisions with a chairman or "head" for each major program area or department.

Charles W. Eliot was an enthusiastic supporter of electives both in colleges and in high schools. He was one of the first to suggest a new school organization in order to provide more choice for high school students. Basically, Eliot wanted to extend the high school courses downward into elementary education. G. Stanley Hall, author of the first book on adolescents and no friend of Eliot's proposal, felt that reorganization was necessary to meet the needs of older elementary pupils who were no longer children. Others believed that the elementary and high schools did not provide a smooth transition from childhood to young adult life. It was felt that the opportunity for advanced elementary education of a general sort as well as some industrial and commercial training should be provided outside the senior high school. The Committee on College Entrance Requirements had recommended the division of elementary and secondary schools into six-year blocks, and the Committee of Ten had considered reorganization of some type.

As a result of these and other suggestions, junior high schools were created in Columbus, Ohio and Berkeley, California in 1909. Other cities soon followed, and the junior high school became a common institution in the United States after 1930. Typically, the elementary school was reduced to six years with junior and senior high schools requiring six years together. This 6-3-3 plan was not always used; some schools retained a four-year high school and used a 6-2-4 system. Reorganization is still in process today with many schools experimenting with a 4-4-4 or other "middle school" plans. The junior high school stressed socialization, guidance, individual differences, and survey or exploratory courses of a general nature.

VOCATIONAL AND INDUSTRIAL EDUCATION

The history of vocational education spans a long period of time in America. Apprenticeship was first used for vocational training when literary and religious education was the only prerogative of the school, but by 1820, a few mechanics' institutes for technical instruction were found in eastern cities. Worcester Polytechnic Institute was opened in 1868, and there were some manual labor schools built along lines suggested by the European educators Pestalozzi and Fellenberg. Manual training demonstrations were given in Philadelphia in 1876. Some cities had manual and vocational courses in high schools by 1890.

Shop work of various kinds replaced manual training in many high schools, but some secondary schools were designated as manual training high schools with no college preparatory courses. The vocational value of shop work was considered part of general education and special trade training was avoided in favor of mechanical principles. Students learned general skills on the transfer-of-training theory rather than how to make specific articles. The need for skilled workers and the desire for high school education for those not bound for college caused the manual training movement to gain speed after 1880. Columbia University began training teachers for manual training classes, and an industrial education association was organized in 1884.

Gradually the movement for training teachers of manual arts spread through the universities. Some labor leaders feared that industrial education would develop a surplus of cheap trained labor, but labor generally approved of industrial and vocational education. In general, manufacturers were also in support of this movement, but the opposition from traditional educators with classical backgrounds was more difficult to overcome.

Smith-Hughes Act.   The vocational school movement continued to grow from 1907 to 1917, receiving its greatest boost in the latter year when the federal Smith-Hughes Act was passed. This law provided federal aid for the states by paying vocational teachers' salaries in the high schools and aiding teacher training institutions in the education of such teachers. The states were required to match the federal grant on a dollar-for-dollar basis. In an effort to provide aid for the child trying to make a choice between vocational subjects, the Vocation Bureau and Breadwinner's Institute was established in 1909. Vocational and manual training also received support from new experiments and theories in education. John Dewey attracted attention by insisting that children learn through activities. His book *School and Society* made this point in 1899. New interest in psychology led to the beginning of professional guidance for students in industrial and vocational schools. Guidance developed slowly, but the first counseling services were offered in the vocational high schools.

Demand for practical vocational skills and scientific information was especially great among the farmers of the nation. Farmers' Institutes started in 1854 and led to an interest in agricultural education on both the high school and the college levels. Colleges which resulted from the Morrill Acts of 1862 and 1890, gave college status to agriculture and the mechanical arts. Demonstration farms, agricultural experiment stations, and training for improvement of agricultural techniques were provided by these colleges and by the Department of Agriculture which was established in 1862. The Hatch Act of 1887 provided federal funds for agricultural experiments. In 1914 Congress passed the Smith-Lever Act which created agricultural extension programs for farmers and led to vocational agriculture courses and 4-H clubs. Many high school students took advantage of vocational work offered because of federal funding, but often vocational agriculture was the only practical course offered in rural secondary schools. There was no attempt to offer general federal aid to public schools until after World War II.

PAROCHIAL AND PRIVATE EDUCATION

Obtaining exact figures on school enrollments before 1900 is difficult because neither schools nor reporting techniques were standardized. Public and private sectarian schools were often reported together as late as 1870. While the states of the West and South were behind those of the North and East in percentages of children enrolled in public schools, it is clear that very rapid growth in all states took place between 1860 and 1900. In the latter year, about ninety percent of the American secondary school students attended public high schools.

Catholic doctrine has always insisted that the state should have only a secondary role in education while the parents and the Church have primary responsibility. Catholic schools existed in such areas as New Mexico, California, and Louisiana early in American history, but intolerance and discrimination prevented rapid growth on the eastern seaboard. In colonial America, only Pennsylvania allowed Catholics to conduct schools. The appointment of Father John Carroll as "Superior of Missions in the United States" and guarantee of religious freedom in the Bill of Rights provided a foundation for Catholic education in America. With the large influx of Irish Catholics during the first half of the nineteenth century, interest in parochial schools increased. By 1840 Catholics had created seventy-five elementary parochial schools, twenty-five high schools, and six colleges. Many Catholic children obviously attended public schools, but there was great controversy over Protestant creeds and the use of the King James version of the Bible in public schools. Catholic children were often punished if they objected to non-Catholic religious practices. In 1854 the Maine Supreme Court rejected a Catholic plea to exclude the Bible from the public school curriculum, although the Ohio Supreme Court upheld a similar Catholic plea in 1872.

The Third Plenary Council of Baltimore in 1884 required all parishes to provide schools for Catholic youngsters. As a result, Catholic parochial schools increased in number to about 3,000 in 1884. Secondary Catholic schools were developed through Jesuit leadership partly in an effort to train boys for the priesthood. Parish high schools were largely an extension of the parochial school. They emphasized Latin, literature, grammar, and religion. Few if any vocational courses were offered. By 1910, there were more than 300 Catholic high schools in operation in the United States.

The largest number of non-Catholic parochial schools were founded by the Lutheran Church. There were also schools created by Quakers, Jews, and other religious groups. Much smaller in numbers than the Catholic schools, these sectarian efforts, nevertheless, provided alternative educational opportunities for students in many parts of the nation. An interesting discussion of these issues appears in *Great School Wars* by Diane Ravitch.

Oregon Case. Bitter public reaction against parochial schools has existed in the United States for many years. Discrimination has been expressed in many ways, but direct efforts have been made to outlaw parochial schools. The most famous case occurred in the state of Oregon in 1925 and has remained unchallenged. The Oregon legislature passed a law which required all children to attend public schools through the eighth grade. The Society of Sisters of the Holy Names of Jesus and Mary and the Hill Academy brought suit against Governor Pierce in an effort to keep their schools. While the Oregon Supreme Court upheld the state law, the Supreme Court of the United

States declared the action unconstitutional. It held that the state has a right to inspect and regulate private and parochial schools, but that the state does not have a monopoly on education.

In addition to religious schools, a number of private schools and academies continued to operate. These were sometimes military schools or elite "college prep" institutions for wealthy children. Military academies declined after the second world war but other kinds of private schools grew rapidly in number.

HIGHER EDUCATION

Colleges and Universities.   Higher education had a steady growth during this period and as a result of the Morrill Act of 1862, almost every state created a land-grant college. Industry and scientific agriculture were emphasized by these institutions, but they were by no means confined to such subjects. The land-grant schools grew slowly at first because they lacked the prestige of liberal arts colleges. However, they had the support of science and were powerful as a democratizing influence. Nine of these colleges developed into state universities, and many added colleges of engineering, home economics, and education. The Second Morrill Act of 1890 made fifteen thousand dollars annually available to each of the original institutions, which caused vast expansion. By 1918, many state universities became major institutions of higher education. Efforts to develop private colleges met with limited success. A high percentage of the sectarian colleges founded before the Civil War closed by World War I, but others were created. Some degree-granting colleges were really only secondary schools, although there were high quality denominational colleges as well as good secular universities.

New University Model.   The most significant development in higher education during this period was the establishment of graduate programs based on the German example. Early supporters of this idea included Henry P. Tappan (later president of the University of Michigan) and Louis Agassiz who developed science programs at Harvard. It was not, however, until Johns Hopkins University opened in 1876 that a real scientific research university existed in America.

Johns Hopkins was a wealthy Baltimore businessman who provided a large endowment for a university which would include a medical school and hospital. Much of the credit for the success of Johns Hopkins University goes to its first president, Daniel Coit Gilman (1831–1908). Gilman was a Yale graduate who became president of the University of California before being selected for Johns Hopkins. He was a keen administrator and a careful judge of talent. Gilman selected professors who had not yet reached national status, but who had demonstrated their potential ability. The new institution had a graduate school aimed at creating new knowledge and supporting scientific investigation rather than merely transferring information and skills. It required graduate students to do research as a regular part of their program and provided the necessary laboratory equipment and other support. Inquiry, observation, freedom to seek truth without institutional restrictions, and high quality scholarship became standard at Johns Hopkins. The idea that faculty members should do research and publish the results of their work also found favor there.

Professional Schools.

Johns Hopkins was the first American university to have a medical college with full-time professors. In the post-Civil War period, professional schools rapidly replaced the private practices of "reading law," apprentice doctors, and self-education for ministers. In 1899, there were 532 reported professional schools operating in the nation, about half of which were departments in colleges and universities. The practice at Johns Hopkins of requiring college graduation for admission to the medical school was rare, and numerous professional programs were offered for short periods of time. Low standards due to a lack of state supervision were common until after 1900 when regulations began to increase. The growth of graduate schools had a major effect on professional schools because of the training they offered to college and professional school teachers. Graduate departments and professional schools began to differentiate between universities and liberal arts colleges, even when such colleges referred to themselves as universities.

Curriculum Changes.

Traditions in education are very strong so that change normally meets with great resistance. College faculties have always been very conservative with regard to altering the curriculum. Nevertheless, colleges did begin to expand their offerings in the period under consideration, in spite of great faculty reluctance. Science and research made the addition of many courses necessary, although most colleges merely added the new programs without altering or eliminating the old. Agriculture, mechanical arts, and military science gained a foothold in higher education because of the Morrill Acts. The sixty-five colleges and universities established under these acts by 1900 obviously had a profound effect on the curriculum. Massachusetts Institute of Technology began instruction in 1865 with theoretical support for scientific and practical subjects provided by Herbert Spencer and T. H. Huxley. Darwin's *Origin of Species* (1859) caused a great deal of interest in the intellectual world, and evolution was soon discussed by such scholars as John Fiske at Harvard. The tycoons of the "gilded age" gave substantial gifts to higher education, and in return, they influenced the curriculum. Practical, utilitarian, and business courses often had the support of philanthropists, as did conservative views of social change and classical economics.

Before the Civil War, it was unusual to allow students free selection of courses or programs in colleges. Although Ticknor had experimented with electives, the real development of the college elective system came when Charles W. Eliot was president of Harvard. By 1894, Harvard required only French or German, English composition, and some work in physics and chemistry; all other courses could be selected by the students. Educational conservatives bitterly opposed the elective system, but leading universities soon adopted it to some degree, although a core of "disciplinary" courses was often required. The major effect of the elective system was to break the hold classics had on higher education and to allow the introduction of popular modern subjects such as history, sociology, psychology, economics, and the sciences. Breadth of the curriculum and the freedom to examine various theories or ideas became part of the university ideal.

While coeducational colleges existed before the Civil War (Oberlin 1833, Antioch 1852, and Iowa 1856), their major development came between 1860 and 1920. By 1880, about half of the colleges and universities admitted women. Vassar, Smith, Wellesley, and Bryn Mawr were women's colleges which offered programs equivalent to colleges for men. Affiliated or "coordinate" colleges for women also were established, such as Radcliffe at Harvard. A wide curriculum was offered for women, but teaching was still the only career generally open to females in 1918.

SCHOOLS AND COLLEGES FOR MINORITY GROUPS

The adoption of the Fourteenth Amendment in 1868 gave black Americans citizenship, but few opportunities for higher education existed then. In 1826, the first college degree granted to a black student went to John Russwurm; only twenty-eight black college graduates were recorded before the Civil War. Northern colleges open to African Americans after 1860 found many ill prepared for college work because of the inadequate segregated public schools from which they came. Progress in literacy rates is clear, however, in the increase in the literacy of black Americans from ten percent in 1866 to over ninety percent in 1936. According to Edward Knight, 132 blacks received Ph.D. degrees in this same time period.

Black schools and colleges in the South developed through the efforts of educators like Booker T. Washington. Hampton Institute for Negro Higher Education had been established in Virginia in 1870 under the sponsorship of the American Missionary Association. Washington became a student there arriving on foot and with only fifty cents to his name. When Washington graduated in 1875, he was recommended by principal Samuel C. Armstrong as a teacher for a proposed black normal school at Tuskegee, Alabama. Under Washington, Tuskegee Normal and Industrial Institute became a model of black education, and its director a national figure. Washington received an honorary degree from Harvard University and became the recognized leader of black education. Realizing the attitudes of white Americans in the South, Washington agreed to a subservient role for blacks in return for practical and vocational education. His Atlanta compromise speech is a classic political concession. At Tuskegee, Washington stressed hard work, vocational skills, and economic advancement. He won wide support among whites in the South, and although his institute became a model for black colleges, his willingness to accept social discrimination has drawn much criticism. Washington always avoided the demand for social and political equality made by W. E. B. DuBois and his followers.

Minority education outside the South grew slowly but steadily during the period between the Civil War and the First World War. A few liberal colleges like Antioch admitted black students early, but discrimination was practiced in most areas of the nation. Numerous black Agricultural, Military, and Normal colleges were established with funds from the Second Morrill Act, and these colleges often included programs for teachers. Federal money was badly needed, and the black A., M., and N. schools soon became as important as Tuskegee and various church-related Black colleges. These colleges admitted Indians, Orientals, and other minority students. Numerous northern state universities were open to minorities, but the number actually admitted was small, due in part to entrance requirements which screened out graduates from the poor public schools. Public school segregation was maintained either legally or de facto almost everywhere.

Native American Schools. Most of the formal education provided for native Americans was through philanthropy or missionary efforts until the Office of Indian Affairs was opened in 1819. Thereafter, schools of various kinds were supported by government grants, although religious organizations continued to operate the majority of mission schools for Native Americans. A number of Native American scholars attended Hampton Institute, and in 1879, a Native American training school was authorized for Carlisle, Pennsylvania. Except for boarding schools on reservations and a few specific programs aimed at training for vocations, very little was done by federal or local government to meet the needs of education for Native Americans.

TEACHER EDUCATION

While colonial teachers were sometimes college graduates, there was nothing available to them which might be called professional training. Academies and female seminaries in the early national period often advertised pedagogical programs which consisted of a review of basic elementary subjects and some lectures on keeping school. It was long considered adequate for secondary teachers to have only a sound knowledge of their subject field without any training in psychology or methods of teaching.

The first normal schools were academically low level institutions, a problem that continued to exist until they were made into four-year colleges in the twentieth century. Early normal schools usually had some sort of practice teaching and a course in mental philosophy, but there was no sound theoretical foundation. Some private normal schools and academies for teachers offered programs with higher academic standards, but they also lacked a professional basis. Nevertheless, the growth of teacher education was rapid in the latter part of the nineteenth century. One hundred fourteen schools for teachers replied to an inquiry about programs and enrollments made by the United States Bureau of Education in 1871. At least 70 normal schools were receiving some state support in 1875. By 1900, there were 345 normal schools reported in the United States. Women outnumbered men in the state normal schools, while the sexes were about evenly divided in private schools for teachers. A great many students in normal schools already held teaching certificates, and most had some teaching experience before entering the program. Large numbers of teachers attended normal schools for short periods, but only about one third of the public school teachers were normal school graduates. Many normal school programs were offered for two years or less and usually were on the secondary school level. Most had meager equipment, insufficient support, poor facilities, and an underpaid staff.

Before World War I, however, these institutions began enlarging their curricula and requiring high school graduation for admission. Some, like Illinois State Normal, were able to erect expensive modern buildings and to develop college-level courses. Both the numbers of and quality of normal schools improved very rapidly in the last decades of the nineteenth century and the first decades of the twentieth. Nevertheless, fewer than half of the trained teachers that were needed to staff public schools were provided by normal schools, high school normal departments, academies, or college departments. District schools continued to be taught by underpaid young women with little or no education beyond elementary school and perhaps a summer institute.

Sheldon and the Oswego Movement.

A much better conceptual framework for the professional training of teachers was provided by Edward Sheldon. Sheldon became secretary of the Board of Education of Oswego, New York in 1853. He visited a number of cities in order to find ways of improving the schools, and in 1859 in Toronto, Sheldon came across a Pestalozzian program produced by the Home and Colonial Training Institution of London. Instruction there was based on charts, pictures, manuals, and objects developed by Charles and Elizabeth Mayo, who had been teachers in schools conducted by Pestalozzi.

Having purchased three hundred dollars' worth of materials and secured the services of Margaret E. M. Jones to demonstrate them, Sheldon proceeded to reform the Oswego schools along lines developed by Pestalozzi. The success was impressive, and in 1866, the New York legislature made Oswego a state normal school. Teachers flocked to the new program and Oswego soon became the most famous teacher-training institution in the United States. Graduates of the school found positions in various parts of the nation, so that the Oswego movement had influence far beyond New York.

Some of the improvement attributed to the Oswego movement came from the enthusiasm of Sheldon himself, but new techniques of learning and respect for the unique personality of the child were also important. Object teaching began with something familiar to the environment of the child and moved to an abstract description of the object. Geography was taught from the local community outward, until the whole nation and the world could be understood. Study and discipline through mutual understanding and respect were also stressed. Unfortunately, the term "object lesson" was also used by textbook companies who merely wanted to sell books, and some other normal schools made highly formalized lesson plans out of what the Oswego movement had intended to be flexible. Nevertheless, Oswego provided a new model of teacher education which included new principles, better psychology, creative methods, and an effort to understand how children learn.

University Departments of Education.   For many years pedagogy and teacher training were excluded from universities. Faculty members in the academic disciplines held all professional education in low esteem and many had only contempt for teacher training programs. In 1879, W. H. Payne, spurred on by the Kalamazoo case, was able to fill the first successful, permanent chair of pedagogy in the nation at the University of Michigan. President Barnard of Columbia was turned down by the trustees when he proposed a department of education in 1882. Instead, he assigned Nicholas Murray Butler to offer Saturday lectures for teachers. The interest was so great that over 2,000 teachers applied for Butler's lectures, but the trustees again refused to authorize a department of education or even a senior elective in pedagogy. Finally, Butler organized the New York College for the Training of Teachers. In 1892, that college was accepted as an affiliate of Columbia University under strong opposition.

Teacher education at the college level began at Washington College in Pennsylvania in 1831 and at New York University in 1832. The University of Iowa had a chair for didactics (education) in 1873. By 1900, professors of pedagogy were to be found in many universities, although sometimes only one professor constituted the whole department. Graduate work in education was offered by New York University in 1887. Starting about 1890, teacher training institutions tended to become degree-granting colleges which required secondary school graduation for admission. The scientific study of education and psychology came to be linked with certification. A body of educational theory slowly developed out of work done in education at universities and graduate schools. Nevertheless, the "normal school stigma" continued to plague departments of education. President Bok of Harvard has recently argued that good teachers will not be produced so long as pedagogy is regulated to the fringes of the universities.

DEVELOPMENT OF EDUCATIONAL PHILOSOPHY

American educational theory was dominated by theology and philosophical idealism before 1900. Contributions to pragmatism were made by William James, Charles Peirce, and John Dewey before World War I, but their influence was much greater during the progressive era of the 1930s. It was so difficult even to provide the rudiments of education to the whole population that little effort was made to define educational goals, to equate theory with psychological principles, or to work out the logical educational positions. Once schools were established, a host of new educational demands were made, and many began to debate the proper role of education. The early influence of Rousseau, Pestalozzi, Froebel, and other European philosophers continued to be felt, but American educational theory also began to develop.

Harris.   William T. Harris, who developed a public kindergarten in 1873 as part of the school system in St. Louis, Missouri, was superintendent of schools there from 1867 to 1880 and United States Commissioner of Education from 1889 to 1906. He was one of the best known school administrators in America, and his ideas had wide influence throughout the nation. Harris was philosophically an idealist, a follower of the German philosopher Hegel, and a traditionalist in education. He believed education should emphasize the cultural subjects and prepare children for harmony with the absolute order of the universe as well as for life in an industrial nation. He accepted some of the methods of Pestalozzi, but was basically opposed to the manual training movement, science, and materialism. As commissioner, a member of the major committees of the NEA, and a leader in the National Herbart Society, his influence was very great. Harris was the great spokesman for the idealistic-traditional theory of education.

Parker.   Quite a different educational position was taken by Francis W. Parker, who was principal of schools in Carrollton, Illinois, before the Civil War. His school career was interrupted by the conflict, in which he served as a colonel in the Union forces. Parker studied in Germany where he became familiar with the practices of Pestalozzi and Froebel. He returned to America to become superintendent of schools in Quincy, Massachusetts, and later was head of the Cook County Normal School in Chicago. Parker was a democratic individualist with a practical outlook. He followed Pestalozzi closely with regard to respect for the creative activity of the child. Parker experimented with many kinds of school programs, including the core curriculum which attempted to relate subjects of the curriculum through such interrelated studies as history and geography. Parker provided the background for the work of John Dewey and the progressives.

The total impact of Pestalozzi and Froebel was relatively light although kindergartens did develop and university scholars began to study the child as an individual. Public education changed very little before the American Herbartian movement started around 1890.

Herbart.   Johann F. Herbart was responsible for a much greater revolution in American education than any previous European thinker had been. Herbart held that the aim of education was attainment of good moral character, which could be acquired only through the process of analyzing the social interests of man to discover ideals appropriate for education. The first step in character realization was the "many sidedness of interest." Although he used the word interest, Herbart was really referring to a stimulus to learning. He once said that the person who lays hold of information, and because of that information reaches out for more, takes "interest" in it. In the study of history and literature, Herbart saw a core for the curriculum which could encompass or could be co-related with all other subjects. His principles of co-relation and concentration, by which he meant relation with emphasis at the core, became central to his doctrine. Despite Herbart's insistence on the social and moral aims of education, he took an intellectual approach to the learning process. He also developed a psychology which is still of some value today.

Herbart was an associationist; that is, he believed that we have to account for every new idea on the basis of ideas already in the mind, and hence we must consciously relate or associate new ideas with previous experiences. For Herbart there could never be a totally new idea. He believed that we receive impressions to the conscious mind (presentation). These presentations are then associated with other ideas which lie together in masses in the subconscious part of the mind. When a new idea in the mind is related, it is transferred from the conscious to the subconscious mind and becomes part of an "apperceptive mass." The idea will not appear in the conscious mind again until it is needed to clarify some new presentation. Herbart's own psychology was not rigid, and his insistence upon the mind as a unity tended to break down the older faculty psychology, which understood the mind to be divided into separate faculties or powers.

American Herbartianism. Herbart's followers in America used his insistence upon association and interests to develop a very rigid educational program. This program came to be known as the Five Formal Steps of Teaching and Learning. They were: (1) preparation, in which old ideas useful in learning new materials are called to the learner's mind; (2) presentation, or the actual giving of the new material; (3) association, in which new material is compared with and related to the old; (4) generalization, in which rules, definitions, or general principles are drawn from specific cases; and (5) application, in which general principles are given meaning by reference to specific examples and practical situations.

These Herbartian steps were made popular by Charles De Garmo, Charles McMurry, and Frank McMurry, who were among the early leaders of the American Herbartian Association. It must be remembered that during the late 1800s, most teachers were largely without training, and there was no rational philosophy of education. The formal steps of the American Herbartianists filled a void in educational theory and hence the influence of Herbart through his American followers became dominant in this country in the 1890s. Unfortunately, the set methods of the followers of Herbart led to a "lock-step" in American education; the same subjects were taught in the same way using the same methods and the same textbooks in every public school from Boston to Berkeley. The beneficial part of this uniformity was that it became possible for children to transfer from one school to another without a change in curriculum or loss of time, but the respect for individuality, new ideas, and creativity, which had been so much in the theories of Froebel and Pestalozzi, were largely lost.

Protest Against Rigid Systems. One of the first to raise a cry against the rigid lock-step school was John Dewey. His influence was first felt in the closing years of the nineteenth century and his importance increased considerably during the first three decades of the twentieth century. Dewey continued to write until the 1950s, but his greatest amount of influence on education came in the 1930s, when the Progressive Education Association was at the height of its popularity. Dewey felt that Herbart and his followers had emphasized formal methods to the extreme, and that they failed to account for natural growth and individual differences. He attacked schools for being antidemocratic and the curriculum for being subject-centered. For Dewey, education must be part of life itself.

Other developments also contributed to the changing climate of opinion out of which new educational theories were developed. In 1859, Charles Darwin published his *Origin of Species*, a book which set off the explosive theory of evolution. Scientific evolution and social Darwinism were theories that challenged the conceptions of man and the universe held by conservative educators. Evolutionary principles contributed to the formation of the philosophy of pragmatism by Charles Peirce and William James. Pragmatism emphasized the practical questions of how we can understand and control the world instead of the metaphysical question of how we can know reality. Herbert Spencer and others applied the theory of evolution to society in order to explain the existence of social classes and social institutions. Resulting studies in sociology altered traditional conceptions of humanity and opened new windows through which to view education. Evolutionary science became part of the curriculum in universities, but it created an issue in public schools where it was often banned. The conflict of religion and science culminated in the Scopes Trial over the teaching of evolution in Dayton, Tennessee, in 1925.

Schools continued to grow in number before World War I. Children tended to remain in school longer, teachers received more training, and education became a subject for university study. New scientific subjects were added to the high schools, and public high schools became the standard American secondary schools. Child study and psychology led to new concepts of method and new interest in the individual child.

THEN TO NOW

Events leading up to the American Civil War and the conflict itself bear a strong relationship to numerous conditions in the modern era. Extremely bitter sectional and ideological arguments not only caused the Civil War but also altered the attitudes of people for generations. Although the union survived, negative feelings about Civil War issues continued to dominate political life well into the twentieth century. Social and educational problems created by the freeing of slaves plagued the nation while the burden carried by the impoverished South caused a very low level of public schooling for both races. Black struggles for equality, reflected by the militant self-help and return-to-Africa movement of Marcus Garvey in 1917 or the civil rights activism of Dr. Martin Luther King Jr. in the 1960s, may be traced to this era. No struggle divided and alienated the American people like the Civil War until the outbreak of the conflict in Vietnam.

American involvement in Southeast Asia during the 1960s and 1970s caused caustic criticism of national policy, especially on university campuses. Like the Civil War, Vietnam raised ugly moral issues, created an erosion of patriotism, and shook the very foundations of the national culture. Just as the Civil War closed schools, promoted illiteracy in most of the South, and led to a system of schools segregated by race, Vietnam also created a major educational crisis. The war caused violence in colleges, alienation of students from the values of their parents, and the withdrawal of financial support to educational institutions. While the two world wars and the Korea action had significant educational influences, only the Civil War and the conflict in Vietnam caused fundamental rifts in the very core of American culture. Tracing the modern issues over desegregation of schools to the Civil War period is easy but the total impact of the Vietnam era on education and the American culture may not be known for generations to come. The quick victory in the Persian Gulf War of 1990-1991 provided some counterbalance to the Vietnam episode, although the difficulty in determining America's role in foreign conflicts such as Somalia, Bosnia, and Haiti continue to be a challenge.

Intellectual and cultural historians argue that life conditions have major effects on the attitudes, values and beliefs of all people. We need to identify the most significant forces that shape values and concepts about the good life for each generation.

Those who grew up in the 1920s held establishment values. They were influenced by World War I, prohibition, and the Model T Ford. Young people were interested in gin and jazz but close family ties and patriotism dominated the nation. Education remained conservative although the Scopes trial, over the teaching of evolution in high schools, created a major issue. By the 1930s the economic crash had taken place and the nation was in the Great Depression. There was mass unemployment, soup lines, and social unrest. Radical economic solutions including socialism were suggested and Franklin Roosevelt became popular with his New Deal. Great emphasis was placed on the value of the dollar and those who grew up in the 1930s are still very security minded. This was the age of progressive education and radical school reform.

At the beginning of the 1940s, the dominant interest was keeping America safe from the Germans and the Japanese. World War II touched every family while patriotism permeated the culture. This was an age of working women, geographic mobility, rationing, and support for the armed forces. People became used to the idea of scarcity and waited for better times when peace would be restored. Education turned back to the basics and the G.I. Bill increased enrollment in colleges. When the war ended, Americans bought all of the things they could not have in a wartime economy. Fifty million TV sets were sold in America, and children began growing up with Howdy Doody and Captain Kangaroo. Crew cuts gave way to longer hair, children were materialistically indulged, and the rock and roll age was personified by Elvis Presley. School desegregation began in the 1950s, and Martin Luther King gained a great following. The Korean conflict was considered a great tragedy, but it did not draw the patriotic support common in the second world war. People growing up at this time were influenced by hedonism, materialism, affluence, and the mass media.

The 1960s saw rapid economic growth, the space program, computers, and Vietnam. Alternative life styles were manifest in the hippie sub-culture while campus rebellion shocked conservative Americans. Those who grew up in this period recall the bitterness over the Vietnam War and the conflict between generations. It was an age of assassination but also of continued financial growth and affluence. Education focused on school integration, equal opportunity, and the needs of the culturally different child. By the end of the decade, deep-rooted value conflicts had divided Americans to a degree quite similar to the era of the Civil War.

By 1970, inflation and a weaker economy were evident. Many people began to fear a return of the conditions of the Great Depression of the 1930s. Some twenty million mothers entered the work force in order to improve family income. The energy crisis was taken seriously and there were concerns about environmental deterioration. Richard Nixon and Watergate caused the erosion of respect for government, while the people began to distrust motives of oil companies and other industrial corporations. Music, the mass media, fast foods, and automobiles were major interests of the young. Drug abuse and alcoholism became widespread among students. Educators concentrated on computer-assisted instruction, a relevant curriculum, and compensatory education for the culturally deprived.

History shows that following wars and periods of social conflict there is often a conservative reaction. At the beginning of the 1980s, such a movement developed throughout American society. There was a demand for an end to social reconstruction through legislation, relaxation of regulations on industry, and opposition to spending for welfare. Education moved back to basics with major interest focused on tests of accountability and training for jobs. Declining economic strength, continued inflation, competition for jobs, scarcity of energy and natural resources, and concern about world peace were major interests. Meanwhile, rapid advances in technological invention and especially in communications continue to alter the environment and to create new life conditions.

Approaching mid-decade of the 1990s, economic cycles continued to bedevil America as an accumulation of the national debt took an ever-greater share of the nation's wealth. Working toward reducing the national debt, while maintaining and augmenting important social programs for the young and the old, became a major focus of Congress and President Clinton. Seeking to reduce the heavy debt load of the 1980s, business and industry downsized and worked to find ways to become more productive and efficient while a major shift from defense spending caused dislocation in employment. The efforts for job creation was a constant goal of the Clinton Administration.

There is a strong tendency in America for each new generation to reject the ideas and the values of the generation just past. John Dewey and the progressives rebelled against the lock-step schools and the rigid systems of the followers of Herbart. The counter culture did not accept the materialism and the need of security so characteristic of the depression era and the period of affluence following World War II. Such beliefs were scorned in turn by the youth of the 1970s and early 1980s. It is also probably true that change in basic value orientation takes place more rapidly in an age of accelerating economic and technological invention than in a more stable environment. If this is the case, present conservative trends in American culture cannot be expected to continue for very many years. The early 1990s saw increasing social, political, and economic fragmentation as individuals, communities, business, and industry sought either to maintain or expand their share of an ever-smaller state and federal budget. Litigation increased in all economic, social, political, religious, and educational institutions during the period. Collegiality gave way to adversarial relationships.

The Civil War was a time of social and ethical conflict. When it ended, not only had the old South disappeared but the whole of American society was altered. The black revolution and the demand for civil rights evolved slowly from the Civil War to the 1950s, but certainly they began in the aftermath of that conflict. Likewise, the whole of American society was changed by the turmoil of the Vietnam era. Changes of this magnitude necessarily have an impact on education and the socialization of the next generation. Periods of revolutionary conflict and social change may be followed by conservative reactions but the culture is never restored to what it was before the conflict. Rapid, though uneven transformation of American society has been evident since the 1860s. American values and the culture of the people can never again be what they were in the antebellum South or the period before the Vietnam conflict.

This is also the case in the rest of the world. The student rebellion in China and the struggle to achieve human rights altered the values of that nation for the future. Events in eastern Europe and the Soviet Union vastly changed perceptions of the Communist Bloc and the concept of the cold war. By 1990, the social and political revolutions in nations like Poland, Hungary, and Romania had altered the nature of Europe and changed global social relationships. These events have great impact upon the world that Americans will occupy in the future. Education must always prepare students for change if it is to be successful.

Educators and politicians, during the 1990s, addressed growing value conflicts through sensitivity training programs and a commitment to moral, ethical, and character education at all levels of the educational system. At the same time home- and private-schooling expanded in part due to the many religious and secular value conflicts in society represented in curriculum content which has been distressful to some parents.

BIBLIOGRAPHY

Beale, Howard. *A History of Freedom of Teaching in American Schools.* New York: Octagon Books, 1974.

Butts, Freeman. *The Education of the West: A Formative Chapter in the History of Civilization.* New York: McGraw-Hill, 1973.

Counts, George. *Secondary Education and Industrialism.* Cambridge, MA: Harvard University Press, 1929.

Cubberley, Ellwood. *Readings in Public Education in the United States.* Boston: Houghton Mifflin, 1934.

Kandel, Isaac. *History of Secondary Education.* Boston: Houghton Mifflin, 1930.

Karier, Clarence J. *Shaping the American Educational Experience: 1990 to the Present.* New York: Free Press, Macmillan, 1975.

Knight, Edgar, and Clifton Hall. *Readings in American Educational History.* New York: Appleton-Century-Crofts, 1951.

Mayer, Frederick. *A History of Educational Thought.* 3d ed. New York: Merrill/Macmillan, 1974.

Nassaw, David. *Schooled to Order.* New York: Oxford University Press, 1979.

Rudolph, Frederick. *The American College and University: A History.* New York: Vintage Books, 1962.

Sheldon, Edward. *Autobiography.* New York: Ives-Butler, 1911.

Vaughn, Preston. *Schools for All: The Blacks and Public Education in the South, 1865–1877.* Lexington, KY: University of Kentucky Press, 1974.

Warren, Donald. *To Enforce Education: A History of the Founding Years of the United States Office of Education*. Detroit, MI: Wayne State University Press, 1974.

Washington, Booker T. *Up From Slavery: An Autobiography*. New York: Doubleday, 1938.

Weinberg, Meyer. *W. E. B. DuBois: A Reader*. New York: Harper and Row, 1970: 147.

Westerhoff, John. *McGuffey and His Readers: Piety, Morality, and Education in Nineteenth Century America*. Nashville, TN: Abingdon Press, 1978.

DEVELOPMENTS IN MORE RECENT AMERICAN EDUCATION 1918–PRESENT

Give me a dozen healthy infants, well-formed, and my own specified world to bring them up in and I'll guarantee to take anyone at random and train him to become any type of specialist I might select—doctor, lawyer, artist, merchant-chief, and yes, even a beggar-man and thief, regardless of his talents, penchants, tendencies, abilities, vocations and race of his ancestors.

John B. Watson

Several volumes could be written on the subject of educational expansion, change, and controversy since the First World War. The most obvious feature has been the tremendous growth in the numbers of students, teachers, and facilities at all levels. Secondary education grew during this period until it became standard for almost all children, just as the elementary school had done in the previous century. Higher education expanded, especially in the years following the Second World War, so that some kind of college or university experience was enjoyed by more than two-thirds of all American high school graduates. Many modern cities in the United States now contain more individuals engaged in formal schooling than could have been found in the entire colonial area at any one time. Sophisticated training offered by industry, early childhood education (both public and private), the federal government, and the mass media are illustrative of agencies and techniques now active in education which are not so significant in earlier times. Education is now big business in terms of money spent on training teachers, using physical plants, developing materials, and serving students.

This magnification of the educational enterprise raised new issues concerning the relationship of the school and the society. Advances in technology, the fluid social order, economic depressions, recessions and recovery, wars both hot and cold, and conflict over the meaning of democracy led to demands for a re-evaluation of educational aims.

World War I	Great Depression	World War II
1919 Progressive Education Association	1932 New Deal Educational Programs	1941 Military Training for National Defense
1925 Oregon Case Guaranteed Right of Private Schools	1930-38 Eight Year Study Confirmed Value of Progressive Schools	1944 G.I. Bill for College Tuition
		1945 UNESCO
1930 School Year Became 172 Days and All States Had Compulsory Attendance		1954 Brown v. Board of Education in Topeka

MAJOR EDUCATIONAL CHANGES

Integration of all Americans into a national community was a goal of such early leaders as Mann and Barnard. Schools were viewed as social ladders for individual and group improvement and as the means for Americanizing immigrants. Since World War II, the civil rights movement, and the black revolution, much more attention has been given to the educational problems of children from various social, economic, religious, ethnic, and racial backgrounds. Desegregation, helping the culturally disadvantaged, and meeting social needs in urban centers have become major goals of American education. Schools have made great strides, but large numbers of children are still excluded from equal educational opportunity, and national unity through social integration has not been realized. Much current educational theory centers upon the role of the school in solving major problems of the culture and upon the kind of education which will be required to prepare the young for meeting the challenges of an uncertain future.

Among the more significant changes in education during the last half century were the following: (a) a broader educational philosophy with social as well as individual objectives, illustrated by progressive education and the social reconstruction movements; (b) a new psychology and more sophisticated learning theories, which led to new teaching methods and curricula based on the needs of children and society; (c) new areas of educational concern such as vocational guidance, scientific testing, and special education for the handicapped and the gifted; (d) reorganization of schools to include junior high schools, junior colleges, night schools, correspondence courses and the like, as well as an explosion of graduate education, changes in graduate and undergraduate delivery systems to include Saturday and week-end classes, on-site classes in industry and business,

Cold War	Vietnam Conflict	
1957 Sputnik	1965 Head Start	1979 Secretary of Education as a Cabinet Position
1958 NDEA	Higher Education Act	
1964 Economic Opportunity Act	Rebellion on College Campuses	1981 Education Consolidation and Improvement Act
	1967 Bilingual Education Act	1983 A Nation At Risk
1965 Elementary and Secondary Education Act	1975 Public Law 94–142 Provided Education for the Handicapped	1990 Massive Educational Reforms in Most States

external degree programs for individuals who cannot take time off from work for further education, home study television classes with proposals for three-year bachelor's degree programs, and college credit for work experience; (e) new emphasis on health, welfare, improved buildings and equipment, and the relationship between schools and the culture; (f) enormous increase in attendance at all levels and an extension of the years of formal schooling for the average student; (g) an extension and improvement of teacher training and the scientific study of education; and (h) the impact of cultural changes such as the mass media of communications, research conducted by private organizations, development of Internet, Bitnet, e-mail, multimedia systems which combine telephone, computer, entertainment, services, research queries, into information superhighways, and the increased role of the federal government in educational affairs. Perhaps the most difficult problem for educators in the United States today is how to provide varied, realistic, general, and individual education for all children and produce the experts necessary for an industrial democracy at the same time. Can we really be equal and excellent too?

Social, Political, Economic Influence.   Many of these changes, and others less dramatic, began in the nineteenth century and were developed in recent decades; but there were also innovations which came about as a result of economic and social changes during the two world wars. Older concerns with physical expansion gave way to new problems of technological discovery and scientific development. Reforms in government pursued legal measures to prevent the waste and exploitation of dwindling natural resources. Contact with the sophisticated culture of Europe during World War I, and the economic crisis which followed the conflict altered many of America's basic conceptions. Woodrow Wilson's failure to persuade America to join the League of Nations, and the isolationism, fatalism, and inflation of the post-war era did not destroy European influences.

However, the decade-long depression which started in 1929 shook American optimism and altered the role of government in economic affairs. When Franklin Roosevelt became president in 1932, the immense task of economic rebuilding began. The New Deal program attempted to place eleven million unemployed persons in various types of meaningful jobs and to establish emergency measures to solve the economic crisis. It was not, however, until the beginning of World War II that the United States found its way out of the depression and into a new era of war boom and post-war prosperity.

The Second World War caused a rapid increase in the rate of technological revolution and stimulated American interest in the international situation, thus leading to an ideological struggle against communism which culminated in the cold war of the 1950s. The impact of space achievements resulted not only in federal support for the advancement of science, mathematics, and foreign languages in the schools but also in efforts to locate and train the exceptional pupil who could be a leader in scientific and military development. Under Truman and Eisenhower, programs were developed which provided a greater amount of social security and a higher rate of employment, but the nation was faced again with a need for protection against external aggression. America became involved in the United Nations (chartered in 1945), and American foreign policy was dominated by a need to develop peaceful co-existence with communistic countries. American efforts to limit communist expansion led to commitments in Korea, Berlin, and Vietnam.

The leadership of John F. Kennedy brought new reforms and policies to the internal social development of the country, including economic stimulation and programs of health and medical care for the aged. Vast increases in federal aid to education, the war on poverty, and greater federal expenditure for education marked the presidency of Lyndon Johnson. It is important to remember that the United States contained a population of about one hundred million in 1918, while it is over 280 million today with increasing numbers of Hispanic, Asian and other immigrants entering the country each year. Social mobility and new industry gave rise to teeming cities with very different educational problems from those of agrarian communities. Americans became the most affluent people in history, and an increase of wealth produced demands for amenities, more education, and solutions to new kinds of problems.

Today, more than fifty percent of our high school students express interest in attending a college or university. While education is still the road to economic advancement, the role of the schools in social change, education for leisure, and the evaluation of major institutions now take on new significance. The trend to begin school earlier and to stay in school longer has by no means reached its zenith. A major educational problem of the twentieth and approaching twenty-first century centers on the need for both general education (common school experiences for all children) and for increased specialization. While cultural changes since World War I are of primary and major importance in the progress of education, we must now turn to specific educational developments.

EVOLUTION OF THE MODERN INSTITUTIONAL STRUCTURE

A serious argument rages among educators over the adequacy of the current educational system in meeting the needs of our young people. Many studies show that children are capable of learning such skills as reading at a younger age than we had previously supposed. Children mature at different rates so that starting all six-year-olds in the first grade is psychologically unsatisfactory. Many students seem to benefit from early childhood education, such as a structured nursery school or a Montessori school. Most American communities now offer some kind of preschool educational experience of a formal kind. While some people became interested in the educational ideas of Maria Montessori as early as 1911, the rapid growth of Montessori programs for young children has taken place only in the last decade. A major problem for Montessori and other preschool programs is that most must be supported by private tuition. A notable exception is the federally funded Head Start program. Often children who could benefit from formal educational experience prior to entering kindergarten are from families unable to pay the fees, and Head Start is not available to all. Since 1970, kindergartens have been publicly supported as part of the public school system in almost all American communities. Before that date, some kindergartens were private and some cities had none at all. Some schools now offer developmental programs for kindergarten age children who are found to be immature by testing. By 1980, a large number of American pre-kindergarten children were in day care centers. Day care centers often have educational programs and most of them teach social skills.

Elementary Programs.   Before the beginning of the twentieth century, the modern school system had emerged as a single track from the elementary grades through college. American schools are still divided into fifty different state systems with a great deal of control vested in local boards and state departments of education. However, the past fifty years have clearly demonstrated a trend to build larger units, standardize programs, and to put more schools under the jurisdiction of centralized administrative units.

In 1893, the National Education Association appointed a Committee of Fifteen on the organization and program of primary and grammar schools. The Committee stressed good English usage including literature, United States history, geography, writing, arithmetic, physical science, and music. Manual training for boys and cooking or sewing for girls were suggested along with Latin for children in the eighth grade. The effect of the recommendations was to standardize the curriculum of elementary schools throughout the nation.

Most modern elementary schools do not extend beyond grade six. Curriculum changes have taken place, but most elementary students still devote the majority of their time to skill subjects such as reading, writing, grammar, and mathematics. History and geography have been combined into "social studies," biological sciences have been added, "new math" has replaced arithmetic, while art and music have somewhat increased in status. Certainly social studies now receive more attention than spelling. Physical education may be organized sports, calisthenics, or merely free play at recess or noon. Many minor subjects such as sex education have been added to the curriculum. Sometimes state legislatures have taken it upon themselves to pass laws requiring additional subjects such as drug education to be taught. Educators have experimented with the curriculum and much new information has been added, but there have been more changes in attitudes and methods than in basic subjects.

Innovations now found in many elementary schools include team teaching, nongraded schools, individualized instruction, open classrooms, and programmed learning. While traditional methods are still dominant, a great many districts are experimenting with innovative plans and programs.

In contrast with the self-contained classroom, team teaching provides for the cooperation of a group of teachers working with children at the same time. A team of teachers with a leader may be responsible for all the instruction of children in a school who normally would be assigned to the primary grades (grades one through three). Teams normally use some large group, some small group, and some individual instruction. Advantages include more time for planning, better evaluation of the progress of pupils, the opportunity for teachers to help one another improve practice, and flexibility in meeting the needs of students. It is difficult to have team teaching in a building designed for self-contained rooms. Success also depends upon the degree to which teachers are able to work together effectively. Many European elementary schools are now organized so that a team of teachers will stay with the same students for several years, thus, getting to know them well. This model is becoming more attractive in America because foreign students often do better than American students on standardized tests.

Nongraded schools allow the child to progress at his own rate without being locked into the content of a given grade. A student in a graded school who is unable to satisfy the requirements of a given area (say third grade reading) must either be retained or promoted at the end of the year. In nongraded schools, a student who needs a year and a half to master third grade reading is neither punished by failing the grade nor promoted beyond his ability to cope.

Children mature at different rates, have different interests, and are not motivated in the same way. Experiments in individualized instruction are designed to meet needs by a flexible program which allows each student to participate in planning his own program of instruction. Some individual instruction plans operate by providing a large number of groups at different levels for various subjects. A low teacher-pupil ratio and adequate support (including a high quality instructional materials center) is needed for successful individualized instruction.

Herbert Kohl and others who advocate the open classroom say that the standard curriculum prevents creativity and good communication. By his standards, not many American elementary schools are "open." However, many schools now offer the pupil a wide choice of activities and provide numerous opportunities for self-expression, the development of interests, and creative activities.

Various kinds of programmed learning, including teaching machines and computer assisted instruction, are used in connection with other innovative programs. They are often found in the media centers of schools with open or individualized plans for instruction. Machines, including closed-circuit television, microfilm, VCRs, tape recorders, CD-Rom, interactive video systems, computer video networks, computer-slide-overhead projector combinations, and projectors for slides and films are also used in traditional schools. In the 1990s, powerful desk top computers including the 486, Pentium systems, and flash chips with networking capabilities are bringing services from financial reports to shopping, travel, and banking into schools, homes, and offices. Students can contact experts in fields of interest through computer mail. As costs decrease, and computers are simplified, more classrooms and homes will have minicomputers with mainframe computer power. Public schools and universities now have e-mail, Internet, Bitnet, and Telnet highways that allow students and faculty to gain ready access to world-wide library, political, social, religious, and economic information. President Clinton has encouraged citizens to contact him through e-mail. His administration updated White House computer systems to enhance government communications systems. It seems safe to predict that multimedia systems will find increased utilization as America moves into a life-long learning society and the information age.

The School Survey. Educational leaders as early as the period of James Carter and Horace Mann had taken a hard look at the adequacy of schools in various states, but it was not until 1910 that a formal survey of schools took place. In that year, superintendent Kendall of Indianapolis was invited to visit and make a report on the schools of Boise, Idaho. His survey covered teachers, the curriculum, the organization of schools, buildings, and the attitude of citizens toward their educational system. By 1914, the school survey was an established practice, but not many were as detailed as that conducted in New York City which cost almost one hundred thousand dollars and required three years.

Early surveys utilized the services of well-known educators and ranked the subject system against others that were regarded as comparable. Nothing more sophisticated than observation was used as a tool for measurement. Criticism of the large numbers of changes recommended, and failure to consider the limitations of resources caused surveys by teams of experts to be unpopular. The Thirteenth Yearbook of the National Society for the Study of Education offered suggestions about how surveys might be conducted by local educators with only slight assistance from experts.

Detailed surveys are still conducted in the United States. They serve a variety of purposes such as planning for consolidation, desegregation, new building, curriculum change, and administrative reorganization. Surveys are also used by organizations for accrediting schools and evaluating programs.

Consolidation

One of the earlier shifts in design resulted from the consolidation of one-room district schools in rural areas. Local elementary schools were first built just far enough apart to permit scholars to walk from their homes. Concentrations of population, the wide use of automobiles, and a reduction of the number of farm families made it possible to build united schools which were larger and more efficient. Just after the First World War, about seventy percent of the public school buildings in the United States were of the one-room variety. Such schools were expensive to maintain, lacking in equipment, poorly supervised, and without specialization. Consolidation has reduced the number of one-room schools to less than five percent of the total. Today, even sparsely populated communities often have modern multiroom physical plants, complete with gymnasium, cafeteria, and modern equipment. Bus service is normally provided by consolidated school districts.

The modern elementary school has changed both in consolidated and urban school districts. Elementary schools are not as directly linked to colleges as high schools. This has allowed more flexibility in the curriculum and in scheduling. Team teaching, programmed instruction, and mini-courses for student electives—such as introduction to foreign languages, vocational education, keyboarding, computer literacy—teaching machines, and computer-assisted instruction are used in connection with other innovative programs in instructional technology. The organization, administration, structure, and curriculum of schools in America is not fixed or final. Further evolution of schools and programs may be expected in the future. Many schools have specially trained teachers for art, speech correction, guidance counseling, and the like. Extracurricular activities such as team sports and a federally subsidized lunch program are commonly found in elementary schools.

Junior High and Middle Schools.   Eight-year elementary schools and four-year high schools are still found in the United States but other organizational plans are more common. Junior high schools increased slowly in number during the first half of the twentieth century but their number increased markedly in the past thirty years. Middle schools or mid-high schools are now found in many communities. Since the middle of this century, the 6-3-3 or 6-6 plan of organization has become more common than the traditional eight-year elementary school followed by a four-year high school. Some cities have experimented with a 6-2-4 or a 4-4-4 organizational plan, while the two-year junior college has sometimes been added as an extension of the common school system. The typical junior high school consists of grades seven, eight, and nine. Part of the theory behind junior high schools relates to a need for vocational or terminal secondary education. Their success may also be attributed to an exploratory curriculum with general courses in science and introductory work in various fields. The student receives guidance concerning his or her abilities and limitations. Fewer subjects are studied, but greater detail is given than for elementary subjects, and the pupil normally has a different teacher for each course. It is assumed that junior high school students no longer need the security of belonging to one classroom with one teacher. They are expected to have a longer attention span than younger children. Perhaps the most important reason for the popularity of the three-year junior high school is that it separates youngsters just starting the adolescent period of life from both older and younger students. This contributes to the development of social skills and avoids cramming children of all ages into a matrix of social and intellectual competition. Junior high schools may be attached to an elementary or high school or may be completely separated.

High Schools.   The most important thing about the American high school in the past fifty years is its phenomenal growth. In the sense that it caters to a range of abilities, interests, and goals, the secondary school has become a school of all the people, just as the elementary school was in an earlier period. In 1920 there were about two and one-half million secondary school students in the United States, or approximately one third of the population between the ages of fourteen and seventeen was in school. In 1965 there were more than fifteen million secondary school students or approximately 85 percent of the high school age group. There are a number of vocational or technical high schools, especially in large cities, but the typical American secondary school has become the "comprehensive" public high school.

Comprehensive is a term used by scholars such as James B. Conant who have studied the program of the high schools in detail. Basically, it refers to a secondary school that has a program designed to meet the various needs and interests of students, regardless of whether or not they expect to attend college. Vocational courses have long been offered by high schools, but the major emphasis is still on college preparation. With the increasing affluence of the American people and the growing scarcity of jobs for which little training is required, college preparation is not likely to lose ground as the major purpose of the high school. According to the *1993 Digest of Educational Statistics* and the *1993 Statistical Abstract of the United States*, college enrollment increased 41 percent between 1970 and 1980 and 20 percent from 1980 to 1992, or from 12.1 million to 14.6 million, a record level. Projected college enrollment for 1994 is 14,373,000. Nevertheless, the purpose of secondary education and the program of the high schools continues to be one of the most hotly debated issues in American education.

Shortly after the Kalamazoo decision insured tax support, the public high school took on qualities of both the academy and the classical school. It offered courses that were practical and cultural on the one hand, and college preparatory on the other. Training of the mind became equated with preparation for life, and the college preparatory course was considered to be the best mental training. Electives were offered in high schools but the curriculum was shaped by what colleges would accept for entrance. The report of the Committee of Ten of the NEA in 1892 emphasized that high schools were for the elite. The twentieth century gave rise to an increase in national wealth, an improved living standard, and a need for a better trained labor force. High schools were forced to cater to the needs of the entire population in a growing industrial democracy. An NEA Commission on the Reorganization of Secondary Education, meeting in 1918, developed the Cardinal Principles of Secondary Education. In contrast with the college-centered and mental-discipline-oriented Committee of Ten, these principles stressed guidance, a wide range of subjects, adaptation of content and methods to the abilities and interest of students, and flexibility of organization and administration. High schools began to stress health, citizenship, vocational preparation, ethical development, and the worthy use of leisure time in addition to fundamental processes and the academic subjects. In short, they became comprehensive.

A demand for experts to improve industry and to help win the cold war resulted in more science courses, while new subjects such as driver training, mental hygiene, and personal relations reflected the needs of individuals in a complex society. The American comprehensive high school has received harsh criticism, especially from those who emphasize traditional subject matter and academic excellence. There is still a question of whether or not the high school should be specialized, and if so, how specialized and how early in the student's career. In 1946, a Harvard committee published *General Education in a Free Society* in which specialization on the secondary level was attacked as unsound. Others have joined the battle to extend general education through the high school on the grounds that modern society demands generalized knowledge of many areas for true human fulfillment and good citizenship. Whatever the criticisms, no other institution has ever provided education beyond the elementary level to all the people of a large nation. This the American high school has done.

Higher Education.

High schools in the United States have never entirely lost their function of college preparation due to the phenomenal growth of colleges and universities. With the exception of the period of the great depression, college enrollments have had a steady increase throughout this century, but the great explosion in size and number of colleges has taken place since World War II. Colleges have become more utilitarian and scientific in nature, although the liberal arts college is still a major American institution. With the addition of colleges of a professional nature (education, agriculture, engineering, commerce, dentistry, and veterinary medicine) to universities, and the organization of separate departments within colleges, higher education has become very specialized. Practical and scientific courses were in demand before World War I, but the expansion of industry and the explosion of knowledge have made college training indispensable to many occupations which previously needed little formal schooling.

Furthermore, hundreds of new special occupations resulted from the changes brought about by scientific research in the universities. Veterans returning from the Second World War demanded and got practical courses from colleges and universities that had previously offered only liberal education. Governmental support of veterans education through the G.I. Bill stimulated a trend toward considerable federal interest in higher education. Large numbers of students attended colleges and graduate schools through grants made by the National Defense Education Act of 1958 or other scholarships. The 500,000 students enrolled in college in 1918 seem a mere drop in the bucket compared with today's figure which exceeds twelve million students. It seems fair to predict that college enrollments in America will follow the same general growth trend as did high school enrollments fifty years ago. Already, graduate schools are growing more rapidly than did colleges in the nineteenth century.

As we approach the twenty-first century, we face many new challenges in higher education. Among them are demands for more information. Higher education institution audits are being explored in many states such as Oklahoma to assure maximum effectiveness in cost control. In addition, Congress passed a *Students Right to Know and Crime Awareness and Campus Security Act* in 1990. Although many college presidents have sought more time for implementation than the 1993 deadline, the bill will be implemented. It requires higher education institutions to publish graduation and crime rates on each campus.

Junior Colleges.   A direct result of the expansion in higher education which could not be accommodated by existing colleges was the junior college movement. Two-year terminal colleges, often staffed by senior high school teachers, began to appear before World War I. There have been both private and public junior colleges, but those with public control and tax support have increased most rapidly in recent years. The government established some junior colleges during the depression years, but the greatest number have been developed by city or state junior college boards. Municipal junior colleges have often provided the first two years of standard college education, thus taking some of the pressure off colleges and universities. Public junior colleges are either free or their tuition charges are very low, and students usually live at home while attending them. The junior college therefore offers an extension of educational opportunity to students who could not otherwise afford higher education. There is a vastly increased demand for more junior colleges of both the terminal and the nonterminal type. One serious problem is financing in communities where all available taxes are required for lower public schools. By 1994, more than 2,500 junior and community colleges were operating with a combined enrollment of 4 million students.

The average length of time spent in school has expanded at both ends of the continuum. Many students now have the opportunity to attend kindergarten before starting public school at the age of six. Quite a large number of school systems have public kindergartens, with the K-6-3-3 or K-4-4-4 plans being most common. Public kindergartens are found in all but the smaller rural schools. Day care centers and Montessori schools for pre-kindergarten youngsters are available in most cities, but they usually require tuition. Head Start programs make an effort to give underprivileged children some of the preschool experiences enjoyed by middle-class youngsters.

SCHOOL FINANCE AND CONTROL

An issue which is developing into a major educational argument in America concerns the location of authority and the source of support for public schools. As the federal government becomes more active in providing money through such measures as the Elementary and Secondary Education Act of 1965, the role of the central government in education becomes larger. Many leaders feel that the schools ought to remain in local hands, and they fear that federal aid to education will eventually lead to complete federal control of schools. On the other hand, national authorities have allowed a good deal of local administration of federal funds when local governments have been unable to raise sufficient money for high quality schools. We can predict that the argument over federal control of schools will continue, although it also seems likely that a larger share of future school finance will be handled by the national government.

Local and State Control.   Educational support and control in the United States has been a curious composite of local, state, and national functions. Because education was not considered a federal responsibility by the founding fathers, each state set up its own unique educational system. Many of the states have similar laws, but each is autonomous with regard to public schools and educational requirements within its own borders. While the states have guarded their authority over schools and generally opposed federal financial aid, local school boards have been granted a considerable degree of freedom in managing the schools. State boards of education have served largely for making policy while state superintendents or commissioners have been responsible for administration and general supervision. States differ widely in their method of selecting boards and executive school officers. Sometimes they are elected, sometimes appointed by the governor, and sometimes appointed by the state legislature.

Most states have well-organized educational offices with specialists for inspecting schools, certifying teachers, and allocating funds that are distributed by the state. There are normally smaller administrative units presided over by township, county, or district superintendents. Cities often have independent school districts with superintendents who work directly for the locally elected board of education, and who perform the functions otherwise delegated to county superintendents. There is no uniformity with regard to the size and type of school districts in the United States. One superintendent and board of education in a metropolitan area may be responsible for hundreds of schools at all levels. At the other end of the extreme is the school board and executive officer governing only one small school building. Although teachers' salaries are uniform in some states, it is still common to find adjacent school districts which differ in money paid to teachers and otherwise expended for the education of children. The inequality of educational opportunity in various districts has encouraged state and federal participation in education.

School Finance.   In the twentieth century, states began to play a much more important role in school finance. State funds originated as early as 1795, when Connecticut sold her vast Western Reserve lands and put the money in permanent school funds. Most states have such funds, drawing money from public land sales, taxes, special appropriations, and the like. Historically, the states have used their meager allotments for giving state aid to local districts that agreed to tax themselves for schools and for making payments to districts unable to obtain sufficient local revenues for a minimum standard. By and large, the concentrated wealth and population of cities has made it possible for urban areas to levy taxes and support schools more easily than rural communities. Local taxes have paid the lion's share of public school costs and the states have confined their administration to a minimum. However, state funds have encouraged the keeping of accurate records of attendance, school inspection, and the establishment of accepted minimum standards. Between 1930 and 1970, the percentage of locally raised public school funds dropped from about 83 to 51 percent. As the proportion of local support has fallen, state and federal support has increased. Quite naturally, the larger governmental units have begun to place more restrictions on the money which they have collected and distributed. Such restrictions have usually been confined to general rules for the use of money, but there is no question that centralized control is increasing. States use a variety of means for funding public schools including sales tax, state income tax, state property tax, fees, and licenses on items such as automobiles. According to a *National Conference of State Legislatures* report, in 1992 at least 14 states earmark a percentage of their lottery money for education. Other states are considering lotteries to fund a portion of their education budget. Often, funds are inadequate, and the relationship between local and state sources creates a political problem. School districts have the power to raise only ad valorem property taxes within district boundaries. If the wealth of the district is low, it may not be possible to meet school funding needs even if the voters in the district support the levy. When this occurs, schools may turn to the courts to force the states to fund a larger part of the school budget. For example, more than 100 school districts in Montana sued the state in 1988 on the grounds that they did not have the power to raise enough taxes to meet state mandated requirements for a basic education. The Supreme Court of Montana agreed with the schools and required the legislature to provide a means for additional state funding for all public schools in Montana.

Historically, the federal government has been interested in the improvement of higher education and specialized training in such subjects as agriculture. Local property taxes are still widely used for school finance, but they are neither sufficiently flexible nor adequate to care for the changing population distribution. Knowledge of the emergence of the federal government as a major educational agency is vital to an understanding of the current issue over support and control of the schools.

FEDERAL PARTICIPATION IN EDUCATION

The amount of involvement of the United States government has increased so much in the past few years that a listing of all the laws is not possible here. Only major areas of activity will be considered. The United States Office of Education has grown rapidly in size and influence, due largely to the need for administering federal funds and advising participants in federal projects. The Office has had a varied history, having been moved from the Department of the Interior and given separate status in 1930, moved again to the Federal Security Agency in 1939, and made part of the Department of Health, Education and Welfare in 1953. Large grants made through H.E.W. to schools and universities contributed to the importance of the Office of Education, and it was made a separate cabinet level position under the Carter Administration. Cutbacks in federal spending in the Reagan Administration created some loss of prestige, and some members of Congress suggested that it should be abolished. The future of the office of Secretary of Education will depend upon politics and federal policy concerning finance.

Support for Industrial and Vocational Education

Among the earlier efforts of the Congress to aid education were acts designed to fill a need for industrial and vocational education. Through the Smith-Hughes Act (1917), the George-Reed Act (1929), and the George-Dean Act (1937), Congress attempted to promote vocational education in public schools. A Federal Board of Vocational Education was created in 1917 and, after 1919, was given the additional task of supervising training of the handicapped. Ten years later, the Capper-Ketcham Act extended the previous Smith-Lever Act to cover education in home economics and agriculture. During the First World War, the government found it necessary to train many technicians, but industrial inactivity during the depression resulted in a great shortage of trained technicians and engineers. The National Defense Training Program of 1940 provided courses for more than seven million workers during World War II. The Rural War Production Training Program trained farm youth for industry and for jobs in food production. Vocational training also benefited from the National Defense Education Act (1958), but the Vocational Education Act extended previous legislation to cover any skilled, technical, or semiskilled occupation and included provisions for keeping potential dropouts in schools.

The original purpose of federal efforts to promote vocational and industrial education was to provide the nation with skilled workers and technicians when other agencies had failed to do so. Clearly, this was the same rationale that fostered the agricultural and mechanical colleges developed from the Morrill Acts. However, Congress has increasingly turned its attention to vocational education which may serve social needs by improving the economy, keeping children in school longer, fighting poverty, and creating new jobs for the unemployed. Further legislation to strengthen vocational education in order to fight against unemployment seems almost certain.

New Deal Acts.

Attempts to improve the national welfare and increase equality of opportunity were made through the so-called New Deal legislation passed during the administration of Franklin D. Roosevelt. The Civilian Conservation Corps employed young men and gave them vocational training, especially in conservation and building trades, while small grants were given to needy students through the National Youth Administration. The Works Progress Administration subsidized teachers salaries for programs in the training of adults and aliens and for nursery schools. The Public Works Administration provided loans for communities to use in building schools and libraries. In 1935, the Secretary of Agriculture was authorized to distribute surplus foods to schools, and this led directly to the National School Lunch Act of 1946, which has made both food and money available to school lunch programs. Loss of tax funds for schools during the depression led to loans to school boards through the Reconstruction Finance Corporation. This trend has been continued in legislation such as the Economic Opportunity Act (EOA) of 1964. Title I of this law set up the Job Corps to train youth between the ages of sixteen and twenty-one for useful employment and citizenship.

Job Corps training centers were built around the nation under this plan. Students were given training in basic skills as well as in vocational subjects. There has also been a work-study program for students still in high school who needed to earn money and a college work-study program for students with financial need. Title II of the EOA authorized aid to adult education and gave cultural enrichment for children from disadvantaged families. The Head Start program was aimed at children from three to five years of age who would not normally have had the advantage of nursery schools or kindergartens.

Wartime Measures.   Wartime activity has also contributed to the involvement of the federal government in education. During the First World War, the government trained technicians and troops drilled on college campuses. In World War II, loans were made to students majoring in subjects like medicine, for which there was a critical need. Congress began giving assistance to those school districts which absorbed large numbers of children of military or defense personnel. Laws aiding such affected areas were extended in 1950 and 1966. In addition, equipment purchased by the government for special war training was later turned over to schools and surplus property was made available to all nonprofit educational institutions.

In an effort to meet the needs of veterans whose schooling had been interrupted by military duty, the Servicemen's Readjustment Act of 1944 (G.I. Bill) was passed. This measure has provided subsistence and school cost allowances for veterans who have continued their education, and it has resulted in the expansion of colleges to accommodate them. The G.I. Bill was revived for veterans of the Korean War and the benefits were increased for Vietnam veterans in 1972.

National Defense Education Act.   A new period of federal activity in education started with the cold war and the Soviet success in launching Sputnik, the first space satellite. The National Defense Education Act of 1958 was designed for the purpose of giving aid to education as a means of strengthening the nation. NDEA loans have been made to prospective teachers in amounts up to five thousand dollars, and half of the loan has been cancellable through service as a public school teacher after graduation. Funds have been made available for laboratory equipment and other materials to improve instruction in science, while fellowships have been offered to persons training to be college professors. State testing and guidance to find and encourage able students, an extension of vocational education, and research on new educational media have also been financed by NDEA funds. Out of the administrations of John F. Kennedy and Lyndon B. Johnson came a host of federal measures designed to promote equality of educational opportunity, to fight poverty, and to strengthen defense. The Higher Education Facilities Act of 1963 made funds available for the construction of college buildings with matching sums provided by the college or state.

Elementary and Secondary Education Act.   Federal aid to education took another big step with the Elementary and Secondary Education Act of 1965. This measure provided funds for textbooks and other instructional materials and services in public and private elementary and secondary schools. The primary purpose was to insure that children from low-income families had access to adequate materials. Control of the funds was in state and local hands rather than those of federal agencies. The act also included one hundred million dollars for research in the field of education to be administered by the United States Office of Education. This act was extended for four more years in 1966, at a cost of about twelve billion dollars. In 1981, the Education Consolidation and Improvement Act provided funds for better quality programs and the encouragement of consolidation efforts. Federal block grants also targeted low income and minority areas for special funding. In the fall of 1993, Secretary of Education Richard W. Riley, reflecting the Clinton Administration theme of reinventing government to make it more effective, proposed retooling the Elementary and Secondary Education Act to improve the lot of poor children. Chapter 1 funding would be directed to schools with high concentrations of poor, neglected, migrant, delinquent, and at-risk children. In addition, states would be encouraged to adopt standards and ways to measure student progress.

Since 1965, the Higher Education Act, which includes the Education Professions Development Act of 1967, has provided large sums of money for the acquisition of books and other library materials in colleges, for improving and extending teacher education programs, for strengthening programs related to community problems like housing and poverty, for supporting developing institutions of higher education, for giving financial assistance to students through grants and loans, and for developing the National Teachers Corps.

Teacher Corps employed specially trained teachers and college students to supplement instruction in schools with numerous low-income students. The education given Teacher Core trainees included living in the neighborhoods near the schools and studying ethnic and minority culture. In 1980, Teacher Core shifted from teacher training to in-service education. Congress has not always appropriated funds for Teacher Corps and many of the training centers were closed during the Reagan Administration. The Higher Education Act provided about twenty-five thousand graduate fellowships for teacher trainees yearly, supported research and development in colleges of education, and established a National Advisory Council on Quality Teacher Education.

Although the federal government entered the educational arena in a big way in the 1960s, new legislation dropped off after the Johnson Administration. One reason is that the shortage of teachers at the time of the National Defense Education Act changed into an oversupply of teachers by 1970. Another reason is the fear of federal control over local schools. In the early 1980s, the mood of the nation favored reduced federal spending and a cut in bureaucracy. Nevertheless, educators now predict a shortage of teachers in the future because of low pay and the impact of inflation. Equality of educational opportunity can hardly be guaranteed with only local taxes. Central tax collection and distribution by the national government appears to be the only way of insuring equal education for the mobile American population. A number of educators have suggested some sort of federal equalization fund to make up for differences in economic support between states. Of course, fear of federal control has also caused many of the states to take steps for the reformation of their own tax laws. Inequality exists within school districts or cities, such as that demonstrated in the Rodriguez case of San Antonio, Texas. Although Rodriguez did not win, pressure was put on state legislatures to make taxation more equitable.

Congressional efforts to aid education have not been uniform over the past several years. Funding of bills passed during the Kennedy and Johnson administrations was not always continued during the presidency of Richard Nixon. Few new federal education measures were proposed during the Nixon administration, but President Ford signed a new elementary and secondary education act into law as one of his first official acts. In spite of the economic recession of the 1970s, efforts to provide federal help for schools and local educational programs have not ended. Less money was provided in the 1970s than in the 1960s, but the impact of federal aid continued. The Department of Health, Education and Welfare used the withholding of funds (or the threat of such withholding) as an instrument for enforcing plans for racial integration. This was continued under President Carter, but President Reagan voiced strong opposition to using the power of the federal government to control local action. The courts have also taken a less vigorous stand in the Los Angeles case of 1981, where busing to achieve racial balance in schools was not supported.

One of the burning issues in American education is the control and support of schools. Public opposition to national educational policy is illustrated by the controversy surrounding the integration of South High School in Boston in 1974. Many laymen fear that local school boards may be vanishing and that an increasing role for the federal government in educational affairs is undesirable. On the other hand, federal funds and programs are felt to be necessary for the success of many schools.

PSYCHOLOGY AND EDUCATION

Assumptions about the nature of mind and the learning process have always been present in education. Plato wrote about the three divisions of the soul and the need to make reason paramount. Locke examined the human understanding and held that ideas enter the mind through the senses. Rousseau saw learning as an extension of natural interests through a series of developmental stages. Puritan schools were predicated upon the belief that the child had an evil nature and that his mind must be "formed" through discipline and effort. Horace Mann supported the phrenology of Franz Joseph Gall, which held that intelligence and aptitudes can be determined by the configuration of the skull.

New respect for the personality of the child came out of the work of Pestalozzi. Froebel, Sheldon, and Parker contributed to an understanding of the psychology of learning. Nevertheless, words like intelligence, consciousness, and mind were still vague and mystical at the end of the nineteenth century. While Herbart had insisted that the mind is a unity, faculty psychology, with its concept of separate mental powers and transfer of training, still ruled educational theory. Mental discipline was the basis of the report of the Committee of Ten and the foundation for almost the entire public school curriculum.

Psychology as a science developed in Europe and to some degree in America before the beginning of the twentieth century. Herbart sought clues to mental development in the facts of physiology. Darwin's work on evolution stimulated others to study the nature of the child from a biological standpoint. Pavlov's conditioned reflex experiments on animals in Russia created a new wave of interest in psychology. Of even more significance was the founding of the first experimental psychology laboratory by Wilhelm Max Wundt at Leipzig in 1878. A great many American psychologists were trained by Wundt, and he is often regarded as the father of structural psychology. Other European leaders included Ebbinghaus, who worked with nonsense syllables to measure memory, and Freud, who developed psychoanalysis from the dynamics of motivation in personality formation.

Although not strictly an experimental psychologist, William James (1842–1910) did much to create a link between education and psychology. His *Principles of Psychology* (1890) was an outstanding contribution which made him internationally known and helped to develop psychology as an independent area of study. James extracted some of the more practical ideas from his major work in psychology and published them under the title *Talks to Teachers*. This was the first attempt to provide psychological guidance for practical educators. Although his work was partly philosophical and introspection was his method, James helped to make psychology a valid field of educational inquiry.

American psychologists, heavily influenced by Europeans, attacked formal discipline and formulated new concepts of mind. Among the first were Edward Titchener, G. Stanley Hall, James M. Cattell, John Dewey, and Edward L. Thorndike. The history of educational psychology is best approached through the various types or schools of psychology.

Structuralism.   Titchener was a student of Wundt and a leading psychologist at Cornell University for thirty years. Concerned with the study of consciousness, Titchener treated psychology as an impersonal science and approached it atomistically. That is, Titchener and the structuralists attempted to isolate and analyze the basic elements of mental processes. He believed that a microscopic examination of the basic blocks of the nervous system and psychic elements would lead to a complete science of the mind. Since structuralism did not concern itself with the living organism, its relationship with education was indirect. Members of this psychological school dominated many college departments of psychology for years.

Functionalism.   William James and John Dewey were the first to identify functionalism as a division of psychology. For them, a study of consciousness could not be isolated from feelings, sensations, thoughts, and activities of the living organism. In 1900, as president of the newly formed American Psychological Association, Dewey called for the application of psychology to social and educational practice. For Dewey the complete act of thought is the same for a child in school and a scientist working on a problem in a laboratory. Both go through the same process which may be described in five steps: (1) activity, (2) problem, (3) data gathering, (4) formation of a hypothesis, and (5) testing. Learning can only occur when students are engaged in genuine activities rather than in artificial ones imposed by the teacher. Problems occur when activity is blocked. Children learn how to gather data from simple sources like their own memories or from more complicated sources like libraries. Hypothesis formation is merely the posing of a possible solution to a problem, and the learner must examine what consequences may occur if the hypothesis is accepted. Only by testing the proposed solution against empirical evidence can learning be completed. Dewey's books *Psychology* and *How We Think* described his functional theories. His *Human Nature and Conduct* (1922) is a statement of the interaction between the individual and his environment.

Other functional psychologists include Harvey Carr and James R. Angell who established laboratories for studying the adjustment of animals to various environments. Functionalism contributed both to education and to other schools such as associationism, connectionism, and behaviorism.

Connectionist Psychology or Associationism.   Edward Lee Thorndike (1874–1949) was a student of William James and James McKeen Cattell. Building on Herman Ebbinghaus's curve of learning and forgetting and studies of animal learning made by Lloyd Morgan in England, Thorndike began a series of learning experiments with animals using puzzle boxes or a maze. After a series of trial and error activities, the animal would chance upon the "solution" which released food. Further trials in the same puzzle box resulted in the animal's making the proper response more rapidly than at first. This led Thorndike to his "law of effect" which he also extended to human activity. He found a very strong effect from rewards, but also discovered that punishment was a less effective means for the control of behavior. Following Pavlov's lead, Thorndike assumed a connection between stimuli and responses. He developed this into S-R bond psychology using the equation: Learning = Stimulus – Response. If stimulus A is known to be associated with response B, repeat A until B is produced without hesitation whenever A occurs. Teachers rapidly accepted Thorndike's laws of learning which they found to be highly useful devices for classroom instruction.

Since Thorndike had an impeccable reputation as a scientist, his pioneering experiments opened new fields of psychological research at the time modern conceptions of pedagogy were being born. He was one of the first to understand that education and psychology were closely linked. Psychology forms the foundation for the science of education, while schools furnish subjects and data sources for psychological research. At

Teachers College, Columbia University, Thorndike stimulated hundreds of students to esteem scientific research. Although his psychology was highly statistical and mechanical, connectionism became the leading educational psychology of the 1920s.

Behaviorism.   The logical extreme of associationism or connectionism gave rise to the psychological school known as behaviorism. John B. Watson (1878–1958) is generally regarded as the founder, but his student Karl Lashley also contributed to this strictly objective division of psychology. Today the best known scholar in the field of behaviorism is B. F. Skinner of Harvard.

Although he had studied with Dewey, Watson believed that psychology should be confined to those activities which could be verified by an outside observer. Behaviorism discarded consciousness as a subject of investigation and refused to use the method of introspection. It limited its findings to laboratory experiments which could be controlled and dealt only with those factors capable of analysis. Behaviorists believe that we have no right to project our feelings or ideas into the subjects we investigate. For example, if a person gives a piece of meat to a dog, it is legitimate to describe the dog's behavior; i.e., the animal jumps up, drools, opens its mouth, and eats the meat. It is not legitimate to say that the dog "likes" the meat since that projects the attitudes or feelings of the human into the dog, and there is no evidence to support the statement.

Watson held that environment is far more important than heredity in the determination of human behavior. He rejected innate ideas and most instincts. His experiments with infants caused him to conclude that almost all emotional responses are learned. Watson held that any normal child could be raised to be a mechanic, athlete, professional man, or thief if the environment could be strictly controlled. Lashley was able to demonstrate that even human glands could be conditioned.

The early work of the behaviorists helped to discredit many theories about learning that were held by other psychologists. They did a great deal to foster objective evaluations of experiments. Sometimes their claims were extravagant and certainly many educators objected to what they described as "rat in a box" psychology and the restriction of investigation to a fractional part of human behavior. Nevertheless, behaviorism won the respect of scientists in other fields, and its rigorous techniques helped to support objective educational research.

B. F. Skinner's work spans the period from early behaviorism to the present. In the late 1930s, he began a series of animal learning experiments in which he taught animals to perform complex tasks. He accomplished this by giving the subject a reward after each step of the task was successfully accomplished. Out of this grew the idea of programmed instruction and teaching machines. During the Second World War, new programs for using electronic devices in teaching were developed by Skinner and his students. Computer assisted instruction, now used in numerous aspects of education, was adapted from the work of behaviorists. Skinner's books, *Science and Human Behavior*, *Walden II*, and *Beyond Freedom and Dignity*, have had a profound effect upon educators in modern America. Few of the findings of Skinner and other behaviorists have been scientifically rejected. The criticism of behaviorism normally comes from those who say it is too narrow, mechanical, and nonhumanistic.

Gestalt.   At about the same time that behaviorism began to influence education in America, German gestalt psychology also became important. Gestalt is a German word meaning "form" or "pattern," and it refers to the whole configuration or sum of integrated experiences present at any one time. The apparent motion created by flashing a series of photographs in the cinema is not explained by examining individual still pictures; nor can music be understood merely through the study of notes. Gestalt psychology was started in Germany by Max Wertheimer, Kurt Koffka, and Wolfgang Kohler. Beginning in 1914, Kohler began a series of experiments on the island of Tenerife using apes as subjects. He concluded that learning takes place as sudden insight, rather than by simple trial-and-error. This led to the examination of the pattern perceived by the learner in his total environment, rather than to an atomistic consideration of essential elements in the learning process.

American gestalt psychologists such as R. M. Ogden and Raymond Wheeler made important contributions to learning theory. Their stress on total understanding of the problem to be solved and the consequences of acting were acceptable to Dewey and the functionalists. Gestalt psychology was adopted by most members of the progressive movement because it dealt with the whole child in context.

Kurt Lewin (1890–1947) was a German gestalt psychologist who migrated to the United States when Hitler came to power. He believed that behavior is the result of energy derived from the needs or wants of the individual and the organism's efforts to meet those needs. Lewin's psychology is called "field theory" because of the emphasis of the "life space" or field of the individual as he perceives it. Lewin used the term "vector" to describe the attractive or repulsive forces which motivate the organism to act.

Learning theories and psychological ideas associated with field theory are still popular in the United States. Most studies of motivation, needs, personality, feelings, and attitudes have been carried on in the light of field theory. Another group of psychologists with similar views of the child and his/her environment are called "holistic." Holistic psychology emphasizes the child as a "whole" and insists that the individual can never be studied and understood except as he relates to the forces present in his entire environment. Modern humanistic psychologists such as Abraham Maslow and Carl Rogers have been highly influenced by gestalt, field, and holistic psychological theory. Members of these schools have had at least as much impact on American education as behaviorists.

Psychoanalysis.   While not strictly an educational or learning psychology, psychoanalysis has contributed to an understanding of childhood experiences and to programs for those with learning disabilities or who need therapy. Sigmund Freud, Carl Jung, Alfred Adler, and Karen Horney were major leaders in this movement. Freud's stress on the sexual attraction of infants and children to the parent of the opposite sex

(Oedipus/Electra Complex) and his discussion of the animal nature of human beings (id) which must be governed by social norms (superego) has had great educational influence. Modern concerns for the impact of conflict and stress on the development of personality as found in the work of Erik Erikson are linked to Freudian concepts. A body of educational literature supporting freedom of choice for students and attacking barriers to personality development is based upon psychoanalytic theory.

Modern Developmental Psychology and Stage Theory.   A major thrust of educational psychology in recent years has been directed toward the relationship of curriculum and methods to stages of development in children. Conflict exists between various theories of development, but there is agreement that poor pedagogy results from attempting to teach information or concepts before the learner has reached the stage at which such information and concepts can be understood.

David Ausubel distinguishes between learning by reception and learning by discovery. Reception learning requires the student to internalize material in order to recall it at a later date (as on a test). Discovery learning does not present material in finished form but sets up an environment in which something has to be discovered or invented by the student before it can be assimilated. In discovery learning, it is the process that is emphasized while reception learning concentrates on the product. While Ausubel contends that discovery learning enables the student to understand how new knowledge is generated and stimulates the learner, it is an inefficient method for delivering large amounts of information. Ausubel therefore believes that there must be a balance between process and product, but that schools which have no discovery learning inhibit the progress of children and make education uninteresting.

Jerome Bruner is recognized for his efforts to apply scientific methods to teaching and for his research on the formation of concepts in children. Bruner is interested in the structure of subject matter. He believes that the teaching of particular subjects can be integrated into the way the students see the world so as to permit learners to discover the basic principles of the discipline under study. Motivation therefore should be stimulated by the subject matter itself and not from external appeals to interest or the arrangement of consequent events. Obviously, this differs from Skinner's operant conditioning. Bruner believes that it is possible to teach any subject in some intellectually honest way to any child at any developmental stage.

Child psychologist Robert Gagné is well known for his contributions to programmed instruction. He believes that children pass through developmental stages of learning which are determined by what is to be learned. Gagné identifies eight conditions for learning. Signal learning occurs when infants learn responses to a general cue, stimulus-response learning is more precise and voluntary, chaining is the result of putting together previous responses, while verbal discrimination is the association of names with objects. More advanced learning includes multiple discrimination to identify and classify groups of stimuli, concept learning or the ability to identify important differences and similarities between sets of stimuli, relation of one complete concept to others or "principle" learning, and problem solving in which several principles are used for dealing with a new situation. Gagné urges educators to give more attention to the way in which instruction is sequenced because he holds that no learning stage can be skipped. Because Gagné believes that it is the nature of the skills to be learned that determines the sequence of stages, the curriculum must be ordered accordingly. Ausubel, Bruner, and Gagné all see the subject matter or the learning tasks as central to learning stages. On the other hand, Piaget holds that stages are related to the maturation and development of children.

Jean Piaget was born in Neuchatel, Switzerland, in 1896. He began his career as a zoology assistant at the age of eleven and published papers on mollusks at the age of fifteen. Piaget worked with Alfred Binet in Paris on standardizing tests of intelligence and became interested in the levels of logic used by children taking such tests. Building on Rousseau and Pestalozzi, Piaget attempted to establish a body of psychology to give support for educational techniques truly adapted to the laws of mental development. For many years he carried out experiments on learning tasks with children in the J. J. Rousseau Institute. He was active in the field until he died in 1980.

Piaget believed that the two fundamental characteristics of a child's learning and cognitive development are organization and adaptation. Organization is described as the systematizing of information into meaningful patterns. These patterns are used to structure new information so that it does not seem random or chaotic to the learner. Adaptation is the process of coping, or integrating new information into existing perceptions and patterns. Intelligence for Piaget must follow from our ability to organize and adapt. Like Dewey, Piaget saw human beings as born active, curious, interested in communication, and with a need to assimilate information. His principles of organization and adaptation are in basic agreement with the theories of Bruner and Gagné. Piaget parted company with other developmental psychologists on the matter of specific stages of growth and development. His stages are determined by genetic development in connection with experience. The stages or levels are related but they are determined by a combination of age and experience.

The sensorimotor stage covers the period from birth to about the age of two. This stage consists mostly of reflexes, but during this time, foundations are laid for later mental growth and development. Trial and error is used for mastering the environment and oral language develops. At about the age of two the preoperational stage begins. From two to four the child is preconceptual and in an intuitive stage of development but experiences vast growth in language use. Judgments are incomplete and modeling is a basis for learning. From three to seven children reach a symbolic stage where drawing, role-playing, size, number, and distance begin to follow some semblance of order. From seven to twelve the child begins to think logically and not in the impressionistic way associated with the preoperational stage. The span of attention expands and a clear sense of time emerges. Children at this level can count, weigh, test solutions, and conserve. They are not, however, able to think abstractly nor are they motivated by delayed rewards. At the stage of formal operations, learners can think hypothetically. They do not require visible concrete cues for each stage of the thinking process. Abstract or ideal concepts are used and the child has a clear concept of time.

Piaget and his followers urge educators to be realistic about what children can accomplish at each stage. Tests have shown that many freshmen entering universities still think on a concrete level. Even after a person has reached the formal level of operations, it is common to revert back to earlier stages under stress. Teachers, in the view of Piaget, must avoid abstract and theoretical tasks if any of the learners in their classrooms are still operating in a nonformal way.

The belief that early experiences are crucial to later development is challenged by Jerome Kagan. For Kagan and his associates, the most recent experiences are more important than the earliest ones. His research shows dramatic improvement when children from deprived backgrounds are exposed to an enriched environment. Rather than dealing with stages of development, Kagan urges teachers to create a stable and positive learning situation. Past experiences of the teacher and of the student are less significant to Kagan than a sense of involvement and experiences that are supportive of intellectual growth. Kagan believes that the environment is all-important, and he is optimistic about programs like Head Start. His cognitive interpretation of child development is a theory which states that learners do best in an environment characterized by moderate discrepancy from their existing world view. Uncertainty and challenge are emotionally satisfying, but the shock of something totally new may create resistance in the learner.

Vygotsky in *Thought and Language* noted that thought and speech are the key to the nature of human consciousness. Thus understanding child development entails a totality of understanding words, thoughts, and motivations. He finds four developmental states: (1) primitive or preverbal thought; (2) experience with physical properties (self and objects around the child); (3) use of external and internal signs as aids in solving internal problems; and (4) ingrowth of constant interaction between inner and outer operations. Vygotsky, like Dewey, placed emphasis on the cultural ingredients in human development.

Other Contributions to Educational Psychology.   The Mastery Learning concept of Benjamin Bloom has had considerable influence on the theory and practice of teaching in twentieth-century America. Mastery Learning calls for individualized instruction with each student going at his or her own pace. Students must demonstrate that each level and condition of learning has been mastered before going on to the next level. Bloom is also known for his two taxonomies, the cognitive and the affective. Values and attitudes in the affective domain must be understood as being different from the intellectual tasks of cognition. This distinction has been supported by split-brain research and its implications for educators. Neurologists like J. E. Bogen and Michael Gazzaniga claim education has stressed verbal skills to a fault and that both language and nonlanguage techniques are needed.

Cognitive psychology contrasts sharply with the behaviorism of B. F. Skinner. It emphasizes complex intellectual processes which cannot be explained by the analysis of simple stimulus-response situations. Since 1970, cognitive psychology has become the dominant theoretical force, but most schools still reflect the behaviorist approach. Cognitive psychologists like Robert Glaser think this will change before the end of the century. Other psychologists such as Albert Bandura and Richard Walters concern themselves with the way people acquire behavior appropriate to social circumstances. Loud expressions and slang language may be appreciated in an informal meeting of peers but is not appropriate in a classroom setting. These psychologists build on the principles of Skinner to form a theory of social learning.

Noam Chomsky of the Massachusetts Institute of Technology has criticized Skinner on quite different grounds. He sees Skinner's learner as a robot responding to external stimuli only. Chomsky believes that all human beings have an inborn inclination to master language, regardless of the environment. His theory of Transformational Grammar states that learners respond not only to the environment but also to internal events.

Another area of psychology that has created considerable educational interest in recent years is described as humanistic and phenomenological. Carl Rogers is known for client-centered or non-directive therapy. He feels that psychology has focused on the experimental laboratory and Freudian theory instead of human growth and the potential of mankind. In books like *On Becoming a Person*, Rogers concerns himself with the infinite possibilities of human development, creativity, and how people can help each other to become more fully human.

Abraham Maslow is one of the best known humanistic psychologists. He has focused on counseling and identified the needs which are basic to the educational environment. Maslow's hierarchy of needs is included in the basic preparation of many American teachers. Basic needs like food and shelter always take priority over others. This is not different from the position of the progressives who believed that before a student can be taught, the school must see that he is properly fed and physically well. Needs for safety and security come next in Maslow's scheme. Beyond security, we all have needs for affection and love. A desire for self-esteem and the respect of others takes the next place on the hierarchy. The final need is for self-actualization.

For Maslow, the best education is one that deals with the real and serious problems of life. In order to understand the wider world, it is necessary to have self-knowledge and to become an authentic individual. Teachers should have deep concerns for children, but teachers cannot be effective unless their own needs are met and they have healthy mental attitudes. Teachers must understand that growth has two components. The learner needs to venture out, to stretch and to be challenged, but the learner also wants to remain safe and in familiar territory. Optimum learning occurs somewhere between absolute safety (with no risk at all) and maximum risk which causes the learner to feel threatened and under stress. Compassionate and caring persons are good teachers. To help a child become a better person requires an atmosphere of acceptance in the classroom and a balance between objective and subjective learning experiences.

CHILD STUDY AND MEASUREMENT

Education as a science or discipline is grounded in psychology, but child study and the measurement movement also provide instruments for research and development. Most of the efforts to measure ability or study children prior to 1900 were not objective. Demands for understanding the nature of the child were made as early as the first century by the Roman educator Quintilian and were repeated by Rousseau, Pestalozzi, and Froebel. However, nothing more sophisticated than the common diary existed as a tool for measuring the ability or characteristics of the child until Francis Galton (1822–1911) developed the mathematics of Karl Pearson into a means of measuring the deviation from the mean between and within groups of children. Galton was a cousin of Charles Darwin, and it was Darwin's research that caused him to become interested in measuring the deviation of characteristics within and between groups of people. Both Galton and Darwin invented tests to measure the abilities or capacities of individuals. Methods for measuring and analyzing quantitative data was the subject of James Cattell's Mental Tests and Measurement (1890). Galton was the first to use curves to express the distribution of individuals in terms of characteristics such as age, height, and intelligence.

While Cattell and Charles Judd were pioneering the measurement movement in America, French psychologists Alfred Binet and Theophile Simon were creating an instrument to measure intelligence. The Simon-Binet test was published in 1906, and ten years later, Lewis Terman produced the Stanford revision of that test. Millions of soldiers were given the Stanford test of intelligence during World War I, which resulted in the first massive data on the subject and created a model for later intelligence tests for use in public schools. The significance of both group and individual testing of intelligence can hardly be overemphasized in the modern history of American education. Test results became the basis for new programs, curriculum changes, ability grouping, and a host of other educational alternatives which are still hotly debated in professional circles.

Another contribution to the statistical measurement of learning began with the work of Dr. Joseph Rice. As editor of the Forum, Rice undertook a study of the achievement of students studying spelling in elementary schools. Having tested 30,000 pupils, he concluded that those who spent only fifteen minutes a day on the study of the subject learned to spell just as well as those who devoted an hour or more to the task. Naturally, there was a negative reaction from those who still supported mental discipline, but in 1912 the NEA went on record as favoring candid investigation of schools and methods. The "Measurement of Educational Products" was part of the *Seventeenth Yearbook of the National Society for the Study of Education* published in 1918. It contained eighty-four standard tests for use in elementary schools and twenty-five for high schools and covered virtually every subject of the curriculum. Thus, Thorndike's scales for measuring academic achievement and Cliff Stone's objective test of arithmetic reasoning (1908) had developed into a set of standardized achievement tests which were published and adopted by schools throughout the United States.

A firm foundation for the quantitative approach to measuring academic achievement had been laid. William McCall, one of Thorndike's students, is credited with the statement, "Whatever exists at all, exists in some amount and can be measured." While educational investigation continued to revise and refine both tests of achievement and of intelligence, mere comparison between students soon gave way to the study of groups. Homogeneous grouping, the effects of social class, studies of educational age, and attempts to diagnose defects of underachieving students became areas of investigation between the world wars. A great many modern issues in education are related to measuring intelligence and achievement. Such measures seldom account for the cultural background of the child. Students with low scores may be discriminated against with regard to future activities such as entering college. Insofar as test scores reflect social or cultural differences, they are unfair measures of comparison between individuals, and this has been the subject of a major debate in recent years. The abuse of individual intelligence testing has also been widespread. If IQ scores are made available to teachers, there is often a tendency to classify the student as "bright" or "slow," on the basis of that evidence alone. Cultural bias in intelligence testing has become a major target of educational research. There is considerable concern today that achievement scores used for meeting accountability requirements (now a legal obligation in most states) may create excessive emphasis on basic skills and information to the detriment of personality development or "affective" learning. Tests for general intelligence had other problems in addition to cultural bias. The Stanford-Binet scales were devised for children fifteen and under. In 1944, David Wechsler, a clinical psychologist at New York's Bellevue Hospital, designed tests of specific mental abilities in adults. These tests measured both verbal ability and performance at tasks. Later the Wechsler Scales were adapted for children and the Stanford-Binet was extended for adults.

Child Study.   Quite a different approach to the study of children and learning came out of the work of G. Stanley Hall (1844–1924). Hall established a center for applied psychology at Johns Hopkins in 1884 and founded the *American Journal of Psychology*. He asked trained kindergarten teachers to test children for their understanding of about one hundred words ranging from common objects to general concepts. From this study he published *The Contents of Children's Minds on Entering School*. In reporting the results of tests on children, Hall included information on social background and sex and remarked on the high degree of emotion and superstition shown by the young. Later, as president of Clark University, Hall brought together the first group of scholars interested in scientific child study. Among his students were Arnold Gesell and Lewis Terman.

Making a formal study of the adolescent child, Hall concluded that emotional development and personality growth were just as important as cognitive learning. As an evolutionist, he sought to combine the culture epoch theory of the Herbartians with the recapitulation theory of biology. He saw childhood play as the recapitulation of man's primitive stage and believed that inhibition of play might result in the expression of violent tendencies.

Child study through the observation of youngsters at play or school, efforts to measure the interests of preschool children, and the stage theory of modern learning theorists like Jean Piaget follow logically from the pioneering work of G. Stanley Hall. The specialties of child and adolescent psychology as well as developmental psychology and the study of exceptional children owe their beginning to his work.

Arnold Gesell's Clinic for Child Development at Yale, A. B. Hollingshead's *Elmtown's Youth* (1949), and James S. Coleman's famous *The Adolescent Society* (1961) represent efforts to understand youth in a cultural setting. Dealing with the personality of the whole child, the efficiency of the school and teacher, or the sociology of education requires methods of evaluation different from those used in the measurement of intelligence or achievement. Interest in human relations and the clarification of values grew out of the realization that the needs of youth are different from those of adults, and that existing educational programs sometimes fail to meet these needs. In 1935, the American Council on Education formed the American Youth Commission which studied problems of youngsters. It found that economic factors, shattered homes, discrimination, and social stratification played major roles in the attitudes of young people and their school achievement. Similar commissions founded by the Progressive Education Association in the 1930s called attention to the fact that schools were subject oriented and not interested in the personal lives of students. Caroline Zachery, chairperson for one of the commissions, insisted that the personality of the individual is formed only through positive functioning relationships with others. She went on to found the mental hygiene movement in American schools. A considerable interest also developed in the area of research on the dynamics of instructional groups and the interactions between students and teachers in a classroom situation.

By 1950, the scientific measurement of groups had developed into a major interest of educational research. European sociologists such as Durkheim and Weber joined psychology and sociology in an effort to understand the psychodynamics of group interaction. Since World War II, there has been a vast increase in the research and literature dealing with the effects of teacher behavior on the student. Some of this has centered on T-groups, group encounter, and sensitivity training. Some has been concerned with the dynamics of instructional groups and is represented by the work of Ned Flanders and Henry Nelson. Sociologists interested in bureaucracies and systems functioning have also contributed to this field of study.

Tests for measuring personality, such as the Rorschach, are also commonly used in education. Temperament, aptitudes, and attitudes of students are understood to have a profound effect upon what they are able to learn and what program best fits their needs. Guidance especially has depended upon aptitudes and job analysis in an effort to fit students into a meaningful curriculum.

Educational testing and measurement now occupies a large share of the time and effort of professionals at all levels in education. Research skills are regarded as important for college and public school teachers alike, and almost all educational programs depend upon research for their support. The literature relating to measurement and testing is now so vast that considerable skill is needed just to find material that relates directly to a given problem or issue. A neglected area of measurement has been creativity and means for identifying the gifted. High IQ scores as used by Terman are not adequate for finding all students who might benefit from programs for the gifted and talented. Julian Stanley of M.I.T. has worked out a way to find and help mathematically talented college students but many gifted youngsters go undetected.

EXPERIMENTS AND INNOVATIONS IN THE TWENTIETH CENTURY

Francis W. Parker tried out many new ideas in school organization and curricula in the late nineteenth century and built the foundations for an experimental program in the Cook County Normal School. John Dewey expanded Parker's beginning into his experimental school at the University of Chicago, which was truly a laboratory for testing educational innovations. The laboratory school lasted only seven years but it was a child-centered school which experimented with democratic organization, nontraditional methods and equipment, and a curriculum based on the natural needs and interests of children (activity curriculum). Many of the ideas which appeared in Dewey's 1916 educational classic, *Democracy and Education*, were tried in the laboratory school, and the Dewey school gave rise to new educational experiments by the progressive educators.

Progressive Education.   Even before the organization of the Progressive Education Association in 1919, schools were being organized according to the liberal ideas of Rousseau, Pestalozzi, Froebel, Parker, and Dewey. In 1907, Marietta Johnson pioneered a "School of Organic Education" at Fairhope, Alabama. Tasks in her school were not assigned by teachers, so students were free to follow their own interests. Natural growth and development according to nature replaced early emphasis on reading and accumulating knowledge. Johnson's program followed Rousseau's *Emile*. The curriculum included nature study, physical education, music, handicrafts, field geography, drama, storytelling, games, and number concepts.

A similar school was established under the supervision of the University of Missouri by Professor Junius L. Meriam. Meriam's school had a flexible time schedule with no rigid periods for drills, exercises, or formal lessons. Others soon followed the lead of Meriam and Johnson. The Cottage School of Riverside, Illinois, and the Little School in the Woods at Greenwich, Connecticut, were activity-centered institutions. John and Evelyn Dewey reported on a number of these efforts in *Schools of Tomorrow* in 1915.

Within a few years of the beginning of progressive education as a movement, the number of private experimental schools increased rapidly. Few sound statistical studies of their programs were made, but they were highly publicized by their founders and others who were critical of "traditional schools."

Progressive Education Association.   Although the Progressive Education Association existed as an organization only from 1919 until 1955, its influence on American education was profound. Marietta Johnson joined with Eugene R. Smith of the Park School in Baltimore and Stanwood Cobb (a Naval Academy instructor) to organize the society. Aimed at the coordination of educational reform among private school leaders, the group was highly influenced by the theories of John Dewey. At an organizational meeting of the Association held in Washington D.C. on March 15, 1919, the eighty-five charter members adopted the following principles:

I. Freedom to Develop Naturally.

The conduct of the pupil should be governed by himself according to the social needs of his community, rather than by arbitrary laws. Full opportunity for initiative and self-expression should be provided, together with an environment rich in interesting material that is available for the use of every pupil.

II. Interest as the Motive for All Work.

Interest should be satisfied and developed through: (1) direct and indirect contact with the world and its activities and use of the experience thus gained; (2) application of knowledge gained, and correlation between different subjects; and (3) consciousness of achievement.

III. The Teacher a Guide, Not a Taskmaster.

It is essential that teachers should believe in the aims and general principles of Progressive Education and that they should have latitude for the development of initiative and originality.

Progressive teachers will encourage the use of all the senses, training the pupils in both observation and judgment, and instead of hearing recitations only, will spend most of the time teaching how to use various sources of information—including life activities as well as books, how to reason about the information thus acquired, and how to express forcefully and logically the conclusion reached.

Ideal teaching conditions demand that classes be small, especially in the elementary school years.

IV. Scientific Study of Pupil Development.

School records should not be confined to the marks given by teachers to show the advancement of the pupils in their study of subjects, but should also include both objective and subjective reports on those physical, mental, moral and social characteristics which can be influenced by the school and the home. Such records should be used as a guide for the treatment of each pupil, and should also serve to focus the attention of the teacher on the all-important work of development rather than on simply teaching subject-matter.

V. Greater Attention to All that Affects the Child's Physical Development.

One of the first considerations of Progressive Education is the health of the pupils. Much more room in which to move about, better light and air, clean and well ventilated buildings, easier access to the out-of-doors and greater use of it are all necessary. There should be frequent use of adequate playgrounds. The teachers should observe closely the physical conditions of each pupil and in co-operation with the home, make abounding health the first objective of childhood.

VI. Co-operation Between School and Home to Meet the Needs of Child Life.

The school should provide, with the home, as much as is possible of all that the natural interests and activities of the child demand, especially during the elementary school years. These conditions can come about only through intelligent cooperation between parents and teachers.

VII. The Progressive School a Leader in Educational Movements.

The Progressive School should be a leader in educational movements. It should be a laboratory where new ideas, if worthy, meet encouragement and where tradition alone does not rule, but the best of the past is leavened with the discoveries of today, and the result is freely added to the sum of educational knowledge. (see *Progressive Education* 1 [April 1924]: 2)

Charles W. Eliot agreed to become the first honorary president of the Progressive Education Association, lending his prestige to the organization. The journal *Progressive Education* appeared in 1924 and continued to be a major publication until 1957.

In the early twenties the membership of PEA consisted largely of teachers and parents in private schools, but by the late thirties there were more than 10,000 members. Most of the professional educators in colleges and universities joined, as did the superintendents and administrators of many public school systems. In addition to the experimental schools supported by the organization, there were annual public conferences devoted to educational reform. Scientific study of pupil development and strong cooperation between schools and the society were major beliefs of PEA. William H. Kilpatrick, developer of the project method, was a major spokesman for progressive education and made the views of John Dewey popular among many educators at all levels. With Ellsworth Collings, Kilpatrick recommended that the school organize its work through a series of activities which would develop the student's purposeful effort. His projects included drills, problems, appreciation activities, and creative or construction projects.

The Progressive Education Association soon broke into camps with quite different interests. The "Social Frontier" group led by George S. Counts wanted to use education as a means for social revolution and reform. Dewey and his followers were interested in a sophisticated educational theory and careful research. Other progressive educators merely developed new methods or supported freedom for children.

Extended School Use.   Not all the early innovations were aimed at the individual development of the child. Intensive use of the school facilities to relieve social problems caused by unexpected urban growth was tried by William Wirt in Gary, Indiana. In an effort to meet the failure of the culture to provide for the needs of city children, the school offered a longer day with workshops, gymnasiums, laboratories, auditoriums, and playgrounds constantly open and supervised. To give all children the opportunity for extended school participation, schools were kept open on Saturday and during vacation periods. Adult night classes were offered, and pupils did their own repair and maintenance work. Costs were kept low by the "platoon system" by which work in classrooms, laboratories, and workshops alternated with activities scheduled in auditoriums, playgrounds, and gymnasiums so as to keep all facilities continuously occupied. This plan for maximum school use spread widely in the United States, and by 1929, more than a thousand schools were using a platoon organization. Today, crowding in some schools is relieved by scheduling one school day early in the morning and another beginning in the afternoon.

Other important efforts to relate the schools to the needs of the society were made by Carleton Washburne in Winnetka, Illinois, and by Helen Parkhurst in Dalton, Massachusetts. The Winnetka plan divided school offerings into "creative and group activities" and "common essentials" like science and basic skills. Work in the essentials was by units and given at the student's own rate of learning, a practice now common in schools using programmed instruction. The Dalton laboratory plan incorporated Dewey's educational principles and many of the methods suggested by the Italian educator Maria Montessori. Both the Dalton and the Winnetka plans sought to develop the "whole child" and were concerned with physical and social as well as intellectual education.

Influence of Experimental Programs.   While the early experimental schools did not become standard in America, they served as models for a different approach to basic educational questions. Ideas put into practice in laboratory or innovated schools were often adopted, with modifications, into the programs of the more traditional institutions. Sometimes new schools were created in response to criticisms of existing conditions and were intended to serve as contrasts with older plans.

Charles W. Eliot prepared a report for the General Education Board in 1916, in which he called for changes in American high schools. Partly at the urging of Eliot, the Lincoln School was established as an experimental arm of Teachers College, Columbia University, and it continued to operate until 1948. Today, many of the leading teachers' colleges and universities which have departments of education maintain laboratory schools. Research and development centers for testing all sorts of educational innovations are appearing in teaching-training institutions. Sophisticated statistical processes and refined methods of testing have given a new dimension to educational testing and the growth of graduate programs has created an explosion in research. Doctoral dissertations in the area of educational psychology alone now provide us with a vast body of knowledge concerning the effectiveness of various pedagogical techniques.

PROGRESSIVE EDUCATORS AND THEIR CRITICS

By 1928 Dewey had become critical of the Progressive Education Association for its lack of sound social philosophy. His arguments against experiments lacking in theory were expressed well in *Experience and Education*, which appeared in 1938. By the 1930s, interest of the progressives shifted from a reaction against formal subject matter and harsh discipline to the social and economic problems of the whole culture. Many of the members continued with their experiments in natural development, the activity curriculum, and the child-centered school, but the possibility of the schools as leaders in improving or reconstructing society became the theme of progressives like George Counts.

While the progressives continued to meet until 1955, their organization was divided into factions with different points of view, and their efforts provoked a growing amount of controversy. Meanwhile, significant projects were being carried on that were to alter major educational concepts. The Eight Year Study of the Progressive Education Association involved thirty high schools interested in experimentation and exploration. They altered the secondary curriculum and made it conform to known laws of learning and the various social environments. The report, published in 1942, showed that students in the progressive high schools did at least as well in college as their counterparts in traditional secondary schools had done, and that they were better oriented to adult life.

Life Adjustment Education.

In 1945, a group of educators launched the Life Adjustment Movement. This group was theoretically related to the progressive education movement and its concern was mostly with those students who were not preparing for college. The Life Adjustment Movement was aimed at a greater equalization of educational opportunity and was critical of any program which was not suitable for the majority of young Americans. The movement was short-lived because of the bitter attacks from many segments of the American people. Life Adjustment had the support of several educational organizations and the United States Office of Education but was bitterly condemned by many college professors and by those interested in the subject-matter curriculum.

Dr. Charles Prosser pointed out that high schools failed to meet the needs of the sixty percent of the students who were not being trained for a vocational skill. In 1947, Commissioner of Education John Studebaker called attention to the twenty percent of the children who did not enter secondary schools and to the forty percent who dropped out before graduation. Attention was also given to the wide range of individual differences among secondary school students and the effect of family or cultural background on achievement. Twenty-nine states developed some kind of curriculum revision associated with Life Adjustment by 1954. Many school systems became interested in how to meet the needs of those who seemed not to benefit from standard courses. Studies were made of the holding power of secondary schools (dropout rate) and of the relevance of programs in the view of students.

Because of the heavy criticism by those interested only in intellectual development and a great public fear that academic standards were being lowered by Life Adjustment, the program was terminated in the late 1950s. Nevertheless, Life Adjustment gave attention to the concern for equal educational opportunities and the problems of cultural deprivation which later brought about such programs as Head Start and the Job Corps. A basic issue remains in American education over whether we should concentrate on educating the whole child or whether intellectual excellence has priority. Many believe that meeting the psychological needs of the child is not enough, nor is developing the mind enough. Few would argue that mastery of the essential subject—particularly those that can be called tool subjects—is not important, but the great challenge is one of relating the experiences of the child to the cultural environment. American schools continue to have large numbers of students who leave school because they are unable to compete, bored, poorly adjusted, or merely uninterested in the programs offered. Today, numerous school systems are attempting to offer alternative high schools, work-study programs, store-front schools, or "schools without walls" in an effort to meet the needs of students for whom the regular educational program is unsatisfactory. This is exactly what the Life Adjustment plan intended to accomplish.

Another progressive innovation, which seemed to offer a possible solution to some of the social problems in modern America, was the Community School. Based on such books as John Dewey's *Schools of Tomorrow,* the concept centered upon organizing the curriculum around the lives of students and involving members of the community as resources. The school was to be used for all sorts of community projects such as recreation activities and as a local center for communications. It was also expected that students and adults would work together on problems that involved the whole community. Experimental community schools were founded by several universities with a grant from the Sloan Foundation in the 1940s, but only a few remain in operation. George Leonard's book *Education and Ecstasy* describes a future school of this kind.

Critics of Progressive Influence.

Idealists, realists, essentialists, and others with a philosophy opposed to pragmatism were critical of progressive education from the beginning. Dewey himself believed that many of the members of the progressive movement had been too quick to adopt new programs or methods without a proper theoretical base. Boyd Bode, one of the outstanding leaders of progressive education, criticized the determination of educational needs by looking at the individual child, rather than the society and the child together. Bode insisted that the meaning of liberty and democracy are linked and that people must make a moral commitment to the kind of society they want before content and authority in education can be established.

In addition to philosophic criticisms, a number of studies of academic achievement revealed certain weaknesses in the students who had attended progressive schools. These studies were not conclusive and most were less impressive than the Eight Year Study which was favorable to progressive schools, but they provided support for those who disagreed with progressive theory. It should be remembered that while the progressive movement had great influence on public elementary schools and colleges of education, the effect on secondary schools was slight and practically nonexistent on the academic disciplines in the universities. Some of those who blame Dewey and the progressives for the ills of education and society, attribute more influence to the progressive movement than the historical evidence supports.

In the 1950s equality of educational opportunity took on a new aspect. Life Adjustment had been concerned with the terminal student but during the cold war years, the great cry was for the academically talented student to receive adequate training. Arthur Bestor, James Conant, John Gardner, and Hyman Rickover were among prominent critics making new demands on education. They claimed that equality of opportunity did not mean the same education for everyone, and that the national welfare demanded special provisions for the gifted. The success of the Soviet Union in launching Sputnik in 1957 shifted emphasis from life adjustment to excellence and led to the National Defense Education Act. This law greatly increased technical and scientific offerings in American high schools and colleges. Not all educators were enthusiastic about the narrow emphasis on quality for the elite or the stress placed on mathematics, science, and foreign languages.

The 1960s were dominated by concerns for equality of opportunity. In the wake of the black revolution following the Brown case and a new concern for civil rights, efforts were made to meet the needs of all children. Ethnic and multicultural studies became popular and bilingual programs were started in schools with many non-English speaking students. Efforts at reorganizing schools to bring about desegregation and the use of busing to create integrated schools dominated the 1960s and 1970s. Efforts were made to help the lower class youngster compete in middle class schools through programs like project Head Start. Critics felt that integration and equality efforts took away from the drive toward excellence and public support for education was in decline by 1980. Others expressed concern about the lack of literary and humanistic emphasis in school programs. These issues will be discussed in detail in the chapter on controversial issues.

ACADEMIC FREEDOM AND THE EDUCATIONAL PROFESSION

Early in this century, American schoolteachers could not smoke, drink alcoholic beverages, or express political preferences without fear of losing their jobs. While this situation has improved, public school staff members are still attacked for what they teach and for their personal activities. Thus, a teacher who asks children to read Huxley's *Brave New World*, or advocates adding fluoride to water, or supports racial integration, may be branded a "communist" by those who fear such ideas. Nor are the schools themselves free from attack. Frequently, a school board, a superintendent, or even an entire school system will find itself under violent fire from organized groups or powerful individuals. During the Joseph McCarthy era, mere accusation of "red influence" was sufficient to frighten many school officials into firing teachers or removing books from the school libraries. In some cases, however, school boards have been willing to stand up to criticism and to make their assailants prove their case, if they have one. In the 1980s, public school teachers came increasingly under attack from the religious "new right" which accused them of teaching values clarification or secular humanism. Teachers have often been unable to fight due to the lack of support from a strong professional organization, a scarcity of financial backing, or the reluctance of some school administrators to take a stand. Thus, a teacher who has a controversial point of view, or who refuses to sign a loyalty oath, may be asked to resign quietly in return for "keeping his record clean." Significant increases in the quantity and quality of teacher training have been made in the last few years, but teachers still lack autonomy to control the admission requirements to their own profession. Teachers find it difficult to identify an agreed upon and enforceable professional code of ethics, or to develop an organization which represents them all. American public school teachers still lack the academic freedom enjoyed by most university professors.

TEACHER EDUCATION

Divergent educational practices in the United States have been reflected in teacher education; today this diversity is becoming less pronounced, but it still exists. Many normal schools early in the twentieth century were more like secondary schools than colleges. For years, a shortage of teachers created a reluctance to enforce general standards of certification. Large numbers of rural teachers were given certificates on the basis of passing examinations or on the strength of a year or two of college work. While temporary or emergency certificates are no longer issued except under most unusual circumstances, state requirements differ with regard to the number and type of professional courses demanded.

Without exception, normal schools did become four-year colleges and most state universities developed departments, schools and colleges of education. The forty-five colleges for teachers in 1920 had grown to four times that number by 1940. Depression years caused the first oversupply of teachers, a condition which gave rise to higher minimum standards. After World War II, most teachers were prepared with a general or liberal college education, specialized knowledge of the field to be taught, professional courses including methods and psychology, and practice teaching. Beyond question, American teachers are better qualified to practice their profession than ever before in history. Nevertheless, there is considerable criticism of teacher education.

The education of American teachers is a persistent national problem. Parents complain about the performance of teachers, university professors question their subject matter competence, administrators feel the universities certify people who cannot cope with school problems, and teachers themselves often feel ill prepared to work with children. Numerous studies of teacher education have been published in recent years, most of which give a negative evaluation. Scholars report that teacher training appears to make little difference in the ability of teachers to affect student achievement. Radical critics like Ivan Illich question having teachers trained and certified at all.

In spite of the dissatisfaction and criticism, it appears that there is still a need for people specially trained to work with children. Public education employs well over two and one-half million people. So long as an institutionalized system of schools is in operation in America, the development and improvement of instructional skills will be required. A shortage of teachers has forced many states to seek alternative means by which teachers may be certified without the standard courses. A few such programs are of good quality, but many put poorly prepared teachers into the classrooms.

Formal and informal surveys and studies reveal that seasoned teachers rate field experience as the most relevant and beneficial part of their training. In 1972, the Commission of Public School Personnel Policies in Ohio reported that 78 percent of the teachers who had graduated from the 53 teacher education institutions in the state thought student teaching was the most valuable part of their preparation. This study also indicated that educational practice or student teaching is insufficient, poorly supervised, and comes too late in the course sequence. Inservice training for teachers already certified and working is also criticized for being of little use to the teacher in actually improving methods, classroom management, communication skills, and techniques for motivation of students.

Alternative programs are being developed each year by colleges and other institutions in an effort to build more relevance and skill into teacher education. Teacher Corps required interns to live and work in school communities (often lower economic areas with large numbers of minority students) while receiving instruction in theory. Colleges of education now offer programs to help middle-class teacher candidates understand the problems of lower-class students.

The major problem of teacher education is providing sufficient field experiences and practice teaching. Institutions of teacher education now usually require many hours of observation and work in schools or with children in other settings prior to practice teaching. There is general agreement that at least one year of internship would be a vast improvement over a semester of practice teaching with one cooperating teacher. By 1980, Florida and Oklahoma had passed laws requiring teacher candidates to spend a fifth year in schools as teacher interns before granting full certification. One problem is that teachers are not paid well enough to justify the extra year of entry level training.

Competency Based Teacher Education, commonly referred to as competency based or performance based teacher education, is now used in many university-based colleges of education. CBTE is directed toward the development of specific skills or categories of behavior which have a direct connection to meaningful and observable learning on the part of the student. Instead of merely having students accumulate credits in various courses, CBTE attempts to offer methods and content selected for their ability to accomplish the goals of professional training effectively and expediently.

Some colleges are now cooperating with urban school districts to provide experiences for teacher interns designed to prepare them for work with the special educational problems of children in the ghettos of large cities. Others have developed "teaching centers" where professional teachers, practice teachers, college professors, and students can have more interaction.

As Charles Silberman has pointed out, new teachers are often thrust into a situation fraught with anxiety and fear, and these fears and anxieties do not necessarily evaporate with experience. The techniques most frequently used to help teachers overcome their problems are inservice training and graduate courses given in colleges and universities.

Inservice programs often include workshops, guest speakers, and seminars, but vary from one district or system to another. Some schools have no inservice education for teachers, and the programs in others are inadequate for real professional growth. The American Association of Colleges for Teacher Education devoted much of its energy in 1989 to identifying a common knowledge base all teachers should share. This proved a difficult task, especially for elementary teachers. There is still much disagreement concerning the make-up of a common knowledge base. Graduate courses in education for teachers are popular because many schools require teachers to obtain a master's degree within a few years from the time of employment, and salary increases are often tied to the acquisition of graduate credit hours or advanced degrees. Graduate work in psychology, administration, statistics, educational philosophy is certainly of value, but there is a minimum of clinical experience or training designed to aid teachers in procedures of instruction and curriculum development. Of course, many teachers use graduate schools of education as a means of preparing themselves for positions as administrators, college teachers, or research workers.

The fact that large numbers of teachers feel that they are poorly prepared and the learning problems of so many students illustrated by failure in achievement is helping to support the development of new programs. With more certified teachers than jobs available, administrators can be more selective if they know what kinds of skills and what type of teacher training is most effective. Many persons now entering the field of education are serious about becoming as skilled and professional as they can. They are demanding clinical training of the sort provided in professional fields such as medicine. Pressures are building for college faculty members to become more directly involved with students and teachers in actual learning situations.

Illich has suggested that teachers should have easy access to "learning webs," centers in which teaching, learning, and communication skills can be developed. Centers where teachers can voluntarily meet to exchange experiences, thoughts, feelings, and suggestions for improving practice are now being suggested nationwide. Such a center was created in Bay Shore, New York in 1972, and pilot programs have been established for teacher centers in Vermont and Florida. In 1993, the National Council for Accreditation of Teacher Education approved outcomes-based standards for the preparation of teachers based upon standards developed by professional subject matters associations such as the National Science Teachers Association. According to Karen Diegmueller in "NCATE Moves Forward in Approving Outcomes for Preparation of Teachers," several states have entered into partnership agreements with NCATE to conduct joint-reviews of teacher training institutions. Some teachers in the mid-1990s were working toward National Teacher Certification.

New Methods.   An effort is made to introduce students to methods such as the use of programmed learning, team teaching, individualized instruction, laboratory techniques, and methods of research. Many states now require student teachers to have some competency in the use of instructional technology before they can be certified. A better understanding of remedial reading and learning disabilities is sometimes demanded. The knowledge explosion, the way learning is affected by mass media, social problems of students, and the development of new techniques require that teachers continue their training as long as they work. An example is the "new mathematics" which required arithmetic teachers to relearn teaching concepts through graduate courses or workshops.

Teacher education has become a topic for debate among educators with different points of view. Most professors of education, leaders of teachers' organizations, and professional teachers and administrators favor present training practices. They agree that teacher training needs to be improved, but they maintain that professional courses must form the core of teacher education. The Land Grant College or Morrill Act of 1862 provided an impetus for professional schools in higher education including Teacher Education Departments and Colleges. There has, however, been continuing interest in what is ultimately worth knowing in teacher education. Several critics who have never had work in professional education nor made a study of teacher-training institutions argued that good teachers are made through mastering subject matter. Admiral Hyman Rickover, American history professor Arthur Bestor, Jr., business tycoon Albert Lynd, and columnist Dorothy Thompson were among the enemies of professional education. They argued that a knowledge of subject matter and a good liberal education can replace a knowledge of child psychology in the training of teachers. This same point of view was expressed earlier by perennialists, the Great Books advocates, and the Council for Basic Education. The Carnegie Corporation provided funds for a study of teacher education conducted by James B. Conant, former president of Harvard University. Conant published his conclusions in 1963, making the colleges primarily responsible for selecting courses for teachers. This study negates the role of the states in certification of teachers. In the late 1980s, California began selecting master teachers and giving them extra pay to coach newly-certified teachers. This mentor project worked well, but as John Goodlad pointed out, it was limited to the techniques of the model master teachers when more revolutionary changes were needed.

Recent Growth. In recent years, there has been an unprecedented growth in schools at all levels from the elementary school through the college. This growth has been accompanied by vast numbers of new developments which affect education. Technological advances have given rise to educational television, filmstrips, motion pictures, overhead projectors, computers for assisting instruction, and the like. Boys and girls who enter the first grade after years of exposure to television and other mass media bring new vocabularies and new experiences into the classroom. Closed-circuit and airborne television programs are received in schools, while new sources of information are found in modern instructional-materials centers. The teaching machine, in both its simple and complicated forms, is now a subject of conversation in schools and homes. While these "new-fangled gadgets" have been viewed warily by school boards and administrators, few informed educators doubt that they will have a part in the educational future of America. Self-instructing machines, team teaching projects, individual assignments, and non-graded organization are now being tested in schools and by research and development centers in colleges of education. Language laboratories, developed by the Army Specialized Training Program, have made a considerable impact on the teaching of foreign languages.

The knowledge explosion has encouraged thinking about a year-round school and the lengthening of the school week through longer hours or Saturday classes. If this is not done, we may still expect the average school year to lengthen from 185 days to more than 200 days within a decade. The proliferation of subjects seems only to have begun as the scientific explosion continues to gain momentum. There is still the task of providing adequate challenge for the gifted child, appropriate work for the retarded, and adequate guidance for all. Even with the work of modern psychologists Jean Piaget and Jerome Bruner, we still have much to find out about the learning process.

The history of American education can never be finished. As this book goes to press, new innovations in education and cultural changes in the society are making new demands. We can only expect that past traditions and trends of development will provide some indication of the future paths of our schools.

THEN TO NOW

One of the great tragedies of American education is that we keep inventing the wheel. Often, ideas that hold great promise for improving teaching and learning are discarded with the movement that brought them about. For example, the psychological concepts of Herbart were rejected by the progressives and by John Dewey himself. This happened because of Dewey's reaction against lock-step programs and rigid systems that developed from the followers of Herbart in America such as Charles DeGarmo. Actually, the ideas of Herbart were well ahead of their time and might have been retained by those who sought to reform teacher-centered methods and formal steps of instruction. Herbart taught that the mind is a unitary organism, and therefore he could not support mental discipline or faculty psychology. He understood the need for relating one subject to another and so developed a core curriculum. Long before psychoanalysis, Herbart studied the relationship of the conscious to the subconscious mind and suggested a logical means by which new ideas from experience may be assimilated and stored by the learner. These ideas were not in conflict with the basic theories of the progressives. Indeed, they might have proved very helpful to the same progressive educators who scorned them because they were identified with the American Herbartian movement. Progressives turned to Gestalt psychology but many current notions about educational psychology were anticipated by Herbart and might have been used to improve the educational environment for generations.

Exactly the same thing happened with progressive education in its period of decline. As we have seen, progressives ruled education in the 1930s, but there was much criticism of their child-centered programs and permissive practices by 1940. The movement ceased to exert much influence after the conservative reaction in education triggered by World War II. Beyond question, many progressives were extreme in their views and their schools were by no means perfect. Nevertheless, progressive education brought about numerous experiments that are of great pedagogical value today. The fact that most American teachers are not well-versed in their own professional history means that they must begin from scratch in order to create new methods and programs. Progressives anticipated and worked with numerous plans and ideas which today are called educational innovations. This point is well made by Judith Ford, in an unpublished doctoral dissertation at University of Oklahoma, in 1977, called "Innovative Methods in Elementary Education: A Description and Analysis of Individualized Instruction in the Progressive Movement in Comparison with the Innovative Modern Elementary School."

Most of the current practices designed to improve instruction were tried in some form by the progressive educators. An exception is computer-assisted instruction, since computers and teaching machines were not available in the 1930s. Some of the most obvious parallels are:

1. *Inquiry based instruction.*   This method is often associated with Piaget and science teaching. John Dewey was a strong advocate of laboratory instruction and discovery learning. Almost all of the progressive schools used inquiry as a major method and records exist of their success.
2. *Mastery learning.*   Modern mastery learning is usually associated with Benjamin Bloom. Recall and application of learning to a problem solving situation was a mainstay of progressive schools. It was best demonstrated by Ellsworth Collings in the McDonald County Rural School in 1905.
3. *Individual contracting.*   Using individual contracts with students to stimulate specific learning is now a practice in many schools. The formal writing of contracts with specific behavioral goals may be current, but the idea of students participating in choosing what they would learn and when goes back to Helen Parkhurst and the Dalton Contract Plan of 1919.
4. *Differentiated staffing.*   Many professional educators now support differentiated staffing. Having all teachers trained in the same way seems inefficient and wasteful. Master teachers, general teachers, learning specialists, teaching assistants, instructional materials specialists, clerks, and nonprofessional staff members might make up a better team for instruction. The progressives used community resource people in their schools. They did not hesitate to bring in people with different training for various school-related tasks. J. Lloyd Trump, who first urged differentiated staffing in schools, was influenced by the progressive experiments.
5. *Flexible scheduling.*   The Gary Platoon Plan organized by William Wirt in 1915 used flexible scheduling. Most of the progressive schools were not tied to the clock or the calendar. They pioneered programs which used whatever time was necessary to accomplish learning without regard to filling days with even blocks of time or earning units of credit. Numerous modern schools use computers to program flexible individualized schedules.

6. *Individualized instruction.*   Today, a body of literature supports the idea that individualized instruction may be superior for many students. Carleton Washburne experimented with such a plan at Winnetka in 1919. Most progressives let students progress at their own speed which required special individual assignments and evaluation. The history of progressive education shows that individual instruction worked better than group instruction for some learning, but that it required more time of teachers. Progressives supported the social interaction of groups for certain subjects (such as social studies) but used individualized projects as well. They understood that each child is unique and that there are many styles of learning. In some ways, the progressive schools were similar to modern alternative schools, almost all of which use individualized instruction.

7. *Open classrooms.*   In spite of all the modern literature on the subject, open classrooms were pioneered by the progressives. Marietta Johnson's School of Organic Education at Fairhope, Alabama, was an early example. Freedom for students to move about, small group activities, an informal atmosphere, inquiry, and freedom of expression were characteristics of progressive education. The best of open classroom instruction is described in progressive literature.

8. *Team teaching and nongraded schools.*   John Dewey himself created teams of teachers to work with students at the laboratory school in the University of Chicago. Like the progressives who followed him, Dewey was aware that several teachers working together can provide a richer educational environment and better evaluation. Although the progressives did not establish nongraded schools in name, they did allow students to learn at their own rate of speed and they were not bound by any external standards. Progressives wrote about the perils of self-contained classrooms and rigid programs which require all children to achieve the same goals within a given span of time.

If American education is to meet the great challenges of the future, it must be efficient, flexible, professional, and stimulating. Schools cannot afford to reinvent and test programs or methods which were tried and tested in the past. Educators need to learn about both the success and the failure of earlier educational experiments and to use those experiments as guides in making a better quality learning environment. The educational reforms of the late 1980s, responding to "A Nation at Risk" and other critical reports, seemed to ignore history. Former Secretary of Education William Bennett wanted to restore a classical curriculum with intellectual rigor for the college-bound elite. Wide support for this by conservative groups and authors like Diane Ravitch and Allen Bloom obscured the goal of progressive education for all. Secretary Cavavos, during the Bush administration stressed greater equality. It is to be hoped that he will not ignore the search for excellence which dominated the history of American education in the previous decade. Secretary Richard W. Riley in the the Clinton administration sought more equality for students at-risk due to poverty and disadvantaged community conditions.

Goals 2000 efforts will continue the search for excellence called for in the reform reports of the 1980s while expanding opportunities for at-risk students.

BIBLIOGRAPHY

Brown, Ellsworth. *The Making of Our Middle Schools.* New York: Littlefield, 1970.

Burton, Warren. *The District School as It Was.* Boston: Lee & Shepard, 1897.

Butts, Freeman. *Public Education in the United States: From Revolution to Reform.* New York: Holt Rinehart and Winston, 1978.

Cremin, Lawrence. *The Transformation of the School.* New York: Alfred A. Knopf, 1961.

Cubberley, Elwood. *Public Education in the United States.* New York: Houghton Mifflin, 1934.

Diegmueller, Karen. "NCATE Moves Forward in Approving Outcomes for Preparation of Teachers." *Education Week* (October 13, 1993):4.

Digest of Educational Statistics 1980. Washington, D.C.: U.S. Government Printing Office, 1980.

Feistritzer, Emily. *Profiles of Teachers in the U.S.* Washington, D.C.: National Center for Educational Information, 1986.

Gutek, Gerald. *An Historical Introduction to American Education.* New York: Thomas Crowell, 1970.

Karier, Clarence. *Shaping the American Educational State: 1900 to the Present.* New York: Free Press, 1975.

Katz, Michael. *Class, Bureaucracy, and Schools.* New York: Praeger, 1971.

McLaughlin, Milbery. *Evaluation and Reform: The Elemental and Secondary Education Act of 1965.* Cambridge, MA: Harvard University Press, 1975.

Pitsch, Mark. "E.D. Officials Begin Task of Marketing Their Proposal to 'Reinvent' the Elementary and Secondary Education Act." *Education Week* (September 29, 1993):22.

Prosser, Charles. *Secondary Education and Life.* Cambridge, MA: Harvard University Press, 1939.

Rippa, Alexander. *Education in a Free Society.* 2d ed. New York: David McKay, 1971.

Tyack, David. *The One Best System: A History of American Urban Education.* Cambridge, MA: Harvard University Press, 1974.

Watson, John B. *Behaviorism.* New York: W. W. Norton and Company, 1924.

CONTROVERSIAL ISSUES IN MODERN AMERICAN EDUCATION

Even if only one child in ten could gain in intellectual effectiveness through a more favorable environment, we would still be bound to make the effort. . . . Individuals do differ greatly in their capacities, and each must be enabled to develop the talent that is in him (her). We believe that every person should be enabled to achieve the best that is in him (her), and we are the declared enemies of all conditions, such as disease, ignorance or poverty, which stunt the individual and prevent such fulfillment.

John W. Gardner

Anything which has already happened is history even if it happened only a moment ago. Making a good historical analysis of events just past is often more difficult than those which occurred in an earlier period. Recent occurrences in educational history are often surrounded by controversy. Very few modern events are free from criticism, and even the educational community often finds itself taking sides. Political groups get involved quite often in current educational concerns and public opinion plays a vital role in numerous decisions. While it was once rare for problems over the schools to result in litigation, it is now very common for educational issues to reach the courts. Books that are critical of many aspects of education now become best sellers while past critics wrote for much smaller audiences. Since education touches all of the American people and since the means of communication are expanding so rapidly, the current history of education is very much the history of controversial issues. While judgments about current events are hard to make, an understanding of history may provide us with the best foundation we can get for placing such events in perspective.

In chapter 9, various positions in the philosophy of education will be discussed. Philosophy is seldom universally accepted, so conflicting ideas and contradictory views are common. Pragmatists and idealists did not agree in the early twentieth century, and they

School Desegregation	Civil Rights Movement	Campus Rebellion
1954 Brown Case Issue	Martin Luther King, Jr.	1966 Coleman Report
1957 Sputnik Issue	1961 John Gardner Published *Can We Be Equal and* *Excellent Too?*	1961–1968 Kennedy-Johnson Legislation
Criticisms of Arthur Bestor, James Conant and Hyman Rickover	1963 Michael Harrington Published *The Other America*	

do not agree today. The same can be said for schools of psychology like Gestalt and behaviorism. The fight over the legal status of private schools that led to the Oregon case of 1925 provides background for the issue of tax support to parochial schools and the legality of tuition tax credits for nonpublic education.

In the past few decades, critical issues have appeared in the schools which pose serious questions for the future of education. There are also controversies in the general society which translate into problems for education. Some of these issues must be solved by members of the educational profession with the help of sound scientific research. Others can be solved only by cooperation between the general public and the profession. Still others continue to be issues for the reason that no solution is obvious or certain, even if the best possible interaction between school people and the public takes place. Altering the curriculum of the public schools to prepare children to cope successfully with future conditions is always uncertain precisely because techniques for future prediction are inexact.

Issues involving the purposes or goals of education concern both the layman and the professional educator in a society which is, to some degree, democratic. This kind of problem is the subject of philosophy of education, but it also involves values, norms, and attitudes which may be understood through sociology, social psychology, and political science. While various groups such as realists and pragmatists have clear-cut educational goals, the educational philosophy of the whole American people is not fixed and certain. In a fluid culture, the aims of education in one period of time are often altered considerably by the next generation. Specific aims, goals, and purposes are hotly debated not only among educators, but by the whole of the body politic. Educational purposes are

Equal Opportunity	Accountability	Return to Basics
1968 Issues Over Bilingual and Multicultural Education	1969 Arthur Jensen Studied IQ and Race	1973 Only 2,500 Black Doctorates in All Fields
Accountability Tests	1969 Theodore Roszak *The Making of a Counterculture*	1979 John Goodlad's *What Are Schools For?*
Compensatory Education for the Disadvantaged	1970 Charles Reich *The Greening of America*	1980s National Critical Reports, *A Nation at Risk, Action for Excellence, Making the Grade*
	Ivan Illich *Deschooling Society*	

certainly going to be the object of much disagreement and discussion in the future as in the past.

The role of the teacher and that of the profession in a problem or issue concerning schools often consists of communication and clarification. The public may be unaware of the existence of problems, or there may be a misunderstanding of the exact nature of those problems. Difficulties concerning poverty, crime, taxation, employment, equal rights, academic freedom, racial integration, discipline, and the like often have educational significance not clear to the casual observer. Explaining what the issues really mean and outlining possible consequences of various plans of action must often fall to educators. Analysis and clarification of hidden issues or underlying problems must often be undertaken before a solution can be reached. Obviously, past experience including a knowledge of history may provide clues to the probable success or failure of alternatives.

A number of approaches may be taken to the history and understanding of current issues and challenges in American education. In this chapter, we will discuss a number of well-known educational conflicts that have reached the courts. Litigation has always been important for educational policy as in the Dartmouth College case, 1819 and the Kalamazoo high school decision of 1874. In contemporary society, many cases handled by the state and federal courts are vital to understanding recent educational history. Earlier chapters examined the ideas of well known philosophers, psychologists, and public officials who influenced education. This chapter will deal with important modern educational critics and spokespersons for major organizations. Critics often serve as guides to significant educational problems. Finally, we will treat a number of current educational issues for which educational institutions and teachers are accountable.

LITIGATION: THE COURTS AND PROBLEMS OF EDUCATION

Religion and Public Schools.   Religion was the major subject in colonial schools, but with the separation of church and state, public schools could teach only interdenominational or nonsectarian religious principles. Still, the curriculum remained heavily influenced by religious writings, prayer, and Christian morality. Bible reading was considered nonsectarian in most communities. The fact that a Protestant Bible was not acceptable to Catholics carried little weight, and Jews were also discriminated against in school programs. Minority groups often chose not to make an issue of religion in the public schools before the twentieth century. If Catholic, Jewish, or other minority religious groups were unable to support their own schools, they normally accepted the rules of the public schools even when the requirements went counter to their own beliefs. In the past few years, however, there have been a great number of court cases over the religious requirements or practices in public schools. While the majority of the cases have decided against the inclusion of religious practices, a large number of Americans have felt that the schools were responsible for moral training which could hardly be given without reference to religion. Beginning the school day with prayer has been attacked by religious liberals and nonbelievers, while Jehovah's Witnesses have claimed that saluting the flag constitutes worship of a "graven image." There is no clear-cut division between patriotic and religious exercises; even the Pledge of Allegiance has contained the words "under God" since 1954. Furthermore, chaplains have been assigned to military units and "in God we trust" has been stamped on coins. The major educational problem, however, concerns Christian Christmas programs, religious exercises, and the reading of Scripture as part of the public school program.

In *Abington School District v. Schempp* (1963), the Court outlawed a 1959 Pennsylvania legislative rule requiring the reading of ten verses from the Bible every day in schools. In *Murray v. Curlett* (1963), the Baltimore School Commissioners were prevented from requiring the reading of a chapter from the Bible or reciting the Lord's Prayer as an opening exercise in schools. These cases led to the publication by the American Association of School Administrators of policy guidelines entitled *Religion in the Public Schools* in 1964. Conservatives called for restoring religion to the public schools and even proposed a constitutional amendment to allow voluntary prayer in schools which was sponsored by Senator Everett Dirksen of Illinois. Nevertheless, the first amendment statement that congress shall make no law respecting an establishment of religion remains the basis for preventing schools from requiring prayer or religious activities. In *Lee v. Weisman* (1992), the Court ruled that public officials violate the Constitution's first amendment if they arrange for a prayer, even though it may be nondenominational, to be included in an elementary or secondary school graduation ceremony. Nonetheless, the Supreme Court declined to review *Jones v. Clear Creek Independent School District Texas* (1992) a U.S. Court of Appeals ruling which held a senior class could vote on whether to include school prayer at graduation as long as the prayers were nonsectarian and nonproselytizing in nature. However, there has never been a rule prohibiting the *study* of religion. Indeed, American history cannot be understood without studying the impact of religion on the development of this nation.

The issue of the role of religion in education is centered on two quite controversial issues: the promotion of religious instruction in public schools, and the use of public tax money to aid nonpublic schools. In 1919 Nebraska passed a law prohibiting private or parochial schools from teaching any subject in any language other than English. The Supreme Court in 1923 ruled the law unconstitutional in *Meyer v. Nebraska*. While holding that the state may require attendance at some school, the Court stated that parents may send their children to private schools where some subjects need not be taught in English. This was a landmark case concerning both religion and the language of instruction.

Two years later the Supreme Court reinforced the right of parents to choose nonpublic schools in *Pierce v. Society of Sisters*. This case made unconstitutional a 1922 Oregon law which required all children between the ages of 8 and 16 to attend *public* schools. There has been no effort to outlaw private or parochial schools since 1925, and the Pierce doctrine remains in force.

The right of the student to be protected from rules that violate his or her religious freedom was at issue in the Gobitis case of 1938. The Gobitis family were members of Jehovah's Witnesses who objected to the school requirement that all students must say the pledge of allegiance to the American flag. The Court upheld the school board in this case, but in 1943 it reversed its position in *West Virginia v. Barnett*. Religious freedom thereafter became a valid reason for children to be excused from school activities which violate their religious beliefs.

In 1947, approximately 2 million public school students were released to attend religious classes during some part of the school week. In *McCollum v. The Board of Education of Champaign, Illinois*, in 1948, the Supreme Court held that releasing students to attend religious classes held in public school buildings was illegal. A later case in New York ended with a ruling that release time does not violate separation of church and state if religious classes are held outside the schools.

Law suits have sometimes resulted in changing educational practices as in the New York Regents' Prayer case of 1962. Using the coercive power of the school to make children participate in religious activities has been held to violate the First Amendment. Although a 1976 Gallup poll found that 70 percent of parents favored compulsory attendance, the Court has held that Amish parents may use the First Amendment as a basis for keeping their children out of high school. By the 1972 case, *Wisconsin v. Yoder*, the compulsory attendance law of the state was set aside to protect the free exercise of the religious views of parents. The 1993 Phi Delta Kappa/Gallup Poll of public attitudes toward public schools found that some two out of three Americans (67%) support choice in public schools, but some seventy four percent opposed allowing parents to send their children to private schools at public expense.

Cases involving public aid to parochial schools have created major concerns in educational circles. In the 1950s, the NEA and the American Association of School Administrators adopted resolutions opposing all efforts to use public funds for nonpublic education. Federal legislation provided school lunches for parochial schools in 1948 and the government allowed G.I. Bill and NDEA funds to be used for scholarships to nonpublic schools. The National Science Foundation made grants to private universities, while the Higher Education Act of 1965 gave money to church-related colleges for nonreligious purposes. Private schools also got libraries and instructional materials under the Elementary and Secondary Education Act of 1965.

In the Cochran case of 1930, the Supreme Court held that while direct aid to private and parochial schools was illegal, the state could use public funds to pay for transportation, lunches, textbooks, and health services which were of benefit to all children. This "child benefit" theory was also the basis for the use of taxes to pay for the transportation of students to Catholic schools in the Everson case. Everson upheld Cochran but the Court was split and the issue has not cooled. Many advocates of the public schools fear that any aid to private and parochial schools will weaken public education. They point out that equality of educational opportunity and integration suffer in nonpublic programs. For them, any aid to private education is a violation of the separation of church and state. They illustrate the difficulty Americans had in obtaining tax support for public schools in the era of Horace Mann and quote Thomas Jefferson on the necessity of keeping religion segregated from government. Several states now prohibit the use of tax money for any kind of aid to parochial schools, whether for child benefit or not. This issue is also tied to the question of tuition tax credits for parents who choose to send their children to private schools and to federal aid to nonpublic education. The arguments were especially heated in the early 1980s. Criticism of public schools caused many parents to demand tuition tax credits while spokespersons for public education held that such credits would weaken the very foundation of public schools.

Although release time for religious instruction, Bible reading, and nonsectarian prayers is illegal in public schools, the issue is not resolved. There is considerable pressure to "restore religion" to the public classroom.

About the same time that Ronald Reagan became a candidate for president, the new "religious and political right" represented by evangelists like Jerry Falwell began to gain strength. Carrying their message on television, as well as in churches and publications, they became a major voice for the "moral majority." This group objects to banning prayer in schools, demands that creationism be taught in place of the theory of evolution, and attacks "liberal" teachings in schools, such as values clarification. The moral conservatives favor banning books which they feel do not support their definition of good child behavior. Since members of this group often send their children to private schools, they support vouchers or the deduction of tuition from income tax returns, as provided by law in Minnesota. They especially oppose what they call "secular humanism," which they believe has corrupted educational practices and the whole culture, and have formed parents groups to rid the schools of "humanist" books. Well organized and well funded, the religious conservatives have taken their efforts into the courts. They have also put great pressure on Congress to "restore prayer" to the public schools. Various conservative and liberal groups representing special interests are entering the political arena to elect individuals at the grass roots level to influence educational decisions.

In *Epperson v. Arkansas* (1968) the Court ruled that an anti-evolution statute was unconstitutional since evolution is a science not a secular religion, and students cannot be restricted from such information. Thirteen years later, on March 19, 1981, the Arkansas Legislative Act 590 or *The Balanced Treatment for Creation Science and Evolution Science Act* was signed into law by Governor Frank White. In *McLean vs. Arkansas Board of Education* (1982), a Federal Court ruled the act unconstitutional on the grounds that it had been passed to advance religion, that it had as a major effect the advancement of particular religious beliefs, and that it created for the State of Arkansas excessive and prohibited entanglement with religion. In *Edwards v. Aguillard* (1987), a Louisiana statute was rejected on similar grounds. The Court ruled that giving equal time to creation science and evolution was designed to discredit scientific knowledge and prevent educators from disseminating such information in violation of the First Amendment establishment clause.

The courts have generally not gone along with book banning. For example, in *Pico v. Board of Education, Island Trees Union Free School District No. 26*, in 1980, the board's decision to ban *Soul on Ice*, *Slaughterhouse Five*, and *Black Boy* was not upheld. More successful have been efforts to control books by influencing the list of approved books for public schools in states like Texas.

Control of the school curriculum through the selection or rejection of materials is an activity in which many groups are now engaged. Conservative groups putting pressure on school systems to reject certain textbooks include the Liberty Foundation, the Stop Textbook Censorship Committee, and the Educational Research Analysis. The last organization, headed by Mel and Norma Gabler, has had much visibility and influence. Some censorship advocates like Phillis Schlafly provide checklists for parents who are looking for morally or politically offensive materials in books. On the liberal side are The American Civil Liberties Union, the Council for Democratic and Secular Humanism, People for the American Way, and the National Association for the Advancement of Colored People. The National Organization for Women has recently become active in gender issues in textbooks.

In the 1960s, the Supreme Court barred state sanctioned prayer and Bible reading in public schools supporting Jefferson's separation of church and state. The Court was silent on such issues for nearly two decades but indicated a new willingness to address First Amendment issues in the 1980s. In 1985, the Court ruled in *Wallace v. Jaffree* that an Alabama law allowing silent prayer in schools violated the establishment clause. The Court has agreed to review *Bender v. Williamsport* which involves the legality of student-initiated devotional meetings held during noninstructional time in a public school. Lower courts barred the meetings but an appeal based on infringement of the rights of students to free access is pending.

In 1984, President Reagan signed into law the Equal Access Act which made it illegal to deny access to students who wish to conduct a meeting, on the basis of religious, political, philosophical, or other content of the speech at such meetings. There is confusion over the intent of this legislation since it appears to conflict with cases like *Lubbock Civil Liberties Union v. Lubbock Independent School District* (1983), which prohibited policies designed to encourage religious meetings. On the other hand, *Widmar v. Vincent* (1981) stated that permitting college students to engage in voluntary religious activities on campus would not violate the establishment clause. Schools which allow a "limited open forum" in which special interests are dealt with on public school property face both equal access and separation issues.

The Supreme Court has addressed this conflict during the administration of President Clinton. In *Lamb's Chapel v. Center Moriches Union Free School District* (1993), the Supreme Court ruled that if schools provide school facilities for some uses permitted by state law, religious groups must have the same access to these facilities.

Additional cases focused on support of nonpublic schools and tax relief for tuition. With current interest in the voucher system, it is noteworthy that in *Mueller v. Allen* (1983) the Court found no violation of the Constitution in tax deductions benefiting parents of parochial school students. The 1977 case *Wolman v. Walter* supported providing nonpublic school pupils with books, tests, and remedial services. The Court objected to parts of the Ohio law providing field trips and instructional services to nonpublic students, since these advanced a sectarian purpose instead of general child benefit. In *Zobrest v. Catalina Foothills School District* (1993), the Supreme Court ruled that public funds may be used for services for a deaf student in a parochial school. The ruling may encourage advocates of public support for some aspects of religious education. Support of teaching "creationism," attacks on textbooks thought to reflect "secular humanism," and demands by conservatives for a more restrictive curriculum will likely be tested in future court cases.

Involuntary Segregation.   Involuntary segregation refers to excluding certain children from schools, usually on the basis of race. The problem of segregation is clearly linked to the period following the American Civil War and to the freeing of the slaves. Public schools for blacks and whites established during the period of reconstruction in the South were quickly eliminated in the 1880s. Thereafter, southern states made laws which required that schools could not admit children from both races to the same classes and segregation began.

As we have seen, federal attempts to provide support to the South for education (as with the Hoar Bill and the Blair Bill) failed. This left a large part of the nation in a condition of poverty and without the resources to provide adequate schooling for its children. The problem was made even more acute by the requirement of a dual school system which was expensive and inefficient. All the schools in the South lacked resources from the 1880s to the 1950s, but the black schools were a cut below all the others.

Northern states did not usually have laws prohibiting racially integrated schools, but many northern schools were segregated because of population patterns. White students did not attend schools with a majority of black pupils until after the Brown Case. Many schools in northern cities were all black or all white according to their location and the demography of the area.

So dubious was the prospect for social equality in the South at the time that Booker T. Washington (1858–1915), thought blacks should accept segregation in return for some access to education. The *Plessy v. Ferguson* case of 1896 affirmed the principle that separate but equal facilities were legal. In 1906, the Niagara movement was started by W. E. B. Du Bois. It led to the National Association for the Advancement of Colored People, which was organized in 1909. The NAACP began to challenge segregation laws in the 1930s, on the grounds that facilities provided to black students were not even remotely equal.

While not attacking the segregation laws on principle, the Supreme Court began to require admission of black students to southern professional schools unless the states could prove that they had equal facilities for blacks within their borders.

Finally in 1950, a direct challenge to segregated education was presented to the Court in *Sweatt v. Painter* where an applicant who had been denied admission to the University of Texas Law School solely on the basis of color claimed that the instruction available in the newly established state law school for blacks was markedly inferior to the instruction at the university; therefore, equal protection of the law was denied. In a unanimous decision the Supreme Court ordered his admission to the white school, indicating that it was virtually impossible in practice, at least in professional education, for a state to comply with the "separate-but-equal" formula.

Following the decision in the Sweatt case, the National Association for the Advancement of Colored People and other organizations pressed the fight against segregation in public schools which resulted in several public school segregation cases. The Court proceeded with a great deal of circumspection and required an unusual amount of investigation by the counsels. Their deliberation was understandable because if segregation in public schools was determined to be a denial of equal protection of laws, it would in all likelihood be impossible to defend segregation in other sectors of public life. The legal foundation of the social structure of a great part of the nation was under attack. By 1954 it had become obvious to the public that black children in segregated states received a much poorer schooling than white students. In 1952, for example, Arkansas spent $102 for the education of each white child compared to $67 for each black child. Black colleges were often substandard, and few jobs were open to black students who had graduated from northern universities. Integration in the armed forces in World War II and the success of blacks who sued for entry into southern universities led to the Supreme Court decision of 1954, *Brown v. Board of Education*.

In this famous case, the NAACP lawyer Thurgood Marshall argued that equality of educational facilities was not the question. Marshall claimed that prestige, teaching standards, the academic surroundings, and the inference of inferiority were important in educational equality. The Court agreed, saying that segregation was construed to deprive minority group children of equal educational opportunity. By its decision, the Supreme Court held that all laws concerning or permitting school segregation were in conflict with the Fourteenth Amendment and ordered involuntary segregation to cease within a "reasonable time." Several major cities like Baltimore, Washington, D.C. and St. Louis made a complete transition to integrated schools on the basis of the 1954 decision.

This decision, as with most decisions, met much opposition. One of the frequent arguments against it is illustrated by an article reprinted from the American Bar Association Journal. Eugene Cook, Attorney General of Georgia, and William J. Potter criticized the Brown decision severely. The opinion of the Court, said these critics, "did not hold that the old 'separate but equal' doctrine, laid down in *Plessy v. Ferguson*, was a bad law. It held that it was bad sociology."

Considerable progress toward desegregation was made in border states, but in the deep South various measures designed to frustrate desegregation were tried. Boycotting or nonsupport of integrated schools, student assignment plans to minimize integration, and the temporary abolition of public schools, as in Prince Edward County, Virginia, took place. Integration of the teaching staff and token integration through bringing in a few minority group students to all white schools were common attempts to meet legal requirements without basic change. Private academies were established in parts of the South in an effort to escape court-ordered integration, especially in areas where black people were in the majority.

A serious problem in many areas has been de facto segregation: segregation based upon school district boundaries which encompass children from only one race. The problem of de facto segregation is by no means confined to the South since blacks, Mexican-Americans, and other minority groups have been forced to live (often for economic reasons) in a single part or section of most cities. Racial boundaries tend to move rapidly so that schools which are planned to serve students from different races or ethnic backgrounds often end up being built in areas where only one race is present. Often some sort of educational park, cluster of school buildings, or central administration assignment of students has been used as an instrument for integration.

Heavy opposition to such efforts is often encountered. Many parents object to having their elementary age children attend schools other than those in their own neighborhoods or within walking distance of their homes. Some fear that integration will have a negative effect on children, such as introducing them to foul language, crime, and drugs. Many school districts have experienced a loss of enrollment as a result of court-ordered desegregation plans. Parents move their families into suburban areas in order to avoid what they believe to be unfortunate aspects of school integration. Perhaps the greatest opposition has occurred when cities have attempted to solve the integration problem by busing students from one school to another in order to achieve some degree of racial balance. A major problem for education has been the mandate given to schools to foster integration while the general public in many communities was unwilling to cooperate. Nevertheless, research indicates that whenever black and white students can be placed together in positive and meaningful educational experiences at an early age, racial tension is reduced and human relations improved.

Delays and circumventions in desegregation have not been confined to public schools. The attempt of Authurine Lucy to enter the University of Alabama in 1956 and the violence created by James Meredith's admission to the University of Mississippi in 1962, are illustrative of the problems of integration in higher education. Nevertheless, colleges and universities have been racially integrated with much less conflict than in public schools.

As the black movement for freedom and integration reached revolutionary levels, plans for school integration were set into motion throughout the United States. Some plans found general acceptance, but most efforts to move large numbers of children from one area of a city to another for integration of schools were bitterly opposed. With the assassination of Martin Luther King, Jr. in 1968, and the Passage of the Civil Rights Act in 1964, desegregation entered a new phase. The Civil Rights Act specified that no person could be discriminated against on the basis of race, color, sex, or national origin in any program which received federal assistance. This meant that federal funding could be withheld from school districts or states that failed to adopt reasonable and acceptable plans for integration.

Some of the southern school districts with the greatest need for financial help have been the least willing to integrate. Plans involving the mass busing of children have drawn fire from parents, politicians, and the public. Federal courts and the Department of Health, Education and Welfare have insisted upon prompt compliance with the law, but the struggle goes on in many communities. School buses were attacked and burned in Michigan. Riots over busing black students to South Boston High School in 1974 caused the closing of the school. Many state legislatures have issued laws against busing for racial balance, and Congress has come close to considering such a law. Meanwhile, schools attempt to follow legal guidelines and carry on the task of public education as best they can.

Although the Supreme Court has continued to uphold the Brown decision, militant resistance to busing has not died out and many school districts still reflect segregation. Sometimes this occurs when the population of a city changes dramatically as in the case of Newark, New Jersey. The Court has held that school boards may not intentionally gerrymander attendance districts to encourage segregation (*Keyes v. Denver*), but some American cities are entirely white or black. In *Milliken v. Bradley*, the Supreme Court reversed the ruling of lower federal courts which said Detroit should adopt a metropolitan desegregation plan to include its suburbs. On the other hand, the Court in 1977 refused to review the decision of Judge Garrity in *Morgan v. Hennigan*. The Court let stand the placing of the school system in federal receivership because the Boston Board had intentionally increased segregation. Numerous other cases are still pending and the mood of the nation seems to be swinging away from support for court-ordered busing plans. Los Angeles was allowed to discontinue busing for racial integration in 1981. Nevertheless, desegregation has worked in many areas, and America will not go back to conditions that existed before 1954.

Following close upon the efforts to end involuntary segregation came attempts to make college education and jobs accessible to a larger number of disadvantaged minorities and to women. Affirmative action plans were established in institutions of higher education to accomplish these goals in recruiting faculty and students. Federal guidelines intended to increase minority enrollment led to setting up a quota for minority students, frequently about 10 percent of the total. Some colleges allowed admission officers to require lower aptitude scores from minorities because research said many tests are culturally biased.

Opposition appeared in the form of the "Committee on Academic Nondiscrimination and Integrity" in 1972. This committee charged that policies favoring minority and female candidates over others better qualified hurt professional performance. Although it recognized the evils of past discrimination, it objected to preferential admission standards for minorities.

In 1978, the Supreme Court agreed to hear arguments in the case of Regents of the University of California v. Allan Bakke. Bakke contended that the quota for minorities at the medical campus at Davis had caused him to be rejected for admission, although his scores were much higher than those of minority candidates who were admitted. The Court ordered that Bakke be admitted on the basis that his rights under the Fourteenth Amendment had been violated. However, it was also stated in the opinion that race and background factors may be considered by institutions making decisions on admissions. In the case of *Steelworkers v. Weber* in 1979, the Court upheld the legality of an affirmative action plan worked out by the United Steelworkers in a challenge similar to that of Bakke.

Litigation and Equality of Opportunity.   Although some part of the educational budget for most school districts is federally collected and distributed, American school support is largely a state and local matter. Traditionally, the federal government has had no role in school finance except where federal funds were involved. This changed dramatically in 1971 with a case brought on behalf of Mexican-American children in Los Angeles. Using the equal protection guarantee of the Fourteenth Amendment, the California Supreme Court ruled that state's system of financing public schools discriminatory in *Serrano v. Priest*. The basis of the argument was that the quality of education provided was a function of the wealth of each district and therefore discriminated against poor children. Following Serrano, more than fifty suits in thirty states were filed against the local property tax systems. Minnesota, Texas, New Jersey, and Connecticut had their property taxes struck down by the courts.

The impact of *Serrano v. Priest* might have been even more dramatic if the Supreme Court had not taken a different stand in *San Antonio Independent School District v. Rodriguez*. A Texas federal district court had ruled the Texas system of local property taxation illegal as in the Serrano case. In 1973, however, the Supreme Court in a five to four decision reversed the district court and held that the system in Texas did not absolutely deprive poor people of education nor discriminate against any definable category of the "poor." In spite of this support for the property tax, attention was brought to the inequality of educational opportunity in various districts within states. Many state legislatures have taken a hard look at their system of school funding since Serrano and Rodriguez. Recent state and federal court rulings require equity provisions for financially burdened school districts. A Texas Supreme Court decision in *Edgewood v. Kirby* (1989) required the state legislature to correct inequities in funding between financially burdened and affluent school districts. In *Rose v. Council for Better Education, Inc.* (1988), a Kentucky State Supreme Court case upheld a lower court ruling that the state had failed to provide an efficient system of common schools. The ruling led to the *Kentucky Educational Reform Act of 1990*, which provided for more effective schools together with equity in taxation to assure a guaranteed minimum level of financial support per pupil for all school districts. New laws have been proposed and others probably will be, because it is hard to justify unequal financial support for education in a democratic society.

Changing educational practices and the characteristics of students have influenced modern litigation. An example is the need many school officials have to search for illegal drugs in schools or on the persons of students. In *New Jersey v. T.L.O.* (1985), the Supreme Court held that the Fourth Amendment does apply to searches conducted by public school officials. However, school officials need not obtain warrants before searching a student nor must they have probable cause before searching. The validity of a school search depends upon its reasonableness under the circumstances. The clause in the Fourteenth Amendment pertaining to equal protection under the law applies also to the rights of students. Older practices of dismissing students from school because they marry, are pregnant, or commit a crime are no longer legal.

Following the demand for accountability, schools were tested on the legality of new requirements for students. Some cases had to do with whether a diploma could be withheld from a student who had passed required courses but who was below par in performance. In *Debra v. Turlington* (1983), the Court ruled that functional literacy tests may be required as a prerequisite for a high school diploma, but the tests must be a valid measure of instruction. The Court also prevented statewide use of tests in Florida until the state showed that discrepancy in passing rates of white and black students were not due to educational deprivations suffered by blacks before integration.

Other Significant Court Cases.   While the most important influence of the courts has been directed toward desegregation, religion, and equality, there have been several other areas of educational importance. A common practice in many American cities was to test children and then to place them in a fixed curriculum according to the ability group into which they fall. This practice was found unconstitutional in 1967 in *Hobson v. Hansen*. This form of grouping, called the "tracking system," tended to promote segregation within schools and make it impossible for students to get out of the track once they had been placed in it.

The right to privacy and to due process under the law has been extended to children in the United States. In 1971 students in Columbus, Ohio, who were suspended for ten days from school without a hearing brought suit. In this case, *Goss v. Lopez*, the Court held that high school students must be granted due process including notice of the charges against them and an opportunity must be provided for them to present their side of the story. Similar cases have protected children suspended for wearing long hair or violating school codes of dress. The Family Educational Rights and Privacy Act of 1974 (also called the Buckley Amendment) requires schools to provide access to records to students over the age of eighteen and to parents of younger students. Another landmark case on children's rights was *Tinker v. Des Moines* in 1969. Quaker students in the Des Moines public schools were suspended for wearing black armbands to protest the war in Vietnam. The Supreme Court found that wearing armbands was a symbolic case of expression and therefore it was protected under the First Amendment, like freedom of speech. Modern courts have also been active in matters concerning loyalty oaths, violations of civil liberties, and academic freedom. As a general rule, schools are prohibited from making any rule or regulation that impinges upon rights that students would enjoy if they were adults.

New challenges to public school finances may emerge from *Franklin v. Gwinnette County Public Schools* (1992) which allowed a student, who alleged she was sexually harassed by a teacher, to seek money damages from the school district under a federal law prohibiting gender bias. The ruling was based on Title IX of the Education Amendments of 1972 and may open school districts to suits dealing with race, ethnicity, age and disability.

With large numbers of children who are not citizens of the United States seeking to enter the schools, especially along the border with Mexico, litigation has emerged. In *Doe v. Plyler* in 1978, a school district's exclusionary policy regarding alien children was struck down. The Fifth Circuit Court of Appeals upheld the decision in 1980. In 1982, the Supreme Court permanently enjoined the state of Texas from excluding undocumented alien children from tuition-free public schools. All children must be served, whether or not they hold citizenship.

Just as compulsory attendance was tested in the courts at an earlier time, so home schooling has more recently become an issue. For a multitude of reasons including control of the values to which children are exposed, some parents are educating their children at home. In *Stephens v. Bongart* in 1937, the court found that home instruction was not equivalent to that provided in public schools partly because of a lack of opportunity for socialization. However, in the Massa case of 1967, it was held that socialization and social development had no place in determining whether home schooling was equivalent to public education. In a recent case, *Mazanec v. North Judson-San Pierre School Corporation* (1985), parents were found entitled to educate their children at home if those parents made a good faith effort to meet certain minimum requirements. However, in *West Virginia v. Riddle* (1981), the court held that the state's interest in protecting children extends to home schools. With growing numbers of home and small religious schools, educators have expressed concern about the role of the public school in carrying the culture to all. This is a major theme in John Goodlad's book *What Are Schools For?*

Other recent cases have involved the treatment of the handicapped, discrimination in staff employment, and the use of federal funds for state programs. In *Bennett v. Kentucky Department of Education* (1985), the Court held that neither substantial compliance or lack of bad faith excused a state from repaying federal funds misspent for readiness classes. Reinforcing the right of due process in *Cleveland Board of Education v. Loudermill* (1985), the Court held that termination must be only for cause and that an employee must have an opportunity to respond to the charges motivating discharge. In another 1985 case, *School Committee of Burlington v. Department of Education of Massachusetts*, the Supreme Court ruled that where a local education agency's proposed placement for a handicapped child is inappropriate, the school authority must pay for a private placement in which the parents unilaterally enrolled their child.

Whatever the future holds for educational litigation, decisions will be influenced by the composition of the courts. If there are a few Supreme Court retirements during the Clinton administration, a liberal swing is likely which will expand various affirmative action programs and strengthen civil rights. Congress and the courts shifted to the right under the Bush administration and the pendulum may swing to the left under the Clinton presidency. A case in illustration is *Grove City College v. Bell* (1984), in which the Court held affirmative action applies only to programs specifically receiving federal funds. The proposed Civil Rights Act of 1984, stipulating that the whole school is subject to affirmative action even if only one program was receiving federal funds, did not pass. Congress subsequently changed the City College decision to include all university programs in affirmative action, not just those that receive federal funding.

MORE RECENT EDUCATIONAL CRITICS

Clashing views on controversial issues have characterized writing in the educational field for many years. Historically, institutionalized education has been characteristically rigid, and that led to criticism by progressives and other liberal writers. On the other hand, business leaders and political conservatives have often attacked the schools for promoting socialistic ideas or for teaching about social issues. Liberal versus conservative arguments over the curriculum, moral training, and the rights of children have been present in the educational literature for generations.

Curriculum matters often tie in with methods and with psychology. When Charles Eliot chaired the Committee of Ten in 1892, specific subjects were prescribed for the high schools. Latin, Greek, English, German, French, Spanish, algebra, geometry, trigonometry, astronomy, meteorology, botany, zoology, physiology, geology, physics, chemistry, history, and physical geography were the subjects that received support. Critics soon pointed out that the high school curriculum lacked vocational subjects, sociology, psychology, and the humanities. The Committee was also highly influenced by the popular educational psychology of the time which stressed mental discipline. Later psychologists were quick to take issue with subjects chosen because of their alleged ability to train the mind. Others argued that the subjects chosen were all intended for college preparatory students while the majority of the high school's population was not college bound.

Critics of education in modern America provide a means by which issues in contemporary schooling may be studied. Some critics find philosophical fault with the aims and purposes of education. Others attack teacher education, the curriculum, or the methods used in schools. Many are concerned about the quality of programs and the products produced by schools. Not only are the critics now numerous and verbal, but also many have established themselves in staunch positions with considerable public support. Some people think that modern critics perform a service by isolating problems and illuminating inadequate aspects of the educational system. Others say that responsible criticism requires offering attainable solutions and working within the system to achieve them. Clearly there are many more people ready to focus on the shortcomings than there are critics with reasonable answers or alternatives. Several critics do have a talent for providing poignant insight into the teaching-learning process and the total school environment. Many critics reach professionals within the educational system who take them seriously enough to attempt change. Colleges of education have been especially sensitive to the charges of critics. Of course, critics also create anger, frustration, disgust, and other negative reactions both inside and outside the system.

During the 1950s, the nation enjoyed a period of relative prosperity and tranquility. The hysterical fear of communism which had caused attacks on academic freedom began to subside. Various social and legal movements toward the achievement of racial equality began to alter the educational system.

This tranquil period came to an end in the reaction against the successful launching of Sputnik. In the wake of fear and criticisms of American educational failures, European schools were compared favorably with those in the United States. James B. Conant, former president of Harvard, called for the reorganization of high schools with more emphasis on excellence. Admiral Hyman Rickover insisted that the major purpose of education is to produce the experts who create the technology and science upon which a modern nation depends for winning wars, hot or cold. These views carried the day, and through such programs as the National Defense Education Act, emphasis was placed upon science, technology, mathematics, foreign languages, and high standards.

In the 1960s, a new wave of criticism arose following the politically, socially, and emotionally turbulent decade marked by civil rights activity at home and war in Vietnam. Critics proclaimed that recent academic reforms had failed or at least were not meeting prevalent needs. Although college board scores indicated that the public schools of the 1960s produced students with comparatively better skills in science and mathematics, questions were raised about the relevance of the curriculum, attitudes produced, individual needs of students, and the role of schools in social change.

In the 1970s, dissatisfaction permeated the social order and the grim realities facing the nation created a diversity of new educational criticisms. Fear that a lasting peace might not be achieved in the world, loss of faith in government following the Watergate affair, and the prospects of unemployment in an economy marked by inflation and recession added to uncertainty about the future. People began to ask how children should be educated to cope with the energy crisis, ecology, the depletion of natural resources, urban congestion, rising crime, a world population explosion, and a changing job market. Others focused less on problem solving and economic survival and more upon the developmental, creative, and human needs of individual students. One group of critics concerned themselves with the way schools mold or shape students. They were sensitive and sympathetic to groups of children who to one degree or another are "victims" of society and therefore of the school system.

By 1980 the focus of criticism had taken a conservative turn. Distrust of big government and bureaucracy caused dissatisfaction with programs for social engineering, school integration, and efforts to aid the poor. Inflation fueled a demand for more job-related training, more efficient use of school time, and less busing for desegregation. A new wave of attacks on teaching the theory of evolution, sex education, and values clarification came from the "moral majority." Multicultural studies and bilingual education became less popular, and there were new demands for accountability. The reputation of education declined as ACT scores continued to slide and many high school graduates proved unable to read beyond an elementary level. "Excellence" and a "return to basics" were the most popular slogans of the times.

During the 1990s, SAT and ACT scores stabilized, educational reform and restructuring continued unabated, and "cultural diversity" was stressed. Political correctness was a term widely used to refer to the influence of various liberal groups.

Samuel Bowles and Herbert Gintis.

Among those who advocate radical school reform or argue that education cannot be improved without a far-reaching social revolution are Bowles and Gintis. Their book, *Schooling in Capitalist America*, called attention to hostility of the school toward the need of the individual for personal development. Like Paul Goodman, Edgar Friedenberg, John Holt, Everett Reimer, and Paolo Freire, these authors call for radical school reform. Bowles has questioned whether education has been of any real economic benefit to minority people, showing that the relative incomes of blacks declined even when the absolute incomes improved. He has also been very critical of the way James Colemen analyzed his data in the Coleman Report. Like Ivan Illich, Bowles and Gintis take an extreme antischool position. They do not think the schools can be reformed without drastic alteration of the underlying social and economic forces.

George Dennison.

George Dennison established the first "street school," which was an alternative educational program for minority children from low-income families on New York's lower East Side. Half of his students came from public schools where they had been given labels such as "severe learning and behavior problems." *In The Lives of Children* (1969), Dennison tells about his experiences with these children, including the violence and obscenity inherent in the daily routines of the pupils. Relating his work with disturbed children to the views of A. S. Neill, John Dewey, Paul Goodman, and Leo Tolstoy, Dennison discusses the needs of those who have been cast off by society or parents. His writings have gained the attention of educators and social reformers sensitive to the depth of individual problems that plague the lives and experiences of many children in the modern world.

John Holt.   An experienced teacher on both the elementary and secondary levels, Holt began expressing himself to other educators in 1964 when he wrote *How Children Fail*. He urged teachers to focus on children and their individual needs rather than upon the formal ingestion of a rigid curriculum. Calling attention to the ominous relationship between the fear and expectation of failing and actual failure, Holt showed how teachers often contribute to a self-fulfilling prophesy. He supports a child-centered approach in which each pupil can develop his or her own activities and abilities at his or her own speed. In other books, *What Do I Do Monday?* (1970), and *Freedom and Beyond* (1972), Holt offered practical suggestions to teachers about how to keep interest alive in schools and what can be done to encourage each student to reach his or her maximum potential.

Ivan Illich.   Any educator who has not heard of Ivan Illich is isolated indeed! In *Deschooling Society* (1971), Illich not only denounced compulsory education but also called upon modern nations like the United States to give up their public systems of education. Illich's background is somewhat different from that of most other educational critics. He was a Catholic priest in New York City, Puerto Rico, and South America until he resigned in 1961 to found the Intercultural Center for Documentation in Cuernavaca, Mexico. As a result of his experiences in Latin America, Illich concluded that mass education has deterimental effects upon poor people. For example, he says that to go to school in Mexico for two or three years and then drop out is worse than not attending school at all. Dropping out makes one a failure in the eyes of society and the learning gained probably is of no use to a poor laboring man. Illich feels that the right of the individual to learn is actually hindered by compulsory attendance and mass education. Schools are used as screening devices to sift out the gifted few or justify the existence of high schools and colleges for the children of the wealthy and powerful. Illich thinks it is not feasible to create schools which will actually meet the educational needs of the masses. Education is the responsibility of society and must not be delegated to schools, which are operated by governments for the benefit of the few. He contends that the disadvantaged would have a better chance if the bond between education and schooling was completely severed. By deschooling society, there would no longer be power or prestige associated with staying in school a long time or acquiring a degree. Probably no one, including Illich, really expects that the United States will abandon its public schools. His criticism is important because it calls attention to the fact that education may benefit one class of society at the expense of others, and that the values fostered by public schools are not necessarily those of greatest use for the survival of the individual and the well-being of the people.

Another group of modern educational critics believes that compulsory public education is detrimental to the purpose and process of learning. Some critics call for an end to "schooling" as a means of social control and value formation.

Herbert Kohl. As a result of his first teaching experience with black sixth graders at East Harlem, Herbert Kohl wrote *36 Children* (1967), which tells how he created a curriculum from his students' experiences and his own imagination. Holding that the standard school curriculum prevents communication between teacher and student, Kohl claimed success in combining creativity and relevant experiences with academic achievement. A more recent book, *The Open Classroom*, is presented as a "handbook for teachers who want to work in an open environment." Kohl has become a leader among teachers and parents who want to foster better community participation in education, and he has worked with various systems in the creation of alternative schools.

Jonathan Kozol. Unlike Kohl, Jonathan Kozol was dismissed as a substitute teacher in a Boston elementary school for deviation from the established curriculum. Concerned about his sincere efforts to communicate with lower-class black students, Kozol shocked the nation with his book *Death at an Early Age: The Destruction of the Hearts and Minds of Negro Children in the Boston Public Schools* (1967). More than a critic of school programs, Kozol is politically sensitive to problems such as minority rights, bureaucratic manipulation by school boards, and the insensitivity of the public to the needs of some groups of children. In 1972 he wrote *Free Schools* and became interested in the efforts to develop meaningful learning programs for children with backgrounds culturally different from those of the majority. Kozol currently writes for educational journals and gives speeches, such as the highly publicized one at the NEA Convention in 1973 which called attention to the inadequate programs he sees in American schools.

Kozol produced another very strong criticism of education in 1985 with his book *Illiterate America*. He said that 25 million Americans cannot read the poison warnings on a can of pesticide or the front page of a newspaper. Another 35 million people in this nation read below the level necessary for success in society. Kozol finds that the United States ranks 49th among the 158 member nations of the United Nations in literacy. He makes a passionate call for educational reform at all levels.

Theodore Roszak. It may be fairly said that Theodore Roszak is spokesman for the "counterculture," which is a world view that pugnaciously criticizes "establishment" ways of conducting society and its agencies. Roszak came to the attention of the public with *The Making of a Counter Culture* (1969), *Where the Wastelands End* (1972), and *A Man for Tomorrow's World* (1970). A history professor, Roszak has had a considerable effect on curriculum development and has addressed groups such as the Association for Supervision and Curriculum Development. He totally rejects compulsory education, which he considers "a product of the rigid social orthodoxy of industrial society." He represents a considerable number of social critics who are disenchanted with modern industrial society and its institutions. Roszak advised students to escape from the restrictions and conformity of modern public schools.

Some educational critics do not take extreme positions but promote their own ideas while taking issue both with existing school practices and the views of other critics. Writers of this sort include Paul Goodman and Charles Silberman.

Charles Silberman.

Charles Silberman believes the school system has some merit. At the same time he opposes the views of those who wish to eliminate schools entirely and those who advocate a child-centered theme. Silberman believes that there is a need for centrality of purpose and a clear educational philosophy in American schools. He attributes failure in recent curriculum reform movements to the fact that educators have not understood the issues that perplexed the progressive education movement or the problems of educating the child for the modern society. Like Goodman, Silberman is an established journalist and a respected scholar. *Crisis in the Classroom* is the best known statement of his educational criticism, and it has been widely read since its publication in 1970. Both Silberman and Kozol warn educators to be wary of past errors. They suggest that we use history as a guide—sifting through past experience to eliminate what is obsolete and ineffective and retain what is beneficial.

Gerald W. Bracey and the Sandia Report.

Bracey wrote "Why Can't They Be Like We Were" in the October 1991 issue of the *Kappan* in which he discussed an alternative view of education. He suggested that reform report conclusions about mediocrity and decline from the "Nation At Risk" forward were often based on faulty data collection and interpetation. Bracey pointed to ambiguity of terms used in the reform reports and found that various linkages discussed such as that between education and international competitiveness were as tenuous as that between education and economic well-being. In the October 1993 *Kappan*, Bracey noted that we need to look at the interpretation of the data about schools afresh, freed from the chronic perception that schools have failed. Robert Huelskamp in the May 1993 issue of the *Kappan* summarized the findings of a national study of education in the United States by the Strategic Studies Center, Sandia National Laboratories in their 1991 research. He reported surprising results that indicated on nearly every measure investigated, there were steady or slightly improving trends. Areas for educational improvement were identified: the need for national agreement on essential changes plus strong leadership to make such modifications; the continuing need to improve the performance of minority, urban, immigrant students; efforts to enhance the status of elementary and secondary schools; and, most importantly, the need to upgrade the quality of the data available on education. The Bracey and Sandia Research efforts suggest many reform reports were issued without careful analysis of available data on education. Bracey, in his third report on *The Condition of Public Education*, Kappan, 1993, reiterated his earlier conclusion that although there are horrific challenges facing American schools, we need to interpret the data more objectively, disregarding the belief that schools have failed.

Critics with Other Viewpoints. While no complete enumeration of modern educational critics is possible here, some of those with special interests or points of view should be mentioned. Sylvia Ashton-Warner, who wrote *Teacher* (1963) and *Teacher in America* (1972), is concerned with the meaning of equality and authority in education. Joseph Featherstone's *Schools Where Children Learn* (1971), warns about "faddishness" and raises the question of whether schools can build a more equal society. The problem of relevance is of concern to George Leonard who wrote *Education and Ecstasy. Teaching as a Subversive Activity* by Neil Postman and Charles Weingartner deals both with relevance and with communication. William Glasser's *Schools Without Failure* and Sunny Decker's *An Empty Spoon* are other examples of the same theme.

Those who claim the schools have not been interested in humanistic psychology include Abraham Maslow and Carl Rogers. Another psychologist, Jerome S. Bruner, believes that too much emphasis has been placed upon the structure of knowledge within the disciplines and not enough concern given to structure in the context of learning and problem solving. Jean Piaget holds that learning takes place at various levels or stages of development which depend upon both maturation and experience. He feels that too little attention has been given to the process of learning and too much to the content.

The wide range of criticisms of American education is not surprising in a rapidly changing, pluralistic, dynamic, and democratic culture. Some critics operate from a scholarly base within the profession, some represent philosophical causes, some are concerned about the role of the school in social change, and others attack education for its support of social values. As long as education is not an exact science and the American society is dynamic and open, criticism may be expected to continue. The problem for the professional educator is understanding exactly what the critics are saying and selecting the best ideas from a host of suggested alternatives.

The School as Agency for Social Action. The role of the school in social change is a philosophical issue, as Theodore Brameld and his critics are quick to point out. So many programs have developed in recent years which seem to use education as a social institution for cultural change that the problem of purpose and function of schools has received new attention.

As James S. Coleman and Edgar Z. Friedenberg have insisted, demands and challenges for the adolescent members of modern society are very great. The impact of social change on the adolescent, pressures on middle-class teenagers, and the problem of youth values in an open society are major concerns for schools. Superimposed upon this are the special problems of low-income students, the children of the urban poor and the youth from African-American, Native American, or Chicano families. These students have more than their share of educational difficulties and are more apt to drop out of school.

Various attempts to compensate for cultural disadvantages and meet the needs of all children and adolescents have been tried.

Ever since the Wechsler Scales for measuring adult intelligence were invented and the Army Alpha and Beta tests were given in World War I, mass testing to establish norms has been used in the United States. Many educators fear that both individual and group intelligence tests are misused in schools, but the first great objection to grouping or categorizing students by test scores came from those who charged cultural bias. It was argued that merely being from a middle-class white environment gave students an unfair advantage on instruments for measuring ability. Efforts to construct culture-fair tests were followed by attempts to remove racism and sexism from textbooks. Most American public school texts before 1960 made black and other minority people "invisible" and fostered definite sex roles for youngsters.

Project Head Start, Vista, Job Corps, Teacher Corps, and Upward Bound are federally funded projects to help disadvantaged students. Job Corps centers were established to teach vocational skills to high school dropouts. Upward Bound attempted to prepare disadvantaged youth for success in college. Other programs used federal funds for more teachers, buildings, and equipment where there were concentrations of low-income or minority children.

The issue of federal projects is still undecided. Supporters of the programs say that gains were made by the disadvantaged as a result of their development and that no harm was done to other students. They call for more money and an extension of the programs on all levels. Others claim that the schools should not be involved in attempts to equalize differences or change society through social action programs. The Coleman Report, Illich's *Deschooling Society*, and the work of Christopher Jenks indicate that these programs made very little lasting difference. Illich does not believe that it is possible for government sponsored school programs to compensate for cultural differences.

Superimposed upon the issues concerning the role of the government in aiding the culturally different were more emotional ones concerning race, heredity, and intelligence. In 1969, psychologist Arthur Jensen published an article in the Harvard Educational Review which suggested that black students average about 15 points below whites on IQ tests. The writings of William Shockley also supported an inferior position for blacks. Jensen tried to point out that his data was not a basis for judging the intellectual capacity of any individual, but there were strong criticisms of his work. Charges of racism and the use of Jensen's studies to prove that integration must fail only further clouded the issue. Authors on both sides allowed their emotions to rule their logic.

Both the number of critics and the depth of concern they expressed increased dramatically in the 1980s. An increasingly popular position is expressed by the political and religious "new right." It eschews any concern for developing moral autonomy in children and supports the teaching of what its supporters deem to be right. People of this persuasion have formed groups to purge the schools of "humanist" books and to restrict the teaching of sex education and values clarification. In practice, these conservative moralists defend educational programs which they believe will create moral character, patriotism, strict discipline, deference to authority, and opposition to secular humanism. They have no problem with the idea that schools should indoctrinate "truth" and ethical behavior patterns in children. They see the current schools corrupted with humanistic values and liberalism.

Another set of critics emerged with the national reports critical of education which were published in 1983 and 1984. Many of these came from fields such as business, engineering, economics, and government. A number of critics also offered their own plans for achieving excellence in education. Chapter Eight deals with the movement toward excellence, including the plans of critics like Boyer, Goodlad, Sizer, and Adler. We shall also see in the chapter on educational philosophy that many powerful lay critics of education exist. These include political figures like Ronald Reagan and members of the religious "New Right," such as Jerry Falwell and Pat Robertson.

ASSESSMENT AND ACCOUNTABILITY

In this section we will treat the modern issue centering on how schools should be held accountable for what they do (or fail to do) and related problems that have to do with the responsibility of educators to the public. As we have seen, many critics of American schools believe that teachers are not pursuing the right methods, curriculum objectives, or educational aims. Others feel that while the goals may be clear, education lacks efficiency in accomplishing those goals. The parents are very much concerned because of decline in measures of achievement such as ACT scores and the constant accusation that "Johnny can't read." Others attack the schools for failure to meet the needs of the culturally different, the non-English speaker, and the exceptional child.

The idea that schools and educators should be responsible for their actions is not new in American education. Annual reports of Horace Mann and the journal articles by Henry Barnard carried criticisms of inadequate or mistaken pedagogical efforts. The means by which teachers are trained has been under fire since the development of normal schools and university departments of education. As early as 1898, the American Association of Manufacturers charged the schools with "repressive brain stuffing," "dulling the intellect," and failing to provide youth with the skills needed to enter the job market. The business community ever since has taken issue with educators over the curriculum and the degree of concentration on courses needed for preparing an effective work force. Educators have also attacked each other as in the rejection of the Herbartian lock-step methods by the progressives and the subsequent rejection of the progressive program by William Bagley and the essentialists. Perhaps the main difference between the past and the present is that today attacks are more widespread and rapid, due to modern communications and the mass media.

American public schools experience periods of ebb and flow both in the interest expressed by the public and in public pressure. Following 1970, criticism of schools and teaching was linked to demands for accountability. The basic concept comes from the field of management, and it is intended to hold someone responsible for performing according to terms previously agreed upon. While serving as Secretary of Defense, Robert McNamara brought the unrelenting evaluative practices of business to government through his program planning and budgeting system. In education, the founding of the accountability movement is usually credited to the works of Leon Lessinger (*Every Kid a Winner: Accountability in Education*, 1970). The sudden popularity of the concept of accountability can be traced to growing dissatisfaction with the quality of schools, a feeling that educators were closing ranks against public criticism, and the ever increasing pressure for more tax dollars to finance education. Many educators have been quite negative about accountability and the issues surrounding it continue to be argued in the 1990s. Total Quality Management and Effective Schools were popular themes in the mid 1990s, as the influence of business and industry efforts toward continuous product improvement as well as customer satisfaction were emphasized in education. Typical of the popular books on effective schools through empowerment was William Byham's *Zapp In Education*, 1992.

As a theoretical concept, few would quarrel with accountability. Teachers obviously need to be responsible for what they do, and the educational profession does not object to evaluation. Teachers do object to the idea that they are guilty of something and must be punished, or to the negative presumption that legislation is needed to make them do their jobs. More significant, questions occur to which no one seems to have the answers. Who is accountable? If the student fails to learn, is that always to be blamed on the teacher and not on the student or the parents? There is massive evidence that schools are responsible for only a part of the child's learning and teachers for an even smaller part. For what are teachers accountable? Information and skills which can be examined on tests surely do not represent total learning. Incidental, collateral or attitudinal learnings are not capable of being organized into objective sequences and are hard to test. Most accountability tests measure only a very limited part of what the student actually learns. John Goodlad had pointed out that timeworn instruments of assessment and archaic criteria for evaluation are poor means for measuring pupil achievement. To whom are educators accountable? The answer to this would seem to be the clients, (students, parents, and employers), but if teachers have had no role in determining educational policy, accountability is unfair. Often the criteria for accountability is determined by state or federal officials with no input from the local community. If teachers are treated as mere employees and not consulted about issues or practices in the schools, they can hardly be held accountable as professionals.

In the past, reputations of teachers were built on some estimate of what constituted "good" teacher behavior. Keeping order in the classroom and grading each student fairly were examples of such behavior. In recent years the measure of good teaching has shifted to the ability of the teacher to produce specific behavioral changes in learners. California's Stull Act requires that the competence of teachers be measured at least in part by the performance of students. This implies that when students do not learn, for whatever reason, the fault is to be placed on certified personnel. Some critics see this as analogous to the ancient practice of paying physicians only if the patient recovers. Accountability has also been tested in the courts. In 1976, the San Francisco Unified School District was sued by a student who had been allowed to graduate from high school although he was unable to read at sixth grade level. Lawyers for the plaintiff argued that the school personnel were negligent in failing to detect and correct his learning problem. In Donohue v. Copiague, a student charged a New York school with failure to cope with his learning disabilities. The plaintiffs were not successful in these cases but the idea of holding teachers accountable to society for the quality and quantity of educational results has clearly been established. Courts in New York and Iowa have reaffirmed that teachers cannot be held liable for poor student performance but the public demand for accountability has not diminished. McCarthy and Cambron-McCabe found that although no educational malpractice claim has yet been successful, some courts have found instances in which plaintiffs might recover damages in an instructional tort action.

In the 1970s, many states passed laws for accountability. Some require the assessment of students on specific tests while others are broad and vague. Seven states involved in the Cooperative Accountability Project require some sort of evaluation but specific measures are determined locally. Some educators fear that business-industrial models of accountability threaten teachers with punitive and often inoperable directives. Others see the schools becoming more rigid and authoritarian with emphasis placed on improvement of test performance and nothing else. Sociologist Robert Havinghurst cautions against a simple form of accountability that makes teachers totally responsible while taking no account of other forces in the learning environment. Both the NEA and the National Commission on Teacher Education and Professional Standards have called accountability unprofessional, inhumane, and arbitrary unless the standards and methods of measurement are developed by the profession itself. These organizations are especially opposed to laws which require the application of business and commercial instruments to education. The American Federation of Teachers has taken an even stronger stand, linking accountability laws to "school-haters" who are looking for scapegoats to blame for social failures. Nevertheless, today most states require some form of assessment and accountability for public schools. The most common means of assessment is a standardized achievement test, and failure often results in the loss of state funds.

Competency Tests for Teachers.　　　Along with accountability, the public has become concerned with weeding out teachers who are poorly prepared or incompetent. Colleges of education are no longer trusted to train teachers or to recommend certification without some external evidence of skills and knowledge of subject matter. Prior to 1978, when Florida passed a bill requiring a comprehensive written examination before certification, three states required beginning teachers to pass the National Teacher Examination. Georgia, New York, Oklahoma, and Wisconsin had plans for some form of competency testing by 1981 and several other states were considering such requirements. After 1978 when the Supreme Court ruled that the NTE was not discriminatory (although more black teachers failed it than whites), other states began to use it. It seems likely that some form of minimum competency test will be required for all beginning teachers in the nation before the end of the century.

Some school districts require new teachers to pass their own tests before they are hired. The Dallas Independent School District had high failure (about half) when tenth-grade verbal and quantitative ability tests were given as a prerequisite to teaching. This alarming rate has done little to enhance the public view of institutions which train teachers. It should be pointed out however, that these tests measure knowledge of subject matter and not skills in teaching. If colleges and universities are to be held accountable, the academic departments that teach mathematics and geography are more vulnerable than colleges or departments of education. Although superior knowledge of subject matter does not necessarily make a superior teacher, the public has a right to demand that teachers are minimally competent in basic subjects. President Albert Shanker of the AFT favors entry-level testing of teacher candidates on the grounds that an improved profession will result. Both the AFT and the NEA oppose tests for teachers already in service.

Since 1970, the public demand for accountability has grown. Interest in voucher plans, cost-effectiveness, community control, and the curriculum has contributed to demands for assessment of teacher performance. More basic concerns revolve around the steady decline in ACT scores and the problem of, "Why Johnny can't read." Most states have passed laws requiring some form of accountability or are planning for such legislation. Holding a teacher responsible for student performance when the teacher does not make school policy and when other factors (including the attitude and ability of the student) may account for inadequate performance is a major issue. Accountability tests are inadequate if they measure only limited aspects of education such as skill in mathematics, and more comprehensive tests are difficult to construct. It has not been determined if tests should be criterion-referenced, norm-referenced or both. Teacher candidates are now required to pass minimum competency tests in many states before they can be certified. There are questions about the effectiveness of such tests in predicting success in the classroom and some concerns about the effect on the projected future shortage of teachers.

Curriculum Concerns.   The entire body of subjects or courses offered in the program of a school is the curriculum. Historically, one of the best ways to understand what a school system tried to accomplish is to study its curriculum. District schools in Colonial New England taught religion, reading, and writing, while the Latin grammar schools concentrated on Latin, Greek, and theology. The use of a core curriculum and the involvement of students in the selection of courses from a wide spectrum of possibilities was a characteristic of progressive schools. In the 1950s, Sputnik and the NDEA produced a discipline-centered curriculum stressing science, mathematics, and foreign languages. With the civil rights movement and a demand for equal educational opportunity came a child-centered program with emphasis placed on ethical, social, and multicultural subjects. This was followed by a "back to basics" movement with more formalized instruction and strict accountability. Within a period of only thirty years, popularity has shifted from Deweyian progressives, to strict academicians, to social reconstructionists, to conservative essentialists. The 1990s promise to be filled with conflicting demands for different curricular choices.

While the debate goes on, teachers and administrators are faced with making curriculum choices and building appropriate programs. Given some basic assumptions about purposes, it is possible to develop a logical and consistent curriculum. In the past, such tasks were undertaken by the central administration or by local or state boards, but now many schools and individual teachers have considerable freedom in curriculum matters. The selection of materials and the stress placed upon certain concepts or examples have a profound effect on the school curriculum. A teacher who feels that ecology should be included in the work of the student can provide ecological materials in a variety of related subjects ranging from biology to civics.

A vast body of literature has grown up around the problem of curriculum development. Curriculum choices can never be made in isolation and the needs and wishes of the public must always be weighed against the teacher's perception of the needs of the child.

Since the middle of the 1960s, two schools of thought have dominated the controversy over curriculum organization and content. One of these is the free, open, child-centered, humanistic, and socially oriented movement. The theory behind this movement is grounded in the work of John Dewey, A. S. Neill, the social reconstructionists, and humanistic-existential authors. The opposite movement calls for standardized subject matter, no-nonsense basic education, high academic standards, and discipline oriented schools. The philosophical foundation for this position reaches back to Plato and has been supported by twentieth-century perennialists and essentialists.

Modern spokesmen for the first movement include Edgar Friedenberg, Paul Goodman, John Holt, Herbert Kohl and Charles Silberman. They oppose the conformity and docility characteristic of the subject-centered school. Accusing traditional schools of indifference to social issues and a meaningless curriculum, these authors demand relevant programs geared to the actual needs and desires of students. For them, the content of the curriculum is less important than the process used and the degree to which the learner is able to relate to the school activities. This means that much of the content of the curriculum must be taken from experiences in the life of the student. The school should deal with social issues, materials drawn from the mass media, and problems of the local community. Sex and drug education are included in the curriculum along with human relations and programs designed to help students understand the racially and culturally different. Calling for free and open education, these authors emphasize the development of self-concept, problem solving, the ability to make reasonable choices, and humanistic attitudes. They understand the need for basic skills like reading, but they have no interest in filling the mind of the student with lots of facts or in "mastering" specific subjects. They wish to foster a positive attitude toward learning and practical skills for dealing with other people and the outside world.

Holding the opposite position are authors like Jacques Barzun, Arthur Bestor, Mortimer Adler, Robert Hutchins, and James Koerner. Their point of view is similar to that expressed by James Conant and Admiral Rickover after Sputnik, that the schools must concentrate on producing subject matter experts and superior scholars to lead the technological society. Koerner has been a spokesman for the Council for Basic Education which opposes the "soft" pedagogy of progressive education and demands a return to "solid" academic subjects. The Council argues against student input into the curriculum, saying that the adults know best what children should study. This is also the position of Hutchins who wants a curriculum composed of those aspects of the culture that have been subjected to the greatest amount of sophistication and refinement (the classics, mathematics, and science). Bestor believes that the function of the school is the teaching of intellectual disciplines, not teaching about current social problems or adjusting students to different cultural groups. This group opposes social engineering in education and bending the curriculum to make it relevant to the student. By 1980 the Council for Basic Education and the "back to basics" movement had gained vast public support, partly from parents disappointed with the level of information and skills learned by their children in public schools and partly from the "Moral Majority" which questions some of the assumptions of an open, humanistic, child-centered, life adjustment programs. In calling for a return to fundamentals and a curriculum of basic studies, Barzun has said, "Nonsense is at the heart of those proposals that would replace definable subject matter with vague activities copied from life or with courses organized around problems or attitudes."

Curriculum Innovations and Methods.   A number of emergent trends have provided persuasive arguments to broaden the public school curriculum. It is not the case that all schools have adopted new subjects, but sufficient demand has been expressed to make them important in the field of curriculum development. They reflect an interest in interdisciplinary approaches to schooling as well as a thrust toward individualization and relevance.

1. Career education is an expression of discontent with the old division between vocational and academic programs. With emphasis on the functional value of career planning for all students, this program claims to be part of general education. On the theory that almost all students will enter some sort of work in the future, career education emphasizes occupational training, career information and guidance, and the involvement of business and community groups. The aim is to make career education available to all students and not just to those in vocational or industrial programs.
2. Consumer education is now part of the social studies curriculum in many schools. The pressures of inflation and the need of all people to make wise choices in purchasing makes consumer education valuable. Courses are often included as part of

economics, or career education, but sometimes consumer education is taught as a separate course.

3. Environmental education reflects a public concern with energy, pollution, ecology, and depletion of natural resources. Population pressures on the natural environment have created a demand for better understanding of environmental issues. Most schools attempt to build environmental content into standard courses in geography and the sciences. Many of these concerns are multicultural ones and have created a new demand for global education.

4. Ethnic and multicultural educational offerings have grown rapidly since the "black revolution" and the emergence of interest in ethnic identity. Some states require schools to include courses in ethnic studies or cultural pluralism and most have policy statements on the subject. The need for identity and recognition of minorities and ethnic groups is clear. Ethnic education is designed to enhance self-esteem of culturally different students and to promote understanding by majority students.

5. Education dealing with drug and alcohol abuse is an expanding program. Because of the widespread problem of abuse and addiction, public demand for such education has been strong. Coordinated programs with law enforcement agencies, community health projects, and former drug abusers are often found. The major criticism of these programs comes from those who do not feel that they are well taught and effective. The transfer of the former education secretary, William Bennett, to the position of chief drug control officer in the Bush administration and the fear of the AIDS virus among drug abusers gave new support to this program in schools.

6. Sex education was placed in the school curriculum because of high rates of illegitimacy, venereal disease among students, the national increase in divorce, and massive evidence that students are sexually active. The sensitive nature of the subject and the belief by many that the school has no business dealing with matters of sex has created considerable controversy over this subject. Yet the evidence is clear that students are not getting appropriate information about sex from their parents, religious institutions, or peers. The number of unwed teenage mothers is increasing at an alarming rate, and very few sexually active students use contraceptives. The traditional units on reproduction in biology classes are hopelessly inadequate and now are supplemented with programs on dating, marriage, parenthood, child care, health, and social responsibility. Expanded sex education classes and programs are addressing the problem more adequately in the 1990s.

While not strictly adding to the curriculum, numerous modifications have been undertaken which alter certain subjects. Courses in mathematics have been changed to allow for metric conversion. Although using the metric system is voluntary, it is expected that mathematical skill in metrics will be needed in the future. Handheld calculators are now part of the equipment of many students and are as common as the slates of the nineteenth century. Teachers have had to adjust to giving less time to practice in manual calculation and more to problems in which electronic calculators are used. Computers are rapidly becoming available in classrooms across the nation. Language and techniques for using micro-computers are included in many courses in science and mathematics at all levels.

The curriculum can never be totally divorced from methods. The same subject matter used for a lecture and in discovery learning will produce very different results in students. As a general rule, conservatives are more comfortable with time-honored methods such as lecture, textbook assignments, homework, standardized tests, and library reports. Liberals tend to promote laboratory methods such as discovery learning, problem solving, and inquiry learning. The activity curriculum and the child-centered curriculum are not popular with the "back to basics" movement although individualized instruction may be used by both liberals and conservatives. Computer-assisted instruction is acceptable to the subject-matter curriculum advocates so long as it does not stray from the subject. Team teaching and flexible scheduling are most often found in schools with a progressive orientation. The activity-centered curriculum which began with William H. Kilpatrick in the 1920s, centers on life experiences such as field trips, group projects, social enterprises, and local centers of interest. Some modern schools support an activity curriculum by working with community groups, social agencies, and governmental institutions. The activity curriculum requires extensive student and community participation.

Competency Based Training and Performance Contracting.   Just as competency based teacher education has become popular, there is a demand that public school students show evidence of mastery of fundamental subjects. The move to place greater emphasis on reading, writing, and mathematics in elementary schools and on English, science, history, and mathematics in secondary schools supports minimum competency testing. Some schools have contracted with private firms to produce specific behavior in specified areas of learning. Such performance contracting (as in Texarkana in 1972) has produced disappointing results, but it is clear that the public demands improvement in the informational levels and skills of students. The pros and cons of testing for minimum competency are much the same as the arguments over accountability.

Demands for stress on basic education and an end to "frills" call for testing students to make sure that they have at least the minimum requirements for each course. Those favoring competency testing want an end to social promotion. They believe no student should graduate from high school without demonstrating proficiency in reading, oral and written communication, and mathematics. Part of the interest in private education comes from the belief that public schools are soft on the fundamentals and try to provide a curriculum that is too broad. "Project 81" in Pennsylvania is an example of a statewide attempt to ensure that all students meet graduation requirements as measured by competency tests. Florida also is a leader in adopting tests for minimum competency. It is argued that merely accumulating the necessary credits is not enough and that testing for knowledge of course content must be universal. Those favoring minimum competency testing usually stress patriotism, strict discipline, homework, dress codes, and teacher-directed activities. They are against innovations in the curriculum, electives, and such "frills" as sex education.

Arguments against competency testing are both theoretical and practical. Many educators oppose a narrow curriculum with no electives. They feel that such programs lack interest and relevance to the needs of students. Those who favor problem solving and inquiry as methods doubt that the tests used are adequate. They say that eliminating the new math, linguistic approaches to grammar, and humanistic studies means a return to the nineteenth century. There are also charges that tests are culturally biased against minorities and ethnic groups. Some believe that it is unfair to prevent a student from graduating because the school has been unable to develop his or her skills. Many argue that the minimum competency tests are directed toward mechanical skills and the memorization of information. They say competency programs detract from higher skills such as reading for comprehension and logical thinking. Only those things which can be easily tested are given emphasis, making the curriculum rigid, narrow, unimaginative, and dull.

Of course, some schools and teachers use contracting with individual students as an instructional method. Giving a grade for specific performance is most often used in schools with a progressive orientation, but it is not different in concept from requiring specific competency for graduation, demanded by essentialists. Whatever the arguments, minimum competency testing seemed to be winning public support in the early 1980s.

Educating the Exceptional Child.   In the twentieth century, vast gains were made in the diagnosis and treatment of students with special problems. Starting with programs for the deaf and the blind, educational institutions developed a variety of effective methods for educating the exceptional child. New facilities for the disabled were built, including ramps and restrooms to accommodate students in wheelchairs. The Rehabilitation Act of 1973 prohibits discrimination against the disabled by failure to provide reasonable facilities and access. Obvious physical and mental disabilities have been understood and dealt with in education for many years, although with varying degrees of success. Learning specialists trained to work with various learning disabilities have been in the schools only for a little over a decade. Programs for the mentally retarded and those with trainable mental disabilities were made to identify and help students with less pronounced difficulties. The gifted and talented were ignored by many schools on the grounds that they would learn in spite of the system. Even today, numerous school systems are just starting special programs for the gifted.

A major issue concerning special students centers on Public Law 94–142. In hearings for this law (passed in 1975), it was pointed out that 1.75 million handicapped children were excluded from school and another 4 million were not receiving full educational services. The law required that each exceptional learner be placed in the least restrictive environment in which his or her educational needs could be satisfactorily served. This meant that children who previously spent their entire in-school time in special classes would be mainstreamed. Disabled children must spend at least part of the day in classes with nondisabled students. The intent of PL 94–142 was to remove the stigma attached to disabled students, to improve social relationships, to provide nondisabled learning models, to allow for a richer and more competitive environment, and to learn to live in the real world outside of the school. Other reasons included allowing more students to be served, providing more cost-effective education, and decentralizing services to reduce transportation costs.

An Individualized Education Program (IEP) is required for all mainstreamed exceptional children. This is a plan for education cooperatively prepared by parents, teachers, and school officials. It covers the content, objectives, means of implementation, and evaluation of each student's program. Usually this plan is drafted by the classroom teachers and modified by parents and learning specialists. An IEP may not be altered without the consent of the child's review committee.

There is no question about the benefit of mainstreaming to the exceptional child. If all children were in small classes and if good cooperation always existed between the learning specialist and the regular teacher, there might be no controversy. This is not the case. Regular classroom teachers often feel that they are not prepared and do not have the time to work well with the disabled. Making and reviewing an IEP for each child requires much time and energy that might be devoted to other tasks. The teachers often feel that they must give most of their time to the special learners while these students are present in the classroom. Parents of nondisabled children often complain that their children are getting less attention as a result of mainstreaming. Others say that the presence of disabled students for a large portion of the day reduces the level of expectation and takes away from excellence. Sometimes the classroom teacher feels that he or she must work harder than the learning specialist and negative feelings result. Although colleges of education usually require a course in special education, many classroom teachers do not feel able to meet the needs of disabled children. It is not always clear just what responsibilities belong to the learning specialist and which ones to the classroom teacher, especially when the specialist is functioning as an observer to review the effectiveness of the program. Mainstreaming seems to be working well in a number of school systems but there is a good deal of criticism and public acceptance is mixed.

The Council for Exceptional Children, in its 1993 spring meeting, noted that "full inclusion" is a step on a continuum of services for all disabled students. The council further noted that inclusion of disabled students (mentally or physically challenged) in regular classrooms throughout the school day is a meaningful goal to be pursued by schools and communities. There are supporters and detractors of the inclusion concept including special education teachers, administrators, parents and students.

Along with increased attention to inclusion, there are several current studies including Mary Wagner and colleagues' *What Happens Next? Trends in Postschool Outcomes of Youths with Disabilities* (1992) that are designed to survey postschool outcomes. These studies indicated significant movement toward social independence and economic improvement within five years of completing high school even though most jobs held are low-skill, low-wage positions.

The Americans With Disabilities Act of 1990 mandated full availability to special telecommunciations systems for over 26 million hearing and speech impaired citizens by July of 1993. As our history demonstrates, an expanded social consciousness continually reaches toward including more of the American populace of all ages, races, genders, and exceptionalities in the nation's educational and social services.

Some of those who oppose mainstreaming of the disabled support programs for gifted and talented youngsters. Demands for academic rigor, excellence, and intellectual development were loud in the era of the cold war and Sputnik. James Conant argued in *The American High School Today* that the academically talented student was not being sufficiently challenged. John Gardner pointed out that excellence is needed not just in scientists and engineers, but also in teachers, scholars, professional people, and social leaders. The White House Conference of 1955 stressed the development of the abilities of especially bright children. Science, mathematics, and foreign languages were considered the major areas of needed excellence. The seemingly antithetical goals of making serious educational demands on students and graduating almost all of them were treated in the 1985 book, *The Shopping Mall High School.*

Following the NDEA, interest in the gifted began to shift toward a better understanding of the exceptionally bright student. It was pointed out that many of the most able students found school boring and a waste of time. Tests of intelligence failed to reveal special qualities such as creative ability. It was found that gifted and talented students often felt socially isolated from other students and sometimes had difficulty in adjusting to group norms. By the 1970s, demands were growing for special programs for all gifted and talented students. Limitations of money slowed the development of these, but legislation was passed which required that special offerings be made available for the gifted. Gifted and talented students must also be mainstreamed, but there is less controversy over this. Most teachers find having the gifted in their classes part of the day much less stressful than dealing with the disabled. It is expected that all schools will provide programs for the gifted and talented by the end of the 1990s. Interest in the academically talented has increased since former U.S. Commissioner Sidney Marland submitted a report to Congress in 1972, which recommended better education for the capable student. Nevertheless, low funding and a lack of trained teachers for the gifted have caused programs to lag far behind the level provided for disabled students.

The Civil Rights Act of 1991 provides regulations for companies with 25 or more employees, and after 1994 for companies with 15 or more workers, to compel them to provide accommodations for the disabled including auxiliary aids, removal of structural barriers, and new construction and alteration standards. By 1993, universities and businesses had worked to remove barriers to equal access to facilities. Elevators, sidewalk modification, and easy access, door-to-door transportation for the disabled have been provided in most major institutions. All institutions will be required to provide equal access in the future.

In 1990, a new federal law, The Older Workers Protection Act, was passed that barred age discrimination in employee benefits coverage as well as employment. Early studies on removal of the age 70 retirement requirement for institutions including schools and universities will have little effect, since most individuals prefer to retire well before that age.

Voucher Plans.   The voucher system is a plan for financing schools with tax money but with parents in control of that money. A voucher is a certificate issued to parents. The parents give the voucher to a school of their choice and the school exchanges the voucher for payment by the government. The system was studied at Harvard University in the 1960s. Voucher plans were tried in the South after 1954 as a means of supporting segregated schools, but these were found unconstitutional. Some states have attempted to use a voucher system for supporting parochial schools, and cases are still pending on their legal status. Modern proposals for voucher plans guard against racial discrimination or the use of taxes to supplement tuition at expensive private schools.

Proponents argue that parents should have a choice as to which schools their children attend. They say the schools would become more competitive and establish many alternatives in curriculum and methods. They point out that without the voucher system, only those wealthy enough to pay tuition can select schools for their children, while the poor must accept whatever the local public schools offer. Properly regulated, a voucher system could bring innovation and reform to schools and give parents much more control over the education of their children. These arguments are especially strong in California where a large segment of the population is supporting a law requiring the state adopt the voucher system. Although the California Voucher System Proposal was defeated in the November 1993 election, efforts to expand school choice will continue.

Many public school people and organizations such as the AFT and NEA are opposed to the voucher system. They believe that the schools would become more segregated with middle-class parents selecting one type while the poor and minorities would be concentrated in others. Competition between schools would foster publicity seeking and teachers would try to be popular rather than professional. Many believe that the system would be unworkable and that it might destroy public education in the United States.

Multicultural and Bilingual Education.   Issues over the inclusion of multicultural studies in the curriculum and providing primary instruction in a language other than English developed in the 1970s and continued into the 1980s. The United States is made up of a large number of people with diverse cultural backgrounds. In addition to a substantial black minority, Chicanos and Latinos, Native Americans, certain European minorities, and Asians are part of the American population. Some members of these groups have been assimilated into the mainstream of the culture but others maintain an ethnic identification and may be regarded as subcultures.

Historically, education has been used as an instrument for bringing foreigners into the national culture. Early arguments for public schools stressed the need to Americanize the immigrants and to make sure that all children learned to speak English. Although this "melting pot ideal" did not result in uniform cultural patterns, the dominant "Anglo" Protestant group managed to require conformity to its language, cultural preferences, and value orientation. Schools not only reflected middle-class interests, they also showed a decided preference for white, Anglo-Saxon, "establishment" norms. Of course assimilation did not include African-Americans, Native Americans, and Hispanics who were segregated and not allowed to fully participate in the majority society. In their cases, they were told to assimilate in the "mainstream" culture.

The civil rights movement called attention to discrimination against minority and ethnic groups. African-Americans were the first to demand equality of opportunity, with Hispanics and Native Americans soon following. As part of the minority revolution, pride in ethnic culture and ethnic identification increased. The unique contributions of minorities to language, art, food, entertainment, and sports were emphasized, together with ethnic histories and distinctive cultural patterns. This increasing ethnic identification led to the concept of cultural pluralism and a growing respect for the contributions made by each ethnic group and minority. Schools began offering programs in cultural awareness and specialized courses like black history and Hispanic studies. Multicultural education was also seen as a means of reducing prejudice through better understanding.

Many schools in America have incorporated elements of multiculturalism in existing programs. Units dealing with Eskimos and Native Americans have been part of the curriculum for years. Textbooks have been rewritten so that black and Hispanic role models are taught along with those from the dominant culture. Attention is given to special events such as Native American Week or Hispanic Heritage Week. A growing interest in international social and economic issues has fostered interest in global education. Where large numbers of minority children are in attendance, courses in ethnic studies or cultural pluralism are sometimes offered. Colleges that train teachers try to encourage the teaching of values which support cultural diversity, ethnic awareness, the exploration of alternative life styles, and an understanding of cultural pluralism. Professional groups, state departments of education, and local curriculum committees are developing methods for multicultural emphasis in all public school classrooms.

Bilingual and bicultural education grew out of the problems non-English speaking and limited-English speaking children were having in schools where primary instruction was in English. Before the civil rights movement, most states required that public school instruction be given only in English. In the 1960s, attention was called to the large number of students who failed or who dropped out of school because the instruction was in a language foreign to them. This was especially the case in Texas where many Spanish-speaking students entered schools in which teachers spoke no Spanish. In 1968, the Bilingual Education Act was passed and appropriations of nearly $160-million for bilingual programs were made by 1979. This act calls for instruction in two languages for children whose native tongue is other than English. Projects using various Native American and Asian languages were created, but most bilingual instruction is in English and Spanish. Support for bilingual education also came from a Supreme Court case in 1974. In *Lau v. Nichols*, the Court held that schools must take steps to aid students who find the educational experiences "wholly incomprehensible" because they do not understand English. The Court stated that the San Francisco Unified School District's failure to provide remedial language instruction to Chinese speaking students constituted a violation of their civil rights under the Civil Rights Act of 1964. This case stands, even though federal funding for bilingual programs was reduced in the budget cuts of the Reagan administration.

Minority and culturally different students often suffer from educational disabilities related to their cultural backgrounds. Studies of Native American children have shown that some Indian youngsters are taught to be quiet in the presence of elders and that their primary learning patterns are very different from those used in most classrooms. While Black English is not one of the bilingual programs, students used to speaking a black dialect often have trouble acquiring language skills in standard English. Educators are beginning to understand that different instructional approaches are needed with different racial and ethnic groups.

Opposition to bilingual and multicultural education is widespread. Obviously the "back to basics" people are against spending time in pluralistic or multicultural studies when that time might be used for fundamental courses. Conservatives regard such studies as another "frill" which should be eliminated from the basic curriculum. Others argue that the multicultural movement tends to promote cultural, social, and economic separation. They want the schools to emphasize the core values of the dominant culture and to assimilate the culturally different into the American mainstream. Some feel that bilingual programs allow children to maintain their first language and discourage the use of English by allowing them to function in school with another language. The idea of a large region of the United States where Spanish is the primary language is considered harmful to national unity by this group. It is feared that the curriculum will be fragmented by attempts to include cultural diversity and cultural pluralism. Educators like Harry Broudy believe that large amounts of material on ethnic diversity tend to "trivialize" the curriculum and may be used to justify a poor quality education for disadvantaged students. Stress on ethnic and cultural differences may lead to cultural separation and have a disunifying effect on the body politic. This seems especially important when educators are trying to find ways to support the values at the core of the democratic society. Americans generally are beginning to doubt that the goals of equal educational opportunity can be achieved through schooling, and there is now much opposition to spending money for social engineering or for ethnic studies. Yet educators realize the American society is based on the principle of equality and that it is improper to force every child into a mode of behavior determined by the norms of the majority.

As Dewey noted, schools are miniature societies. Forms of discrimination such as sexism, racism, class, cultural and linguistic conflicts infecting society also are reflected in our schools. American's historical treatment of Hispanics, Asians, and Native Americans have left wounds that often still require healing efforts. Fred Kierstead and Paul Wagner in *The Ethical, Legal, and Multicultural Foundations of Teaching* call for transcultural education designed to provide for an interchange of cultural ideas for human improvement. In this sense multicultural education's divisive components would be replaced by the study of cultures because of their contribution to humanity as a whole. Rather than dividing ethnic and culturally diverse groups within a macroculture like America, transcultural education would study cultures for their unifying themes. Multicultural education in its present form stresses differences rather than commonalities, and Kierstead suggests that a new phase of multicultural education, a transcultural phase, would promote more tolerance, interdependence and respect for human dignity.

The Changing Role of Women in Education.

The struggle for equal rights for women has a history as long as that for minorities. Vast change has occurred since Emma Hart Willard began a boarding school for girls in her home in 1814 and Mary Lyon opened Mount Holyoke Seminary in 1837. Elizabeth Blackwell became the first American woman to earn the M.D. degree while astronomer Maria Mitchell was appointed the first female science professor at Vassar in 1862. Florence Bascom became a geologist with the U.S. Geological Survey in 1896 and a fellow of the Geological Society of America in 1894. In 1920, Florence Sabin, who took one of the first medical degrees from Johns Hopkins University, was the first woman to be elected to the National Academy of Sciences. Alice Evans was elected the first female president of the Society of American Bacteriologists in 1928, while Maria Mayer won the Nobel Prize in 1963 for physics research. Other prizes went to Rosalyn Yalow for medicine in 1977 and to Barbara McClintock in physiology and medicine in 1983.

Historian Darlene Clark Hine, in her two volume *Black Women in America: An Historical Encyclopedia* (1993), provided a reference book that described the role of black women in American history from the 17th century to the present. From an account of Africans put ashore from a Dutch ship at Jamestown in 1619 to the 1992 election of Senator Moseley Braun of Illinois, detailed accounts of the struggles for progress and survival are provided.

Edward Stevens and George Wood, in their *Justice, Ideology, and Education*, note that the civil rights movement of the 1950s, anti-war protests, and counter-culture groups helped create a climate of liberation. Currently, sexual harassment programs and seminars are held for employees in most of society's institutions. Sexual discrimination has been addressed in Title IX of the Educational Amendments of 1972. Currently the *Educational Law Reporter* contains an increased number of cases dealing with sex discrimination and harassment.

The Civil Rights Act of 1991 includes a section dealing with Civil Rights and Women's Equity in Employment and The Glass Ceiling Act or Women's Equal Opportunity Act, which provide awards for firms that demonstrate extensive efforts not only to create opportunities for women and minorities but also to assist them in advancing to upper management positions. Major corporations, leading universities, and other institutions provide valuing-diversity workshops, seminars, and training sessions that deal with retaining and promoting culturally diverse employees. Sensitivity sessions are utilized to deal with issues of sexual harassment, hate crimes, and subtle forms of discrimination against women and minorities.

Melora Sundt in *Effective Sexual Harassment Policies* refers to a federal court decision in *Ellison v. Brady* (1991) to illustrate increased awareness of harassment issues for educators. The Ellison case developed the "reasonable woman standard" to deal with harassing behavior that creates a hostile working environment.

Since the early national period, a majority of the nation's teachers have been women. Traditionally, the work of women has been viewed as less valuable than that of men, which has helped to keep status and salaries low. Prestige for women in education was enhanced by the selection of social studies teacher Christa McAuliffe for the ill-fated Challenger space flight in 1986. Nonetheless, men still hold the majority of high-paying administrative positions in the schools. In spite of decades of work to eradicate sexual stereotypes from textbooks and the call for gender equity by the National Organization for Women, discrimination still exists. Research shows that girls are still discouraged from seeking careers in science and mathematics. A large number of American women, especially single mothers, live in poverty. Hunter College professor Ruth Sidell in *Women and Children Last*, calls for a more humane set of social policies to deal with poverty, work and welfare, and the rights of women and children. Equality for women in education will continue to be an issue through the 1990s.

TAKING SIDES TODAY AND TOMORROW

In this chapter, we have discussed issues, court cases, and contemporary critics. In every controversy, there is a connection to earlier arguments, writers, or litigation. Nothing which is at issue in modern American education is without historical foundation. The current question of the proper role for the federal government in educational matters relates to the land grants of the Northwest Ordinance and the Morrill Acts. The caustic criticism of schools in *Deschooling Society* is not far removed from the attack on society and education in *Emile*. Rousseau and Illich are separated by centuries, but the positions they represent are much the same, and the relationship between the schools and the wider society is still debated. The appeal made by citizens of Kalamazoo to the courts in the 1870s is an illustration of using litigation for resolving educational conflicts. This was true for the desegregation cases of the 1950s, the equal opportunity cases of the 1970s, and litigation over financial support of schools which continues into the 1990s. Some aspects of the social and educational milieu stir up public emotion and debate at an extreme level. An example is the *Roe v. Wade* case legalizing abortion and the strongly held opinions about whether it should be upheld or reversed. Another is the question of whether small school districts with scarce resources must bear the whole cost of educating severely-handicapped students. Few object in principle to PL 94–142 which requires local educational agencies to ensure an education in the least restrictive environment for handicapped children in the district. However, McCay Vernon cites a situation in New Jersey where the cost of educating one child with extreme hyperactivity places an added tax burden of $1,500 per year on each citizen of the county. This problem has not been solved for the future, and it is sure to be an issue for years to come.

Sometimes, a local reaction to a wider controversy may so divide a community that education is affected for a long period of time. We have seen that there is national strife over the selection and adoption of school textbooks and book censorship. In Kanawha

County, West Virginia, textbook selection by two committees (from state approved textbook lists) were sent forward to the board. The board unanimously voted to accept the recommendations and made the collection available for public review. By the winter of 1975, many of the books were labeled as "dirty, anti-Christian, or anti-American" by some parents and local groups. Local ministers were divided on the issue but the flames were fanned by organizations as diverse as the NEA, the Council of Parents and Teachers, the NAACP, the National Library Association, the Ku Klux Klan, and the John Birch Society. The board ended up by banning books depicting racial strife, demeaning patriotism, supporting alien forms of government, debasing religious or ethnic groups, encouraging sedition, or which used offensive language. The judgment about these themes was very broad so that a great many books were removed from the schools.

Underlying this turbulent issue over textbooks were social conflicts of a more basic kind. Kanawha County was made up of about 200,000 people, two-thirds of whom were relatively affluent. The remainder were rural poor, who made a living in the coal fields of Appalachia. This group felt exploited and denied an adequate standard of living. Another problem was that the schools, including the textbook committees, had little or no parental involvement in their decisions. In the aftermath of the Kanawha County controversy, it is clear that conflict over textbook selection was triggered by a much deeper community conflict. We can anticipate future educational arguments whenever there is a serious value conflict within the culture. For example, in communities containing both fundamentalists and religious liberals, it is to be expected that arguments against evolution as the only credible theory of the origin of life will be posed by creationists.

Many of the results of taking sides on issues such as involuntary segregation are now history. Heated debate continues over the unfavorable comparisons of American and foreign students on standardized tests of achievement. Decades of federal support for equalization, illustrated by programs like Head Start and Upward Bound did not support high levels of achievement. The "Nation at Risk" report triggered emphasis on competition, excellence, and high academic standards. In the Reagan administration, Secretary Bennett gave his support to programs like the great books of the western world and the Paideia proposal of Mortimer Adler. The classical-perennialist curriculum of James Madison High School and the highly general liberal arts program became the rage of the 1980s as a model of quality secondary education. Regardless of the merits of this kind of schooling, critics say that it is not for everyone. Washington D.C. school superintendent Floretta McKenzie argues that the perennial approach fails to provide vocational training, specific skills needed for employment, and comprehensive instructional strategies to accommodate different learning styles or poorly-motivated students. Dr. McKenzie is not only a prominent practicing educator but also a leading advocate of minority education and equality. She feels that the great books program of the Paideia Proposal will lead to a dual system of education and an increase in the dropout rate. The problem is especially central to states like Texas where half of the three and one half million school age children are black or Hispanic. Former education secretary Lauro

Cavazos and current secretary Richard Riley are keenly interested in equality of opportunity as well as learning outcomes for all of the nation's students and propose to fight for a lower dropout rate and higher achievement levels. This issue will not be easily resolved in the near future and may be expected to be of concern through the year 2000. John Gardner may have put it best when he asked, "Can we be equal and excellent too?"

With the fifty separate state educational systems, the problems of funding American schools and providing equality of opportunity by eliminating differences between the number of dollars supporting each child within states is a continuing issue. Courts have recently ruled the states of Texas and Montana in violation of required equalization rules. The fundamental problem is that of securing adequate taxation to support schools, especially in areas where the economy is weak or where other priorities such as roads get more support. Attitudes of the public are critical and may be affected by activities such as teacher strikes. After a 16 month labor dispute culminating in an 11 day strike which closed the schools, Los Angeles teachers won a 24 percent pay raise over three years. This strike in the nation's second largest school district put half a million students out of school. In addition to the $600 million pay plan, teachers won more authority (empowerment) over curriculum and methods. This was an impressive gain, but it remains to be seen what the effect on the attitude of the public in California may be.

Other ongoing controversies center on bilingual programs and education for the handicapped. Bilingual instruction was especially needed in states like Florida, California, and Texas where Hispanic children were at great disadvantage if instruction was only in English. George Sanchez found that students in Texas with Spanish family names received an average of only one-fourth the years of formal education of those with Anglo names. About five million children now come from homes where English is not the primary language. Federal help comes from Title VII of the Elementary and Secondary Education Act and Chapter 1 of the Education Consolidation and Improvement Act. State and local funds are also needed. There are strong arguments against bilingual education beyond the costs of providing it. Some think time and energy spent on instruction in two languages robs students of resources that should be spent on basic education. That argument is used also by those who feel mainstreaming of disabled students focuses attention on special students to the detriment of nondisabled children. Another criticism is historical. Formerly, when minority groups came to the United States, they were assimilated into the culture and became English speaking. Assimilation was the theory behind the Lau decision which required the San Francisco schools to provide language instruction for its Chinese speaking students. The Spanish speaking minority, however, continues to use Spanish after receiving bilingual instruction. This is the reason that some states have passed legislation which makes English the official language. Still other critics like Diane Ravitch say that bilingual programs grew out of the civil rights movement and ethnic political pressure and that there is no proof that they work.

Ever larger numbers of American children are assessed to need some sort of special education. With a growing number of minority children and new global awareness, it is unlikely that the Bilingual Education Act of 1968 will be repealed. Multiethnic education, an approach to making schools pluralistic, attempts to integrate education and to avoid reliance on English and Anglo-Saxon values. It will continue to be debated into the next century.

Because of the dynamic nature of society and the fact that education is an enterprise that involves our most important resource, children, we can expect a high level of controversy in the future. Only a few issues are fully resolved. Most of the arguments over educational issues will continue into the future and new ones are almost certain to emerge.

BIBLIOGRAPHY

Adams, James Truslow. *Frontiers of American Culture*. New York: Scribner's, 1944.

Ballantine, Jenne. *Schools and Society: A Unified Reader*, 2d. ed. Mountain View, CA: Mayfield Publishing, 1989.

Bloom, Benjamin. *All Our Children Learning*. New York: McGraw-Hill, 1980.

Bowles, Samuel, and Herbert Gintis. *Schooling in Capitalist America*. New York: Basic Books, 1976.

Bracey, Gerald W. "Why Can't They Be Like We Were?" *Phi Delta Kappan* (October, 1991):104–117.

Bracey, Gerald W. "The Third Bracey Report on the Condition of Public Education. *Phi Delta Kappan*, (October, 1993):105–117.

Byham, William C. *Zapp In Education*. New York: Fawcett Columbine, 1992.

Cordasco, Francesco. *Bilingual Schooling in the United States: A Sourcebook for Educational Personnel*. New York: McGraw-Hill, 1976.

D'Amico, R., C. Marder, L. Newman, and Mary Wagner. *What Happens Next?: Trends in Post School Outcomes of Youth With Disabilities*. Menlo Park, CA: SRI International, 1992.

Elam, Stanley M., Lowell C. Rose, and Alec M. Gallup. "The 25th Annual Phi Delta Kappa Gallup Poll of Public's Attitudes Toward the Public Schools," *Phi Delta Kappan*, (October 1993):138, 150.

Ellis, Arthur, John Cogan, and Kenneth Howey. *Introduction to the Foundations of Education*. Englewood Cliffs, NJ: Prentice-Hall, 1981.

Estes, Nolan, and Donald Waldrip. *Magnet Schools: Legal and Practical Implications*. NJ: New Century Education Corporation, 1978.

Gardner, John W. *Excellence: Can We Be Equal and Excellent Too? New York:* Harper and Row, 1961.

Gatti, Richard, and Daniel Gatti. *New Encyclopedia Dictionary of School Law*. West Nyack, NY: Parker Publishing Company, 1983.

Hewett, Frank, and Steven Forness. *Education of Exceptional Learners*. Boston: Allyn and Bacon, 1977.

Hine, Darlene Clark. *Black Women in America: An Historical Encyclopedia.* Brooklyn, NY: Carlson Publishing Co., 1993.

Huelskamp, Robert M. "Perspectives on Education in America." *Phi Delta Kappan*, (May 1993):718–721.

Jones, R. L., ed. *Mainstreaming and the Minority Child*. Reston, VA: Council for Exceptional Children, 1976.

Kierstead, Fred, and Paul A. Wagner. *The Ethical, Legal and Multicultural Foudations of Teaching*. Madison, WI: W. C. Brown and Benchmark, 1993.

Kozol, Jonathan. *Illiterate America*. Garden City NY: Anchor Press/Doubleday, 1985.

La Follette, Marcel Chotkowski. *Creationism, Science, and the Law: The Arkansas Case*. Cambridge: M. I. T. Press, 1993.

McCarthy, Martha M., and Cambron-McCabe. *Public School Law: Teachers' and Students' Rights*. Boston: Allyn and Bacon, 1992.

Nieto, Sonia. *Affirming Diversity.* New York: Longman, 1992.

Noll, James. *Taking Sides: Clashing Views on Controversial Educational Issues.* Guilford, CT: Duskin, 1980.

Ormstein, Allan, and Daniel Levine. *An Introduction to the Foundations of Education.* 2d ed. Boston: Houghton Mifflin, 1981.

Powell, Arthur, Eleanor Farrar, and David Cohen. *The Shopping Mall High School.* Boston: Houghton Mifflin Company, 1985.

Pratte, Richard. *Pluralism in Education.* Springfield, IL: Charles C. Thomas, 1979.

Prosser, Charles. *Secondary Education and Life.* Cambridge: Harvard University Press, 1939.

Stevens, Edwards, and George H. Woods. *Justice, Ideology, and Education.* New York: McGraw Hill, 1992.

Sundt, Melora. "Effective Sexual Harassment Policies: Focus on the Harasser and the Campus Culture." In *Synthesis: Law and Policy* 1993 4(4):333.

Tyack, David. *The One Best System.* Cambridge: Harvard University Press, 1974.

Wagner, Mary, Ronald D'Amico, Camille Marder, Lynn Newman, and Jose Blackorby. *What Happens Next? Trends in Postschool Outcomes of Youth with Disabilities.* Washington, D.C.: Office of Special Education Program, U.S. Office of Education, 1992.

Webb, Rodman, and Robert Sherman. *Schooling and Society. 2d ed.* New York: Macmillan, 1989.

Wise, Arthur. *The Bureaucratization of the American Classroom.* Berkeley, CA: University of California Press, 1979.

(Most of the controversial issues in education are well-covered in electronic data bases such as ERIC.)

8   IN SEARCH OF EXCELLENCE: EDUCATION IN THE 1980s AND 1990s

Tomorrow's systems of education will evolve if present arrangements are dynamic . . . [and] schooling and education are not synonymous. . . . Hope for the future rests with our ability to use and relate effectively all those educative and potentially educative institutions and agencies in our society—home, school, church, media, museums, workplace and more.

John I. Goodlad

THE GREAT AMERICAN EDUCATIONAL REFORM MOVEMENT

As demonstrated in previous chapters, the period of American history from the administrations of Presidents Kennedy and Johnson to that of Presidents Reagan, Bush, and Clinton was dominated by the social reform movement. Rejecting the old Darwinian concept of survival of the fittest, social engineers and educators joined forces in an effort to attain equality of opportunity and create the "Great Society." Aside from school lunch programs and health measures, the first such programs concentrated on racial desegregation of the schools. These efforts were soon followed by egalitarian programs focusing on the culturally deprived, the urban poor, and the disadvantaged. Thus Projects Head Start and Upward Bound and mainstreaming were superimposed on integration plans such as busing to achieve racial balance and magnet schools. The influx of vast numbers of Spanish-speaking children fostered bilingual programs, while federally sponsored enrichment agendas were followed in the cities. Progress was made toward an equal and democratic society in the 1960s and 1970s, although not at a rate that satisfied critics like Illich and Kozol. Almost all of the federal money for education was earmarked for these projects and virtually every school district was affected to some degree. When new ideas for the improvement of education appeared in the early 1980s, such as

195

Nixon	Ford	Carter
1974 Watergate Scandal Loss of Respect for Government	1976 Bicentennial NEA Politically Active	Continuation of Social Engineering in Education
High Inflation, Revolt of Taxpayers	1979 Separate Department of Education	Bilingual Programs for Growing Hispanic Minority

B. Othanel Smith's *A Design for a School of Pedagogy*, there was insufficient public support for implementation.

It should have come as no surprise that concentration on access to schooling and equity would have a leveling effect on overall achievement. After all, when the population of students expanded to include minorities, the disadvantaged, and those with exceptional needs, some regression might have been expected. College boards, for example, once taken only by elite, college-bound high school students, declined as the numbers of pupils taking them expanded. John Gardner, among others, had previously raised the question of whether the public schools could be both equal and excellent. The two goals are not mutually exclusive but sterling success in scholarship requires effort and money which equality also demands.

Reform Reports.   More than thirty examinations of public education in the United States followed closely on the publication of "A Nation at Risk." Some of these were sponsored by special interest groups, several emerged from the work of commissions and professional organizations, while a few represented individual efforts. Among the most important were:

> *A Nation Prepared: Teachers for the 21st Century*, Report of the Carnegie Task Force on Teaching as a Profession, 1986.
>
> *A Place Called School: Prospects for the Future*, John Goodlad, 1983.
>
> *Academic Preparation for College: What Students Need To Know and Be Able to Do*, Educational Equality Project, The College Board, 1983.

Reagan	Bush		Clinton	
Stress on Basics	1980's *A Nation at Risk*	1986 Gramm-Rudman	1993 National Service Trust Fund	
New Power of Political and Religious Right	Other National Reform Reports	1986 Holmes Group		1994 Whitewatergate
Conservative Social and Fiscal Policies and Rise of the Fundamentalist "New Right"		1984 Responses by Ernest Boyer, John Goodlad, and Theodore Sizer		
		1988 Shortage of Teachers		

Action for Excellence: A Comprehensive Plan to Improve our Nation's Schools, Task Force on Education for Economic Growth, Education Commission of the States, 1983.

Cultural Literacy: What Every American Needs to Know E.D. Hirsch Jr, 1987.

High School: A Report on Secondary Education in America, Ernest L. Boyer, The Carnegie Foundation for the Advancement of Teaching, 1983.

Horace's Compromise: The Dilemma of the American High School, Theodore R. Sizer, 1984.

Horace's School: Redesigning the American High School, Theodore, R. Sizer, 1991.

Investing in Our Children, Report of the Committee for Economic Development, 1985.

Making the Grade, Report of the Twentieth Century Fund Task Force on Federal Elementary and Secondary Education Policy, 1983.

Results in Education: 1990, Report of the National Governor's Association, 1991.

Savage Inequalities: Children in America's Schools, Jonathan Kozol, 1991.

Shared Vision: Policy Recommendations for Linking Teacher Education to School Reform, Calvin Frazier, 1993.

Teachers for Our Nation's Schools, John Goodlad, 1990.

The Forgotten Half: Non-College Youth in America:An Interim Report on the School-to-Work Transition, Report of William T. Grant Foundation's Commission on Work, Family and Citizenship, 1988.

The Paideia Proposal: An Educational Manifesto, Mortimer J. Adler, on behalf of the members of the Paideia Group, 1982.

Time for Results, National Governors' Association, 1986.

The Troubled Crusade: American Education 1945-1980, Diane Ravitch, 1983.

A Study of High Schools, Theodore Sizer, co-sponsored by the National Association of Secondary School Principals and the National Association of Independent Schools, 1984.

In Search of Excellence: Lessons from America's Best Run Companies, Thomas Peters and Robert Waterman, 1984.

A Nation at Risk.   "A Nation at Risk," issued by the National Commission on Excellence in Education, had an impact similar to that of Sputnik in 1957. The report has been criticized by educators as focusing too much on high schools, using too narrow a sample and dated information, being biased in favor of a business model, and comparing comprehensive American schools with limited-population elite schools in Germany and Japan. Nevertheless, "A Nation at Risk" caught the attention of the public and educators alike. The report made a strong case for the urgency of reform if the nation was to retain its place in the modern world. It was followed by a myriad of other studies and reports, but there is no question that "A Nation at Risk" had the most influence.

In international comparisons, the report showed that American students never were first or second and often were dead last as ranked against other industrial nations on nineteen academic tests. About 13 percent of the nation's seventeen-year-olds were functionally illiterate while the percentage for minority youth was 40. Some 23 million adults could not pass simple tests of reading, writing, and comprehension. Half of the population of gifted students failed to match their tested ability in school performance. The average achievement of secondary students was lower than in 1957. Nearly 40 percent of the high school seniors could not draw inferences from written material and only one third could solve a mathematical problem requiring several steps.

The report pointed out that college boards (SAT test scores) declined steadily from 1963 to 1980. On the average, verbal scores dropped 50 points and scores in mathematics 40 points. Achievement in English and science had dropped, while the proportion of students demonstrating superior achievement had also declined dramatically. Between 1975 and 1980, remedial courses in mathematics offered by four year colleges increased by 72 percent, so that they came to make up one-fourth of the mathematics curriculum. Average achievement scores of college graduates also fell between 1975 and 1980. Business and military leaders were cited as saying that high school graduates were so deficient in such basic skills as reading, writing, spelling, and computation that they were forced to spend millions of dollars for remedial training courses just to bring workers and trainees up to ninth-grade level.

"*A Nation at Risk*" was credited with creating the momentum for educational reform but it did not offer a model for high quality education. Almost nothing in the report deals with pedagogy while concentration was on mechanical solutions, regarded by the profession as bureaucratic and simplistic. No means of implementing excellence while maintaining equality was suggested. The report asked for more of the same, more basic courses, more homework, longer school years, more required courses, and better pay for teachers. Most educators saw this as a Band-Aid solution when a major new direction was needed. They saw little help for improving schools such as Eastside High School in Patterson, New Jersey, where principal Joe Clark won both admiration and blame for maintaining discipline with a bull horn and a baseball bat. The report had little to say about how to reform schools with significant problems.

After nearly twenty years of neglect except for social measures, education again became a top national priority in the 1980s. It was a major agenda item for the presidential elections of 1984 and 1992. In 1984, thirty governors organized task forces on schooling, as did hundreds of school boards. Universities made efforts to strengthen relationships with schools, and the private sector offered its own reform package. The National Governors' Association in its report, *Time for Results,* advocated a national board to certify teachers, performance and pay links, school choice, school buildings open all year, and academic bankruptcy for schools and school districts not meeting standards. In 1991 the same group issued a report, *Results in Education: 1990,* evaluating the results of earlier proposals for sweeping educational reforms. The report concluded there was uneven and slow implementation of the proposals.

Calvin Frazier in *A Shared Vision: Policy Recommendations for Linking Teacher Education to School Reform,* noted few results from the reform reports of the 1980s and suggested part of the fault was in teacher training institutions. Frazier called for more input from lawmakers, clear assignments for everyone involved in school reform, clear standards for teacher education programs, licensure of new teachers, and additional funds for effective school reform. Sizer in *Horace's School: Redesigning The American High School* discussed his eight years of managing the Coalition of Essential Schools. He also found the reform movement of the 1980s to have little effect on the lives of his fictional English teacher or his students. Some of the most salient ideas may be gleaned from an examination of the most influential publications.

The Business Model.   "A Nation at Risk" took economic competition as its cause for being. *Action for Excellence,* by the Task Force on Education for Economic Growth, stressed America's position in a changing world market. It argued that public education must prepare students with greater scientific and economic knowledge and provide them with computer literacy. It suggested a partnership of state and corporate support while delegating the needs of specialized groups and minorities to state and corporate leaders. "America's Competitive Challenge," a report by the Business-Higher Education Forum, argued that federal funding should upgrade university facilities but it also proposed that industry should invest more in the education of its workers. It suggested that industry and the universities work together for better utilization of all educational resources.

As Naisbitt and Aburedene pointed out in *Reinventing the Corporation*, in 1985, American corporations spend $60 billion annually on education and training. Their programs are so vast that they offer an alternative to traditional university training and, of course, these corporations apply business measures of efficiency and cost effectiveness to their programs. Much of this is very similar to support of the *Cult of Efficiency* at the turn of the century, well described by Raymond E. Callahan in 1962. It shows how schools came under the influence of efficiency experts once before.

There should be little surprise in the discovery that business corporations feel they have the best models for educational reform. Successful commercial enterprises have been able to compete in a changing world market and have their own measures of efficiency. The most popular book of the period dealing with the ways in which business and industry have tried to recapture excellence is *In Search of Excellence: Lessons from America's Best Run Companies*, written by Thomas J. Peters and Robert H. Waterman in 1982. Their belief is that what works for the private sector can also be used by public institutions like schools. Their suggestions include:

1. A bias for action: doing something—anything—is better than the status quo.
2. Learning the preferences of the customers and catering to them.
3. Breaking up the corporation into small units and encouraging independent thinking.
4. Productivity through people: making all workers responsible and allowing them to share in rewards.
5. Insisting that executives keep in touch with essential business and have direct involvement with workers.
6. Concentration on the business at hand rather than pursuing secondary goals.
7. Simple structure with authority at lower levels and few top administrators.
8. Fostering a climate that stresses dedication to the central values of the company combined with tolerance for the activities of all who accept those values.

Clearly these concepts were acceptable to educational institutions. The question remains, however, of applying the incentives of a profit making corporation to schools. This was not the first time that business has set itself up as a model for educators to follow. The difference in the 1980s was that reform was demanded and successful corporations provided a pattern with much public support.

The Paideia Proposal. Mortimer Adler, long-time advocate of the Great Books curriculum and philosophical companion to Robert Hutchins, wrote the *Paideia Pro-*

posal in 1982. This plan advocated giving the same quality of schooling to all. It required a program of study that is both liberal and general. All sidetracks, specialized courses, and vocational training were eliminated. The basic course of study to be followed in twelve years of schooling allows only one choice, that of a second language.

Adler identifies three distinct modes of teaching and learning, rising in successive gradations of complexity and difficulty from the first to the twelfth year. All three modes are essential to the overall course of study. Mode One represents the acquisition of organized knowledge by means of didactic instruction, lectures and responses using textbooks and other aids, in these subject areas: language, literature and the fine arts, math, natural science, history, geography, and social studies. Mode Two represents the development of intellectual skills (skill of learning)—by means of coaching, exercises, and supervised practice—in operations of reading, writing, speaking, listening, calculating, problem solving, observing, measuring, estimating, and exercising critical judgment. Mode Three represents enlarging the understanding of ideas and values by means of Socratic questioning and interaction with major contributions to literature.

In addition to these three main modes of learning, the required course of study would include physical education, care of the body, computer skills, manual arts, and an introduction to various careers. Adler was convinced that children judged unable to pursue his curriculum simply had not yet had their minds challenged by such requirements.

The Paideia plan gained advocates among those favoring liberal education and thinking skills. It was almost the exact opposite of the models proposed by "A Nation at Risk" and the business sector. While no powerful organizations or political groups embraced the Paideia Proposal, it has influenced the movement away from early specialization in the high schools and the strengthening of general education requirements in colleges and universities.

Boyer, Goodlad, and Sizer.

Three names which appeared constantly in the reform literature of the mid-1980s were Ernest Boyer, John Goodlad, and Theodore Sizer. The three had long been associated with studies of education before the critical reports emerged and each had developed a plan for improving schools. Boyer's most important contribution was a report for the Carnegie Foundation for the Advancement of Teaching in 1983, *High School: A Report on Secondary Education in America*. Goodlad, a recognized expert in curriculum, made a major contribution to the reform literature in *A Place Called School: Prospects for the Future*, published in 1984. Sizer also published his *Horace's Compromise: The Dilemma of the American High School* in that year. Patricia Cross of Harvard, in a *Kappan* article called "The Rising Tide of School Reform Reports," credited these three with the most influential reform books from within the educational profession.

Boyer's detailed studies of secondary education tend to support some of the disturbing accounts of teaching conditions described earlier by sociologists like Dan Lortie in *Schoolteacher*. He sees the teaching profession as in deep crisis in this nation and says teachers are fully aware of their situation. Teachers are deeply troubled not only about low salaries but also about loss of status, bureaucratic pressures, lack of recognition, and a poor public image. It makes no sense to talk about recruiting better teachers for the future unless the conditions of teaching are improved. The professional ethos which attracted many teachers in the first place has withered under public criticism and an outmoded school structure. He argues that the push for excellence must begin by improving the conditions which drive out good teachers. Fewer students choose to enter teaching as a profession and those who do are not the best students. Boyer is also critical of college programs for the preparation of teaching and the methods by which states handle certification.

Flexibility and freedom are keys to Boyer's ideas of reform. He wants a comprehensive modernization process that will free teachers to innovate on the individual school level. The average high school teacher with six classes a day and only 54 minutes of preparation time is hard pressed to pursue excellence. Reviewing subject matter, preparing lesson plans, grading papers, advising students, and making out report cards also take time that might be given to improving teaching techniques. The nature of the classroom and working conditions must change for excellence to be achieved. Flexibility and decentralization need to replace top-down decision making and bureaucratic standardization. Unless teachers at the local level are supported by the public and given real professional status, Boyer thinks reform will fail.

A Place Called School also calls attention to the plight of the profession and the crisis of schooling. In fact, Goodlad thinks that the problems of schooling are of such crippling proportions that the entire system of public education may collapse. Monetary solutions are not sufficient to regain excellence. Nonproductivity, low achievement, high dropout rates, poor attendance, low teacher morale, and loss of public confidence are symptoms of severe problems. Mere application of business practices or piecemeal measures like higher standards for high school graduation will not do. There is, however, a mandate for change which legitimizes drastic action. Goodlad, therefore, finds an opportunity in the crisis of the 1980s.

In his plan for educational renewal, Goodlad does not abandon the quest for social equality which dominated schooling in the 1960s and 1970s. He is keenly aware of the denial of access to knowledge and access to effective teaching for racial minorities and those regulated to lower tracks through testing. The disadvantaged students are those who might gain most from varied pedagogical techniques and individualized instruction. They are the least likely to benefit from those reforms which pursue excellence by increasing the proportion of failures.

Goodlad's concept of educational reform requires that we focus on entire schools as opposed to "tinkering" with structure and curriculum. To do this, the community must be involved, and Goodlad has even suggested that the community ought to be the major educator of the child. Colleges and universities should be linked in partnerships aimed at improving both public schools and teacher education. Not content merely to write about renewal, Goodlad announced his sponsorship of twelve such school-university partnerships at the AACTE meeting in Chicago in 1986. His *Teacher's for Our Nation's*

Schools called for autonomous centers of pedagogy in colleges and universities in order to have the same authority exhibited by medical and law schools.

Theodore Sizer also supports more experimentation on the local school level as a means for altering the high degree of standardization and sameness common to educational institutions. A decentralized model with school-based management and delegation of authority to district or school building levels is preferable to the line-staff model in vogue. By designating certain schools as experimental units with license to try innovative approaches, better techniques of instruction can be developed. The school principal must have authority for allocation of resources and must act as instructional leader. *Horace's Compromise* recommended that individual schools be relieved of mandated curriculum, allowing experimentation based on the unique conditions of each community. Schools within schools would be set up as laboratories. School-based management should be used to move more authority to individual units and provide more instructional options. The involvement of teachers, parents, students, community leaders, and representatives of business and industry should be encouraged.

Sizer is very much concerned about the inability of high school teachers to get to know their students well enough to coach them toward excellence. For example, in learning to write well, students need a lengthy interaction with one teacher who goes over each theme, makes corrections, suggests improvements, and gives encouragement. This is impossible for an English teacher who has five different classes of thirty students. In order for the teacher to know the mind of the child well and to serve as a mentor or coach, the ratio of teachers to students must be reduced. Sizer suggests having secondary teachers offer more than one subject to the same students. English teachers might have the same students for English, sociology, and American history. This would require broader teacher training but it would allow for better results.

Comment and Criticism. *Action for Excellence, Making the Grade*, and *A Nation at Risk* were political documents. They gave vivid accounts of American education in decline with little regard for accuracy. Their aim was to get action from state and federal policy makers and from the public. The practical school administrator got very little guidance from these reports as means for actual school improvement.

The drive for educational excellence should also include at-risk children, as noted in *Investing in Our Children, Savage Inequalities: Children in America's Schools*, and *The Forgotten Half: Non-College Youth in America: An Interim Report on the School-to-Work Transition*. All of these works call for greater recognition of these children's education, social and economic needs, and aspirations. Non-college-bound students deserve the same opportunities to excel in society and in the workplace. The drive for excellence should not be excessively focused on college-bound students.

There was also a suggestion in E. D. Hirsch's *Cultural Literacy* that stipulated that all educated persons ought to have knowledge of the best ideals of humankind. Lack of such knowledge, Hirsch noted, is at the base of our literacy challenge.

Academic Preparation for College synthesized the judgment of hundreds of high school teachers and college professors concerning the knowledge and skills students should bring from high school to college. It set high standards and a rigorous course of study for such subjects as English, mathematics, science, social studies, foreign languages, and the arts. There was also the requirement for students to master competencies in reading, writing, speaking, reasoning, mathematics, and study skills. On the negative side, many educators felt that the report was idealistic and far-fetched. It appealed mostly to elite schools, where most students are college bound and where resources are adequate. Many who are concerned about dropouts and teaching minimum competencies to average children saw the report as unrealistic. Nevertheless, *Academic Preparation for College* provided a comprehensive curriculum model and a specific plan for reform.

A number of common points run through most of the reports. Although in trouble, public schools are a mainstay of American society. In spite of vouchers, tax rebates for private school tuition, and alternative schools with tax support, no serious proposals for ending public school education are made. Education is correlated with economic growth and high-quality schooling is essential to the national well being. Neither the individual nor the nation can prosper without high-quality education. Education is the universal right of all people in a free society. Education is a lifelong process and the foundation for it must be laid in elementary schools. Access to post-secondary education is dependent on the quality of high school programs for all. It is not satisfactory to push one segment of the population through a low-achievement secondary education and into the work force. This implies that the process of learning is as important as content.

Education must be accountable. No sector of society is without responsibility for teaching and learning. It is in the national interest for the federal government to regulate, legislate, and fund national school programs. Local districts are responsible for implementing programs, the delivery of educational priorities, legislation, regulations, and funding. The fundamental building block of educational renewal consists in the recruitment and training of high-quality teachers.

The reform reports and studies of the 1980s and 1990s had many points in common. They called for revised curriculums and the strengthening of requirements in English, mathematics, social studies, physical education, art, music, computer sciences, and foreign languages. All called for higher student efforts including tests for promotion and graduation, better discipline and more homework. Some suggested beginning education earlier and extending the school day and year. Most asked for additional programs to benefit the gifted and talented and others to give special help to slow learners. There were several calls for upgrading textbooks, establishing a core curriculum, and eliminating tracking. At least eight studies demanded a revision of vocational courses. Most required incorporating outside learning experiences into the curriculum and several emphasized the need to improve reasoning skills. Almost every study said something about higher college admission standards.

The reports disagreed about how all of this was to be accomplished and who would pay for it. It is always easier to call attention to a problem than it is to provide a viable solution. Many school leaders were dismayed to find the national reports gave them very little practical advice about how to achieve the excellence demanded. Much of the state-level activity that followed the reports was directed toward regulations such as teacher and pupil testing, stronger academic standards, and mandated curriculum requirements. A student of history might wonder if the 21st Century will be spent correcting for the overregulation of the 1980s and 1990s. These decades were spent addressing the per-missiveness and neglect of earlier decades, but will possibly be part of the problem rather than the solution for the next century.

School Effectiveness.   The dismal statistics which pointed to failure and medioc-rity in American education in the 1980s were by no means descriptive of all institutions. Averages ignore data which falls at the upper or lower ends of the scale. Many have drowned in rivers which average only 3 feet in depth. Numerous communities know very well that their schools are outstanding and that they have achieved the excellence demanded in the national reports. The educational profession by 1984 was identifying characteristics of effective schools that could be used as tools of evaluation and for ascer-taining which schools could serve as models of superiority.

Older studies of school effectiveness have been used as the basis for new research. Weber's 1970 study of reading achievement in inner city schools found that strong lead-ership, high student expectations, a good atmosphere for learning, use of phonics, indi-vidualization of instruction, careful evaluation, and adequate numbers of trained reading teachers made an outstanding program. In 1981, Zerchykov cited administrative leader-ship, an orderly school, frequent monitoring of student progress, redirection of resources toward basic instruction, a good atmosphere, stress on basic skills, and realistic instruc-tional expectations as factors creating school effectiveness.

By 1985, studies of school effectiveness were in progress throughout the nation by school districts, state departments of education, professional organizations, and universi-ties. Two critical factors emerged from these studies to be added to those previously iden-tified. Effective schools must have the support and involvement of the community and school principals must be dynamic instructional leaders. Boyer also addressed this ques-tion and found that effective schools:

1. have clear goals and a commitment to public education
2. identify a core of learning common to all students
3. attract the best teachers in the area
4. promote mastery of communication skills and language use
5. prepare for work and for further education
6. use flexible patterns of instruction
7. have ties with business, college, and community leaders
8. use technology effectively, and
9. develop strong administrative leadership.

National leaders involved in "A Nation at Risk" had their own agendas for bringing about effective schools. In 1983, Education Secretary Bell called for high schools to require four years of English, three years each of mathematics, social studies, and science, and passing of examinations in all of these areas. He also said that by 1989, SAT and ACT scores should surpass the 1965 levels, dropout rates should be cut by 10 percent, and entry-level teachers' salaries should be competitive with those of business and engineering. Neither Bell nor Secretary William Bennett, who followed him in office, provided a specific plan for how these things might be accomplished or how they would be financed.

Two other terms were widely used in the school effectiveness literature of the mid-1980s. "Time-on-Task" dealt with the actual part of each day spent on instruction, as opposed to time used for announcements, passing through halls, taking attendance, and the like. "Efficiency" focused on the most cost effective means of accomplishing educational goals in order to maximize scarce resources. Defined as academic learning time or engaged learning time, time-on-task did allow for a higher part of each day to be spent by students in paying attention to their studies. Students are on-task when they are actively engaged in activities which match their abilities and interests and on which they succeed most of the time. However, the California Beginning Teacher Evaluation Study of 1977, which studied this topic in detail, showed that only rather small gains can be made by cutting down wasted time. Current research shows that sizable increases in achievement require sizable increases in time, if time is the only variable modified. Better use of time is essential but it may not be sufficient to achieve excellence. Likewise the effective school research shows that, as efficiency increases, there is little room for additional improvement through more efficient methods. For example, in January of 1983, 85 percent of high schools, 68 percent of the middle schools, and 42 percent of the elementary schools had microcomputers in use for instruction. The amount of idle time was so small that better efficiency in the utilization of computers would accomplish very little. Real improvement in computer linked instruction must come from buying more machines or making existing computers available during hours when school is not in session, because they are already nearing maximum use during the regular school day.

The Bush and Clinton administrations, reacting to the 1990 work of the National Governors meetings on education, adopted six national education goals for the year 2000 designed to encourage more effective schools through focusing on learner outcomes. The goals were:

1. All children will start school ready to learn.
2. The high school graduation rate will increase to at least ninety percent.
3. Students completing grades 4, 8, and 12 will have demonstrated competency in academic subject matter including English, mathematics, science, history and geography.
4. Students in the United States will be first in the world in mathematics and science achievement.

5. Every school will be free of drugs and violence.
6. Schools will offer an environment conducive to learning.

Although the goals were widely heralded as a base for educational excellence, few professional educators believed they would be achieved by 2000 due to restricted financial resources, plus potential social and political roadblocks to reform.

Reform Initiatives in the States and Cities.   The pursuit of excellence in the several states did not begin with "A Nation at Risk," but the national reports certainly stimulated renewed activity. According to Action in the States, by the Education Commission of the States in 1984, school reform was a high-priority item everywhere. All but five states had legislatively enacted initiatives or were awaiting action by the legislature or the state board. The states have generally followed the public demand to cut down on curriculum offerings not considered basic, such as art, music, and physical education, while requiring more "solid" courses. Most states have chosen to mandate the basic curriculum with emphasis given to courses such as English, mathematics, science, and social studies. Action plans for renewal are usually collaboratively developed by governors, legislatures, and state and local boards. Hearings for the public have been conducted in most of the states with comprehensive action plans. Educators and business leaders have been invited to participate.

State educational reform is diverse because of demographic factors, the existing level of educational achievement, and the economic conditions. Nevertheless, all the states share some of the same concerns. In addition to upgrading the curriculum, they wish to strengthen standards for high school graduation, raise teacher certification requirements, improve salaries for teachers, promote business involvement in education, and integrate technology into instruction. Competency testing for promotion and especially for high school graduation is part of the plan in most states. Some states also call for continuous staff development, school-based accountability, and curriculum updating through reaccreditation.

As a rule, state efforts aimed at educational excellence in the mid-1980s were conservative. Economic and political forces caused the states to opt for strengthening existing schools rather than designing a new approach to education. State plans tended to call for more testing, more homework, more hours in the school day and school year, and emphasis on basics in the curriculum. Foreign language requirements and computer literacy also received attention in many state programs. Career education and preparing for the world of work were addressed because of the strong expressions of concern by business leaders. With the increase of single parent families and latch key children, state plans dealt with school responsibility for health and nutrition. Some reflected public interest in environmental, nuclear war, and energy issues as well as international and multicultural concerns.

The 1980s and 1990s witnessed several state and city school administration reforms and fiscal restructuring. They all dealt with what Linda Darling-Hammond, Director of the National Center for Restructuring Education at Columbia University, referred to as a new school reform model designed to develop communities of learning, grounded in grassroots of democratic discourse. She saw this as a way for empowerment and educational freedom.

The *Chicago School Reform Act of 1988* required basic changes in Chicago public school governance. The act sought more involvement and input of local stakeholders in school governance and policy making. Forsyth and Marilyn in *City Schools Leading the Way* (1993) noted that the Illinois State Law provided for increases in parental input in Chicago's school policy. Forsyth and Marilyn also noted that Boston was another city school system that moved toward decentralization, accountability and increased input from parents, teachers and administrators.

The trend toward increased decision making at the school site level, although spreading, is yielding mixed results. Further restructuring, modification, and experimentation are to be expected in the years ahead. Collective bargaining, restricted finances, and teacher strikes will require continued work in conflict resolution to achieve effective schools.

The concept emerging in the state and city school reforms responded to Arthur Wirth's call for more democratic participation in public school policymaking. Yet, pitfalls exist in implementing reform when there is failure to recognize that the educational enterprise is complex, that there are many voices representing many interests, and that politics involves compromise and consensus to achieve necessary funding for implementing innovative educational reforms as McKersie noted. Impediments to educational reform in addition to funding limitations include increased costly litigation as various interest groups seek to implement their own agendas often to the detriment of the overall school programs.

Local Reform Initiatives.   Historically, some of the most impressive efforts to achieve excellence in education have been initiated at the local or district levels. Examples include the Dalton Plan of the Progressive Era and the Philadelphia Parkway Program of the 1960s and 1970s. Urban school reform in Atlanta in the 1970s under the leadership of Superintendent Alonzo Crim also showed how a failing district could be made into an outstanding one with local effort. Most of the alternative schools in the United States were developed without state or national leadership. Laboratory schools, schools-without-walls, and magnet schools intended to draw students to a superior and specialized program were created by school districts. Larger school districts with considerable resources, a highly professional staff, and active community leaders have been able to establish models of excellence in education. Sometimes the leadership has come from the superintendent and sometimes from school boards, the parent-teacher's organization, or reform minded citizens. John Dewey insisted that the school and the community must work as a unit for high quality education. John Goodlad has stated many times that the community should be the major educator of the child. Educational historian Lawrence Cremin argued that the community should serve to interlock all educative agencies within and outside of the school.

Following "A Nation at Risk," most local school districts in the United States began to evaluate performance standards and accountability. Student outcomes were evaluated in terms of behavior and competence. While state boards focused on learner achievement, many individual schools looked at the relationship between the curriculum and student performance.

Financial Crunch.   The Reagan administration created the National Commission on Excellence but made it plain that the federal government would not fund its recommendations. According to the NEA, it would cost almost $24 billion to implement the recommendations, and if the school year is lengthened, about $40 billion. Even decreasing class size by one or two students would require millions of dollars, while increasing teacher's salaries across the nation carries a staggering bill. President Reagan maintained that schools need more discipline not more money, while his educational leaders (T. H. Bell and W. Bennett) said that states and local districts would have to finance the reforms.

This, of course, was more realistic for some states than others. California was in better shape to finance reform than states that had suffered recession, such as Michigan, Oregon, and the industrial Northeast. Sun belt states which were doing well before the decline in oil prices were hit with major cutbacks in 1984. The decline was most dramatic in Louisiana, Oklahoma, and Texas. None of the states which depend on agriculture for revenue were able to adequately fund reforms or salary increases for teachers. In every state, education must compete with demands for prisons, bridges, roads, and sewer systems. Educational reform also bumps up against needs to repair physical plants or meet safety requirements. In 1983 it was estimated that $25 billion was needed by local school districts just to repair buildings, replace defective equipment, and eliminate hazardous asbestos. By 1994, many states including California and Florida had difficulty funding the educational effort due to a sluggish economy.

Much of the money for excellence in education must be raised at the local district level, but this was becoming increasingly difficult in the mid-1980s. Arkansas, for example, traditionally a poor state and one ranked low in educational achievement, passed tough new standards for schools, to be implemented in 1987. It was estimated that the cost of these standards would be $298 million. Part of the funding was to come from state revenues, but local districts were required to bear the costs of employing new teachers for subjects not formerly offered. A shortfall in the collection of state taxes in 1985 reduced the school fund by $25 million. Local millage elections were held in 120 districts in 1984 and 242 in 1985. In 70 percent of these elections higher millages were passed, indicating strong local support for high-quality education. Nevertheless, the local efforts were not enough, and Arkansas trailed the national average per pupil expenditure in 1986 by $1,136. It is not realistic to expect local districts and state governments to fund reforms without federal help. By 1986 most states were experiencing great difficulty in paying for better educational programs.

States are being asked to assume most of the costs for educational excellence at a difficult time. The taxpayer's revolt characterized by Proposition 13 in California, which limited spending in that state, was followed by balanced budget legislation in seventeen states between 1977 and 1981. States like Idaho, Montana, California, and Michigan are unlikely to pass new taxes without significant improvement in their economies.

In *Nordlinger v. Hahn* (1992) the Court upheld the constitutionality of California's Proposition 13 which protected the rights of existing homeowners. By mid 1993 six State Supreme Courts had ordered legislatures to fund schools more equitably. Most states in 1993 faced severe financial restrictions with increased demands for educational staff and facilities in face of growing enrollments and decreased finances.

Gramm-Rudman Amendment.   The Gramm-Rudman Bill, passed by Congress in 1985, severely hampered the financing of educational reforms. Reflecting President Reagan's supply-side economics, the bill called for slashing the federal deficit by reducing federal expenditures for social and welfare programs. National defense, social security, and interest on the national debt were exempt so that all cuts aimed at reducing the deficit had to come from programs like education, highways, and welfare. The administration opposed any new taxes and threatened to veto any that were passed. The theory offered by White House economists was that the U.S. economy would grow at a sufficiently brisk rate to create adequate revenues to fill state and local coffers. Educational reform would therefore be supported at levels other than the federal, which was consistent with Reagan's philosophy.

The immediate impact of Gramm-Rudman was to cut programs which have improved education. Chapter I, a program that undeniably helped raise the reading and mathematics scores of disadvantaged youngsters, was a target. Head Start and vocational programs were also singled-out for loss of funding. The administration's student-aid proposal chopped funding by $2 billion, removed $775 million from the school lunch program, and reduced special education programs by $50 million annually.

The federal cuts created a double problem for achieving educational excellence. First, continued financing of programs traditionally funded by the federal government fell to the states and local districts. Money that might have gone to strengthen the curriculum, improve teacher's salaries, or create innovative programs was diverted instead to maintain important existing agendas. Second, Gramm-Rudman cuts in revenue sharing to states and to costly programs like highways and welfare, forced states to assume funding responsibilities that made fewer state dollars available for education. Even if the economy eventually improves enough to offset the federal cuts, the immediate impact on state and local support was devastating.

The Clinton Administration's advocacy of a national service program envisioned in his book *Putting People First* was designed to have a *National Service Trust Fund* to guarantee every American who wanted a college education the means to obtain one. The National and Community Service Trust Act passed by Congress in 1993 provided jobs for over 20,000 young people in 1994, with over 33,000 in jobs by 1996. Under the plan, students would receive $4,725 a year for full time service (1700 hours) and $2,362 for part time service (900 hours), for post secondary education or training tuition. Their jobs would be working in the areas of environmental, educational, safety programs and would provide a wage, child care and health insurance. Based on his work with educational apprenticeship programs while Governor of Arkansas, President Clinton sought a national school-job link to be funded based on states' willingness to engage in a systematic school-to-work program.

Many of those advocating educational reform, especially the spokespersons for national commissions and the federal government, say that the way to improve schools is not to spend more money. Most educators agree that "throwing" money at a problem will not make it go away, but they are convinced that many vital reform programs are expensive. The theory that economic growth will be sufficient to offset federal cuts is disputed by both educators and economists. There was considerable national feeling that Gramm-Rudman would not achieve a balanced budget and that the cost to society was too high. Several constitutional challenges to the bill were made in late 1986.

Meanwhile, the price of keeping the existing system in operation continued to climb. NEA figures showed that Americans raised their spending for K–12 programs by $9.1 billion in 1985–1986. Enrollments increased nationwide by an estimated 109,000 to a total of 39.5 million students. Secondary enrollment declined slightly but was more than offset by elementary gains. The classroom teachers increased by 13,670, raising the nation's teaching force to 2.178 million. Although the per student expenditure varied considerably from state to state, schools spent an average of $3,677 per pupil in 1985–1986 and $5,195 in 1992–1993. Alaska spent the most with $8,044 per child and Utah the least with $2,297 per pupil. Average salaries for teachers rose by 7.3 percent nationally to $25,257 in 1985–1986 and $35,000 for 1992–1993. Revenues also increased 7.2 percent but the federal share fell for the seventh consecutive year to an estimated 6.4 percent. It is obvious that state and local efforts are hard pressed to meet basic needs and to increase teacher's salaries without the additional burdens of new programs for excellence and replacing programs lost through federal budget cutting.

Rebuilding v. Restructuring.

The American school system was designed in the early national period under the leadership of school reformers like Horace Mann. It reflected the influence of the old New England colonial district and catered to the needs of a new democracy. The nation then was dominated by agriculture, making a common school with summer vacations and local control quite acceptable. With the rise of industry, standardization of the curriculum and a delivery system based on a Newtonian mechanistic model was adopted. The school system became a closed machine with top-down administration, predetermined standards, lock-step definitions of content by grade, and fixed rules of behavior. Obviously the system worked well to prepare students for the factory or the office. With its emphasis on assimilation, conformity, and traditional values, it was able to handle the masses of European immigrants and the growing American population. Mass production philosophy and assembly line concepts lent themselves to efficiency in the production of trained workers at low cost.

New needs began to emerge with the world wars, the great depression, social unrest, the rising affluence of the middle class, the human rights movement, and the demands of minorities for status. Superimposed upon these changes were the new requirements of the information age, a service economy, and a global culture. New programs were tried in an effort to cope with changing life conditions, social mobility, and new expectations. These included open classrooms, individualized instruction, alternative schools, non-graded schools, team teaching and magnet schools. By-and-large, these innovations were added to the existing system but they did not become the dominant pattern. Many were simply tried for a time and then withdrawn, allowing the old system to emerge again. Most of the current reform movement is aimed at modifying the basic traditional schools. There are those who think a piecemeal approach is not adequate and that it is now time for a holistic redesign of the whole structure.

Some of those who would restructure education have moved their children outside the system. The home school movement of the mid-1980s is an example. With individual computers, communications networks, and many parents working at home, it became possible to give children a basic education without recourse to the schools. While many students are kept at home by parents for religious or cultural reasons, the home school movement is growing among well-educated citizens who prefer to provide their own educational programs for their children. States have initiated testing programs to evaluate the learning of home educated children when they wish to transfer to public schools.

Private education in the United States represents another alternative which has not lost its popularity. Many private and parochial schools are very traditional. They often have high achievement because of a select student body, strong parental support, high quality teachers, and a demanding curriculum. Nevertheless, private schools are not subject to state regulations and controls (unless they request state accreditation). They are therefore free to pursue innovative programs and alternative learning techniques. Very few private schools had adopted radical or innovative programs by 1986. The growth in private education has been among religious fundamentalists and others dissatisfied with the quality of public education. Evangelical fundamentalists such as Jerry Falwell gave support to private religious schools in the 1980s. Others in cities like Seattle choose to send their students to private schools deemed to be of high quality. Both groups support the Reagan administration's plan to provide vouchers for schooling.

At best, federal responses to the reform demands of the 1980s and 1990s must be described as piecemeal. One thrust is the policy of deregulation, first applied to the airlines. Deregulation attempts to remove federal controls from business and industry in keeping with the free market theory and competition. Of course, most of the federal regulations concerning schools were applied to the use of federal money. As fewer dollars flow from the national treasury into school programs, the question of federal control becomes less significant. However, Milton and Rose Friedman argued in *Free to Choose* that governmental rules and regulations restrict the freedom of citizens in educational matters. Of course, most laws regulating education are by the states and it is unlikely that those will be repealed. The free market concept also supports funding plans, which would allow parents to spend their vouchers at a school of their choice, public or private. Many educators believe that vouchers would dismantle the public school system, especially in the large cities where there are many disadvantaged and minority children. The Clinton administration proposed programs to vaccinate all children, to create pilot enterprise schools with empowerment zones, and to create year-round community centers in urban and rural communities for the disadvantaged. Another proposal was *Goals 2000: Educate America Act* to increase equity among schools without federal mandates.

Barn raising, or helping neighbors replace farm buildings destroyed by fire or weather was a community effort in colonial days through the 20th century. Efforts to rekindle a spirit of service and helping others has been spreading through America's school districts. The Reagan, Bush and Clinton administrations stressed the importance of volunteerism in America. Several states in 1993 were exploring mandatory community service as part of high school graduation requirements. Maryland was one of the first states to make student service mandatory for graduation. Students were given opportunities to choose things they were interested in and later to use their experiences for class papers. Community volunteer agencies were receptive to student assistance.

Goodlad's call for focus on entire schools, not just teachers, curriculums, or organization, is a more holistic approach. The Rand Corporation's study of school effectiveness argued that increased expenditures on traditional practices would do little good. Patricia Cross of Harvard called attention to the mechanical solutions to the crisis of the 1980s and suggested that the old educational structures may be inadequate to cope with modern diversity. Others describe current reforms as ordinary and conventional. Henderson, in *As Schools Start Up: Reform Shifts from Spending to Seeing Results* (1993), noted that the 1990s saw improvements in teachers' salaries to an average of over $36,000, longer school years, strengthened academic requirements together with a focus more on achievement and performance outcomes than increased spending. Lawton in *Verbal, Math Scores on S.A T. Up for the Second Straight Year* found that although S.A.T. scores were up verbal scores were still 1 point below the 1983 average. Improvement in S.A.T. scores were attributed to increased nationwide demands for more rigorous academic studies.

No doubt there will be improvements in the American education system as a result of the quest for excellence. The question remains of whether or not the system itself must be reformed to meet the needs of the future.

ACHIEVING EXCELLENCE IN TEACHER EDUCATION

As the public system of education experienced change in America, there have been major consequences for teachers and teacher educators. In periods of teacher shortages, colleges and universities with teacher education programs have been been under great pressure to admit more students and to feed the market. This often caused officials to pay slight attention to standards, especially when the funding for the institutions of higher education was enrollment driven. The shortage ended with the matriculation of the baby boom generation, but it is likely to return with heavy competition for skilled workers, relatively low salaries, unsatisfactory working conditions, and the retirement of a major segment of the teachers in service. At this writing, New York City, California, and Texas already face a large shortage of teachers and the problem is expected to become nationwide by 1993.

Status of Teachers. The 1980s may be characterized as a period of professional decline at the very time when better professional performance is demanded. Teaching was one of the first professions open to women in the United States. As more men entered the teaching field, the low salaries of teachers became unacceptable, and teachers began to organize in order to improve their situation. Such organizations as the NEA and the AFT eventually became powerful enough to influence federal policy. The creation of the office of Secretary of Education in 1978 was at least partly a response to the growing power of teachers' organizations, and the reduction of the scope of that office in the Reagan administration cannot be separated from what President Reagan viewed as political opposition by teachers. Strike and work stoppages have not improved the image of teachers in the public mind, nor have the professional organizations. Although able women now have the choice of many professions outside teaching, traditional lower salaries for teachers have contributed to inequality for women since the teaching force remains heavily female. The difficulty of attracting and retaining high quality teachers remains in part because the salaries are still not competitive with those of college graduates working in other fields. The early 1990s represented a period of attempts to recreate and renew education through a variety of reform proposals. Efforts to increase faculty, staff, and administrative salaries continued toward mid decade. In many states, restricted finances prevented much progress toward salary increases.

In 1984, for example, Marvin Cetron found that the average starting salary of an American teacher was $14,500. He compared this with $19,344 for a librarian, $20,484 for an economist, $24,864 for a computer analyst, $26,844 for an engineer, and $42,978 for a personnel director. Even workers with no college degrees were paid better than teachers, with sanitation workers starting at $20,290 and city bus drivers at $22,906. Salaries are certainly one reason why professional organizations in education are viewed as militant by many noneducators. It is unfortunate that so much of the effort of teachers through their organizations has been used to fight for better wages and working conditions instead of for better standards and a stronger curriculum, because this has hurt the professional image. Still, by 1985, the low pay and low status of American teachers had gained the attention of state legislatures. Most states at that time were examining ways to improve teachers' salaries through career ladder plans, incentives for master teachers, or state salary schedules. Unfortunately, at the very time when states were realizing that higher salaries for teachers are imperative if excellence in education is to be achieved, federal cutbacks in funding under the Gramm-Rudman legislation and a sluggish economy, due to factors such as the decline in oil and agricultural prices, limited the power of many governing bodies to address the situation. Many LEAs have also reached their limits of raising money through higher millage elections.

The *Occupational Handbook*, 1992–1993, included data noting that the average elementary teacher's salary was $32,400 and the secondary teacher received $33,700 in 1991. The national average public school teacher's salary in 1991–1992 was $34,213 according to the American Federation of Teachers. The AFT reported average salaries for beginning teachers in 1991–1992 was $22,171. The Occupational Handbook 1993 noted that, in 1991, starting salaries ranged for accredited librarians from $23,400–$27,000, entry level economists from $17,000–$25,000, computer analysts from $17,000–$21,000, starting engineers from $31,900–$36,200, entry level personnel managers from $17,000–$21,000, sanitation workers from $17,000–$25,700, and bus drivers $22,000 a year. However, entry level salaries for Arkansas teachers for the 1992–1993 school year was $19,569. Still, although states and the federal government were facing financial restrictions in 1993, many efforts were underway to increase at least minimally teachers' salaries through various state and local tax increases as well as through lotteries.

Other Negative Factors.   Low salaries were by no means the only problem facing teachers in the 1980s. Ernest Boyer reports in *High School* that teachers are deeply concerned about the loss of status, a negative public image, little recognition for their work, and heavily bureaucratic pressures imposed by the board or the administration. Recruiting better students to become teachers is difficult when many teachers in service feel frustrated or are seeking to leave the profession. Traditionally, teachers have been the best recruiters, suggesting that their better pupils consider the teaching field. This trend was definitely in decline by 1986 when numerous teachers, along with parents, advised students not to become teachers. In May 1985, the Corporate Forum on Education and the Economy created a Task Force on Teaching as a Profession to study the declining ability of the profession to attract promising future teachers. Boyer, reflecting an earlier study by Emily Feistritzer on the teaching profession, stated that students preparing to teach have lower SAT scores than other college students and that the standards in colleges of education are low.

As departments, colleges, and schools of education began to strengthen entrance requirements in response to the national criticism, state departments were slow to deny teaching positions to unqualified people. Feistritzer reported in 1983 that all but two states made provision for issuing an emergency or other substandard teaching credential. The same boards that directed their departments to license only teachers who passed tests such as the NTE failed to shut the door on temporary certificates. As the predicted shortage of teachers materializes, state departments will come under increasing pressure from local superintendents to allow them to fill teaching positions with any available warm body. Recruiting high-quality teachers or enforcing higher professional standards will be very hard if state departments bend to this pressure. Education is the only field in which unqualified persons may be hired in the place of professionals. Certainly this does not occur in medicine, law, or engineering.

Challenges to the education profession also include increasing crime on school campuses. James Hellegaard in *Fear Stalks The Hallways* noted that in 1993, Secretary

Riley reported there were over three million thefts and violent crimes on or near school campuses every year. In many school districts student absenteeism was growing due to fear of being victimized on school grounds. Nationwide over 160,000 children skip classes daily for fear of physical harm. In Florida, one of the nation's most populous states, criminal offenses ranging from thefts to assaults and homicide rose over 34% in one year, from over 46,000 incidents in the 1990–1991 school year to over 61,000 in 1991–1992. Teachers and administrators are not immune to the rapid increase in school crime. Over 6,000 teachers nationwide are physically attacked by pupils each school day according to the Florida Educational Coalition Crime and Violence Survey. Holmstrom in *The Art of Undoing Violence is Finding Its Own Place in Classrooms and Streets* reported that 100,000 children take guns to school every day, and many schools and school districts have initiated anti-violence, and conflict resolution programs from kindergarten through high school.

Educators believe causes of increased school crime include social fragmentation, single parent families, latch key children, easy access to drugs, finding a sense of belonging through gang membership, and easy access to weapons. Hate crimes are growing on our public school and college campuses. Workshops, seminars, and sensitivity training sessions are being developed to address the issue. In 1993, Secretary of Education Richard W. Riley sought legislation for a safe school program targeted to assist poor districts in high crime areas.

Changes in Teacher Education.   The National Commission on Excellence and other groups created awareness for the need to improve education. At first the focus was on secondary schools but this soon spread to colleges in which teachers are prepared. Not much progress toward excellence can be made unless the quality of teacher education programs is addressed.

One of the first reactions by SCDEs (schools, colleges, and departments of education) was that while teacher education needed improvement, the criticism fell almost exclusively upon them. When teachers fail in basic skills, such as reading, writing and mathematics, it is not the SCDEs which teach those skills. Likewise, a physics teacher weak in his or her subject matter did not study the discipline in a SCDE. The general public was slow to understand that teachers take only one fourth to one third of their work in professional education. Professors of education argued that the entire university faculty has responsibility for preparing teachers, including professors in arts and sciences. Nevertheless there was a clear mandate for SCDEs to revise their programs in order to achieve excellence. Organizations like the National Council for Accreditation of Teacher Education (NCATE) had started this process long before the national reports appeared. More stringent NCATE standards were adopted in 1984. Not all SCDEs are NCATE accredited but many states also adopted the standards of the organization as a model for quality teacher education programs.

A survey undertaken by the American Council on Education in 1984 showed that nine of ten colleges with teacher education programs had minimum requirements, while eight of ten had initiated higher admission standards. Most were requiring some exit test for certification, such as a satisfactory score on the NTE. Graduation and certification requirements are not always the same but colleges were attempting to conform to the state testing requirements. Curriculum changes included a larger general education component, heavier concentration on a subject matter discipline, a familiarity with computers, extended practice teaching, and more concentration on communication skills. The SCDEs were already requiring tests and measurement, a course in the exceptional learner, child and adolescent psychology, social foundations of education, and appropriate methods courses. Several institutions required two courses in reading for all teachers. Virtually all SCDEs had educational practice as a requirement and most also expected candidates to have field-based laboratories before the practice teaching experience.

A 1985 survey funded by the National Science Foundation, the U.S. Department of Education, and the National Endowment for the Humanities was based on a sample of 1,040 colleges with teacher education programs. It found:

> SCDEs admit students after the freshman year or at the start of the junior year.
>
> Seven of ten institutions require a minimum GPA in university wide courses for entry. The average GPA requirement was 2.4 (NCATE now recommends a 2.5–2.7 GPA for entrance).
>
> Two in five programs require exit testing. Most others plan to initiate exit testing. The NTE is the most used exit test.
>
> The average number of credit hours required for graduation was 127. Of these, the average number in education was 43 for elementary majors and 30 for secondary. This included practice teaching for which an average of 10 credit hours is allowed.
>
> Secondary students spend an average of 85 clock hours in practice teaching and elementary students 113.
>
> Most SCDEs require mathematics, science, and communications of all candidates; about half require computer science. Speech, hearing, and writing tests, together with personal interviews and recommendations are becoming common for entry. About half the institutions also require standardized or proficiency tests. Almost all have a special requirement in English.

The strengthening of teacher education programs satisfied state and NCATE standards and conformed to the major suggestions found in the national reports of 1983. However, many professional educators argued that a four-year college program was not adequate to prepare candidates for the new demands of the teaching field. At the very least, it was suggested that an entry level teacher with a baccalaureate degree needed further education along with experience in order to become a master teacher. In-service programs for teachers were therefore stressed as a means of continuing the education of new professionals and upgrading the skills of teachers with longer service. By 1986, it was agreed that a four-year college commitment and an equal or longer commitment by a school district to continue the education of teachers was needed for a competent profession.

Five-Year Programs and the Holmes Group.

Long before "A Nation at Risk" was published, some major universities like Stanford had given up undergraduate teacher education to concentrate only on graduate studies. They argued that the research based in education has grown so large that teachers and administrators need high quality graduate work and that many now wish to enter the profession after having completed an undergraduate degree in another field. Certainly it is true that growing numbers of teachers take advanced courses and most expect to earn a master's or specialist degree during their careers. By the mid-1980s numerous universities were offering graduate level courses for certification to accommodate degree holders and transfer students from other fields, even if they continued to offer the basic four-year teacher education program. Some states like New Jersey allowed local districts to provide the training for certification to prospective teachers with degrees in subject fields.

A similar approach was taken by a subset of the National Association of State Universities and Land-Grant Colleges, called the Holmes Group after former Dean Henry Holmes of Harvard's Graduate School of Education. Under the leadership of Deans Judith Lanier of Michigan State and John Palmer of the University of Wisconsin, the organization is committed to a broad strategy of reform for teacher education. The Holmes Group intends to make the education of teachers intellectually sound, to create relevant and defensible standards of entry into the profession, to connect schools of education with public schools, and to base teacher education on state-of-the-art research. Some of the fourteen original member universities insist that a five-year teacher education program is a minimum for these goals. In 1986, the Holmes Group invited 123 leading research universities with colleges or departments of education to join the coalition. The Holmes Group is another major organization of professional leaders in education which may influence the course of teacher education as has occurred with NCATE, AACTE, ASCD, and AERA. *A Nation Prepared: Teachers for the 21st Century* recommended giving teachers more control over schools tied to increased accountablity together with phasing out undergraduate education programs. By 1993, several colleges and universities added a fifth year education major eliminating undergraduate programs. The move is controversial with some educators who view the move to five and six-year programs as detrimental to future educators in part due to added time and cost of their training.

Most professional educators and teacher educators in the universities believe that the real key to excellence, which is absolutely vital to the future well being of the nation, rests upon our ability to recruit, educate, and retain high quality teachers. The criticism of the national reports may offer an opportunity to make education a real profession on a par with law and medicine. Certainly the knowledge and research is adequate if resources can be found to strengthen and extend professional training. All critics agree that a well-founded general education and in-depth knowledge of the subject matter discipline are essential for teachers. The field experience and pedagogical parts of teacher education must be vastly improved to develop a true teaching professional committed to lifelong teaching and learning.

The Holmes Group argues that education for teachers must not just be improved but restructured. Boyer and Goodlad hold that the entire school community must be involved in a partnership with the universities to create a professional climate in which teacher candidates may learn to be professionals. A fifth year internship with continued formal education had been used in Oklahoma. Much greater stress is now placed on continuous in-service education for teachers after they begin teaching. Continuous updating of methods and the application of the latest research to teaching situations will be part of the professional activity of all future teachers. The United States demands and deserves the best possible teachers for the information age. There are still arguments about how to design and support a teacher education that will produce such professionals. Meanwhile, the teacher shortage has caused many states to provide some sort of alternative certification for would-be teachers with college degrees but no preparation in pedagogy.

REFORM IN EDUCATIONAL ADMINISTRATION

Educational administration underwent major changes in the 1980s and 1990s, both in the universities where administrators are prepared and in the field. Doctoral programs in school administration became much more research oriented and management skills taken from business administration were added. Many educational administrators seek more practitioner-oriented doctoral programs and question the applicability of research-oriented programs to their ongoing careers. More efficient methods of operating the schools were developed. Superintendents learned more about school law, school finance, personnel management, litigation, and site-based management. Principals devoted more time to evaluation of teachers, planning in-service training, and serving as instructional leaders. Accountability and effective schools became key words in the administration field.

Educational administrators traditionally were successful teachers who were promoted and then learned management skills on the job or with continued graduate training. This pattern still exists to some extent in America, but the level of required training has increased to the point where administrators must expect to spend additional years in the graduate classroom taking advanced coursework before assuming a principalship or a superintendency. State requirements for administrative certification have also been strengthened, demanding a specific course of study as well as experience to qualify. Alternative certification programs designed to encourage managers from industry and business to become school administrators have been implemented in some states. Competition for the better jobs is keen and the salaries are high by educational standards. Administrators who can articulate goals, inspire workers to work harmoniously toward those goals, maintain good relations with the public and school board, and demonstrate leadership, are in demand. Nevertheless, the pressures in urban school districts are such that the average longevity of superintendents in large urban areas is less than three years. High turnover and early burnout continued to plague the field of school administration in the closing years of the 1980s and the early 1990s.

Professional improvement and information sharing have been greatly enhanced by the major organizations in administration. These provide a forum in which administrators can discuss problems and evaluate possible solutions with peers from similar school districts. Administrator organizations publish journals, maintain links to professors in the leading universities, and appraise administrators of changing regulations. The National Association of Secondary School Principals is one of the oldest and best respected professional organizations. The American Association of School Administrators holds major conventions and attracts superintendents from across the nation as well as political and academic leaders. The National Council of Professors of School Administration and the University Council for Educational Administration serve the needs of those who train administrators and foster the dissemination of research. Elementary principals have their own organization and all major associations have local and state affiliates. Much of the debate over the best responses to the reports demanding school reform have taken place in these organizations.

Most of the educational reform reports of the 1980s and early 1990s stressed the role of the principal and superintendent in exercising leadership for improving instruction. Administrators were expected to develop a positive organizational climate to facilitate staff development and improve learning processes. Reports urging increased mandated standards, more testing of students and teachers, more discipline, an end to "soft" subjects, and strict control of the educational process clearly called for a firm hand. By 1985, however, educators began to stress the importance of the human element in the schooling process. Education is a complex process and caution must be used in implementing massive changes envisioned by the reports. Literature in administration began to reflect the impact of "unintended multipliers" such as elitism, teacher flight, lower morale, loss of creativity, and high dropout rates when oversimplified solutions are applied.

Little was said in the "A Nation at Risk" report about the principal as instructional leader. In the early national period, it was intended that principals perform that role, but in the twentieth century they became managers. School principals in the 1960s often gave most of their attention to discipline, scheduling, the physical plant, reports, busing, extracurricular activities, and other functions not directly related to instruction. Research shows that administrative leadership at the school-building level is critical. The Connecticut School Effectiveness Project of 1982 cited instructional leadership by a principal who understands and applies the characteristics of instructional effectiveness as one of seven measures of good schools. (The others were a safe, orderly environment, a clear school mission, a climate of high student expectation, high time-on-task, frequent monitoring of student progress, and positive home-school relations). Other studies found that principals in effective schools spend time in classrooms to identify problems and to help teachers develop strategies for dealing with them. A school principal who can achieve balance between strong leadership and maximum autonomy for teachers will help to achieve excellence. Some of the critics say that the studies of principals as instructional leaders conducted in inner city schools may not apply to others. Goodlad doubts that principals can maintain a higher level of teaching expertise than the teachers. Not all principals have the ability to become the exceptional, charismatic leaders that the researchers describe. It is clear, however, that principals must devote much of their time and energy to instruction if excellence is to be achieved.

Educational administrators in the 1980s accepted many ideas from business, such as the Peters and Waterman conclusion that excellent organizations have profound respect for individual workers and stimulate unusual effort by ordinary people. They sought university programs to help them deal effectively with multiple changes in a democratic system of education. To the themes of accountability, organizational climate, and managing change for excellence were added collective negotiation with teachers and fact finding for bargaining. Other trends for educational administrators were increased emphasis on ethical values, maintaining order and discipline in schools, and dealing with federal disengagement from the schools.

In *Educating for a New Millennium*, Shane and Tabler stipulated the importance of basing the organization and administration of education on local control so that those most familiar with community needs would make priorities and deploy resources. They also called for an alternative to the bureaucratic model of administrative structure common to schooling and business. A diversified concept of organizational life in which individuals have flexibility and freedom is supported also by both Goodlad and Boyer. Former UCEA director Jack Culbertson argues that the administrators will have to become more effective in utilizing computer data in decision making as well as coping with the exploding information and rapid expansion of technology. He also stresses good management training in a period of declining resources for schools. Good working relations with school boards, state officials, departments of education, and political leaders are critical to the modern administrator.

Since the responsibility of enforcing laws rests on school administrators, they must be especially sensitive to the legal aspects of reform. Following the lead of the Supreme Court in the Brown decision of 1954, education has become a legal right for all citizens. By the 1970s, this right was extended to those with special needs such as the handicapped. The 1975 Education for All Handicapped Children Act made it incumbent on all districts to provide education to children with special needs, in the "least restrictive environment." Superimposed on this law were the various state regulations concerning excellence. Every state in the nation made some effort to improve education through legislation in the 1980s. Laws mandated curriculum reform, graduation requirements, student evaluation, longer school days and years, and plans to reward teachers through career ladders or master teacher programs. Another responsibility was responding to the increased number of lawsuits brought against schools. These have increased dramatically since 1980, and range from cases involving accidents to those accusing schools of failing to provide equal access to education.

Goodlad has argued that principals and superintendents are self-selected. He means that those interested in administrative positions have pursued the necessary training and entered the job market. He suggests that future schools would be better served if the system chose teachers having good administrative potential, determined by some testing procedure. Goodlad believes that the profession should determine which of its members ought to pursue administrative careers.

Partly in response to the national demands for reform, vast improvement in administrative training and practice occurred in the 1980s. Accountability, quality control, the principal as instructional leader, effective schools, and standards for graduation were concepts that ruled the decade. Nevertheless, the criticism directed toward education in general focused on administrators in particular. In 1986, Assistant Secretary of Education Chester Finn called for throwing out school administrators and replacing them with businessmen or retired military officers. Even high officials had no concept of the professional role of the administrator or the sophisticated scholarly discipline upon which it rests.

BIBLIOGRAPHY

Arkansas The Lone State In Registering Double-Digit Growth in Teacher Pay. (American Federal of Teachers Report), Springdale Morning News, August 30, 1992.

A Nation Prepared: Teachers for the 21st Century. New York: Carnegie Forum on Education and the Economy, Report of the Task Force on Teaching as a Profession, 1986.

Adler, Mortimer. *The Paideia Proposal*: An Educational Manifesto. New York: Macmillan, 1982.

Alexander, Lamar. *Time for Results*. New York: Report on Education by the National Governor's Association, 1986.

Ashton, Patricia, and Rodman Webb. *Making a Difference: Teacher's Sense of Efficacy and Student Achievement.* New York: Longman, 1986.

Boyer, Ernest. *High School: A Report on Secondary Education in America.* Boston: Houghton Mifflin, 1984.

Carnegie Forum on Education and the Economy. *A Nation Prepared: Teachers for the 21st Century.* New York: Carnegie Corp., 1986.

Centron, Marvin. *Schools of the Future: How American Business and Education Can Cooperate to Save Our Schools.* New York: McGraw-Hill, 1985.

Cross, Patricia. "The Rising Tide of School Reform Reports." *Phi Delta Kappan* 66(3).

Darling-Hammond, Linda. "Reframing the School Reform Agenda" *Phi Delta Kappan*, June 1993: 753–761.

Education Commission of the States. *Action in the States: Progress Toward Educational Renewal.* A Report of the Task Force on Education for Economic Growth, July 1984.

Fantini, Mario. *Regaining Excellence in Education.* New York: Merrill/Macmillan, 1986.

Feistritzer, Emily. *The Condition of Teaching: A State by State Analysis.* Princeton, NJ: The Carnegie Foundation for the Advancement of Teaching, 1985.

The Forgotten Half: Non-College Youth in America: An Interim Report on the School-to-Work Transition. New York: William T. Grant Foudation Commission on Work, Family and Citizenship, 1988.

Frazier, Calvin. *A Shared Vision: Policy Recommendations for Linking Teacher Education to School Reform.* Denver, CO: Education Commission of the States, 1993.

From Risk to Renewal: Charting a Course for Reform. Washington, D.C., Editorial Projects in Education, 1993.

Gardner, Howard. *Frames of Mind: The Theory of Multiple Intelligence.* New York: Basic Books, 1983.

Goodlad, John I. *Teachers for Our Nation's Schools.* San Francisco: Jossey Bass, 1990.

Goodlad, John. *A Place Called School: Prospects for the Future.* New York: McGraw Hill, 1984.

Hellegaard, James. "Fear Stalks the Hallways". *Gainesville Sun,* Sunday, June 6, 1993: 1A.

Henderson, Keith. "As Schools Start Up, Reform Shifts from Spending to Seeing Results." *Christian Science Monitor* (August 30, 1993): 1,14.

Hirsch, E. D., Jr. *Cultural Literacy.* Boston: Houghton-Mifflin, 1987.

Holmes Group Consortium. "New Standards for Quality Teacher Education," U.S. Department of Education, 1984.

Holmstrom, David. "The Art of Undoing Violence Is Finding Its Own Place in Classrooms and Streets." *Christian Science Monitor* (September 1, 1993):1,4.

Holt, John. *Teach Your Own: A Hopeful Path for Education.* New York: Delacorte Press/Seymour Lawrence, 1981.

Investing in Our Children. New York: Committee for Economic Development, 1985.

Kozol, Jonathan. *Savage Inequalities: Children in America's Schools.* New York: Crown Publishing Company, 1991.

Lawton, Millicent. "Verbal, Math Scores on S.A.T. Up for Second Straight Year". *Education Week* (September 8, 1993):10.

Leary, James. *Educators on Trial.* Farmington, MI: Action Inservice, 1981.

McKersie, William S. "Philanthropy's Paradox: Chicago School Reform." *Educational Evaluation and Policy Analysis* 15(2): 109–128.

Naisbitt, John, and Patricia Aburdene. *Re-inventing the Corporation.* New York: Warner Books, 1985.

National Coalition of Advocates for Students. *Barriers to Excellence: Our Children at Risk.* Boston: Author, 1985.

National Commission on Excellence in Education. "A Nation at Risk: The Imperative for Educational Reform." Washington, D.C.: U.S. Government Printing Office, 1983.

Owen, David. *None of the Above: Behind the Myth of Scholastic Aptitude.* Boston: Houghton Mifflin, 1985.

Peters, Thomas J., and Robert H.Waterman, *In Search of Excellence: Lessons From America's Best Run Companies.* New York: Harper & Row, 1982.

Results in Education 1990. Washington, D.C. The Governors' 1991 Report on Education, 1990.

Rosenthal, Neal H. and Ronald E. Kirtscher, *The Occupational Outlook Handbook 1992–1993.* Washington, D.C: Bureau of Labor Statistics, 1992–1993.

Sarason, Seymour B. *The Predictable Failure of Educational Reform.* San Francisco: Jossey Bass, 1990.

Shane, Harold Gray, and M. Bernadine Fabler. *Educating for a New Millennium: Views of 132 International Scholars.* Bloomington, IN: Phi Beta Kappa, 1981.

Sizer, Theodore R. *Horace's School: Redesigning the American High School.* Boston: Houghton Mifflin Co., 1992.

___. *Horace's Compromise: The Dilemma of the American High School.* Boston: Houghton-Mifflin, 1984.

Tallerico, Marilyn. "Governing Urban Schools," eds. Patrick B. Forsyth, and Tallerico, *City Schools Leading the Way.* Newbury Park, CA: Corwin Press, 1993:239–240.

Woods, Peter. *Inside Schools.* Boston: Routledge & Kagan Paul, 1986.

CONTEMPORARY PHILOSOPHIES OF EDUCATION

Only in education, never in the life of farmer, sailor, merchant, physican, or laboratory experimenter, does knowledge mean primarily a store of information aloof from doing.

John Dewey

Educational issues occur and recur, but underlying philosophical contentions remain. Our historical perspective would be incomplete without an exploration of alternative views of what is ultimately worth knowing and the various aims, policies, and ideologies expressed in school and society throughout our educational history. These themes blend the past to the present and build bridges for the future.

INTRODUCTION TO EDUCATIONAL PHILOSOPHY

Webster defines philosophy as the "love of wisdom" which is a literal rendering of the Greek word. Philosophy deals with ultimate questions such as the nature of truth, what is real and what is of value. Speculative, reflective, and theoretical attempts to answer questions about the basic purposes, goals, and outcomes of formal education are philosophical in nature. Those questions dealing with the nature of knowledge, the characteristics of the educated person or the structure of the curriculum are the broadest issues for philosophy of education. Those dealing with methods of teaching or the length of the school year have a somewhat less abstract nature. Although the terms are sometimes used interchangeably, educational theory is more focused and narrow in scope than educational philosophy. Before the twentieth century, most American educational philosophy was derived from the great systems or schools of philosophy, especially idealism and realism. While these positions are still supported with vigor by many policy makers in education, they have been challenged recently by contrasting views expressed by pragmatists, existentialists, futurists, and analytic philosophers, among others.

1200–1800	1800–1900
Aquinas (1225–1274)	Kierkegaard (1813–1855)
Locke (1632–1704)	Spencer (1820–1903)
Berkeley (1685–1753)	Peirce (1839–1914)
Rousseau (1712–1778)	Whitehead (1861–1947)
Herbart (1776–1841)	Russell (1872–1970)

Traditional philosophy is, like other fields of discipline inquiry, divided into categories. These are important because they focus the arguments between schools and illustrate what is most important to individual philosophers. Idealism and realism deal equally with all divisions, pragmatists have little to say on questions of ultimate reality, and analytic philosophers concentrate on rules of valid thinking. The basic divisions are metaphysics, epistemology, axiology, and logic.

Metaphysics is concerned with reality and existence. For education, the conception of reality reflected in the curriculum and the experiences of the student are paramount. Formal education describes and defines reality as it is understood by those in control of the learning environment. Obviously, reality would appear differently to an Athenian citizen in the age of Pericles, a Puritan minister in colonial New England, or an x-ray astronomer gathering data on a distant galaxy.

Epistemology is the theory of knowledge and includes the study of how we know. Does knowledge begin with sensations from objects as realists think? Do we create knowledge by interaction with our environment as pragmatists say? Are idealists right in saying that knowing is the recall of absolute ideas that have an independent existence of their own? The answers imply stimulating questions about the learner, problem solving, and the utilization of sensory stimuli. Clearly, knowing and knowledge are critical to any theory of education.

The division known as axiology includes ethics, aesthetics, and the formation of values. Ethics examines moral values while aesthetics deals with the values of beauty and art. All teachers must be concerned with the formation of values by children and the encouragement of behaviors that conform to some conception of that which is true, good, or beautiful. Many educational theories such as idealism and realism hold that values are valid in all times and places (objective theory of value) while pragmatists and social theorists say that they are culturally or ethically relative. Many of the major conflicts over the impact of the school in the formation of character and guiding behavior are grounded in axiology.

The final division, logic, is concerned with the rules of valid thinking. The study of logic was once required of all university students. Logic is now limited to the discipline of formal philosophy, but it is still basic to the rules of correct argument. Analytical philosophy relies on logic while existentialism subsumes it under personal feeling and individual freedom. Inductive logic is associated with empiricism and pragmatism; realism

Modern	
James (1842–1910)	Foucault (1926–1984)
Dewey (1859–1952)	Habermas (1929–　)
Buber (1878–1965)	Rorty (1931–　)
Wittgenstein (1889–1951)	
Skinner (1904–1990)	

and perennialism rely on deduction from first principles. A very good way to understand philosophers or schools of philosophy is to study their position on metaphysics, epistemology, axiology, and logic. Questions about ultimate reality, the nature of knowledge, values, and rules of thinking (even when a given theory is silent on the topic) will reveal a great deal about any philosopher or philosophy.

Schools of Educational Philosophy.　　　Neither educational philosophy nor philosophy itself falls automatically into neat categories. The discreet schools, or "isms" as they are often called, have no validity apart from the thinkers whose systems of thought they represent. Just as Aristotle found it helpful to group plants and animals into classes according to their similarities, students of philosophy find classifying a good tool for understanding theoretical positions. We must remember, however, that individual members of a school or "ism" do not always agree on every point. There is no substitute for a biographical approach in which the lives and major works of intellectual giants are individually studied. Still, the schools of thought may be useful as a beginning point, because they illustrate common ground between members and are easily contrasted with opposing philosophical views.

Everyone agrees that Plato, Hegel, Kant, Berkeley, and Horne are representatives of idealism, while Bacon, Locke, and Hume are British empiricists. On the other hand, Albert Camus is called both a logical positivist and an existentialist; some philosophers defy classification altogether. Names may also be confusing. For example, John Dewey only slightly modified his position during his long career but is classified as a pragmatist, an instrumentalist, and a progressive by different authors. Most commonly used categories provide a foundation for the study of educational practice grounded in philosophy, but classification schemes may vary. For example, J. Donald Butler in *Four Philosophies and Their Practice in Education and Religion* includes naturalism as a school while J. Arthur Cooper created a division in his recent book called "eternalism." Most of the authors included under naturalism or eternalism will be identified in other standard categories.

As we examine the schools, one other disclaimer should be kept in mind. Some famous philosophers such as Rousseau and Whitehead devoted much of their attention to education while others like Hegel and Bergson did not write on the subject. There are major educational theorists, Comenius and Pestalozzi for example, who are not recognized as important to general philosophy. Sometimes educational ideas from a variety of nonphilosophical sources may be incorporated into a theoretical school. Educational futurism draws from sociology, economics, communications theory, and cybernetics as much as from philosophy.

As we have seen in previous chapters, American philosophy of education was slow to develop. Early schools in the colonies, and later in the United States, were simple in curriculum, goals, and organization. As long as the general public, consisting largely of farmers and factory workers, was satisfied with the three "R's," history, spelling, and some religious or moral training, conflict was minimal. Common values were easily identified in a fairly homogeneous population keenly interested in a better standard of living but not much concerned with intellectual or social issues. Before the Kalamazoo decision made possible the vast expansion of the high school, secondary education was confined to the college-bound elite. Colleges dictated both the educational theory and the curriculum of the high schools. In turn, the colleges and universities reflected the beliefs of their boards, presidents, and faculties. Religious idealism was strong in denominational colleges; Scottish realism dominated the state universities, while the special form of religious realism called Thomism governed Catholic institutions. Science had a difficult time gaining a foothold in colleges and high schools, and no alternative values were tolerated.

Not only was philosophic conflict rare in American education prior to this century, but the important ideas were imported from Europe. Comenius, Locke, Rousseau, Pestalozzi, Froebel, and Herbart were the respected leaders in educational theory until the early twentieth century. Even today, philosophers from outside the United States contribute most of the thought to many educational theories. Even after the political changes in the Soviet Union, one quarter to one third of the world's children are in schools which follow some form of Marxism, but only a handful of Americans accept or contribute to contemporary Marxism. Existentialism is largely European, while analytic philosophy is split between American and international theorists. On the other hand pragmatism, behaviorism, and social reconstructionism are unique to America.

Modern Realism.   Modern realism has flourished in the scientific era. We have seen how Herbart combined sense realism with psychology to produce an influential theory of education that dominated professional education in the 1890s. Contemporary realism has benefitted from the work of Alfred North Whitehead (1861–1947) and Bertrand Russell (1872–1970). These two people made their reputations in the field of mathematics, coauthoring the famous Principia Mathematica. Whitehead was very much interested in education and produced a book called *The Aims of Education and Other Essays*. He was concerned about process and what he called "living ideas." Such ideas are connected with the experience of learners and are capable of being articulated and communicated to others. He saw this organic process pattern of education as different from the learning of "inert" ideas of the past. An excellent statement of Whitehead's position is found in Harry Broudy's *Building a Philosophy of Education*. Russell urged a temperate approach to science and said that education held the key to a better world.

He conducted some practical experiments in private education himself with his Beacon Hill School in Massachusetts, and was active in a number of social movements against the atom bomb and all wars. Modern realism has many faces, depending on point of view. All realists agree that sense objects exist, that instruction should be organized according to intellectual disciplines, and that the role of the teacher who presents the curriculum is crucial.

Perennialism.   Realists and idealists are in fundamental opposition on the nature of reality, but their educational theories are much more similar than different. Both want a subject matter curriculum and see the school as an institution designed for the cultivation of human intelligence. Education ought to concentrate on basic moral, ethical, aesthetic, and religious principles drawn from the collective experience of culture, especially western culture. These ideals have recently been expressed under a new rubric—perennialism. While the term is of recent origin, perennialism presents a conservative, traditional view of human nature and education. It would not be amiss to say that the founding fathers held perennialist views since they grounded their beliefs in religious idealism and made the basic assumption that certain ethical principles apply to all people at all times. This is so for the eternal truth from God that was the foundation for Harvard College and for Franklin's nondenominational academy in Philadelphia. The idea of universal and unchanging truth was not foreign to those who advocated the separation of church and state in the Bill of Rights or to Horace Mann in his struggle to keep schools free of sectarian control. Assuming the rational nature of human beings, realists held that education should stress the recurrent theme of human life as well as knowledge about the objective world.

The metaphysics (and epistemology) of perennialism is basically that of realism with its scientific/humanistic orientation and its belief that knowledge is relatively stable. Perennialists want a subject-matter curriculum which includes history, language, mathematics, logic, literature, the humanities, and the sciences. Such a program of study reflects the most important aspects of the learned disciplines as they have developed over the centuries, and it is best represented by the classical literature or the great books of the western world. The most articulate spokespersons for the perennialist position are Robert Hutchins (1899–1986) and Mortimer Adler (1902–). Hutchins and Adler established the Great Books Program in 1946 and devised an index by which the answers of classical authors to the great questions could be compared. Hutchins, who was chosen dean of the Yale law school at a very early age, became the president of the University of Chicago at the age of 30 in 1929. There, he stressed cultivation of the intellect and held that only educational institutions have the power to do that. He opposed specialized or vocational education but favored those subjects designed to develop the mind. Adler has recently reentered the field as a voice for perennialism with his book, *The Paideia Proposal* (see Chapter 8). He has recently had the support of former education secretary William Bennett who shares the basic tenets of perennialism. Another major statement of perennialism, very popular with the intellectual community, is found in Allan Bloom's *The Closing of the American Mind*, which was published in 1987.

Pragmatism.   Pragmatism (from the Greek word meaning a thing well done) emerged as a uniquely American philosophy just before the end of the nineteenth century. Educational theories such as progressivism, John Dewey's experimentalism, and social reconstructionism are branches of pragmatism. Founded upon modern science and evolution, pragmatism developed a distinctive empirical epistemology opposed to idealism and rationalism. Its themes were practicality, change, growth, and uncertainty as opposed to the order, finality, and fixed truth dominant in older systems. Pragmatists stressed incompleteness, contingency, the consequences of human experience, and a wide open universe. George H. Mead contributed to the movement with his social concept of the human mind as expressed in his *Mind, Self and Society*, but the major figures in pragmatism were Charles S. Peirce (1839–1914), William James (1843–1910), and John Dewey (1859–1952).

A classic statement of the philosophy by Peirce appeared in an article called "How to Make Our Ideas Clear" in the *Popular Science Quarterly* for January, 1878. Peirce said that if we consider the practical effects that an object of our conception might have for our lives, these practical effects define the object. That is, an object only exists "for us" to the degree that it has practical bearings on our life space—our own existence. Since objects far distant in space called quasars have only recently been discovered, they did not exist for Peirce, but they have important practical bearings (and therefore are real) for modern astronomers and for all of us who have altered our conception of the universe on the basis of their discovery.

Peirce argued that the only genuine road to knowledge is the scientific method which is based on human experience and subject to empirical testing. The truth of an idea must be based upon agreement by an infinite community of informed observers and knowers. Such truth may be relatively stable because of continuing agreement by competent observers, but it can never be fixed or final. Just because learned men once thought the earth to be the center of the solar system does not make that concept true. We must live today by the best "truth" we can get but be ready to call it falsehood when new information or new techniques improve our powers of observation. Most Americans accept this theory as it is applied to science or medicine, but many object to its use in ethics, the rules of social behavior, or religion. It is not widely supported in nonscientific cultures such as those of the third world. Peirce was never a popular writer, and many of his concepts were complex; still, his principle of verification in actual experience became the foundation for pragmatic philosophy.

In an earlier chapter, William James was treated as a major contributor to educational psychology. Like his brother, Henry, he was a famous author with a national reputation and enormous influence in intellectual circles. In *Pragmatism: A New Name for Some Old Ways of Thinking* (1907), James agreed with Peirce that truth is not absolute but depends on the "workability" or consequences of an idea in actual life. Human experi-

ence is of paramount importance for James, and he often spoke of the "stream of experience," or the serial course of events which make up our individual concrete reality. James
was not such a "hardheaded" experimental scientist as Peirce and believed that truth is
not always objective but that meaning is sometimes found in personal experience that is
nonverifiable.

Thus, there is an existential strain in James which is reflected in his keen interest in
extrasensory perception. James called upon philosophers to abandon universals, abstractions, and essences in favor of studying human experience (in the laboratory) and reflecting on personal experience (introspection). Peirce was a more systematic thinker than
James and soon became upset over what he considered the "bastardization" of pragmatism (even inventing the term "pragmaticism" to distance himself from James), but James
remained popular, and his theories were closely related to those of Dewey.

By any measure John Dewey was the most important educational philosopher ever
produced in the United States as well as a major founder of pragmatism. Born in
Burlington, Vermont in 1859, the year *The Origin of Species* was published, Dewey had
an average boyhood dominated by New England Puritan values and Protestant Christianity. At the University of Vermont, an edge was put on his intellectual appetite by a
course in physiology in which the theory of evolution was taught. Dewey turned to philosophy as a means of bridging the gap between the new science and his belief that the
world was shaped by God's moral will. After graduation, Dewey taught school in rural
Vermont and Oiltown, Pennsylvania, before entering Johns Hopkins University as a
graduate student in philosophy. There, he studied under the idealists, George Morris,
G. Stanley Hall, and Charles Peirce. Morris introduced Dewey to a system of thought
which declared that matter was only illusion. Dewey took his Ph.D. and for ten years
taught philosophy at the universities of Michigan and Minnesota. During this time, he
became interested in the vigorous rate of change in technology and society, the growth of
democracy, and the economic and social changes caused by industrial expansion and
urban development. He became disenchanted with a system of unchanging spiritual reality and began to reject Hegelian idealism for what William James called the "wide open
universe."

By 1890, Dewey was converted to pragmatism and started his own version of the philosophy, called instrumentalism or experimentalism. Dewey made pragmatism a comprehensive system of thought dealing with all problems generated by conflicts within the culture. Instrumentalism served to restore integration and cooperation between beliefs about
the world in which we live and beliefs about the values and purposes which guide conduct. As much a method as a philosophy, instrumentalism concentrates on the scientific,
experimental tools for clarification of ideas about social issues and moral conduct.

Dewey saw the task of philosophy was not to know the nature of ultimate reality but
to understand and control the world. The human mind is an instrument which must be
sharpened by experience for use in problem solving and adjustment to the practical situations of human life. Experience, especially collective human experience, provides the best
means for coping with a world always in flux. Anticipating Alvin Toffler and the futur-

ists of today, Dewey held that problems cannot be solved with any degree of finality because of constant change and the unknown. Human intelligence and knowledge enable us to adapt our environment to our needs and to adapt philosophic goals to the reality of the situation of life-space in which we exist.

Like Locke, Dewey was concerned about the origin of ideas and the problem of how the mind functions. The first of his many books dealt with functional psychology. He accepted the empirical principle that ideas come from experience and are verified by comparison with objective reality. Since action must precede knowledge, there are no a *priori* ideas. Dewey drew upon the naturalistic theories of Rousseau and Froebel but also from biological sciences, sociology, and Darwinian evolution. He saw human survival and the progress of the race tied to the means available for solving essential problems. Natural intelligence combined with reconstruction of past experience can be the means only if antecedent action is able to trigger a scientific, rational approach to solutions. Past beliefs, grounded in tradition or drawn from authority, may actually inhibit the survival of man. For this reason, Dewey wanted to submit every tradition, attitude, or belief to the experimental test with its corollary of verification by experience.

As a psychological functionalist, Dewey understood that the mind is set in motion by the organism's desire to meet its needs and solve its problems. Although the human organism is of infinite complexity, intelligence may be defined as the use of experience in solving problems. Mind is an organic function used by humans to reduce drives and satisfy needs in interaction with the environment. People are not naturally passive, and the experiences they undergo become the building blocks of meaning. Dewey understood that what people think about is related to what they do and the totality of environmental influence. Intelligence and learning must be equated with the scientific method of problem solving. Since the individual is not isolated, intelligence must be directed toward social efficiency or community issues as well as individual needs.

A central theme in Dewey's educational theory is "the complete act of thought." Although described in many of his writings, his little book *How We Think* (1910), gives the most detailed analysis of the problem-solving process. Dewey held that learning grows out of ongoing activity which must be meaningful to the learner. Activity involves the individual in the relationship between an act and its consequences. This implies that schools must foster purposeful activity by building on the common interests of children, such as communication, inquiry, construction, and artistic expression. Although activity is required for learning, no progress will be made so long as the activity is routine and the student operates on the basis of habit.

Learning actually begins when a difficulty or problem creates a barrier and prevents an activity from continuing. The problem must be genuine (not imposed from outside by the teacher) and must be defined by the learner, so that he or she knows exactly what blocks the activity. The problem provides motivation, the driving force or interest required for thinking. At this point, information or data concerning a possible solution is gathered. This may be done merely by remembering prior experience or by more sophisticated means such as consulting an expert or using a library. The next step is forming an hypothesis—an educated guess as to how the problem may be resolved. The learner does not jump at once to any hypothesis but first reflects upon the probable outcomes and the possibility of undesirable consequences if the hypothesis is accepted. Finally, the learner chooses the most likely hypothesis to solve the problem and puts it to the empirical test of experience. If it works, the barrier to the activity is removed; if not, the learner has gained further data upon which to operate and may continue the process. Dewey's complete act of thought (activity, problem, data, hypothesis, testing) was taken directly from the scientific research model and is the basis for his pedagogy.

In *Experience and Education*, 1938, Dewey defined education as the process of continuous reconstruction of experience with the purpose of widening and deepening its social content while, at the same time, helping the individual to gain control of the methods involved. In Democracy and Education he called education a process of living and not merely preparation for future living. Dewey also claimed that education is growth, and as long as growth continues, education must continue as a social process. As the title suggests, *Democracy and Education* argues that the social process of education is best served if the school is a democratic community. Dewey once said that if we are willing to conceive of education as the process of forming fundamental dispositions, philosophy may be defined as the general theory of education.

Dewey's critics often point to the contradictions and inconsistencies in his work. One reason these are found is that he continued to be a prolific writer until his death in 1952, so that few have studied all of his books and articles. Another is that he continued to develop his philosophy throughout his life. On becoming chairperson of the Department of Philosophy at the University of Chicago, Dewey gave equal attention to the teacher education unit of which he was also in charge. He became a critic of rugged individualism, free enterprise without controls, outmoded social institutions, and a narrow definition of democracy as a form of government. His educational experiments at the laboratory school in the University of Chicago were used as models by many of his progressive followers, but he became very critical of progressives when he felt their activities were not philosophically sound. In 1916, his *Democracy and Education* was published, making him a national figure in both fields.

After leaving Chicago for Columbia University in 1904, Dewey devoted more of his attention to social and moral issues. Rejecting the idea that philosophy defines ends and education provides means, he held that ends must always be kept in view and adjusted as progress is made. Ends never justify means. Dewey was the enemy of philosophic dualisms. He saw no conflict between the school and society, the student and the curriculum, or interest and effort in education. Although vitally interested in the concepts of community and democracy, Dewey insisted upon leaving open the possibility that better social relationships might be invented in the future. To view the democratic society as an end or a goal would have violated his principle of continuous reconstruction of experience and constant adjustment to the conditions of life.

Dewey supported child-centered schools without stiff authoritarianism, but he also stressed the importance of integrated subjects in the curriculum and saw the school as a place where experiences could be simplified, purified, and ordered. His open-ended universe and pluralistic reality would not allow him to place limits on what might be studied, but he did think people could be educated so that they could control their own affairs and attain a more satisfactory collective life. Scientific method and experimental thinking can help us improve life and invent better social institutions. While rejecting supernatural beliefs, as well as militant atheism, Dewey supported a humanistic religious position in books like *A Common Faith*. He also gave considerable attention to aesthetic development, especially in *Art as Experience*.

Dewey was not only the most articulate spokesman for pragmatism and the theoretical founder of progressivism but also the most influential American philosopher of education. He had legions of followers, and many may still be found in schools and institutions of higher education. Many colleges of education such as Teacher's College of Columbia University, Illinois, Texas, Ohio State, and Stanford remained centers of Dewey's theory long after his death. Several of his followers like Boyd Bode, Gordon Hullfish, William Kilpatrick, and Bruce Raup became well known in their own right. Critics were also numerous. These ranged from the serious philosophical issues raised by idealist Herman Horne or the attack on relativism voiced by Allan Bloom to the unfounded political rhetoric expressed by Max Rafferty and Albert Lynd.

Social Reconstructionism.   From ancient times, educational institutions have had the function of transmitting cherished values and preserving the culture. Schools have rarely been the focus of radical social change but they have been an instrument for social improvement, especially economic improvement. Horace Mann and other early national leaders fostered utopian ideals in education, such as equality of opportunity and ending poverty. Interest in this utopian theme accelerated during the progressive era in American history and the rise of populist parties. The Utopian theme was also influenced by reforms such as women's suffrage, civil rights for minorities, the attack on graft, and the work of muckraking authors who exposed corruption and inequality. Progressive education was also a force in social reconstruction as illustrated by the appearance in 1932 of *Dare the Schools Build a New Social Order?* by George Counts. This was a call for complete social revolution and was considered radical even by most members of the Progressive Education Society, but it did raise the question of the role of the school in changing society.

Dewey's belief in education as an instrument for the continuous reconstruction of experience, his championship of democracy as a way of life, and the pragmatic theme of understanding and controlling the world contributed to this position. In 1935, Counts was joined by W. H. Kilpatrick, John Childs, Bruce Raup, and Harold Rugg in founding the John Dewey Society for the Study of Education and Culture. The Society began publishing the journal *Social Frontier* which attacked the evils of capitalism and called for active participation of educators in social change. This journal was responsible for much conservative criticism of progressive education, but it was also the focal point of those progressives who felt that schools should be active in altering society.

The most important figure in social reconstruction is Theodore Brameld (1904–1987). Brameld saw a crisis in the modern society with mass confusion regarding goals and many contradictions. He agreed with Isaac Kandel that setting up a utopian model is dangerous because there is no empirical way to define what an ideal society should be. Still, he felt that we must take a holistic approach to alternative possibilities. Brameld's arguments are expressed in books like *Toward a Reconstructed Philosophy of Education, Education as Power,* and *Patterns of Educational Philosophy.* If the crisis, illustrated by wars, the rich-poor gap, pollution, international terrorism, the population explosion, resource depletion, and accelerating technological advance is real, then merely transmitting dominant social values in traditional schools will not suffice. Brameld wanted to solve the pervasive problems of humankind and direct us toward a global government.

He agreed with Karl Mannheim and Robert Heilbroner that we are about to witness the very end of civilization unless we can quickly and drastically reconstruct our priorities and patterns of behavior. He saw mass confusion about goals and inadequate responses to the world crisis. He thought that nationalism is no longer adequate and that we must create a world government to control nuclear arms and stop environmental destruction. In *Education as Power,* he argues that knowledge is power and that the reconstructionist theory of value might be transmitted through schooling to produce a utopian "civilized civilization." Since values are man-made, it is possible to define ends through social consensus. It is assumed that world peace and economic cooperation are such goals, but no one wants them to be imposed by an outside authority such as a national government. In *Toward a Reconstructed Philosophy of Education,* Brameld says education is a means for guaranteeing sufficient income to all families, meeting reasonable standards of nutrition, medical care, shelter, dress, and schooling, and utilizing all of the world's natural resources in the interests of the majority of people. This position is shared by many social theorists and most futurists.

While many agree that the world crisis is real and cannot be resolved by the United States alone, a global civilization and a world government do not seem realistic. Schools under the direction of local or national governments lack the power to engage in global reconstruction. They can, as futurists argue, provide information on what is happening in our world and prepare students for problem solving and better communication in an age of rapid change.

From a practical standpoint, social reconstructionism has waxed and waned depending upon the political climate. Progressives in the 30's and 40's were successful in persuading school authorities that children learn best if they are safe, healthy, properly nourished, and enjoy a pleasant physical environment. This "whole child" philosophy led to hot lunches, health care, counseling services and the like. The civil rights movement of the Martin Luther King era, the war on poverty, and the liberal social policies of the Kennedy and Johnson administrations fostered social engineering in schools. Racial integration, bilingual programs, special education, Head Start, and Upward Bound are examples of such efforts at the federal level. At one time, it appeared that congress might pass a national equalization law which would provide the same financial support for every American child regardless of the state or district in which the student lived. While not totally abandoned in the administrations of Reagan and Bush, these efforts at social engineering received less support under conservative presidents. Major support for reconstructionist theory is now found mostly among futurists and critics of existing educational goals. The Clinton Administration will encourage Congressional action on a variety of social legislation issues including Child Care, Universal Health Care, and College Student Assistance programs. There will be continuing efforts toward social engineering under his administration.

Essentialism.   Essentialism is a conservative educational theory which emphasizes the value of certain "basic" subjects and the authority of the teacher. Educators have always attempted to identify what is essential to the knowledge of a learned person, but those subjects have not always been the same. Ancient Athenians thought it essential for boys of the citizenship class to learn the *Iliad*, but they did not think it good for slaves or women to study Homer. Most modern Americans now think computer literacy is basic, but this would not have been the case two decades ago. Educational history is filled with debate over what constitutes basic knowledge, who should receive it, and how it should be transmitted. The essentialist movement in America began as a response to what was considered "soft pedagogy" or "permissive" education supported by progressives. It was recently reflected in the charge of former education secretary William Bennett that schools emphasized process and not content.

In 1938, a group of prominent educators led by William C. Bagley (1874–1946), started a movement which called for intellectual training in schools instead of "child growth and development." They said the essential skills of reading, writing, and arithmetic should be found in every elementary curriculum together with history, literature, and geography. For the secondary school, the curriculum was the western cultural heritage, including the academic subjects in the arts and sciences. Bagley favored observed data over a strictly rational approach and, like the realists, supported scientific examination of physical phenomena. He was soon joined by Michael Demiashkevich, Robert Ulich, and W. E. Hocking. By this time, progressive education was on the decline, and essentialism attracted a great deal of public support.

Bagley was an articulate spokesman for the essentialist theory. He served as editor of *School and Society* from 1939 to 1946, and his position at Teacher's College gave him status with educators. In "An Essentialist's Platform for the Advancement of Education" (1938), he claimed that schooling requires hard work and attention as well as respect for genuine authority. He stressed the logical sequence of subjects and called for a "back to basics" movement to combat the lowering of academic standards. There is no question that some progressives had ignored content in favor of process (although those who did were not following Dewey) and that some students were weak in factual information. Although the Eight Year Study showed that students from progressive high schools did well in college, Bagley's argument had merit, and the political climate was right with the conservatism of the World War II era.

Essentialism was soon supported by many other authors with quite different views who were determined to attack not only progressives but all those they labeled "educationists." Arthur Bestor, Jr., in *Educational Wastelands*, 1953, Albert Lynd in *Quackery in the Public Schools*, 1953 and Max Rafferty in *Suffer Little Children*, 1962, were especially shrill in their condemnation of all educators. While their motivation was largely political, they did attract a great deal of public support and caused essentialism to become the focal point for all criticism of public schools and teacher education programs. In discussing the "diminished mind," Mortimer Smith accused John Dewey of destroying the ability of Americans to think. Some of the arguments were no better grounded in fact than the anticommunist "witch hunts" of Joseph McCarthy, but they got a similar response from the mass media and "education bashing" became popular by 1960.

More serious, if less colorful, were the arguments for more rigor in curriculum after the formation of the Council for Basic Education in 1946. Indeed, modern educational history describes a pattern of back to basics movements followed by liberal responses like team teaching and nongraded schools, followed again by back to basics. Sometimes the cycle is fostered by comparison with foreign schools as was the case with Admiral Hyman Rickover and James B. Conant following the Soviet success with Sputnik in 1957. More recently, the cycle was initiated by education secretary T. H. Bell and his National Commission on Excellence in Education which produced "A Nation at Risk" in 1983.

Essentialism in education has recently been encouraged by demands of governing bodies for new requirements for high-school graduation, better college board scores, assessment, and accountability. It has always been possible to illustrate that some students do poorly on a test of essential knowledge. In 1989, a widely televised Barbara Walters' Special called attention to the lack of geographic knowledge on the part of American secondary students. Public reaction to such media events brings pressure for the elimination of "non-essential" subjects, concentration on basics, and more testing. The same arguments are used by ultra conservative groups like the fundamentalist Christian "new right" to get rid of subjects they dislike such as sex education and environmental studies.

Unfortunately, the current essentialist movement has lost the logical basis provided by Bagley and has become merely a protest against educational change and innovation. Many professional educators think the current back to basics movement has run its course and that a new cycle may be starting. With the appointment of Secretary Lauro Cavazos in the Bush administration, educators anticipate more attention to equality of educational opportunity and serving the needs of all students instead of concentration on basics. Should this prove true, history indicates the strong probability of yet another back to basics movement sometime in the future.

Humanism.   Humanism is not so much a philosophy of education as a point of view based on literary studies and the assumption that the proper study of mankind is man. All systems of philosophy give some attention to human values and the human condition. The roots of humanism go back to ancient Greece where the sophists claimed that "man is the measure of all things." In Europe, during the 14th and 15th centuries, it flourished as the intellectual core of the Renaissance. Desiderius Erasmus (1466–1536), contributed to humanism by trying to move the church away from ceremonies and toward ideal Christian living. Early American literary humanists rejected the Puritan belief that man is sinful by nature and agreed with Comenius that the human condition could be improved through education. Franklin, Jefferson, Emerson, and Thoreau are counted among American humanists, as are all Deists.

Literary and classical humanism flourished after World War I and was represented by such advocates as Nicholas Murray Butler, Abraham Flexner, and Mark Van Doren. Drawing from the newer disciplines of psychology, political science, anthropology, and sociology, they spoke less to the supernatural nature of man than to his distinctively human faculties as a guide for moral conduct. Humanists support the utilitarian concept of the greatest good for the greatest number but oppose the dominance of science, materialism, and values drawn from mass behavior. Humanistic educators find too great an emphasis on vocationalism and technology in schools and urge more attention to literature and the classics.

There is a strong tie between humanists and perennialists. Indeed, Robert Hutchins and Mortimer Adler may be classified as both perennialists and humanists. Humanists say that man has distinctive qualities quite different from animals such as reason, moral conscience, aesthetic taste, and religious instinct. While giving priority to the literary and linguistic arts, humanists stress the heritage of Western culture, especially the classics of Greece and Rome. Such subjects lead to a well-rounded development of the intellectual, moral, aesthetic and religious capabilities of humankind.

Neo-Thomists and main line Protestants support humanism while fundamentalist Christians do not. Using the powerful tool of the television ministry, many "born again" Christians have launched a particularly vicious attack on what they call "secular humanism." Although the term seems to have been invented for atheistic humanists, as used by Jimmy Swaggart and Jerry Falwell, it includes liberal Christian ministers and all professors in secular universities. This blanket definition which includes odd bedfellows such as scientists and Biblical scholars under the rubric "secular humanism" has confused the issues. Falwell has claimed that "secular humanism" is a religion, something that all humanists would deny. Literary humanists have suffered from the conservative attacks and their influence in education has been weakened. A curriculum example is the support for giving creationism equal space with the theory of evolution in school textbooks.

Analytic Philosophy of Education.   The analysis of concepts in philosophy is as old as the formal study of ideas while logic can be traced back to Aristotle. Certainly the meaning of various concepts and arguments is central to building any philosophy or educational theory. Pragmatists like Peirce wanted to make ideas clear, but Dewey used terms like "democracy," "interests," and "growth" without giving them precise meaning.

With the decline in emphasis on formal logic in universities and the rise of political and media slogans, the use of logic and the analysis of language gained in importance. Many departments of educational philosophy in universities are now dominated by analytic professors. They point out the absurdity of taking a phrase such as "self actualization" from Maslow and making it an educational goal without understanding what Maslow really meant or how hard it would be for all students to attain it. They challenge political statements of the "Lake Wobegone" sort which say all students should be better than average.

While the roots of analytic philosophy are found in logic, British empiricism and nineteenth century efforts to clarify meaning in literature, its major foundation is contemporary realism and logical positivism. An Englishman, George E. Moore (1873–1958), developed the analytic branch of realism with emphasis on ordinary language. His colleague Bertrand Russell leaned toward formal language and the precise terms used in the sciences and mathematics. Moore's *A Defense of Common Sense* dealt with the meaning of propositions found in common language and pointed out that many issues in philosophy are due to misunderstanding because of abstract and technical language. Russell's formalistic approach became popular with scientific Americans, especially after he began lecturing at Harvard in 1914. The logical positivist roots of analytic philosophy originated with a group of European scientists and mathematicians known as the "Vienna Circle." Ludwig Wittgenstein (1889–1951) was an Austrian philosopher who contributed to positivism and greatly influenced the Vienna Circle. He studied with Russell at Cambridge and became a British subject after World War I. Wittgenstein held that the job of philosophy is not to discover truth but to resolve problems and clarify ideas obtained from other fields. He wanted to deal with the language about data as opposed to the study of metaphysical statements from the great philosophical systems. Vienna Circle members Rudolph Carnap and A. J. Ayer interpreted Wittgenstein to mean that all propositions must be verifiable in logic or by statements of sense perception if they have meaning.

With the growth of modern science and new disciplines, special language has been used by experts. An example would be the terms in computer languages like BASIC or COBOL. Analysts foster communication by dealing with the real meaning of terms, their truthfulness, and their reliability. They translate specialized language into ordinary meaning which can be used for educational policies.

Because of increased specialization and advanced technology, communication between experts in different fields has become more difficult. Information that comes through the mass media shows a vast range of truthfulness, reliability, and validity. Clearly, an analysis of knowing such as Gilbert Ryle developed in *The Concept of Mind* has value now.

Modern analytic professors of education like Israel Scheffler, R. S. Peters, Jonas Soltis, Henry Perkinson, and Richard Pring offer no metaphysical statements or models of schools. Instead, they clarify meaning so that those who make policy or develop curriculum may understand exactly the theories upon which they build and the consequences of their own position statements. Analytic philosophy is not a speculative system but it provides a means for making educational ideas clear, precise, and meaningful.

Behaviorism.   In earlier chapters we have seen that psychology and education are closely related. Dewey and James were psychologists, as well as philosophers and progressives, and adopted Gestalt psychology as their own. A few modern psychologists have developed a position sufficiently broad and with enough followers so that it is meaningful to speak of their educational philosophies. Among these are Jerome Bruner, Abraham Maslow, Carl Rogers, and especially Burrhus Frederick Skinner (1904-1990). While best known for his programmed instruction derived from the principles of operant conditioning based on laboratory experiments with animals, Skinner has moved behavioral engineering into the realm of utopian planning, the nature of man, social values, and a definition of the good life.

Born in Susquehanna, Pennsylvania, Skinner taught psychology at the University of Minnesota and Indiana University before returning to Harvard where he had taken his Ph.D. Earning a reputation as one of the most important contemporary psychologists, his work on animal behavior is a major contribution to knowledge. Building on the foundation of Ivan Pavlov (1849–1946), who began experimentation on conditioned reflexes in Russia, and the American behaviorists Edward Lee Thorndike (1874–1949) and John B. Watson (1878–1958), he developed laws of behavior and created teaching machines. Had he confined his work to "rat-in-a-box" psychology, as it is sometimes called, there would be no behavioristic theory of education, but he went beyond the experimental laboratory in his books *Walden II*, 1976 and *Beyond Freedom and Dignity*, 1971.

Behaviorism is grounded in realism, especially the materialistic branch which maintains that behavior is caused by environmental conditions. Instead of concentration on mind or consciousness, behaviorists look at observable facts, capable of empirical verification. Skinner thought errors had been made by philosophers who attempted to deduce a concept of human nature from *a priori* generalizations or introspection. While not denying genetic influence, he opposed the traditional views of humankind which assume there are internal drives and hidden forces that define humans. Humanists argued that human beings possess distinctive qualities absolutely different from animals and which are not the product of evolution. Skinner treats humans as animals subject to the same environmental controls and evolutionary forces as any other living organism.

Increasingly in contemporary society, our behavior is controlled by environmental forces. Some of these, like inflation and population growth, may be accidental while others, like advertising to make us want particular products, are intentional and manipulative. Skinner argues that since we understand the power of such forces to modify behavior, we ought to use them deliberately to construct a society of the most benefit to all. This was the theme of the utopian new Walden where everything was done with cooperation but according to plan. Few are neutral about Skinner's theories. A common charge is that he abolished "mankind" through scientific analysis. He is interested in the complexity and uniqueness of people but he sees people as mechanical and animal in nature. Critics suggest that the same behavioral engineering techniques he advocates might produce a nightmare society such as Orwell's 1984. Skinner replies that we are likely to get such a society by not planning or attempting to control and modify human behavior.

Skinner believes in a sophisticated science of human behavior and maintains that value judgments are just as much a part of science as any other field, including philosophy. Behavior (including aggressive behavior) is explained by positive reinforcement. It is not helpful to condemn the culprit in crime or the extermination of Jews in World War II. Rather, we should look for ways to remove the positive reinforcement of such behavior. Knowing is not just a cognitive process but it is environmental, behavioral, and psychological as well. The "good" for Skinner is merely that which is rewarded, and if we want to shape cultural evolution, we must find ways to reinforce that behavior which the culture defines as desirable. He points out that historically, cultural change has been blind, accidental, or random. He holds that while we may not have a blueprint for the perfect society, we can develop better social arrangements, and education is one of the best ways to design a better culture. Again, positive reinforcement (not punishment) is the most effective way to alter institutions because human action is shaped by rewards. Obviously, behavior depends upon actual possibilities. In ancient Athens, the automobile was not a possibility and it had no part of shaping the culture. For modern American adolescents, driving an automobile is rewarding, it gives a feeling of power and freedom, and the teenage subculture regards "wheels" as one of the most important status symbols. For contemporary culture, the automobile is very important and our behavior of driving and prizing cars is reinforced.

Behaviorists view the child as a highly conditioned organism even before entering school. Whatever has gone on before, including contradiction in the values exhibited by parents or the environmental control of institutions like churches will have an impact on the school environment. Since teachers must engage in the modification of behavior, it is important that they know what goals they wish to achieve and how to reach them with efficiency. Skinner does not see this process as evil, but as a means for expanding possibilities and developing a preference for a better kind of civilization.

Behaviorists can demonstrate that operant conditioning actually works. Successful techniques for classroom management and control are grounded in the theory, as well as instructional methods such as those of Madeline Hunter. Skinner's influence is enormous in spite of strong opposition to his ideas. The author of this book once heard a university president introduce Skinner as "the devil." Nevertheless, behaviorism is a growing educational philosophy, especially in the United States.

Existentialism.   Not a systematic philosophy, existentialism (and its psychological counterpart, phenomenology) is a protest against institutional controls, formalism, and social norms. Existentialism provides a means for examining life in a personal way, reflecting on commitments and choices, and considering the temporary nature of human life. Existentialists do not believe that we inhabit a meaningful or explainable world. The philosophy includes a theme of hope but there is also the theme of desperation and anguish. One cannot find a model of a school based upon existentialism. The closest thing might be the schools of the American Summerhill Association (based on the work of A. S. Neill in England) which stresses freedom of choice, authenticity and personal development. Martin Buber (1878–1965) offered some suggestions about education in *I and Thou* while critics like Holt, Leonard, and Illich reflect an existentialistic point of view. The philosophy forms a foundation for taking issue with almost all of the activities which take place in public and private schools.

Roots of existentialism go back to the admonition of Socrates to "know thyself" and the sophists who said "man is the measure of all things." Descartes, Pascal, and Dostoevsky stressed the idea of personal freedom and responsibility. The modern theme was developed by Albert Camus, Gabriel Marcel, Friedrich Nietzsche, and Edmund Husserl, who founded phenomenology. The influence on American education has come since the Second World War and is largely based on Soren Kierkegaard (1813–1855), Martin Heidegger (1889–1976), Jean Paul Sartre (1905–1980), and Martin Buber.

Existentialism's primary focus has been on the nature of human existence. As Sartre put it, existence precedes essence and we are "condemned" to be free. Unlike realists or idealists, existentialists think people create their own essence by choosing what they will be. This is quite different from Kant's charge that we have a duty to be moral or Mill's belief that we must act in the best interests of the greatest number. We must choose to conform, rebel, commit suicide, live independent from social norms, love, hate, or be directed by peer values. While others seek to impinge upon our freedom to make choices, we are totally responsible. The authentic person is one who is aware of his or her freedom and is willing to take the responsibility for self-direction and self-definition. Choices and the manner in which they are made determine what human beings we will become. Each person's situation is unique, the world is only temporary and each of us must carry the burden of his own upcoming death. Existentialists will not tell us that our choices are right or wrong, only that our freedom is total, our existence is determined by the choices we make, and that the universe is indifferent to human wishes and desires. We may choose to keep up with the Joneses, take our values from the mass media, or work only for money in a meaningless job, but such choices lead to an unfulfilled life of desperation and anguish and cut off possibilities of loving, creating, and being.

The very nature of existence poses a metaphysical question of central interest to existentialists and the theory of value is important but the philosophy is not concerned with logic or epistemology. Some aspects of phenomenology relate to the formation of values and ethical questions in education. Examples would be Abraham Maslow's stages of development and the theory of moral development in the work of Lawrence Kohlberg. Since schools operate on rules, conformity, acceptance of the curriculum, homework, following directions, teacher authority, and the like, students who insist on individual choice and challenge regulations are hard to manage. Some existentialists think that schools should not exist. Others like George Leonard object to the "hidden curriculum" of social expectations and peer values which are transmitted by the school environment. They think that once the veneer of civilization is stripped away, the savage nature of man and the misery of the human condition will be revealed. No set of values or established body of knowledge can replace individual experience with its personal motives, choices, and responsibilities. To accept a philosophy or religion from others denies our right to create our own values and imposes a barrier to answering the question of what we have chosen to be. These views are also reflected in the criticism of Ivan Illich (treated in Chapter 7).

Existentialism is very troublesome for educators because it attacks the fundamental assumptions of systematic philosophies upon which schools rest. The themes of desperation, alienation, death, and despair are not compatible with schooling. Absolute freedom to choose is a challenge to all social organization and the institutions of civilization. Yet the awful price we pay for giving over our choices to others and allowing them to determine our fate is the basis for a critical examination of all philosophies. An example is the Jonestown mass suicide in Guyana where many lost their lives by totally trusting in others. The influence of existentialistic writers is increasing and can hardly be dismissed by policy builders or those who create educational theory, even though it is difficult to deal with in schools.

Social and Futures Philosophy.

Strongly related to social reconstructionism and the theories of John Dewey, social and futures philosophies are emerging as important bodies of thought aimed at understanding a world of accelerating change. Joel Feinberg tells us that social philosophy is less well defined than most of the other conventional branches while social philosophy of education is even more elliptical since it embraces philosophical matters from political science, sociology, and anthropology, while including skills of analysis and critical thinking. While the theory has roots in the Enlightenment and in the works of Comenius, Locke, and Rousseau, it is mainly a twentieth century development.

Social and futures philosophy is especially concerned with the study of the school as a social institution and concepts like freedom, human rights, leadership, ideology, power, equity and justice. Social and futures thinkers rely as much on work from other disciplines as on philosophy. William F. Ogburn's *Social Change*, Marshall McLuhan's *Understanding Media*, Arnold Toynbee's *A Study of History*, and Kenneth Boulding's *The Meaning of the Twentieth Century* are examples. This interdisciplinary basis means that these theorists are interested in all social issues. General statements of the futures philosophy are found in the works of Alvin Toffler and Edward Cornish, while the educational theory has been developed by Jim Bowman, Christopher Dede, Draper Kauffmann, Fred Kierstead, and Harold Shane.

Insofar as social philosophers deal with ultimate reality, they accept the metaphysics of realism. Logic is of little interest to them although many accept the urge to clarify language as voiced by analytical thinkers. The real thrust of the movement is epistemology and axiology. These philosophers have historically criticized "received" notions such as the accepted social role of the school, the end of preparing to enter the job market, and the notion that existing bodies of knowledge define the path to the good life. They look to

Educational Philosophy	Influences	Rationale	Curriculum
Perennialism (Neo-thomism)	St. Thomas Aquinas Jacques Maritain Robert M. Hutchins Stringfellow Barr Max Rafferty Mortimer Adler	Stresses intellectual attainment and the search for truth	The Great Books The Classics Liberal Arts
Idealism (Essentialism)	Plato Josiah Royce Immanuel Kant Ralph Waldo Emerson Herman Horne	All material things are explainable	History Biography Humanities
Realism (Essentialism)	Alfred N. Whitehead Aristotle John Amos Comenius Johann F. Herbart John Locke Harry Broudy	Propositions are true only if they correspond with known facts	Science Mathematics Quantitative subjects Foreign language
Pragmatism	Boyd Bode John Dewey William James Charles Peirce William Kilpatrick	Search for things that work Experimental Democratic	Core curriculum Student centered Revolves around the interest of the student
Reconstructionism	Theodore Brameld George Counts Harold Rugg Ivan Illich John Holt Paul Goodman	Seeks to reconstruct society through education	Current events Social problems Futures research Sociology Political Science
Existentialism	John Paul Sartre Soren Kierkegaard Martin Buber Albert Camus Martin Heidegger A. S. Neill Carl Rogers	Importance of the individual Subjectivity Discover the inner nature of things and people	Individual preference Psychology Human Relations

Developed by Timothy J. Bergen, Jr., University of South Carolina.

Educational Philosophy	Teacher	Method of Teaching	Examinations
Perennialism (Neo-thomism)	A taskmaster—philosophically oriented and knowledgeable about the Great Books	Lectures Discussions Seminars	Essay
Idealism (Essentialism)	Serves as the ideal A good role model	Lectures Discussions Imitation	Essay
Realism (Essentialism)	Presents subject in a highly organized and very exact manner	Lectures Demonstrations Sensory experiences Teaching machines	Objective
Pragmatism	A guide One who can present meaningful knowledge with skill	Discussions Projects	Gauge how well people can problem solve
Reconstructionism	Social activist	Real-life projects	Student select, administer and evaluate Gauge ability as an activist
Existentialism	Very committed individual Person who is both teacher and learner One who provides a free environment to learn	Learner is encouraged to discover the best method for him/herself	Student should learn to examine him/herself

Educational Philosophy	Preferred Architecture	Criticism	Educational Outcome
Perennialism (Neo-thomism)	Classical	Very elite and aristocratic Must be accepted on faith and absolute truth	An intellectual scholar
Idealism (Essentialism)	Traditional	Elite	An intellectual scholar
Realism (Essentialism)	Efficient Functional	Often fails to deal with social change	Technician Scientist
Pragmatism	Flexible Natural	Permissive Very democratic Replace history with social studies	Good problem solver
Reconstructionism	Non-school setting "Schools without walls"	Very utopian Very impatient	Social activist
Existentialism	Individual preference	Unsystematic Rejects all authority	Inner-directed Authentic person Committed, involved, cares

the kind of information a learner must have for survival in the future, and they consider how the society might be reconstructed through education to meet new technical, social, and environmental needs. This aspect of the social philosophy has, in the current century, taken on a strong normative component, as it attempts to set forth new designs and scenarios of teaching and learning, research and study, knowledge and values, and the theoretical dimensions of special institutions. Spencer Maxcy of Louisiana State University has developed a statement of social philosophy of education, as has Harold Hodgkinson.

As the name implies, social philosophers of education are concerned with the deeper, more theoretical dimensions of social issues as they are related to education. They have criticized the accepted social role of the school. Futurists are interested in those social arrangements that will allow us to survive with a maximum realization of the human potential. They see education as a means of inventing the future and restructuring society so as to resolve the most pressing human problems and to take advantage of new opportunities provided by technological invention. This aspect of social philosophy of education has a strong value orientation as it attempts to set forth new designs and scenarios of teaching, learning, research, and study. Values and ethics, freedom, human rights, equity, justice, ideology, leadership, and the proper use of power are major areas of interest for futurists and social philosophers.

Qualitative methods of educational inquiry are used because of the limited value of statistical projections for predicting the future. William Pinar talks of the need to reconceptualize education, to move from traditional means of telling the truth about schooling to a better understanding through psychological/biographical/literary techniques and the adoption of more naturalistic methods. Philosophy, social science, and futurism join hands to provide a more workable set of solutions to the social problems facing human society. A branch of social philosophy called hermeneutics argues that the primary function of thought is seeking an understanding of the conditions we face as humans. The business of social and futures philosophy is edifying, rather than providing data or statistical analysis of present conditions and interpreting social change.

These philosophers hold that in our swift technological transformation into the information age and the post-industrial society characterized by computers and cybernation, we have failed to address matters of value and ethics. They argue that industrial-age schools and materialistic/individualistic values are not appropriate for the future. In *The Minimal Self* (1984), Christopher Lasch is critical of personalistic and individualistic theories. A philosophy of self for the future should stress survival, protecting the environment, collective needs, and the global nature of society. In the last half century, Americans have seen major changes which require new ethical standards. Husband and wife both work, children are sent to daycare centers, television illustrates sex, violence, and greed, gangs create havoc in cities, drug use is epidemic, and children are having children. These things point to a need for a major shift in the teaching and formation of values, but many schools behave as if the world has not changed since 1950. Teachers and principals working toward a future's social philosophy must be sensitive to the ethical dimension of preparing citizens for a world filled with significant human problems.

Ultimately, social philosophy is pledged to the idea that education is a flawed enterprise that may be improved through reflective thinking and "unpacking" the curriculum. Cleo Cherryholmes tells us that textbooks have rarely been scrutinized for what they leave out and that American school textbooks are bland and uniform in their treatment of critical social issues that we must face as a nation. According to Peter Wagschal, the future studies program at the University of Massachusetts concentrates on social change and the most equalitarian educational arrangements for preparing tomorrow's citizens.

Social philosophers since the Enlightenment have focused upon the issue of freedom and liberty. Huston Smith has proposed that the traditional binary distinction between freedom and authority must be examined again in the light of new developments. He thinks that genuine freedom is not respondent to "ceiling authorities" but rests on certain "floor authorities" which make it possible to respond to change. A social theory of educational future is similarly concerned with the notion of freedom that will underwrite the future in a global community. There is an equal interest by both groups in the relationship of freedom to human rights. Of course, the matter of human rights and their status in a state have puzzled social philosophers for centuries. Supporting six billion people on earth by the year 2000, protecting the global environment, providing economic opportunity, preventing war, and addressing the AIDS epidemic are examples of problems that make the issue more critical. There is also keen interest in what values need to be taught or developed in order to provide a reasonable foundation for the future. Clearly, the Puritan ethic, materialistic values of the market place, competition, or exploitation of resources for economic gain are not satisfactory.

Futurists and social theorists are interested in the complex problem of leadership. Jurgen Habermas has argued that one of the problems of the modern industrial/capitalistic society is that administrators concentrate on achieving goals but never question the worthiness of these ends. Since the process-product equation has come into vogue in school administration, principals see children as "products" rather than as people. Futurists find this model appalling, especially when we are moving out of the industrial era and into the information age, or the age of cybernation. Both theories support democratic participation in running the schools and the empowerment of teachers and students to participate in the decision-making process.

Perhaps the most important theme facing social and futures philosophers concerns the kinds of social arrangements most conducive to human survival and maximum realization of the human potential. Ought we live under a monarchy, an oligarchy, a democracy, or in anarchy with no government at all? Can existing arrangements be modified for the future, or will we need to invent quite different arrangements? Dewey suggested that this might be necessary when he argued that democracy was the best social arrangement yet developed but that it might be improved upon in the future.

Postmodernism.   Jurgen Habermas, Jean Francois Lyotard, Michel Foucault, Henry Giroux, Richard Rorty, Michael Apple, and Barry Kanpol discussed various aspects of an ideology known as postmodernism. Rorty's writings build on the basic philosophical premises of John Dewey. The other authors offer alternatives to the philosophical ideas of the enlightenment era. Concepts of structure, dogmatism, rationalism, modernism, positivism and any other preconceived notion of knowledge are replaced in postmodernism by ideas of ambiguity, questioning, unsystematic narration of perceptions, and freedom from any superimposed knowledge systems. Even language and its structure is under intense scrutiny because of its limitations on truly knowing. Postmodernism is a blend of the liberating message of existentialism with the humanism of pragmatism, and critical theory of Marxism.

Postmodernists criticize any universalistic explanations of the cosmos replacing them with a transformation of liberation that includes concerns of "marginalized" people. (Those who have not always been heeded by mainstream thinkers). This celebration of diversity focuses on liberating individuals from age, class, gender, and race-based prejudices. Reaching the feelings, attitudes, and aspirations of individuals through exploration of their own account of educational politics and struggles within their school settings is achieved through micronarratives (or present oriented dialogue). These insights into the attitudes of educators about their individual struggles and triumphs within schools provide meaning structures that can be interwoven in metanarratives of school research findings.

As with pragmatism, postmodernism finds democracy and its institutions always in flux, change and modification. As Dewey noted, change is always prevalent in a democracy. Change gives democracy its uniqueness and ability to meet conditions requiring innovation in theory and practice. As in existentialism, postmodernism seeks meaning in situational context, texture, and consciousness raising. The Marxist call for liberation from forms of modernism or industrialism that encroach on human freedom, is found in postmodernists attunement to an age of post-industrialism or global communication/information networks.

Postmodernists seek to build a more humane society through reaching all levels, gender, ages, and races. They seek to recreate and reinvent democracy to achieve more economic and social justice. Susan Hekman, Kate Campbell and other feminist authors find postmodernism helpful in delineating alternatives to masculine oriented theories from the Enlightenment forward. Erikson's account suggests that this is a necessary liberating approach as can be seen from the 1637 trial of Ann Hutchinson whose banishment from Massachusetts Colony was due in no small part to Governor Winthrop's view:

> For if she had attended her household affairs, and such things as belong to women, and had not gone out of her way and calling to meddle in such things as are proper for men, she had kept her wits, and might have improved them usefully and honorably in the place that God sent her.

The feminist struggle for liberation continues through postmodern literature as we approach the 21st century.

THEN TO NOW

The philosophies of education discussed in this chapter are certainly the major ones in contemporary America but many educational decisions are made without any obvious link to a theoretical foundation. As Dewey once put it, philosophers may argue with one another, but the world is run by "burly sinners." It is certainly true that many of the people who make decisions about education do so without a philosophic foundation or one that is pragmatic in the narrow sense of the word.

An example is an article called "Education for Economic Growth" by former North Carolina governor, James Hunt, which appeared in the *Kappan* in April, 1984. Hunt probably reflected the opinion of many Americans when he argued that the real function of schooling is to make technologically and scientifically literate citizens able to compete for jobs in the world market. As chairperson of the Task Force on Education for Economic Growth, Hunt saw education as the means for improving the economy and believed that the measure of good schools is that students get good jobs. He favored minimum competency tests for all potential high school graduates and identifies the purpose of education as higher productivity, higher profits, and a better life based on income and spending power. He also thought that governments at all levels have a right to expect the outcome of better competition in the economic sector, because they provide the funds to support schools. Hunt's views are shared by many but they represent an extremely narrow and nontheoretical concept of educational goals. Job preparation, economic growth, and competition in the marketplace have always been among the purposes of American schools, but seldom the major or only goal.

Only a few philosophical positions such as existentialism would be in total opposition to Hunt, but most would think his views myopic to the extreme. Idealists and perennialists would argue that job preparation is secondary to character building, value formation, citizenship training, and a broad understanding of western civilization. Social and futures theorists would say that Hunt's position is counterproductive to meeting even his narrow objective because future economic growth depends on solving social problems, protecting the environment, and creating a stable world order.

It is reasonable to expect that a child born today will be a functioning member of the society of the middle of the twenty-first century. If conditions change at the rate of present experience (and there is good reason to think they will alter even more rapidly) the world of 2050 will be a different one indeed. Some philosophic systems are based on the assumption of unchanging reality and the permanence of forces which shape human life. They offer less illumination for the future of education than those which focus more directly on the problems of today and the possibilities of tomorrow.

There is a seeming contradiction between the support for individual freedom found in Rousseau's *Emile* and his effort to develop a social contract for the inhabitants of Poland which had mechanisms of social control and public schools. Futurist Fred Kierstead has expanded this conflict in order to define the meaning of the "general will" as the authority for making educational decisions. For Rousseau, the will of the people, expressed through popularity polls or single votes, was not as trustworthy as the general will. The general will was the true belief to the people as a body over time. If there is validity in the theory, we then have the problem of how to find the general will today and in the future. Media campaigns, political pressures, personalities of leaders and current events may cloud our perception of what the people truly want. Philosophy may be the best tool we have for clearing away these barriers to making educational policy. The ideas of Rousseau may yet have direct bearing on the way we educate future generations.

Other philosophic positions also carry into the future. John Dewey's concept of continuous reconstruction of experience as the basis for solving problems and planning action is compatible with the writings of futurists like Alvin Toffler, Arthur Wirth, or John R. Platt. Dewey argued that democracy was the most conducive form of social organization for human life owing to the fact that only in a democracy are people free to inquire. By possessing this freedom of inquiry, the mechanisms of democracy can be upheld and sustained. Modern social philosophers who see democracy as the most suitable "form of life" as Dewey did, think democratic education is the means by which people can secure the civil and political freedoms necessary for the good life. By the mid 1990s, major movements toward a more democratic culture in the Soviet Union encouraged futurists to believe that democratic schooling might become a reality even in nations with a Marxist orientation. Now that Russia and China are moving toward a free market, futuristic thinkers are even more optimistic about global democratic schools. Certainly the ideas of Dewey are as relevant for the global post-industrial society as they were for the progressive educators of the 1930s in America. We may expect that forthcoming educational issues will reflect differences in philosophy even when the major players lack clearly defined theoretical positions

Arthur Wirth, in his *Education and Work For the Year 2000: Choices We Face,* noted that we must give ourselves freedom and flexibilities to explore alternatives and opinions. Wirth's book, as Maxine Greene noted, dealt with the continuing tension between our democratic tradition and demands of technological revolution. The aims and ideologies of education expressed through the various philosophies of education articulated in this chapter are those that lay a foundation for educational policies. Hidden agendas reflected in ideologies are always evolving, judging, and weighing alternative routes to political, economic, and social goals.

The Clinton Administration's goals of a people-centered administration may evolve with elements of Postmodern theory, with emphasis on "celebration of diversity." Clinton's government appointments were designed to reflect diversity in gender, race, and ethnicity. Many members of his team reflect the ideologies of change, process, and "deconstructionism" (the reassessment of what is really known at any time for any circumstances). Many of these concepts are currently being discussed in academic communities. African-American, Hispanic-American, Asian-American, gender, and women's studies classes and programs reflect the postmodern theories of Richard Rorty, H. A. Giroux, Michel Foucault, and Michael Apple that are now part of many university agendas.

Unlike the West Germans or the Japanese, ordinary Americans are directly involved with the governance of their schools. Americans are also inconsistent in the way they choose or represent values and philosophies. Thus, school board members often share a vague belief in an idealistic world order or universal mind while spending their time on such mundane matters as buying busses, reviewing complaints about "lax" discipline, or trying to head off the demands of teachers for better pay. Parents and community citizens may exhibit keen interest in the success of the local high school's varsity football team and very little interest in the school curriculum, although they would not list varsity sports as the purpose of secondary education.

Former education secretary William Bennett was an extremely articulate spokesperson for perennialism. He was also a critic of professional educators and contributed to the "teacher bashing" which has been a popular activity in America since the 1930s. His well-stated educational theory received far less coverage in the press than his attacks on "educationists" or his caustic remarks about schools. It is curious that many Americans have a negative attitude toward the public schools or the "educational establishment" but good feelings about the local education their own children receive. Scores of surveys conducted in the 1980s and 1990s revealed that some people who were highly critical of education at the national or state levels gave high praise to their local schools and teachers. This curious situation is reflected in expressions of disdain for education and educators combined with support for local school millage and bond elections.

Consistency is not a characteristic trait of Americans, and this probably contributes to a lack of clarity in educational theory. Some schools attempt to follow conflicting goals at the same time without analyzing the problems this creates. Obviously, better understanding of the theoretical basis of education is required to clarify issues and meet the needs of the future. Education secretary Reilly is moving toward social reconstructionism in American Education following the Clinton Administration education agenda.

BIBLIOGRAPHY

Apple, Michael. *Ideology and Curriculum*. London: Routledge & Kegan Paul, 1979.

Bestor, Arthur. *The Restoration of Learning*. New York: Knopf, 1955.

Bestor, Arthur. *Educational Wastelands*. Urbana: U of Illinois Press, 1953.

Brameld, Theodore. *Patterns of Educational Philosophy*. New York: Holt, Rinehart and Winston, 1971.

Butler, Donald. *Four Philosophies and Their Practice in Religion*. New York: Harper and Row, 1957.

Campbell, Kate, ed. *A Critical Feminism: Argument In the Disciplines*. Philadelphia: Open University Press, 1992.

Cherryholmes, Cleo. *Power and Criticism*: Poststructural Investigations in Education. New York: Teacher's College Press, 1988.

Comish, Edward. *The Study of the Future*. Washington, D.C.: World Future Society, 1977.

Cooper, J. Arthur. *Exemplars in Educational Philosophy*. Minneapolis, MN: Alphia Editions, 1988.

Cuban, Larry. *How Teachers Taught: Constancy and Change in American Classrooms, 1890–1980.* New York: Longman, 1984.

Dewey, John. *Democracy and Education.* New York: Macmillan, 1916.

____. *Experience and Education.* Toronto: Macmillan, 1938.

Erickson, Kai. *Wayward Puritans: A Study in the Sociology of Deviance.* New York: Wiley and Sons, 1982.

Fineberg, Joel. *Social Philosophy.* Englewood Cliffs, NJ: Prentice Hall, Inc., 1973.

Giroux, H. A. *Postmodernism, Feminism, and Cultural Politics.* New York: State University of New York, 1991.

Giroux, Henry. *Theory and Resistance in Education*: A Pedagogy for the Opposition. Boston: Bergin & Garvey, 1983.

Gutek, Gerald. *Philosophical and Ideological Perspectives on Education.* Englewood Cliffs, New Jersey: Prentice-Hall, 1988.

Habermas, J. *The Philosophical Discourse of Modernity.* Cambridge, Mass: M.I.T. Press, 1987.

Hekman, Susan J. *Gender and Knowledge: Elements of a Postmodern Feminism.* Boston: Northeastern University Press, 1990.

Horne, Herman. *The Democratic Philosophy of Education.* New York: Macmillan, 1935.

Hutchins, Robert. *Great Books: The Foundation of a Liberal Education.* New York: Simon and Schuster, 1954.

James, William. *Pragmatism: A New Name for Some Old Ways of Thinking.* New York: Longman, Green, 1981.

Johanningmeier, Erwin. *Americans and Their Schools.* Chicago: Rand McNally, 1980.

Kanpol, Barry. *Towards A Theory and Practice of Teacher Cultural Politics: Continuing the Post Modern Debate.* Norwood, NJ: Norwood Publishing Co., 1992.

Kliebard, Herbert. *Forging The American Curriculum: Essays in Curriculum History and Theory.* New York: Routledge, 1992.

____. *The Struggle for the American Curriculum.* Boston: Routledge and Kegan Paul, 1986.

Kneller, George. *Existentialism and Education.* New York: John Wiley, 1958.

Lasch, Christopher. *The Minimal Self: Psychic Survival in Troubled Times.* New York: W. W. Norton, 1984.

Lather, Patti. *Getting Smart.* New York: Routledge, 1991.

Lynd, Albert. *Quackery in the Public Schools,* Boston: Little Brown, 1953.

Lyotard, J. *Post Modern Explained.* Minneapolis: University of Minnesota Press, 1993.

____. *The Postmodern Condition: A Report on Knowledge.* Minneapolis: University of Minnesota Press, 1984.

____. *Toward the Post Modern,* Atlantic Highlands, New Jersey: Humanities Press, 1991.

Meadows, Donela, and Dennis Meadows. *The Limits to Growth.* New York: Universe Books, 1972.

Morris, Van Cleve. *Existentialism in Education.* New York: Harper and Row, 1966.

Neill, A. S. *Summerhill.* New York: Hart, 1960.

Ozmon, Howard, and Samuel Craver. *Philosophic Foundations of Education.* New York: Merrill/Macmillan, 1986.

Park, Joe, ed. Selected *Readings in the Philosophy of Education.* New York: Macmillan Co., 1958.

Perkinson, Henry. *Since Socrates: Studies in the History of Western Educational Thought.* New York: Longman, 1980.

Rafferty, Max. *Suffer, Little Children.* New York: Devin-Adair Co., 1962.

Rorty, Richard. *Objectivity, Relativism and Truth.* New York: Cambridge Press, 1991.

____. *Philosophy and the Mirror of Nature.* Princeton, NJ: Princeton University Press, 1987.

Russell, Bertrand. *Education and the Modern World.* New York: W. W. Norton, 1932.

Sarup, Madan. *Marxism and Education.* London: Routledge & Kegan Paul, 1978.

Simpson, Douglas, and Michael Jackson. *The Teacher as Philosopher.* New York: Methuen, 1984.

Skinner, B. F. *Beyond Freedom and Dignity.* New York: Alfred A. Knopf, 1971.

Strike, Kenneth, and Jonas Soltis. *The Ethics of Teaching.* New York: Teachers College Press, 1985.

Toffler, Alvin. *Future Shock.* New York: Random House, 1970.

Whitehead, Alfred. *The Aims of Education and Other Essays.* New York: Macmillan, 1929.

FROM NOW TO THEN: EDUCATION IN THE FUTURE

Societies . . . are not machines and they are not computers. They cannot be reduced so simply into hardware and software, base and superstructure. A more apt model would picture them as consisting of many more elements, all connected in immensely complex and continually changing feedback loops. As their complexity rises, knowledge becomes more central to their economic and ecological survival.

Alvin Toffler

History has its own intrinsic value, but most of us are interested in the past because of its practical value in understanding the present and its ability to suggest the probable course of future events. Teachers must of necessity be oriented toward the future. Children now entering kindergarten may reasonably be expected to be alive and active in the middle of the twenty-first century. Colleges that train teachers are currently working with teacher candidates who will directly influence the citizens of the twenty-second century. In a period of very slow cultural change such as the Middle Ages, significant spans of time were not critical. Today with accelerating invention in many fields, the explosion of research and knowledge, careening technology, electronic communications networks, and computers, the rate of change does indeed approach future shock. If the twenty-first century is as different from the twentieth as the twentieth was from the nineteenth, children entrusted to the care of educators may expect changes that stagger the imagination. All indications point to an even faster rate of change, and not even an economic depression would reverse the trend. The existing school program with a curriculum derived largely from the past is inadequate to meet the future needs of children. Because we cannot know the future in advance, it is necessary that we prepare future citizens for as wide a variety of alternatives as possible. It is extremely difficult to give future generations the skills and information (to say nothing of the attitudes and values) they will require for future survival, but anticipation of events to come seems fundamental to the attempt. The worst we

255

Industrial Era	Computer Age	Information Age	
1969 Apollo Moon Landing	1970 Toffler's *Future Shock*	1980 Worldwide Telecommunications Networks	
	Transistor Computer	1982 Naisbitt's *Megatrends 2000*	1990 Naisbitt's *Megatrends II*
First Generation Vacuum Tube Computer	Explorer Launched		
	Toffler's *Powershift*	Microcomputer in Homes	

can do is to send students into the next century armed only with an education based on the ideals and needs of nineteenth-century agrarian America. It is said that education always looks to the past and that invention in the schools comes slowly, but it is imperative that teachers become students of the future and that they do their utmost to give students the best tools possible for coping with a variety of probable futures.

On first reflection, history may seem an odd means for approaching the future. Further analysis will show that past recorded events do shed light on how human beings expected things to go, how things actually did go, and what consequences followed. The television series "Connections" is an example of the way one scientific discovery led to another until the whole shape of technology and even of human society was drastically altered in unexpected ways. An illustration is the invention of the chimney during an unusually cold period in the twelfth century which made it possible to heat numerous rooms on more than one floor. One result was a dramatic change in architecture, because buildings no longer had to be built around one fireplace with a smoke hole in the roof. An educational example is furnished by the social revolution which took place in Athens during the fifth century B.C. A new class of rich people emerged who made their money from banking, shipping, and the manufacture of goods for export. These men wanted to obtain an education for their sons similar to that provided for the young men from the old aristocratic families. For this purpose they hired migrant teachers called Sophists such as Protagoras, Gorgias, and Antiphon. The Sophists were skilled at teaching oratory and grammar, but they also criticized conventional morality, religion, and law. They taught practical ways of getting ahead in the world and clever means for evading rules. The Sophists drastically changed the values and norms of Athenian society and eventually altered the entire social order.

History may also be used as an instrument for analyzing and evaluating major forces or trends in the culture with the purpose of anticipating the future. Robert Heilbroner

Post-Industrial Age	2000		Communications Era	
Socialization and Basic Learning Through Home Computers and TV	2000 Genetic Engineering Common	2005 Automated Highways	2015 Human Travel by Light Beam	2030 Mind to Mind Communication
				Nanotechnology
	Microengineering		Brain Wave Analysis	
1990 All Students Skilled in Computer Languages	Six Billion Humans on Earth	2012 Drugs for Raising Intelligence	2020 Worldwide Guaranteed Minimum Income	Cheap Energy from Fusion

has done exactly that in his books *The Future As History* (1959) and *An Inquiry into the Human Prospect* (1975). In the first book, Heilbroner looked at longstanding trends in American culture as a means of defining the crucial problems that must be resolved if a viable future is to be achieved. He made no effort to play the role of prophet but gave detailed accounts of the revolutions in the twentieth century to show what must occur if liberal society is to survive. The second book treats the global situation in a similar way. Heilbroner looks at world economic trends, the challenges to political democracy, exploding population, environmental destruction, and obliterative weaponry. His conclusion is that neither industrial capitalism or Marxist socialism in their present forms have the necessary strength to avoid global catastrophe. While he is pessimistic about what is happening in the modern world, Heilbroner uses history as a tool to spell out exactly what we must do if the consequences of our past activities are not to result in disaster. Many futuristic writers use history as an instrument for examining societal propensities and suggesting alternatives.

History is filled with examples of attempts to foretell the future. Some of the earliest legends and artifacts deal with predicting things to come and rationalizing the plausibility of those predictions. The difficulty is that forecasting the future has seldom proved accurate, and predictions which did come true were rarely accepted more widely than those which failed. One of the major difficulties is a human tendency to assume that the future will only be an extension of the present. Those without an appreciation of history believe that the future will consist of a massive dose of today. This is a serious error in a period of dramatic and accelerating change as futurists are fond of pointing out. In general, the record of forecasting future events is not a good one, partly because changes in behavior and values of people are not as easy to predict as weather patterns or oil production. As Harry Broudy puts it: Human behavior cannot be extrapolated in any simple linear fashion. We can extrapolate the increasing need for energy by using the current rates of consumption as a base. But we cannot predict that the demand for energy, as measured by the demand for air conditioning, electrical heating, and household appliances, will increase at the same rate as it has in the last decade.

Many of those who claim to be futurists draw an analogy between well-established scientific or materialistic trends and what they believe will be the life conditions of the future. These extrapolists usually have the support of those in control of wealth and power who desire and expect that known general tendencies will merely accelerate. They ignore the possibility of radical changes in values, social behaviors, or attitudes. Herbert Spencer's doctrine of inevitable progress and the steady advance of technology leading to a utopian world for man was so popular and so widely accepted that few took seriously the dystopian predictions of H. G. Wells. Yet Wells, in such books as *The Time Machine*, *War of the Worlds*, and *The Shape of Things to Come*, anticipated world war, space travel, and the breakdown of the social order. Like Jules Verne before him, Wells made predictions that turned out to be far more accurate than those of his more "respectable" contemporaries. The same can be said for Huxley in *Brave New World* and Orwell in *1984*. C. Owen Paepke in *The Evolution of Progress, 1993* envisons an emerging concept of progress which will make human traits and abilities the subject rather than the source of change as the agenda of the next century. Paepke finds lengthening the life span and discovery of genetic sources of exceptional mental abilities and other favorable traits to be a present and future possibility.

Joseph F. Coates identified twelve transforming issues for the future at the 1993 meeting of the Society for Human Resource Management.

1. Labor, seeking to overcome management power on the rise since the 1950s, will organize, sue, strike, sabotage employment, and seek legislation to enhance their power.
2. With the information fiber optic superhighways, more work will be done away from offices due to people wanting flexible schedules, and for cost effectiveness.
3. African-Americans have made "enormous progress" in corporate America in the last 50 years. Coates estimates more than two-thirds have a "handhold on the upper mobility ladder." Because of this, the issue is no longer one of equal access but of performance.
4. There will be increased business cooperation and coordination on research and development for minimal individual company risk. Efforts will be made to develop a corporate culture and equity among groups from different organizations.
5. The future will hold widespread genetic testing, personality, and skill level tests so employers can evaluate their investments.
6. Automation, training, teamwork will be increasingly utilized to enhance productivity.
7. Global networking for increased world markets will be used to improve quality and exports.

8. Due to increased employee costs, there will be exponential growth in part-time, contract, temporary employees, doubling in the next decade from 25% to 50% of workers.

9. There will be an increase in women executives who will push for flexible work schedules as well as a new corporate culture.

10. Education will increasingly be under scrutiny to find ways of improving quality of the product.

11. Future worklife will encompass more attention to quality of life cycle including child and elderly care.

12. Increased attention will be given to improving the quality of executive leadership.

We must conclude that science and the most sober human reasoning are conditioned to look only at the immediate past for causes of human problems. Human intellect and judgment are not well adapted to interpreting the behavior of social systems, anticipating radical changes in values or understanding that existing governments are inadequate to manage the affairs of people in the modern world. One reason for this is that training has become so sophisticated and therefore so specialized that very few are educated broadly enough to see the whole picture. Futurism centers upon the interrelationship of human activities, the wide range of possible alternatives for human action and the opportunities for consciously altering or inventing the future.

Intellectual activity does not always merely follow change in the materialistic and technological spheres. Ideas, such as those of the world's great religious leaders, have the power to change not only values but also priorities and views of the good life. Those who have really changed the world are the thinkers who have challenged basic theories, beliefs, values, and myths. Rousseau, Marx, Darwin, and Freud are examples of such thinkers.

Both qualitative and quantitative research provide insights into educational history and help build a setting for understanding growth and development of educational systems. Qualitative research can enrich and enhance our becoming engaged in living history. Data collection through interviews, field observation, and records research helps one explore thinking, feeling, attitudes, opinions, and perceptions of educators within a particular time frame and setting. Flexibility, creativity, and humaneness emerge from many qualitative studies.

M. K. Motherwell, Educational Coordinator of the Shiloh Museum in Springdale, Arkansas, has put together an award winning qualitative study based on a letter written by a mother to her son in November of 1866 in the aftermath of the Civil War. The five-minute video tape, *In Dreadful Conflict*, explores little known facts of the last years of the Civil War in Northwest Arkansas through the eyes, heart, and perceptions of a mother who lived through the period. Backed by views of the various Civil War battles, grave sites in Northwest Arkansas, breakdown of law and order with roving bandits taking possessions at random, and explanations of the hard economic times, a vibrant view of history is revealed. Studies such as these provide guides to the value of conflict resolution in the future.

Educators must be students of the future if they are to make any real progress in meeting the needs of students in the world of tomorrow. Scholars in many fields are speculating about the future and examining trends in the current world. While much of the futuristic writing sounds a warning about what may happen, some of the work is optimistic in tone. The ancient Chinese wrote the word "crisis" as a combination of the symbols for "danger" and "opportunity."

THE FUTURES MOVEMENT

Ever since Alvin Toffler wrote *Future Shock*, people in America have been more aware of what experts in certain fields have known for decade—that the rate of change in modern society is rapidly accelerating. A new group of scientists and authors, known generally as futurists, have taken issue with the standard assumptions implicit and explicit in modern civilization. They question the idea of progress leading to ever-greater production of goods, the expenditures of enormous quantities of energy, the rapid depletion of the nonrenewable natural resources, and the development of a worldwide market for materialistic consumer goods. Futurists build on the social theories of Karl Marx, Karl Mannheim, Pitirim Sorokin, Oswald Spengler, and Arnold Toynbee, among others. They are aware of the culture lag theory, which suggests that human beings cannot cope with the shattering stress and disorganization that results when materialistic invention comes too rapidly for social adjustment. Problems such as the exploding world population, the threat of nuclear war, pollution, runaway technology, the knowledge explosion, and environmental destruction, cause many futurists to doubt the survival of civilization and its institutions, unless radical adjustments can be quickly made.

In *Cybernation: the Silent Revolution*, Donald N. Michael shows how poorly prepared modern people are for the revolution now in progress. Kenneth Boulding refers to the automation-biological revolution as "The Great Transition" and ranks it as significant on human growth and development as the discovery of agriculture or the industrial revolution. In *The Coming of Post-Industrial Society*, Daniel Bell forecasts the most radical changes which have ever faced the human race. In *Overskill*, Eugene Schwartz argues that the present trend toward increased technological and materialistic expansion cannot be maintained. Lester Brown illustrates the growing economic gap between the rich and poor in *World without Borders*. He points out that the whole world is becoming poverty stricken in terms of the earth's total ability to sustain life and predicts that a stable world order depends on meeting the basic needs of all people. Radical economists like John Kenneth Galbraith and Robert Theobald maintain that the present socio-economic system in the industrial nations like Japan, West Germany, and the United States cannot ensure survival. In The Prometheus Project, Gerald Fineberg calls for a new and revolutionary set of long-range social goals while Donella Meadows insists that for future survival there must be limits to growth. John R. Platt believes that a science for human survival is needed to examine social and individual priorities. He thinks greater care must be taken to avoid ecological disasters such as the Exxon oil spill off the coast of Alaska in 1989.

Arthur Wirth in *Education Work for the Year 2000* finds the United States facing two alternatives. One would entail adhering to our current course of education while ignoring increasing segregation of Americans by income and social disarray among the disadvantaged or making a major shift in national priorities. The second option would require ensuring that all children regardless of race or class have equal access to the best education possible.

Some futurists see humanity as an endangered species clinging precariously to a life-support system which its own actions may destroy. Others are concerned about efforts to maintain wealth and privilege in an overpopulated world, where equality of distribution of resources is badly needed. Barry Commoner believes that our technology is responsible for deterioration in the quality of the environment and that a new and better technology is needed to prevent massive biological degradation. Almost all see overgrowth, increased industrialization, urbanization, unemployment, psychological alienation, environmental destruction, polarization of rich and poor, expansion of the population, and demands for resources beyond the capacity of the earth to provide them, as major problems of the present and the future.

Most futurists are painfully aware of the danger of prediction and the terrible record of forecasting human events previous intellectuals have had. Still, most of our basic institutions and beliefs depend upon the assumption that things will remain pretty much as they are, an assumption which plainly runs contrary to fact. Electronic media and the invention of the computer have joined to produce an explosion of information unlike anything previously experienced. New knowledge can be quickly disseminated and applied to tasks that stagger the imagination, such as landing human beings safely on the moon. Each new technical development creates new possibilities for invention and the rapid exchange of ideas, plans, and programs which grow at an exponential rate. Linking information systems and machines creates cybernation. The possibility of a highly refined automated, cybernated system of production is now very real. There are also very great breakthroughs in areas of science such as biology and genetics, the results of which are not yet clear, but certainly highly significant. Every day much more is learned about human behavior and the learning process.

Futurists use different terms to refer to the transformation now taking place. The unknown state into which we are passing is labeled "post-industrial, post-civilized, automated, cybernated, super-industrial, information-era, communications-era" and the like. Futuristic writers do not agree on exactly what form the great revolution will take, but they agree that it is already in process. The transformation offers great hope for achieving a higher level of human potential and "inventing the future"; however, it also poses the danger that people will be unable to adjust rapidly enough to change. Obviously, futurists have little faith that education can be guided by ideas of the past, such as the collection of classics known as the Great Books of the Western World.

METHODS OF FUTURES RESEARCH

Futures research is concerned with collecting information and developing the processes by which alternatives are determined and policy is made in a variety of disciplines. It concentrates on anticipated developments, the probability that various events will occur in a given time period, and the consequences of alternatives. Much attention is given to the impact of one event upon another and the way two or more events may interact to change future conditions. Futures research is action-oriented and realistic rather than utopian. It assumes that human action can and should make a difference in increasing or decreasing the probability of various possible futures. Futures research concerns itself with conceptualizing and inventing the future by examining the consequences of various plans of action before they become tomorrow's reality.

Delphi.   The delphi technique is a means of forecasting based on the consensus of a group of specialists or experts. Delphi methodology involves first the selection of knowledgeable people in a given field or problem area. Each member of the group is asked to render forecasts individually. After all forecasts are collected, the results of the total survey are returned to each member of the group. Members may then revise their earlier forecasts or explain their reasons for not being in consensus with the other members. The process of collecting and distributing the survey results is carried out until each member understands all other positions and all have reached final conclusions on their individual positions.

Cross-Impact Matrix.   This is a refinement of the delphi technique which purports to determine the impact of future events upon each other. A delphi procedure can be used to measure the relationships between forecasted events. A computer analysis of the matrix can also be used to develop a set of probabilities for a complex set of events.

Digital computers, which have the capability of solving hundreds of equations within short periods of time, provide the researcher with the means for dynamic systems modeling. Mathematical simulation through computer analysis can facilitate knowledge about inherent lags between normative and exploratory forecasts. The computer, however, can only simulate a system to the extent that operating equations accurately describe behaviors in the real system. Theobald stresses that "the computer is a very good servant and a very bad master."

Simulation and Gaming.   Simulation and gaming processes encompass a broad range of methodologies. They usually involve an analysis of alternative future systems. They may be confined to particular fields of futurist interests using the computer (as described above) or they may involve more simplistic models such as three-dimensional (pencil and paper) games and experience compression techniques (brainstorming). The simulation may also involve a cross-impact analysis such as George Koehier's game, Futuribles, which provides participants with 288 possible futures in areas such as education, religion, energy, government, transportation, and the like.

Perspective Trees.   In this process, the researcher first examines the forces of change (rather than solutions to problems) within a given parameter. Second, a list is devised containing broad categories (poverty, health, war) as well as specific categories (government regulations, subcultures). Next, numerous relations or perspective trees are produced. While perspective trees do not provide a whole method for forecasting, they are instrumental in the planning process. They are especially helpful when used in conjunction with the delphi technique, trend extrapolation, or computerized cross-impact analysis.

Trend Extrapolation.   This technique entails an analysis of past and present trends in order to predict future trends. The central thesis is one of continuity; future trends will resemble past behaviors. A major problem in trend extrapolation is the selection of parameters. First, parameters are quantifiable at best. A subjective analysis of trends does not satisfy this methodology. Second, parameters must be selected which provide sufficient historical data. Third, regularity of patterns must be established. Fourth, the researcher should determine the interaction of past trends and changes in relationships between past and present parameters. Trend extrapolation may be used as a method itself or it may be incorporated into other methods. Extrapolation assumes no discontinuity with the past and is widely used by business, industry and government.

Scenario Concepts.   A scenario is usually a study of possible futures. Scenario conceptualization of the future is often limited by its subjective, nonquantitative format. It does provide, however, a creative means for analyzing futuribles without dependence upon past projections. This method is particularly important in the realm of social values. It is extremely difficult to model a hierarchical social system and to forecast value changes. Scenario conceptualizing facilitates a profile of social thresholds and provides descriptions of possible alternatives which oblige an individual to examine goals and priorities. The writing of scenarios is not only a research method, it is one of the best ways for students to learn how to deal with the future. The construction and evaluation of scenarios has become one of the most common classroom activities.

SCHOOLS OF FUTURISTIC THOUGHT

Because of the diversity of futures theories, it is helpful to divide them into groups according to general principles and shared beliefs. Just as in philosophy, there is some overlap, and a few individuals do not fit any given category. Nevertheless, some system of classification is essential for treating assumptions and selecting the positions from which a futuristic philosophy of education may be constructed.

Optimistic Extrapolists or Technological Enthusiasts.   As the name implies, optimistic extrapolists are hopeful about the future and often accuse critical theorists (like Robert Heilbroner) of crying "wolf." One of the best known representatives of this group is the late Herman Kahn of the Hudson Institute. Kahn predicts a future society where technology has provided people with all possible comforts and leisure time. Support for Kahn and the Hudson Institute comes from business and government. Optimistic extrapolists analyze existing trends and attempt to forecast future needs and markets. Kahn and his colleague Bruce Briggs say that there is no such thing as pollution, only resources which we have not yet learned to recycle. Extrapolists use think tanks to study trends and to propose alternative courses of action related to specific problems in industry. They have pioneered new methods of research such as delphi, computer-assisted trend analysis, and the cross-impact matrix.

Optimistic extrapolists or technological enthusiasts see growth and technological development as natural and good for the whole world. They believe that we will discover new resources and learn how to better utilize existing ones so that there will be ample support for a high quality of life, even for people in underdeveloped nations. This optimism is reflected in Daniel Bell's *The Coming of Post-Industrial Society*. Other examples of the position are found in Olaf Helmer's *Social Technology*, and *The Image of the Future* by Fred Polak. The educational need of the future will be more and better-trained scientists, engineers, and planners.

John Naisbitt's books, *Megatrends* and *Megatrends II* define the pervasive directions in which modern society is moving. Based on the analysis of national newspapers in the United States, he attempted to extrapolate the major trends that shape our world. Naisbitt is a cautious optimist, pointing out that a bright future is likely only if we understand the trends and alter our lives in order to take advantage of opportunities and avoid serious technological or societal traps. Naisbitt's megatrends include shifting from:

- an industrial society to an information-based society
- a forced technology to a high tech mode
- a national economy to a truly global economy
- short range planning to long-term planning
- centralization to decentralization
- institutional help to self-help in fields like health
- representative democracy to participatory democracy
- authority dominated hierarchies to networking
- dominance of the North, in America, to dominance of the South, and
- single option choices to multiple option choices.

Some concepts in *Megatrends* fit a systems model or a participatory democratic model but the book is mainly directed at understanding the most important existing trends that shape our lives.

Future Constructors.   These futurists often have experience and training in science or engineering. They use laboratory experiments and empirical data for proving the points they wish to make. Future constructors plan to control the future and education will play a major role in bringing about the society they prescribe. One of the best statements of how this might be accomplished is found in B. F. Skinner's *Walden II*. Future Constructors believe that people can be educated to cooperate with planners and to make whatever adjustments are required for survival. They feel that future events cannot be left to mere chance or to individual wishes but must be designed for optimum benefit of all people. They say we must make better use of technology and do more with fewer resources. The future will most certainly not take care of itself, but planning, limiting growth, and social engineering can lead to the construction of a better future for all. Many writers in this group feel that very little progress has been made toward planning the future and that time is running out. As R. Buckminister Fuller put it, we must choose either utopia or oblivion.

Donald N. Michael warns in *The Unprepared Society*, that people are not ready for the onslaught of the future, but he argues that utopia is possible through careful planning. He understands that a complete break with the past is impossible, but human activities can be controlled, and the future can be altered in a positive way. Constructors wish to produce a future that provides human satisfaction, some degree of choice, and well-adjusted individuals. Of course, this implies that major social, economic, and environmental problems can be resolved. This is possible only if the best trained planners and engineers are given the power to alter many of the priorities of the present industrial era. John R. Platt makes the point very well in his book *The Step to Man* and in an article in *The Science Teacher* called "Science for Human Survival."

Systems Futurists.   The popularity of general systems theory is reflected by those futurists who see the world as a series of interrelated systems. They point out that change in one area will often create vast and unexpected results in another. Systems futurists believe that our resources are finite on the "spaceship" earth and that we must use them carefully. Members of this group use computer models to study the interaction of such variables as population growth, resource allocation, food supply, land use, and industrial growth. They believe that human survival depends upon a change of attitude among the peoples of the planet who must now recognize the necessity of living within certain constraints. These futurists want to work closely with leaders in government and business to make them aware of thinking globally and adopting a systems approach to planning the social and economic future. Systems futurists are opposed to what Thorstein Veblen called "conspicuous consumption." They believe that education must provide experiences in holistic problem solving and stress the need to limit demand for scarce resources.

Lester R. Brown's books *World Without Borders*, *The Twenty-Ninth Day*, and his yearly *State of the World Reports* are examples of treating demography, agriculture, and economics on a global scale. The "limits to growth" theory of Dennis and Donella Meadows reflect systems thinking. Jan Tinbergen is typical of the systems theorists associated with the Club of Rome. Hazel Henderson's *An End to Economics* and Ervin

Laszlo's *The Systems View of the World* are statements of the position of systems futurists.

Participatory Futurists or Transformationists.   Numerous futurists, especially those with backgrounds in the social sciences and economics, fall into the category of participatory futurists. They agree with John Dewey that all mature human beings should participate in the decisions that affect them. In *Alternatives For America II*, Robert Theobald stresses the need for free access to unbiased information, open communication, dialogue, and authority based on use rather than status. Participatory futurists want to examine all available alternatives in order to bring about consensus on plans of action. This may require the altering of the economic system, educating for problem solving, more cooperative styles of life, and abandoning values of the industrial era.

In *The Everyman Project*, Robert Jungk speaks of forming communication networks to foster social responsibility. Alvin Toffler pointed out in *Future Shock* that the accelerating rate of change makes it dangerous to rely on past experience or modes of thought. In *The Third Wave*, Toffler calls for decentralizing authority and solving most problems, at the local or community level. Like other participatory futurists, Toffler recognizes the existence of tremendous problems but he is convinced that all the people working together can resolve them.

Participatory futurists have recently addressed the need for a hands-on humanistic approach to the management of business and industry. In 1985, Toffler wrote *The Adaptive Corporation*, which called for a new kind of administrative leadership. Managers now need nonlinear skills which will enable them to understand and adapt to swiftly changing conditions. The key to this is found both in superior knowledge of what is going on in the world and creating a work environment in which all employees participate. A similar note is struck by Peters and Waterman in their analysis of the best run companies. They argue for a participatory leadership style in which all workers pull together for excellence in the unit. While these concepts are intended to apply to business organizations, they also can be adopted to education and government.

Evolutionary Futurists.   Emphasis on moral and spiritual values rather than on technological growth is characteristic of evolutionary futurists. They view the future with optimism because materialism and the rapid consumption of vital resources will be replaced by a new consciousness and more humane lifestyles. Evolutionary futurists have roots in the past, especially in classical literature. Some of the concepts fostered by this group can be found in Maria Montessori's *The Absorbent Mind*, 1967. These futurists envision a world in which human beings undergo a transformation to a higher form of spiritual awareness and achieve integration of body, mind, and spirit. Living in harmony with themselves and the universe is their goal. They believe that leadership should be in the hands of those people who demonstrate a strong sense of moral and ethical responsibility.

Willis Harman's *An Incomplete Guide to the Future* and E. F. Shumacher's *A Guide for the Perplexed* are typical of the works of these futurists. They are concerned about improving the quality of human life on earth. They believe that natural and human resources are gifts which must be used with wisdom. Education should foster a strong sense of moral and ethical responsibility. Education is the means by which wisdom and spiritual values are acquired. Schools should be used to discipline the mind and aid understanding of the broad range of alternatives open to everyone. Mass media values, keeping up with the Joneses, and specialized job training are just the opposite of what the evolutionary futurists want. They are interested in general education for moral development which would include the classical wisdom of ages past.

Humanistic Futurists.   George Leonard's classic *Education and Ecstasy* is a statement of many of the beliefs of the humanistic futurists. These people believe that the actions we undertake now create or invent the future. Humanistic futurists believe that modern society places too much emphasis on role playing, competition, status, and materialistic success. This has distorted human nature and makes it difficult to pass from the industrial era into an age of awareness. People must remove their masks, become more sensitive to others, and learn compassion. Leonard feels that until people are more aware of their own bodies, feelings and intellects, they cannot live fully in the present or create an adequate future. All of us need to deal honestly with our own emotions and discover what is of real value in life. *Transpersonal Education: A Curriculum for Feeling and Being*, edited by Gay Hendricks and James Fadiman, suggests the kind of schooling humanistic futurists desire. They want to see the earth kept beautiful and safe to stimulate joy in living. This requires better protection of the environment and limits to economic growth. Teachers should be co-learners and role models in an open, trusting, sensitive learning situation. Learning must be an integral part of the total human experience and students must get in touch with their own emotional being. In addition to creating sensitive and compassionate human beings, this group wants to challenge the values of the current industrial age. Humanists believe we have moved too far toward the kind of world described in Orwell's *1984* and Huxley's *Brave New World*. In order for each person to achieve his or her full potential, the highly technological structured world of business and industry must be abandoned. Affective learning is as important as cognitive learning. The study of alternative lifestyles, dream sharing, and sensory awareness activities would be part of the curriculum. This is the theme of Bob Samples' *The Metamorphic Mind: A Celebration of Creative Consciousness*.

Visionaries and Radicals.   Two smaller groups with quite different conceptions of the future are the visionary futurists and the radical futurists. Those who fall into the visionary category refuse to be bound by the constraints of common-sense reality. They stress imagination for freeing people from the shackles of the past and enabling them to leap into a new era. They envision a future in which a complete transformation of human nature will occur and universal consciousness will develop. They believe Jules Verne and H. G. Wells were able to anticipate future events because their imaginations were unlimited. The idea that intelligence and awareness may transcend known human capacity is used in television programs like "Star Trek" and in the books of Arthur Clarke, Harlan Ellison, and Kurt Vonnegut, Jr.

A leading visionary spokesperson is F. M. Esfandiary. In *Optimism One* and *Up-Wingers*, he argues that such problems as resource allocation, energy, world peace, and pollution are irrelevant. By attaining cosmic awareness, new generations will have the whole universe at their disposal and decisions will be made by all humanity through an instantaneous universal referendum. Adrian Berry, in *The Next Thousand Years: A Vision of Man's Future in the Universe*, speaks of electronic brain stimulation and expanding human horizons through linking the brain to computers. Those who do not share these optimistic views are not considered futurists at all by the visionary futurists.

The best known book by a radical futurist is Illich's *Deschooling Society*. Illich, like Paul Goodman, Arthur Waskow and Everett Reimer, believes schools foster bad social values and that they cannot be reformed. Radicals want to overthrow the existing power structure and drastically alter society to gain personal freedom and ensure the well being of future generations. They think the past is repressive and should be forgotten. Distrusting all forms of authority, radical futurists view economic growth as just another form of exploitation. They say individuals must be freed from the burdens of economic and governmental oppression. For them, technology is to be feared when it is in the hands of a power elite.

IMPLICATIONS FOR EDUCATIONAL THEORY

A great deal of the history of American education is the history of conflict over future aims and goals. When Comenius wrote about his concept of pansophia and his belief that human beings could better themselves through schooling, he was preparing for a better future. Locke, Rousseau, Pestalozzi, and Herbart concerned themselves with the kind of education that they thought would bring about a utopian society. Most speculative plans for educational reform have been directed toward the kind of world that would be free of the problems and weaknesses of the present. Those who wrote plans for a national system of education in 1795 and Jefferson's plan for public education in Virginia were also futuristic in the sense that they aimed at producing a better society and a more democratic one in years to come.

It is easy to trace elements of futurism in the educational theory of John Dewey. His pragmatic philosophy centered on the question of how we can know and control the world. Dewey created an educational theory to meet the needs of a growing, dynamic, urban, industrial society which was in constant flux. His principle of the continuous reconstruction of human experience in the light of new learning is one commonly found among futuristic writers. The idea of making a better society through the schools is central to social reconstructionists who followed Dewey.

The futures field has been heavily influenced by economics and sociology, but it is interdisciplinary and broadly based. No adequate theory of education for the future can ignore the wide range of forces that influence the human condition. Marshall McLuhan has attacked the "fragmented unrelation" of the industrial era school curricula and pointed out that any subject studied in depth at once relates to other subjects. A futuristic educational philosophy must be global, open, synergetic, interdisciplinary, and oriented toward cultural synthesis.

Americans and citizens of the other industrial nations appear to be caught up in the pursuit of hedonism and what Veblen called "conspicuous consumption." Little effort is made to understand the past or to trace roots of the culture so that people seldom appreciate their cultural heritage. Looking with apprehension at the future, many opt for a life centered in the present and pursue the immediate gratification of desires. Following the crowd to materialistic values and situational ethics as fostered by the mass media and commercial advertising is a poor approach to the future. Those with no sense of the past cannot locate themselves in historical perspective or live vicariously through their posterity. This is not to say that the future should be approached by way of a rear view mirror image of the past. A traditional mind set and the uncritical acceptance of earlier values may prevent us from accepting change or making the best choices among alternatives. Values of the Puritan ethic are not helpful in guiding the use of leisure time nor can we expect an optimum future to be shaped by the ideals of the industrial era. Education must encourage the study and the use of the past to take maximum advantage of collective human experience, but it must not allow the future to be subsumed under the values of the past or the present.

An accelerating rate of technological change together with the emergence of new problems in the adaptive nonmaterial culture is accepted as a fact of life by most futurists. There are disagreements about limiting technological growth and about the kinds of technology that may be most important for the good life of the future but very few advocate a "back to nature" movement or a smashing of machines as the Luddites tried to do in the nineteenth century. Rapid change and invention will almost certainly continue unless there is a total breakdown of civilization resulting in a new dark age or total annihilation. Certainly, the knowledge explosion and the growth of electronic communications networks will have a major impact on education. If learning is to be an instrument for survival, it must prepare people to understand and control technological change. Change for its own sake or for mere economic growth is not necessarily healthy but many of the most important problems require a technological solution and little progress can be expected unless people have access to new information and the tools for using it. The great task for educational theory is clearing the way for social inventions that will match expansion in technology and keep up with rapid change.

This change continues to occur at a rate that staggers the imagination. In 1986, it was estimated that the world contained some 5 billion computers. Granted, many of these were mere chips small enough to fit into credit cards but nevertheless computers outnumbered people on this planet. In the same year, 7,000 new articles in the scientific fields appeared every day, while new fiber optic communications cables made a quantum leap in the capacity to carry information. Interactive television made distance learning a viable option by 1990, vastly increasing the opportunity to carry formal learning to remote sites.

Many serious scholars including Robert Heilbroner and Cristopher Lasch are not at all convinced that a Malthusian apocalypse or a nuclear holocaust can be prevented. Nevertheless, any hope for inventing the future by human action is predicated upon the assumption that people can understand and control the forces which shape their world. In the past, people beset by obscure problems and difficulties often adopted the "whatever will be will be" attitude and abandoned faith in human capacity. This "failure of nerve" which has occurred periodically in human history makes planning impossible and abandons reason for fate. Even when problems appear to be insurmountable, educators must have faith in the ability of human intelligence to comprehend the world and to control the destiny of humanity. The belief that wisdom and rational action cannot alter the future is a self-fulfilling prophesy which education must combat.

There is a tendency for writers in futurism, especially science fiction authors and utopian novelists, to suggest desirable goals without saying how these goals are to be achieved. Futurism in educational theory will do well to consider John Dewey's argument that means and ends can never be separated and that the ends do not justify the means. Goals, ends, and aims in future education must be evaluated not only on the basis of their desirability but also on the criterion of the possibilities for implementation. Simple solutions to complex problems often have side effects that are as bad or worse than the original problems. It must be remembered that nothing is done in a vacuum and what is involved in reaching a goal is just as important as the goal itself. In society and education, as in ecology and economics, any change or alteration will have widespread and often unpredicted effects beyond the primary area in which the change takes place.

Maximum realization of the human potential cannot be achieved unless people work together to resolve the really crucial problems such as preventing nuclear war, protecting the natural environment, and meeting the basic needs of all people for scarce resources. Solving basic problems is necessary but not sufficient for realization of the human potential. There must also be the opportunity to achieve the good life, the life of greatest value. This, in turn, implies the availability of alternatives and the ability to choose. Schools often set arbitrary limits to choice and inhibit creativity. Limits are also set by society in that models are taken from the industrial era with its emphasis on materialism, production, exploitation, and growth. It is incumbent upon future educators to make sure that education clearly delineates the problems, provides learners with necessary tools and information, and encourages the selection of sane alternatives. Every educational plan for the future must show that it enhances the chances for human survival and the quality of life.

CHARACTERISTICS OF FUTURISTIC EDUCATION

Some leading educational futurists have suggested specific changes in order to help bring about a viable future for the citizens of tomorrow. While these alternatives are speculative, they do address the problem of the inadequacy of existing bureaucratic schools to meet the needs of the next century. Their purpose is to criticize certain characteristics and practices in current educational institutions and to offer possible substitute practices more likely to meet future requirements.

Replacing Linear with Synergetic Processes.   Institutions are established to meet certain human needs. They are apt, however, to become self-sustaining bureaucracies with goals of self-aggrandizement and immortality. The school, like most bureaucracies, has a dominant nonhuman priority—its own survival. The objectives of the institution are necessarily more important than individual objectives. It is possible to change this aim of permanence by changing two other essential characteristics of the bureaucracy—its linear design and division of labor.

American institutions have been, by Theobald's analysis (1970), successful in the recent past by concentrating on major goals while ignoring secondary and tertiary consequences. This, he specifies, is a consequence of linear design. He cites seven inherent weaknesses which are characteristic of linear organizations. They are most applicable to the school.

1. The school can only receive information that it is designed to receive. This requires that information must be adjusted to the classification system. Schools are primarily designed to receive state-approved textbooks. Information must conform to specialized courses. Teachers cannot easily provide new materials because of the cost and time involved.
2. Linear organizations can only make linear decisions. This implies that educators must extend existing patterns. Administrators cannot make decisions from the perspective of students or teachers.
3. Linear institutions are easily overloaded. Teachers often have too many students, activities, and information to process in short periods of time. Decisions become difficult to administer properly.
4. Linear organization people tend to be promoted until they reach a level of incompetence. In education, upward mobility requires many teachers to become administrators.
5. Linear organizations are capable of reproducing. This is especially true in higher education as departments attempt to gain strength through numbers.
6. Linear organizations tend to repress unfavorable information. Educators rarely pass unfavorable information up or down the organizational hierarchy since it may reflect upon an individual's competence.
7. Linear organizations are only capable of controlling people who wish to be controlled.

A synergetic system is proposed as an alternative to linear organization. In its early stages, it is perceived as an "ad-hocracy," which is Toffler's term for the creation of task forces which move within bureaucracies to complete temporary tasks. In a more advanced stage, this would be replaced by what Theobald labels "consentives." Consentives already exist in the form of buyers' cooperatives, community ecology groups, and Ralph Nader's Raiders. In education, the alternative of a synergetic, process-oriented organization first requires a distinction between training and education.

Education Is More Than Training.   The educational system is designed to carry out a process of training. Training perpetuates existing information and reinforces current trends. It is usually a memorization/regurgitation, short-term method of learning. Whenever, for example, students are expected to memorize the presidents of the United States, they are being trained. The true purpose of education, however, is to study the principles operant within an activity in order to facilitate new questions and new answers. In essence, education requires an environment in which students are not asked questions for which the answers are known; if the questions involve predetermined conclusions, the process is training.

Both education and training should be provided in the school. There are, obviously, skills such as keyboard usage and welding in which many students would choose to be trained. The problem is that training has dominated the curriculum. It is suggested that many school problems are attributable to students' growing resistance to training. Even on college campuses many students are questioning the assumptions inherent in the present system. For them, learning through training is not "relevant" because it does not provide an atmosphere for re-examination of society's priorities, classifications, habits, and values. Although training was an asset to the industrial revolution, the emerging communications era requires an educational system which will enhance the development of new values and behavior patterns. It will also add to the ability to solve problems and to communicate in a meaningful way.

Education for the Unknown.   Throughout the history of education, students attended schools to learn what they did not know from teachers who were presumed to know. A grave error in traditional education was that it gave insufficient attention to fielding problems for which there was no known answer. Learners emerged from the schools with little skill in inquiry or in probing for new answers. Now, however, focus must be on working together to deal with probabilities and uncertainties. Experts may be used to clarify aspects of problems, but the most important human and societal difficulties cannot be resolved by experts alone. Students need to think of learning as a technique of cooperative problem analysis and sharing of sources of information. Information must become knowledge and knowledge must become wisdom before unknown issues can be resolved. At this point in time, we do not have the answer to many of the most important problems, such as controlling nuclear arms, ending international terrorism, and providing basic human services to all the people of the world. Future education will fail, unless it moves away from exclusive treatment of what is well understood and toward helping students cope with the unknown. Problem solving, communication skills, and willingness to risk making mistakes are critical to such efforts. As George Leonard has argued, real learning means that the student must be prepared to change and to risk having his or her prejudices altered. It is very clear that survival depends on learning how to cope with major problems that are as yet unresolved.

Structural Authority versus Sapiential Authority.

Structural authority provided an important rationale in the industrial-era world view. Railroads were built, assembly lines were developed, and warfare was accomplished through the principle of structural authority. This authority, which is derived from one's position or rank, is the dominant pattern in educational institutions. The organizing prerequisite of the school is one whereby professors "teach" and the students "learn." Under the auspices of structural authority, the student is expected to accept the information, assume that it is correct, ingurgitate it as accurately as possible, and regurgitate all information deemed significant by the teacher. The critical factor is that the authority of the teacher is established by position rather than competency.

Sapiential authority, a term developed by Robert Theobald and Tom Paterson, is proposed as a future alternative form of authority. Sapiential authority is not based upon title or rank. It depends upon no sanctions from governments, schools, or other institutions. Rather, sapiential authority is based upon the possession of information, knowledge, or ideas which find support among others. A model for this exists today in the learned societies and professions. When a paper is read or a thesis is presented, it is accepted or rejected by those most knowledgeable about the field, and one's institutional position does not protect one's words from peers' scrutiny. A major qualification of sapiential authority is that all participants have the opportunity for critical analysis of any given piece of information.

Many people fear that the breakdown of traditional authority will result in chaos. This is particularly true of the new religious and political conservatives who became powerful in the 1980s. They want to return to earlier conditions as a psychological rejection of uncomfortable change. They urge schools to "return to traditional values" with stress on basic, noncontroversial curriculum materials and reliance on the authority of the teacher. The new "right" appears to be moving education far back into the past at exactly the time it needs to look to the future.

There are those in every organization who have been promoted beyond their level of competence and fear any attack on structural authority because it threatens their security. Schools, like other bureaucratic institutions, use structural authority to protect incompetent individuals and useless regulations. Even though sapiential authority has not yet received serious attention, it is a necessary part of education for future survival. One qualification is necessary: this authority should not be interpreted as license or made to support the belief that any idea is just as valid as any other. But the problems of the present and the future are so vast and so difficult that every individual's best contributions are needed. Education must, therefore, provide conditions that allow for perception of sapiential authority by each individual and for development of each individual's full potential.

School Learning versus Life-Long Learning.   The schools of the industrial age have become so specialized that there is no longer room in the curriculum for developing a broad understanding of the world. In his book *Overskill*, Eugene Schwartz shows that specialization is self-defeating. Civilization cannot be saved by a group of highly trained specialists who do not understand other fields.

Technology for the information age requires experts but there are many places in modern society where specialized information and skills can be obtained. In order to facilitate life-long learning, the school must focus on more education (rather than training) and sapiential authority instead of rigid structure. There must be an atmosphere conducive to interdisciplinary studies and humanistic values. Modern world problems are interrelated and their solution depends upon what Fuller calls a concept of synergy. He means that the unique behavior of whole systems cannot be predicted by any behaviors of their component functions taken separately.

As Dewey often said, school should not be separate from the community, and the child need not be in conflict with the curriculum. Dichotomies between theory and practice or between idealistic and technical subjects may become academic as learning is understood to be a life-long practice. The mass media is already engaged in education. Xerox has an educational program which is almost of university status and many corporations train their own computer operators. Adult and continuing education will surely grow. So long as the concept of reaching a certain educational plateau (such as high school graduation) and then ending education to enter the work force remains in vogue, specialized training will remain paramount. We are, however, entering a learning society and an age of information. People must now expect that they will go on learning throughout life, not only as preparation for earning a living but also for avocations and leisure activities. Preparation for a life of learning should replace the idea of terminal schooling in the theory and practice of education.

Replacing Games with Cooperation.   Educational institutions rely primarily upon the use of positive and negative sanctions which result in an "I win-you lose" competitive structure. Grading practices often lead to sorting children into success groups and failure groups. Educators talk about cooperation but enforce competition between students. As John Goodlad has pointed out, grades in school are good predictors of further success in school but not good predictors of success in jobs or in life. Good workers, compassionate human beings, caring parents, and concerned citizens are not made by winning high grades in a competitive school environment. Winners tend to be disproportionately middle-class, white, and affluent. Of course, the winners are also losers because they have been taught to perpetuate competition in work and in world affairs. This is a zero sum game in which everyone eventually will lose. The ecological crisis is one physical representation of this problem. Competitive attitudes put stress on limited natural resources and endanger wildlife. They are no longer useful in giant industrial cooperations that control goods and manage markets.

Learning how to cooperate is a future survival skill which educational institutions must now begin to practice and to teach. Students trained as passive, noninvolved spectators in the classrooms are not apt to be involved in cooperative activities outside. The mass media (especially the medium of television) also tend to promote isolation, noninvolvement, and spectatorism. School activities need to be made more cooperative and action-oriented with all students emotionally involved. Education involves change and the school situation must promote change in the learner. A passive attitude does not promote change and neither does competition. At the very least, students must be prepared to risk their prejudices if learning is to take place. If education is the process that changes the learner, the traditional school environment will simply not do. Within the existing school system, the competitive environment has precluded all efforts of teaching cooperation. In the future, it may be possible for educators to teach a healthy competitive perspective within a cooperative framework. At present, schools pick up competitive attitudes to control and manipulate children.

Skill in Evaluation. Students in the twenty-first century will regard it as curious that learners once thought teachers and textbooks were unquestioned authorities. In the information age, so many sources of knowledge exist that a constant examination of what is "true" and what is "useful" must be made. Literacy exercises like checking one written account against another and the comparison of various interpretations will be supplemented by computer checks of validity of facts. Priority must be given to critical viewing at a time when vast amounts of information are transmitted by the medium of television. No person in the future will be educated unless he or she has learned to detect subtle psychological persuasion, false logic, emotional appeals, and similar tricks used to make people believe what is not true. If unbiased information and the ability to apply that information to problems is critical to future well-being, all students must be good at evaluation. The argument of Postman and Weingartner that all students need a built in "crap detector" will become even more valid as the information age develops. The ability to analyze and evaluate information was not stressed in many of the industrial age schools and it is not a part of many of the reform plans that followed "A Nation at Risk." Nevertheless, the lifelong learner and problem solver of tomorrow must be an expert at critical evaluation. Since our information becomes obsolete rapidly, Alvin Toffler argues that in the future, the illiterate person will be one who has not learned how to "learn, unlearn, and relearn" (Toffler, 1970, 414).

The Future School: A Problem Analysis/Resource Distribution Center. In the future, educational institutions at all levels must become resource centers for the distribution and creation of unbiased information. Universities have long been expected to achieve this goal on a national and international basis. The linking of telecommunications and computers makes vast quantities of information available to any group or individual. Data banks for information may now be found in schools and even in many homes. Obviously schools will need to stop concentrating on the memorization of bits of information and start stressing how to find and use information. The process of comparing conflicting accounts of events and evaluating the validity of available data must take a much more important role in education. The research function of determining whether or not information can be trusted can no longer be left to universities alone. Each future citizen must have unbiased data upon which to make vital decisions, and the skills of judging information must be taught early in life.

It should be pointed out that critical viewing is also a survival skill since a great deal of our knowledge about the world comes to us through television. Raw data and unorganized information are not very useful in solving problems. Knowing how to quickly find and systematize information will surely become a vital part of tomorrow's education. Even when it is identified and organized, information is not knowledge and knowledge is not wisdom. Students must learn to make evaluative judgments, to analyze, clarify, generalize, and understand. Many futurists have said that we are drowning in data and information. It is knowledge and wisdom that must be developed through the process of education.

Much that passes for education today is of little value in helping students learn to solve problems. Giving information to the pupil is an inadequate means of producing self-directed scholars and future citizens. The questions for which answers are unknown are the most significant ones. Theobald's contention that everything already discovered should be called training and the term education should be used only for unresolved issues has implications for problem analysis centers. Future problems will certainly require input from individuals with different backgrounds and training, therefore students need to learn how to cooperate to reach consensus. Inquiry, discovery, and scientific methods of learning must take precedence over lectures, reading texts, and selecting answers from multiple-choice tests. The problem analysis/resource distribution centers can be modeled on some of the best of existing practices and earlier experiments such as those of the progressives. It is not necessary to invent a totally new process but merely to change the focus of education from the acquisition of information to the application of data to problem situations in a cooperative and action-oriented environment.

FUTURES CURRICULUM

Professional educators are not waiting for futures programs to gain acceptance in all schools before taking action. The popularity of the annual meeting of the Education Section of the World Futures Society, attended by hundreds of classroom teachers, attests to the interest many have in futurism. While formal courses in futurism are most often found only at university level, thousands of teachers incorporate elements of futures studies into the classes they normally offer. Communications networks and publications exist to promote various methods and materials used in the futures education movement. Some universities such as the University of Massachusetts and the University of Houston at Clear Lake offer degree programs in futurism. Such universities also conduct courses and workshops for teachers interested in giving a future focus to the subjects they teach. Some of the characteristics of futures programs in elementary and secondary schools are as follows.

Interdisciplinary Approach.   Futurism in education is not confined to any single discipline or subject area. Indeed, the overarching feature of treating the future in the curriculum is the interdisciplinary focus. The idea of a core curriculum as invented by Herbart and used by the progressives is central to futurism. Relating history to sociology and economics, or stressing the connections between biology, psychology, and ecology are common practices. A characteristic of futures is that the impact of one field of human endeavor on another is studied. The symbiotic relationship of plants and animals living in the same environments or the impact economic development may have on natural ecological balance is analyzed. The word "synergy" describes the change that altering one aspect of world may have on another. Synergetic, symbiotic, integrated, holistic, core, interdisciplinary studies are found in the futures curriculum. It is believed that the narrow boundaries of disciplines and narrow specialization may interfere with the complete understanding of an issue. Future problem solvers must be able to bring together information from a variety of subject areas if their solutions are to be viable. Innovative methods need not be for the elite only. A 1989 study in Orange County, California, found that poor achievers gained most by problem solving and creative classroom activities.

Problem Analysis Focus.   Most futures courses attempt to help students analyze the problems around them. To say that things cost more because of inflation or that food is scarce in Africa because the soil is thin represents inadequate understanding. In order to solve problems and to select wisely between alternative futures, it is necessary to distinguish between probable causes and glib explanations. Futures courses are known for probing deeply to find the underlying causes of difficulties, especially social ones. When the reasons for failure in some human endeavors are understood, students are in a better position to evaluate possible, probable, and preferable futures. The study of trends and probable projections is strengthened if students have learned to be critical and to search for reasons when things do not go as expected. Inventing the future is not mere speculation about personal and societal preferences, it involves being realistic, critical, analytic, and careful. Futures courses also stress the power of the individual and the group to alter the future. The notion that "whatever will be will be" and the belief that human action can make no difference in the course of human events is not accepted. Fatalism is replaced with a pro-active orientation and a belief that many alternative futures are possible. Participation, involvement, creativity, and choosing are stressed by futurists as ways of getting people to take the initiative instead of waiting for the future to shock them.

Faith in Human Ability to Control the Future.   In spite of the critical and analytic aspects of futures courses, the field is generally optimistic. Obviously the world is in crisis and the possibility of such a catastrophe as thermonuclear war is real, but futurists believe that the major dilemmas with which societies are faced are capable of being solved. There is considerable skepticism about the viability of current technological solutions to global problems but futuristic literature is not highly pessimistic. Futurism stresses the power that well-educated citizens have in controlling their own lives and tends to support the belief that human action can prevent the apocalyptic end of civilization. Stress is placed on the notion that what we do today will determine the shape of the future. While some attention is given to forecasting coming events, futures courses attempt to develop insight into the major current problems, in an effort to show what must be done to prevent disaster and ensure a desirable tomorrow.

Open-Ended, Inquiry Based Methodology.   Futures courses attempt to avoid the mere imposing of facts and information on students. Much of the curricula is hypothetical, especially where possible and probable alternative futures are concerned. Evaluation of student written scenarios and classroom delphi polling are often used. Schools usually do not have access to sophisticated instruments such as the computer-based cross-impact matrix, but students can be involved in trend extrapolation, modeling, and various kinds of futures games. Teachers attempt to avoid authority relationships or any attempt to dictate the right answer but they try to promote logical thinking and careful analysis by students. The teacher as facilitator promotes problem solving, informed speculation, creative imagination, and systematic thinking. Student involvement does not mean that one future alternative is just as good as another or that the courses have no intellectual rigor. Students are encouraged to project themselves into a variety of probable future situations and to think logically about the problems and opportunities such situations might create. The use of science fiction literature, exploratory predictions, attitude surveys, and brainstorming techniques is common. A major goal is creating individuals who will be more likely to manage their own future in a pro-active way.

Value Teaching in Futuristics.   A strong value component is found in most futures courses. Values usually emerge whenever alternative futures are considered because of the nature of the choices students must make. For example, continued economic growth produces pollution, the destruction of natural resources, urban congestion, and materialism. If these by-products of expansion are to be avoided, future citizens must be willing to live on a lower standard or to adopt other styles of life. The question of whether or not affluence brings about the good life can hardly be considered without challenging cherished values. Futurism requires students to constantly re-examine adherence to the values of the current industrial era. Concepts like simple living, appropriate technology, environmental protection, zero population growth, and world political stability imply serious reconstruction of personal and societal values. Most futurists think that the present trend toward preparing for higher grades and better scores on college boards does not support values education or treat ethical issues.

FUTURE TRENDS

While we cannot be certain about what will take place in the immediate future and long range forecasts are always risky, there are certain trends in American education that seem likely to continue and some worldwide forecasts can be made with a high degree of probability that they will occur. Of course, any real major change such as a new technique of learning or a war would alter trends in a dramatic way. If some degree of stability continues in the next decades the following educational speculations seem safe:

1. Education will become lifelong and will continue throughout the year. The present nine-month school will be replaced by learning opportunities available at any time. Mass media and home based microcomputers will be used as educational aids for the very young. Adults will not finish school but will continue to learn throughout life. It will be necessary to retrain constantly in order to keep up with changes in various fields. Cycles of learning and work will replace the present pattern of school first and work later. Learning for life and leisure will be more important than job training.

2. As new ways of obtaining an education emerge, the old system of semester terms and units of credit will be altered. Means will be found to certify that the learner has the necessary level of skill and information to enter a new learning environment without showing academic credentials. Since much of the learning will be fostered by industry or given in courses, transcripts will be less significant. There will be a variety of educational delivery systems, including independent study degree programs.

3. The curriculum will be very much enlarged to include new discoveries, leisure and avocational skills, travel, human values, group therapy, and psychological guidance. The idea of a curriculum as broad as life itself, which Comenius suggested, will finally become a reality. There will be nothing which cannot be formally studied if the students are interested.

4. Fewer classroom teachers will be needed but there will be an increase in the number of people engaged in teaching and learning. Long years of training may be required before a person is allowed to manage a future learning environment. However, much learning will be informal and lifelong so that the distinction between the teacher and the taught will erode away. Learning facilitators will perform a variety of functions and educational centers will have differentiated staffing. Computers and teaching machines will carry on many teaching tasks but specialists will be available to help with any learning disability and to stimulate students.

5. There will be less competition, less standardization, less grouping by ability, and less pressure on the student. More attention will be given to growing, developing, problem solving, communication, and personal goals. Since learning will be an activity for life, knowing how to learn in an efficient and joyful way will be a very highly prized future skill.

6. Age specific compulsory learning institutions (called schools) will be replaced by a variety of diversified learning environments. Young people will be able to take responsibility for their own learning at a much earlier age. It will be common to find children and senior citizens in the same learning situations. A learning society

will emerge, which means that most people will spend a great deal of every day of their lives in some kind of learning environment.

7. An emerging contingent workforce with an ever increasing number of part-time workers who have little job security and few health benefits will require flexibility in educational aims, content, and length of schooling. The National Association of Temporary Services, based on a DRI/McGraw Hill survey of 200 temporary help employment firms revealed explosive expansion of part-time, temporary work for the forseeable future. The number of temporary employees increased some 17.3 percent in 1992 to 1.3 million.

Senator Howard Metzenbaum of Ohio saw the possibility of 50 percent part time workers by the year 2,000. He finds such a possibility alarming for the nation's standard of living. With corporate downsizing, overtime work is used instead of new hires. When additional employees are needed, part time and temporary workers are used to keep costs down. The challenge for education is to prepare individuals for job market reality.

8. Technology will make possible many new educational possibilities. Telecommunications and computers will make information available to everyone. People will be able to link themselves electronically with others who are interested in the subjects they wish to study and to contact the best known experts in the field. Chemical and electronic learning aids including brain stimulation will be used to help concentration and eliminate learning blocks. The skill required to quickly find and evaluate any information on any subject will become as common as reading is today. New companies will develop which will produce and market educational materials as well as entertainment computers and a myriad of new communication networks.

9. Education will stress the understanding of the forces in the environment that must be controlled in order to ensure the maximum realization of human potential and the good life. Problem-solving centers will emerge and students will become skilled at finding alternative solutions to all major difficulties. Greater attention will be given to world understanding and to the issues that involve all of the people on earth. All major new developments in the world (and perhaps in space) will immediately take a place in the curriculum. At the same time, much educational activity will occur with small interest groups, or it will be directed toward the solution of community problems. The ability to analyze data, to think in a systematic way, and to be realistic about the possibilities of the future will be skills everyone will need to develop.

As this book has tried to point out, the past, present, and future are always related. A real understanding of what has happened in American education and why it happened is essential for guiding action now and for inventing the future. As Lasch argued in *The Culture of Narcissism*, those without an appreciation of history have no interest in the future because they live only for the present. Our hedonistic culture may stress the importance of living now and letting tomorrow take care of itself, but such an attitude is devastating to the teaching profession. Toffler in *Powershift* noted that for over three hundred years the world was perceived as a great clock or machine, in which knowable causes led to predictable results. He believes we are witnessing one of the most important changes in the history of power. Toffler stated that it is clear that knowledge, a source of the highest quality of power, is gaining importance in our society and world. He projects that the most important powershift is the hidden shift in the relationships between violence, wealth, and knowledge as societies speed toward their collision with the future. Toffler in *War and Anti-war* calls for an understanding of the linkage between knowledge, wealth, and war.

Educators must be future-oriented if they are to prepare students for a world of tomorrow which surely will be vastly different from today. The background of historical understanding and the appreciation of issues and conflicts of the past provides the best foundation we can have for predicting trends and preparing for a viable future. Perhaps the most important use of history is that it shows us how far short of our own traditions we have fallen and stimulates us to strive for a higher realization of our individual and collective potential in the world of the future.

BIBLIOGRAPHY

Botkin, James, Mahdi Elmandjra, and Mircea Malitza. *No Limits to Learning: Bridging the Human Gap*. New York: Pergamon Press, 1979.

Bowman, Jim, Fred Kierstead, Chris Dede, and John Pulliam. *The Far Side of the Future: Social Problems and Educational Reconstruction*. Washington, D.C.: World Future Society, 1978.

Boyer, William, *America's Future: Transition to the 21st Century*. New York: Praeger, 1984.

Boyett, Joseph, and Henry Conn, *Workplace 2000*. New York: Plume-Peguin, 1992.

Bright, James. *Practical Technology Forecasting*. New York: Industrial Management Center, 1978.

Brown, Lester. *The Twenty-Ninth Day*. New York: W.W. Norton, 1978.

Cetron, Marvin. *Schools of the Future: How American Business and Education Can Cooperate to Save Our Schools*. New York: McGraw-Hill, 1985.

Cornish, Edward. *The Study of the Future: An Introduction to the Art and Science of Understanding and Shaping Tomorrow's World*. Washington, D.C.: World Future Society, 1978.

Didsbury, Howard, ed. *Challenges and Opportunities from Now to 2001*. Bethesda, MD: World Future Society, 1986.

Dillin, John. "As 'Good' Jobs Become 'Bad' Jobs, Congress Takes a Closer Look". *Christian Science Monitor* (June 18, 1993):1, 4. ___. "Temps Getting More Work," *Tulsa World* (June 27, 1993):2G.

Dunn, Joe, and Howard Preston. *Future South-A Historical Perspective for the Twenty-First Century*. Urbana: University of Illinois Press, 1991.

Glines, Don. "Can Schools of Today Survive Very Far into the 21st Century?" *NASSP Bulletin* 73(514). February 1989.

Hipple, Theodore, ed. *The Futures of Education 1975–2000*. Santa Monica, CA: Goodyear, 1974.

Jungk, Robert. *The Everyman Project: Resources for a Humane Future*. London: Thames and Hudson, 1976.

Kadaba, Lini S. "Futurist (Joseph Coates) Identified Issues That Will Transform Corporations," *Tulsa World* (June 13, 1993):4G.

Kierstead, Fred, Jim Bowman, and Christopher Dede, eds. *Educational Futures: Sourcebook*. Washington, D.C.: World Future Society, 1979.

Naisbitt, John. *Megatrends*. New York: Warner Books, 1982.

___. *Megatrends 2000: Ten New Directions for the 1990s*. New York: Morrow, 1990.

Paepke, C. Owen. *The Evolution of Progress*. New York: Random House, 1993.

Pulliam, John, and Jim Bowman. *Educational Futurism: In Pursuance of Survival*. Norman, OK: University of Oklahoma Press, 1974.

Roffler, Alvin, ed. *The Adaptive Corporation*. New York: McGraw-Hill, 1985.

___. *The Third Wave*. New York: Morrow, 1980.

Rubin, Louis, ed. *The Future of Education: Perspectives on Tomorrow's Schooling*. Boston: Allyn & Bacon, 1975.

Scileppi, John. *A Systems View of Education: A Model for Change*. Lanham, MD: University Press of America, 1984.

Theobald, Robert. *An Alternative Future for America II*. Rev. ed. Chicago: Swallow Press, 1970.

___. *Turning the Century*. New York: Knowledge Systems, 1992.

Toffler, Alvin, ed. *Learning for Tomorrow*. New York: Random House, 1974.

___. *Future Shock*. New York: Random House, 1970.

___. *Powershift, Wealth and Violence at the Edge of the 21st Century*. New York: Bantam, 1990.

___. *War and Anti-War*. New York: Little Brown, 1993.

World Future Society, ed. *The Future, A Guide to Information Sources*. Washington, D.C.: World Future Society, 1979.

Wirth, Arthur. *Education and Work for the Year 2000: Choices We Face*. San Francisco: Jossey-Bass, 1992.

GENERAL BIBLIOGRAPHY

Bailyn, Bernard. *Education in Forming of American Society*. Chapel Hill, NC: University of North Carolina Press, 1960, 147pp. This is a critical essay on American history of education from the cultural standpoint. It surveys the main themes of educational history yet to be written. There is a useful evaluation of earlier movements in American cultural history, such as Puritanism, philanthropy, race relations, and the growth of sectarianism.

Butts, Freeman. *The Education of the West: A Formative Chapter in the History of Civilization*. New York: McGraw-Hill, 1933. A very sound general history by one of the best known American educational historians.

____. *Public Education in the United States: From Revolution to Reform*. New York: Holt, Rinehart and Winston, 1978. The work is outstanding for its detail and depth of study. It is the best account of legislation and court cases in recent years.

Commager, Henry Steele, ed. *Documents of American History*. New York: Appleton-Century-Crofts, 1963, 739 pp., including index. Contains 665 noteworthy documents significant in the shaping of American history. Documents pertinent to education are included.

Cremin, Lawrence. *The Wonderful World of Ellwood Patterson Cubberly: An Essay on the Historiography of American Education*. New York: Columbia University Teachers College, Bureau of Publications, 1965. An interesting and delightful treatment of the first great American educational historian by a leading modern scholar in the same field.

____. *Public Education*. New York: Basic Books, 1976. A treatment of the history of American education with attention given to public policy, the emerging role of government, and the issues over control of schools.

____. *American Education: The Colonial Experience 1607–1783*. New York: Harper and Row, 1970. An analysis and description of the formative period of American education during the drive for independence.

____. *American Education: The National Experience 1783–1876*. New York: Harper and Row, 1980. An analysis and description of American education during the period of building and unifying the nation.

____. *American Education: The Metropolitan Experience 1876–1980*. New York: Harper and Row, 1988. A portrayal of American education as the nation achieved world power status. Identification of three persistent elements of American education—popularization, multitudinousness, and politicization.

____. *Popular Education and Its Discontents*. New York: Harper and Row, 1990. A compilation of three essays that explore increasing dissatisfaction with education, radical changes in society and education, and a continuing effort to solve social problems indirectly through education rather than through politics.

Curti, Merle. *The Social Ideas of American Educators*. Patterson, NJ: Pageant Books, 1959, 613 pp. including index. Contents: Part I, (1) Colonial Survivals and Revolutionary Promises, 1620–1820, (2) New Conflicts and a New Solution 1800–1860, (3) Education and Social Reform: Horace Mann, (4) Henry Barnard, (5)

The Education of Women, (6) The School and the Triumph of Business Enterprise, 1860–1914, (7) Education in the South, (8) The Black Man's Place: Booker T. Washington, 1856–1916, (9) William T. Harris, The Conservator, 1835–1908, (10) Bishop Spalding, Catholic Educator, 1840–1916, (11) Francis Wayland Parker, Democrat, 1837–1902, (12) G. Stanley Hall, Evolutionist, 1846–1924, (13) William James, Individualist, 1842–1910, (14) Edward Lee Thorndike, Scientist, 1874–1949, (15) John Dewey, 1859–1952, (16) PostWar Patterns. A conclusion and bibliographical notes follow and there is a treatment of recent educational history. This book provides an excellent social understanding of American educational development. Also useful is Curti's *The Growth of American Thought*. New York: Harper & Row, 1951.

Curtis, Stanley J., and M. E. A. Boultwood. *A Short History of Educational Ideas*, 3d ed. London: University Tutorial Press Ltd., 1964. 615 pp., including index. A standard text in Western educational history, paying considerable attention to American education and American educational leaders. Helpful bibliographical information is given at the end of each chapter.

Dworkin, Martin. *Dewey on Education*. New York: Columbia University Teacher's College Press, 1959. The best quick reference to the work of Dewey for those who do not wish to use Dewey's own books. Also suggested is Dewey's own *Democracy and Education*. New York: Macmillan, 1916.

Fantini, Mario. *Regaining Excellence in Education*. New York: Merrill/Macmillan, 1986. A very good analysis of the reform movement in education resulting from "A Nation at Risk" and other reports of the 1980s. This book deals with future trends as well as the responses of state and local groups to the demand for educational reform. Reports and sources are well documented and succinctly presented.

Gatti, Richard, and Daniel Gatti. *New Encyclopedic Dictionary of School Law*. West Nyack, NY: Parker Publishing, 1983. A complete analysis of laws and court cases that altered the shape of American education. Concentration is on the recent trends in the courts and the philosophical shifts that have created new trends in the relationship between schools and governing agencies.

Good, Harry, and James Teller. *A History of American Education*. 3rd ed. New York: Macmillan, 1973. A detailed history of American education complete with index and extensive bibliography. It is especially useful for the period prior to the twentieth century.

Johanningmeier, Erwin. *Americans and Their Schools*. Chicago: Rand McNally, 1980. A superior text which is both very detailed and interesting. It would be an excellent choice for a text in a graduate level history of American education course. Johanningmeier is an interesting author to read and he puts to rest a number of common myths about education in this nation.

Karier, Clarence J. *Shaping the American Educational State, 1900 to the Present*. New York: Free Press, 1975. A collection of essays and documents on the most important forces at work in developing the modern American educational system. Karier deals with issues and problems as well as ideas and movements.

Knight, Edgar W. *Fifty Years of American Education*. New York: Ronald Press, 1952, 484 pp., including index. Other standard works on the subject by the same author include: *A Documentary History of Education in the South Before 1860*. Chapel Hill: University of North Carolina Press, 1949 and *Education in the United States*. Boston: Ginn, 1951.

Levine, Daniel, and Robert Havinghurst. *Society and Education*. 6th ed. Boston: Allyn and Bacon, 1984. A very complete sociology of education calls attention to the social forces in American education that have shaped modern conditions. It provides the student of history with an in-depth understanding of modern social attitudes and trends.

Mayer, Frederick. *American Ideas and Education*. New York: Merrill/Macmillan, 1964. Mayer's book is an intellectual and social history of American education which is especially useful for the student of ideas, attitudes, movements, and people. Mayer includes a large number of quotations from the leaders with whom he deals.

Meyer, Adolphe, E. *The Educational History of the American People*. 2d ed. New York: McGraw-Hill, 1967. This very readable text presents the material in a refreshing way. It does assume some basic knowledge of American history on the part of the student.

Monroe, Paul, ed. *A Cyclopedia of Education*. New York: Macmillan, 1911–1913. Five volumes, including illustrations, charts, diagrams, and references. This monumental work is dated, but still the only one of its kind and a valuable source of information. A revised edition is in progress which will include modern material.

Mulhern, James. *A History of Education*. 2d ed. New York: Ronald Press, 1959. Parts W and V contain a wealth of material pertaining to the growth of and the changes in the American educational system.

Naisbitt, John. *Megatrends*. New York: Warner Books, 1982. The student of history interested in the future will find a very interesting presentation of the major forces operating to shape our world in this book. Naisbitt describes the most important trends and suggests alternative courses of action to cope with them.

Perkinson, Henry. *Since Socrates: Studies in the History of Western Educational Thought*. New York: Longman, 1980. Perkinson gives a fresh account of the development of educational thought in the western world, with stress placed on intellectual and cultural history.

___. *Two Hundred Years of American Educational Thought*. New York: McKay, 1976. This book contains one of the best accounts of the critics of American education to be found anywhere in the literature.

Potter, Robert E. *The Stream of American Education*. New York: American Book, 1967, 522 pp., including a list of sources and index. Potter's book is one of the most complete single volume treatments of American education available. It is especially useful for the study of current educational issues and problems.

Power, Edward J. *Legacy of Learning: A History of Western Education*. Albany, NY: State University of New York Press, 1991. A contribution to understanding the evolution of curriculum development in American education.

___. *Main Currents in the History of Education*, 2d ed. New York: McGraw-Hill, 1969. A useful general treatment of major American educational ideas.

___. *Transit of Learning: A Social and Cultural Interpretation of American Educational History*, 1979. Contextual treatment of curriculum development in the United States.

Pratte, Richard. *Ideology and Education*. New York: Wiley, 1977. A useful account of the theories and philosophies of education. It treats individual thinkers and the social conditions that contributed to their ideas.

Rusk, Robert, and James Scotland. *Doctrines of the Great Educators*. New York: St. Martin's Press, 1979. A new account of the contributions to education made by those who really changed the basic conceptions about education.

Thayer, V. T. *Formative Ideas in American Education*. New York: Dodd, Mead, 1965. Professor Thayer presents the philosophic views and changing theories held by leading educators in the United States. The detail in which significant ideas are presented makes Thayer very good reading for serious educators.

Toffler, Alvin. *War and Anti-War*. New York: Little Brown, 1993. Viewpoints of a futurist on the impact of technology on the individual, society, and the world community.

Travers, Paul, and Ronald Rebore. *Foundations of Education: Becoming a Teacher*. 3rd ed. New York: Allyn and Bacon, 1993. A university professor and public school superintendent author a textbook for prospective teachers which combines historical, philosophical, and social perspectives on education.

Tyack, David B., ed. *Turning Points in American Educational History*. Waltham, MA: Blaisdell, 1967. Some of the most significant writings and documents in the history of American education are presented with introductions by the author. This is a well-selected collection of the most significant materials relating to the subject of schooling in America.

Warren, Donald, ed. *History, Education, and Public Policy*. Berkeley, CA: McCutchan, 1978. This collection of essays and documents gives a clear account of the way education and public policy in the United States are related.

Webb, Rodman, and Robert Sherman. *Schooling and Society*. 2d ed. New York: Macmillan, 1989.

Wirth, Arthur. *Education and Work for the Year 2000: Choices We Make*. San Francisco: Jossey-Bass, 1992. Analysis of choices facing American Society between status quo and need for changing priorities to provide for increasing numbers of individuals at risk.

GLOSSARY

Academic Freedom. The liberty of teachers and scholars to pursue scholarly questions without fear of control or chastisement by administrative personnel of educational or governmental institutions.

Academy. An American secondary school of the colonial and early national era which stressed practical subjects like bookkeeping rather than the classics.

Accountability. The requirement that schools be responsible to the public for how well students do. This is done by testing of the students.

Activity Curriculum. A school program or curriculum chosen by the students themselves with the guidance from the teacher. The activity curriculum was used in some schools associated with progressive education.

Apperceptive Mass. The term used by the philosopher-psychologist Herbart to describe interlocking related or associated ideas in the subconscious part of the mind.

Associationism. The school of psychology which holds that learning should emphasize the relationships of concepts or ideas. Herbart was an associationist in this sense.

Bargaining, Collective. A provision for negotiating with a school board by which teachers are represented not as individuals but as a group. A union or a professional organization may be the bargaining agency.

Behaviorism. A school of psychology started by John B. Watson in 1912 which assumes nothing about people or animals and bases its conclusions entirely upon the observed reactions or "behavior" of subjects when they are exposed to a given stimulus.

Child-Centered School. A school in which the primary concern is with developing the whole child rather than with subject matter. John Dewey and the progressive educators developed child-centered schools in which they tried to follow the natural needs, interests, and abilities of children.

Child Study Movement. The scientific study of the nature of children and learning, started about 1900 by G. Stanley Hall.

Common School. A school for all of the people. In the United States, free, public, elementary schools were the first "common" schools, but the term is now applied also to public high schools.

Compensatory Education. Systematic efforts to overcome problems of the culturally different student as with Head Start or bilingual teaching.

Competency-Based Teacher Education. A requirement that teachers demonstrate minimum competency in the subjects they will teach before they are certified. Competency testing of students to see how well they can perform is now often required before graduation.

Comprehensive High School. A secondary school which attempts to cater to the needs of all students by offering more than one course of specialization in its program. Comprehensive high schools usually have a college preparatory course and one or more scientific or vocational courses which are terminal.

Compulsory Education. School attendance which is required by law on the theory that it is for the benefit of the commonwealth to educate all the people. Today, the practice is under attack by critics.

Core Curriculum.   A program in which the different subjects of the curriculum are related to a central group of studies. History and geography are combined into the social studies core. Model core curriculums often relate foreign languages with other subjects.

Dame School.   A low-level primary school in the colonial and early national periods usually conducted by an untrained woman in her own home. Dame school teachers taught only the bare fundamentals for which they received small fees or presents.

De Facto Segregation.   A condition of segregation or separation of races into different schools caused by district boundaries which include children from only one race in a given school. This differs from segregation dejure which is a legal requirement for segregated schools (illegal since 1954).

Deism.   The belief, held by many liberal colonial leaders, that God created the world and then withdrew to let it operate according to natural law. This means that man is on his own because God does not interfere with the affairs of men.

Developmental Stage.   The theory that learning depends upon the maturity of the learner, and that it is necessary to reach a certain level of development (physical or mental or both) before certain kinds of learning can take place.

District System.   A scheme of school organization, originating in Massachusetts, in which the local geographical unit or district is the legal authority for a school or schools. Modern districts, within state systems, are the legal areas covered by the services of a given school or schools.

Early Childhood Education.   Any systematic effort to teach a child before the normal period of schooling begins. Froebel and Montessori were pioneers in the field. Project Head Start is a modern example of early childhood education.

Empirical Principle.   The belief, as expressed by John Locke, that the measure of the truth of an idea is its comparison with common-sense reality. Many nonempirical theories hold that truth is tested by logic, revelation, or innate feelings.

The Enlightenment.   A pattern of thought which protested against authority in religious and secular life. The Enlightenment stressed science, reason, and the dignity of all men, and it helped to create the shift of thought which made the American Revolution possible.

Essentialism.   An educational theory which is a protest against progressive education and consists of an effort to identify the most important practical skills which are then taught to children as the basic or essential subjects.

Experimental Schools.   Schools in which new methods or materials are tried in an effort to select the best. Experimental schools may be conducted by universities, school systems, or private groups. Normally, careful records are kept in order to measure the progress of pupils using a new curriculum or technique against those using more established ones.

Faculty Psychology.   The belief, which was the basic psychology of educators in the nineteenth century, that the mind is divided into separate faculties or powers like willing, memory, and reasoning. Exercise of the faculties was supposed to strengthen the mind; thus the study of Latin grammar would transfer to or improve the ability to use logic.

Futurism.   A philosophical position and a movement in education designed to shift emphasis from the current era to the needs that will emerge in a period of rapid change.

General Education.   Education which is not specialized and which is designed for general living or good citizenship rather than preparation for a vocation. There is an issue over just what should be included in general education as well as how many years should be devoted to it.

Graded School System.   A division of schools into groups of students according to the curriculum or the ages of pupils as in the six elementary grades. Early schools were not graded and a substantial number of modern elementary schools are experimenting with nongraded systems, although grading is still the common practice.

Great Awakening.   A religious revival in colonial America which was responsible for the creation of many schools and church-related colleges. Jonathan Edwards is credited with starting the Great Awakening among Puritans about 1733.

Herbartian Method. The formal system of presenting subject matter to students by the American followers of Herbart, using the five formal steps of preparation, presentation, association, generalization, and application.

Hornbook. A single printed page containing the alphabet, syllables, a prayer, and other simple words which was used in colonial times as the beginner's first book or pre-primer. Hornbooks were attached to a wooden paddle for ease in carrying and covered with a thin sheet of transparent horn for protection.

Humanism. A movement to attain knowledge of life and institutions through the study of the Latin and Greek classical authors. Humanism influenced the American colonies and had a profound effect on the development of American schools. Modern humanism is concerned with the needs and values of people.

Idealism. A major school of philosophy which holds that only ideas are real and that objects cannot exist outside some mind. Idealism was used by Berkeley to signify the opposite of realism. Jonathan Edwards and W. T. Harris were American idealists who influenced education.

Inclusion. Full inclusion of disabled students in regular classrooms.

In Service Training. Continuing education for teachers who are actually teaching or in service. Such training may be conducted in a school as a workshop or extension course, or teachers may attend classes in a university at night or in vacation periods.

Intelligence Quotient (IQ). A number which is obtained by dividing mental age (found by a standard or normal test) by chronological age. Intelligence quotients are widely used for placing children in school programs, although they are by no means perfect measurements.

Involuntary Segregation. Forced separation of students on the basis of race, color, or creed. Racial segregation may not be required by law in

the United States since the Supreme Court decision in the Brown Case of 1954.

Kindergarten. A "garden of children" or an institution where small children may grow and develop. The term was coined by Froebel who began the first schools for children aged four, five, and six years. Kindergartens appeared in America about the time of the Civil War and are now schools for five-year-olds.

Knowledge Revolution. The tremendous explosion of information in almost every field, which makes it difficult for scholars to be aware of the new knowledge discovered in their own and related fields. The knowledge revolution is accompanied by a vast increase in sources of information, especially computers.

Laissez-Faire. The idea, based on Adam Smith's Wealth of Nations, that the government should not interfere in any way with the laws of supply and demand. Laissez-faire theory holds that the best government is one which governs least.

Land-Grant College. Colleges or universities founded or supported by a gift of public land. Many American agricultural and mechanical colleges were established by the Morrill Land-Grant Act of 1862.

Latin Grammar School. A classical secondary school with a curriculum consisting largely of Latin and Greek, the purpose of which was preparation for college.

Lock-Step. A rigid or uniform organization and curriculum in which each grade or course is the foundation for each higher grade or course and there is no flexibility. The influence of the American Herbartianists led to the lock-step in our public schools after 1890.

Mainstreaming. The process, required by Public Law 94-142, of placing exceptional learners in the least restrictive learning environment. This means that handicapped students spend at least part of each day in a "normal" classroom.

Mental Discipline. A theory, associated with faculty psychology and transfer of training, which holds that the mind must be disciplined or exercised through drill, memorization, and the study of difficult subjects.

Middle School. A modern school organizational plan. Middle schools may be imposed between elementary and junior high schools or they replace them. A 4-4-4 plan uses the term "middle school" for the middle four years.

Modular System. Flexible schedule in a school, organized around modules of time (usually 15 minutes each) to allow for different time periods for various subjects and individual needs.

Monitorial Schools. Schools developed by Joseph Lancaster and Andrew Bell in which one teacher taught a number of bright students or monitors who, in turn, taught other groups of children. Monitorial schools were brought to America in the early national period in an attempt to provide cheap charity education for poor students.

Multi-Track System. The educational program, found in Europe and in the American colonies, which provided one kind of education for the wealthy elite and another kind for the ordinary people.

Nation at Risk. One of a series of national reports critical of American schooling which appeared in the early 1980s. These reports created a demand for excellence and a movement for school reform.

Naturalism. In philosophy, the belief that the world contains only forces which require no supernatural explanation. In education, the belief that children should be free to follow their own interests, desires, and needs. Rousseau was a naturalist in education.

Nongraded School. A school which is not divided into specific grades for each age group. Nongraded schools may have children grouped according to social needs, ability, or progress, or not grouped at all.

Normal School. An American teacher-training school or college. Nineteenth century normal schools were often two-year institutions on about the same level as high schools. Modern teacher-training colleges are four-year institutions and many offer graduate training.

Object Lessons. Teaching by means of objects and activities rather than through abstract symbols and words. The object lesson of the Swiss educator Pestalozzi was first introduced in America at the Oswego Normal School by Edward Sheldon in 1850.

Old Field School. A colonial educational institution developed in Virginia by families who would cooperate to build an elementary school on one of the fallow "old fields." These schools were the counterparts of district schools in New England.

Open Classroom. A modern educational innovation in which self-contained classrooms are replaced with an open plan with individualized instruction and freedom for the child to move about the school.

Pedagogy. The scientific study of education, or the curriculum of teacher-training institutions with regard to how to teach.

Perennialism. A term used by Theodore Brameld to describe a position which opposes pragmatism and progressivism, and which looks toward a restoration of the absolute or ultimate value system of ages past. Robert Hutchins and many Catholic educators may be described as perennialists.

Pragmatism. The school of philosophy which holds that only the practical results of a belief give it meaning and that arguments which have no practical consequence are meaningless. Charles Peirce coined the term and John Dewey is a good example of a pragmatist in education.

Programmed Learning. Any learning device which may be used by a student in such a way that a reaction to his activities is immediately supplied. These range from simple, printed notebooks to computer-assisted instruction, and the learner is not dependent upon a teacher in order to progress.

Progressive Educators. A term applied to a group of educators who objected to subject-centered schools, followed the philosophy of John Dewey, and applied the doctrines of Rousseau, Pestalozzi, and Froebel to education. Francis W. Parker was an early progressive, but the term is usually associated with members of the Progressive Education Association which was founded in 1918.

Project Method. The method of William H. Kilpatrick and his followers. Any learning activities in which pupils have an opportunity to choose, direct, or plan their own work under conditions similar to those of real life.

Rate Bill. A scheme for supporting schools that was a transition from fees to tax-support. Each child was charged a rate or graduated amount for schooling, according to what the parents were able to afford.

Sapiential Authority. A term used by futurists like Theobald to mean authority based in truth or use value of information rather than upon status or position.

Scientific or Sense Realism. An effort to relate education to the "real" or common-sense world, which was started by scientific thinkers like Copernicus, Galileo, and Bacon. John Locke and Benjamin Franklin were scientific realists who influenced American schools.

Sectarianism. A term which refers to religious denominations. Early schools were under the control of particular church groups or sects until the Bill of Rights required that public schools be secular because of separation of church and state in America.

Secularism. The principle of religious freedom applied in such a way that the sphere of influence of religious groups or religious leaders does not extend to public institutions like the schools.

Single-Track System. An educational program in which all the students have the same kind of educational opportunity, rather than one school system for the elite and another for the masses.

Social Darwinism. The theory of evolution applied to society rather than to biology. Social evolution was used by Sumner and Spencer to justify the existing social conditions and the concentration of wealth in the hands of the few.

Social Reconstruction. The belief that society can be made over or changed. Some social reconstructionists in education have held that the schools can reconstruct society, while Theodore Brameld believes that schools should have some role in social change.

Special Education. A school program designed for the child who is exceptional, that is, either gifted or below normal in ability. The study of exceptional children is now well established and most American school systems have special education classes.

Subject-Centered School or Curriculum. The traditional educational program which is organized around subject matter or around major concepts in the organized fields of knowledge or disciplines. This is in opposition to the child-centered curriculum which emphasizes individual differences, needs, and interests of children.

Sunday School. A movement started by Robert Raikes in England and transferred to the United States in the early 1800s, which attempted to teach the fundamentals to children who worked in factories all week.

Tabula Rasa. As used by John Locke, the theory that children have no innate ideas at birth, and that the mind comes to be furnished with ideas through the sense organs or sensation. All learning comes through experience, and the mind is blank at birth.

Team Teaching. A plan by which several teachers, organized into a team with a leader, provide the instruction for a larger group of children than would usually be found in a self-contained classroom. Team members may handle classes together, or one member may teach a large number of children while the others work with individuals.

Terminal Education. Education or schooling which is not designed to lead to further or higher schooling. Vocational programs in high schools which lead directly to jobs rather than to college are examples of terminal education.

Theocracy. Civil and political power vested in the same person or group. Separation of church and state in America is guaranteed by the Bill of Rights, but the early New England governments were theocracies.

Time-on-Task. An effort to improve schools by paying close attention to the time actually spent by students in paying attention to their subjects as opposed to time devoted to activities such as passing in halls or listening to announcements.

Transfer of Training. The theory, associated with faculty psychology and mental discipline, that learning one subject will aid, or transfer to, the study of another subject.

Utilitarianism. In education, the doctrine that the school curriculum should be governed by its usefulness for vocational success or public utility.

Vocational Education. Training which is intended to prepare the student for a particular job or to give a basic skill needed in several vocations.

Voluntary Segregation. The practice of establishing a school or other institution which is not for the use of the general public but which is under the control of a specific group. Parochial and private schools are examples of voluntary segregation.

INDEX